I0797923

By Jon Meacham

*American Struggle: Democracy, Dissent, and the Pursuit of a More Perfect Union: An Anthology* (editor)

*The Call to Serve: A Visual Biography of President George Herbert Walker Bush*

*And There Was Light: Abraham Lincoln and the American Struggle*

*His Truth Is Marching On: John Lewis and the Power of Hope*

*The Hope of Glory: Reflections on the Last Words of Jesus from the Cross*

*The Soul of America: The Battle for Our Better Angels*

*Destiny and Power: The American Odyssey of George Herbert Walker Bush*

*Thomas Jefferson: The Art of Power*

*American Lion: Andrew Jackson in the White House*

*American Gospel: God, the Founding Fathers, and the Making of a Nation*

*Franklin and Winston: An Intimate Portrait of an Epic Friendship*

*Voices in Our Blood: America's Best on the Civil Rights Movement* (editor)

# AMERICAN STRUGGLE

# AMERICAN STRUGGLE

*Democracy, Dissent, and the Pursuit of a More Perfect Union*

AN ANTHOLOGY

JON MEACHAM

RANDOM HOUSE
*New York*

Random House
An imprint and division of Penguin Random House LLC
1745 Broadway, New York, NY 10019
randomhousebooks.com
penguinrandomhouse.com



Hardcover ISBN 9780593597552
Ebook ISBN 9780593597576

Text permission credits are located on pages 481–482.

Printed in the United States of America on acid-free paper

1st Printing

FIRST EDITION

BOOK TEAM: Production editor: Dennis Ambrose · Managing editor: Rebecca Berlant · Production manager: Richard Elman · Copy editor: Nancy Elgin · Proofreaders: Claire Maby, Ruth Anne Phillips, Rachael Clements, Caryl Weintraub · Indexer: Charlee Trantino

*Book design by Simon M. Sullivan*
*Title-page spread: U.S. Marines raising the flag on Mount Suribachi on Iwo Jima in February 1945*

The authorized representative in the EU for product safety and compliance is Penguin Random House Ireland, Morrison Chambers, 32 Nassau Street, Dublin D02 YH68, Ireland, https://eu-contact.penguin.ie.

In memoriam
Charles Peters, 1926–2023

Nations reel and stagger on their way; they make hideous mistakes; they commit frightful wrongs; they do great and beautiful things. And shall we not best guide humanity by telling the truth about all this, so far as the truth is ascertainable?

—W.E.B. Du Bois

# CONTENTS

## PART IV · THE FIERY TRIAL · *1860–1865*

## PART V · A TROUBLED PEACE · *1865–1932*

## PART IX · FRAYING CONSENSUS · *1969–*

INTRODUCTION

# "I DO NOT DESPAIR OF THIS COUNTRY"

*Jon Meacham*

THE NEWS WAS GRIM. In a majority opinion delivered from the bench of the United States Supreme Court in Washington, D.C., on Friday, March 6, 1857, Chief Justice Roger Taney issued the verdict in the case of Dred Scott, an enslaved man who was suing for his liberty after being taken from the slave state of Missouri into free federal territory. One lower court had agreed with Scott. Another, the state supreme court of Missouri, had ruled against him, and the case had gone to Washington in 1856. Five of the justices of the Supreme Court, including Taney of Maryland, were from slave states, and they joined with two others to issue a sweeping decision on this late-winter Friday. Scott could not prevail in his bid for freedom, the court ruled, for Scott had no standing in the American order other than the fact of his enslavement. Black people, Taney announced, were not protected by the Declaration of Independence's assertion of innate human equality. They could not be considered citizens. And the 1820 Missouri Compromise, which had banned slavery in the northern regions of the Louisiana Purchase, was held unconstitutional. "In the opinion of the court, the legislation and histories of the times, and the language used in the Declaration of Independence," Taney said, "show, that neither the class of persons who had been imported as slaves, nor their descendants, whether they had become free or not, were then acknowledged as a part of the people, nor intended to be included in the general words used in that memorable instrument." Black people, the court decided, had long been considered subhuman, and so they remained. "They had," Taney read, "for more than a century before been regarded as beings of an inferior order, and altogether unfit to associate with the white race, either in social or political relations; and so far inferior, that they had no rights which the white man was bound to respect."

It was a breathtakingly proslavery ruling. There was a lively debate in America that turned on whether *all* were encompassed in Thomas Jefferson's assertion that "all men are created equal"—a debate the Taney court was attempting to end with a single strike. "All the powers of earth seem rapidly combining against [the enslaved person]," Abraham Lincoln said in Illinois. "Mammon is after him; ambition follows, and philosophy follows, and the Theology of the day is fast joining the cry." Reading the news in Rochester, New York, where he had settled after escaping enslavement in Taney's Maryland, the abolitionist, editor, and orator Frederick Douglass reacted not gloomily but defiantly. "Come what will, I hold it to be morally certain that, sooner or later, by fair means or foul means, in quiet or in tumult, in peace or in blood, in judgment or in mercy, slavery is doomed to cease out of this otherwise goodly land, and liberty is destined to become the settled law of this Republic," Douglass told the American Anti-Slavery Society. "I base my sense of the certain overthrow of slavery, in part, upon the nature of the American Government, the Constitution, the tendencies of the age, and the character of the American people; and this, notwithstanding the important decision of Judge Taney. I know of no soil better adapted to the growth of reform than American soil. I know of no country where the conditions for affecting great changes in the settled order of things, for the development of right ideas of liberty and humanity, are more favorable than here in these United States." To the *Chicago Daily Tribune,* "The remedy is—UNION, ACTION, THE BALLOT BOX! There is on the side of the Free States the population and the power—the votes—and whenever these votes shall agree, 'that Slavery shall not be the fundamental law of the land,' that decree will be omnipotent."

And so, on the eve of the Civil War, as the 1850s ran along, there was a fundamental conflict between visions of liberty and of slavery, of principle and of power, of right and of wrong. The tensions of that cataclysmic hour were extreme—as Lincoln would note, it was because of slavery that the war came—but as the documents collected in this volume show, they were not exceptional. America has been defined by the perennial struggle between the appetites of the few and the privileged and the aspirations of the many who have rightly insisted that the nation live up to its self-professed creed of sacred rights and equal justice under law.

As this anthology shows, that struggle is not the work of a day. It is, rather, the animating force of our history. The story of how fully or how meagerly America recognizes and acts upon the implications of the Declaration of Independence and the Constitution—which Douglass called a "Glorious Liberty Document"—is the story of the country.

And that story is not a fairy tale. It is not an uncomplicated saga of inevitable progress—for progress is anything but inevitable—nor is it an entirely uplifting drama of good prevailing over evil. We do ourselves no favors by pretending that American history is either cheerfully grand or unrelievedly bleak, for American history is a human undertaking and is as subject to selfishness and to greed, to cruelty and to injustice, as we are in our own lives. Yet it is also true that the United States of America has grown stronger, freer, and more just when it has opened its arms rather than clenched its fists; built bridges, not walls; and understood that the promise of the Declaration includes not some but all. Conscience and history call on us to honor liberators, not captors; builders, not destroyers; the respectful, not the grasping.

Nativism, xenophobia, cultural populism, and broad political fear have shaped the Republic from the beginning, and always will. Such is the nature of life in a fallen world; anxiety and its manifestations in the public square ebb and flow. (Truth be told, they mostly flow, which is the occasion of our conversation here.) The American Founders understood this. "If men were angels," James Madison wrote, "then no government would be necessary"—and given that men were so self-evidently unangelic, the American government was designed to check our passions and to balance our failings.

In our own unangelic moment, the speeches, letters, and essays collected here remind us that American politics is inherently dramatic and tends toward the inflammatory and the superlative. Candidates and partisans and commentators from age to age depict every election not just as a choice, but as an existential battle; not only as contests of opinion, but as clashes of worldviews.

Progress has been forever contingent; the republic has always been fragile.

This perennial contingency and fragility is especially acute in the first decades of twenty-first-century America. We live in a polarized era, and history itself is a subject of political contention. Roughly put, many on the right seek to see America as perfect; many on the left argue that the national experiment is fundamentally flawed. The truth, I believe, lies between these oft-expressed extremes. America has had shining hours; it has also dwelt in darkness. This anthology seeks to put our best and our worst before a divided and often dispirited nation—and to remind us that conscientious citizenship is essential to bringing out the more perfect Union envisioned in the Preamble to the Constitution. To know what has come before is to be armed against despair. If the people of preceding generations, with all their flaws and limitations and ambitions and appetites, could press on through ignorance and superstition, racism and sexism, selfishness and greed, then perhaps we can, too.

This is no time for sentimentality. That things worked out in the past—slavery fell; Hitler was defeated; legalized segregation was undone—does not mean that things will work out in the present or in the future. Yet history is one means by which we can assess the scope of the issues at hand and orient ourselves in the battles of the hour. A sixteenth-century edition of Plutarch, translated into French, put the matter this way: History was "a certain rule and instruction which by examples past, teacheth us to judge of things present and to foresee things to come, so as we may know what to like of and what to follow, what to mislike, and what to eschew." The passions and hopes and fears evident in this collection give the reader a grasp of ages past—and ages past tend to illuminate ages to come.

This book is a window on the complicated, sometimes disappointing, but always essential story of American democracy—a story that has the capacity to remain a vital force for freedom, opportunity, prosperity, and justice. From Lexington and Concord to Gettysburg to Omaha Beach to the Edmund Pettus Bridge, we have nudged the world toward an ethos of liberty rather than tyranny. The future belongs to the men and the women, in power and far from it, who insist on equal justice for all, on what Lincoln called "an open field and a fair chance." How do we know the future belongs to such people? Because the best of the past belongs to those who did precisely that.

Change in democracies requires persuasion—the molding of what Lincoln referred to as "public sentiment." In a popular government such as ours, even with its inherent checks and balances, unity, defined as a commonly held set of facts and basic values, is essential, for without common agreement on ends, the battles over means become the central and consuming reality, crowding out the possibilities of progress. The need for unity is an ancient American insight. From Thomas Paine's *Common Sense* to Jefferson's Declaration, from the Declaration of Sentiments at Seneca Falls to the writings of Frederick Douglass, the architects of the nation have argued for a unified assent to the principle of fair play.

No age is perfect. There are derelictions and debacles, dreams deferred and hopes dashed. Yet the lesson of American history is that we're at our best when we at least agree on the facts at hand, on the efficacy of compromise, and on the legitimacy of our institutions. "We can succeed only by concert," Lincoln told the Congress amid the Civil War. "It is not 'Can any of us *imagine* better?' but 'Can we all *do* better?' "

Doing better requires a grasp of what the best of us have been able—and unable—to accomplish in the past. One lesson that emerges from these pages is that nothing about American democracy is guaranteed, except perhaps that it will never manufacture the kingdom of heaven on earth. "The sad duty of politics," the theologian Reinhold Niebuhr observed, "is to establish justice in a sinful world." It is a duty that can end only beyond time.

In the aftermath of the *Dred Scott* decision—a time when, as Lincoln noted, everything seemed to be conspiring to preserve slavery—Frederick Douglass insisted that the darkness of the moment could not long endure. A few years before, in an address at Corinthian Hall in Rochester, New York, on the fifth of July, Douglass had declared a basic faith in the American experiment. "I do not despair of this country," he had said. "The fiat of the Almighty, *'Let There Be Light,'* has not yet spent its force." Now, with Taney's haunting words in the headlines, Douglass reaffirmed his convictions. "The Constitution, as well as the Declaration of Independence, and the sentiments of the founders of the Republic, give us a platform broad enough, and strong enough, to support the most comprehensive plans for the freedom and elevation of all the people of this country, without regard to color, class, or clime," Douglass said. As rickety as it may seem, the platform in which Douglass put such faith remains beneath our feet. It has fallen to us to repair it, restore it, and then summon the courage to stand upon it, however ferocious the struggle.

# PART I

# IN THE BEGINNING

## *Origins to 1776*

We must delight in each other; make other's conditions our own; rejoice together, mourn together, labor and suffer together.

—John Winthrop, 1630

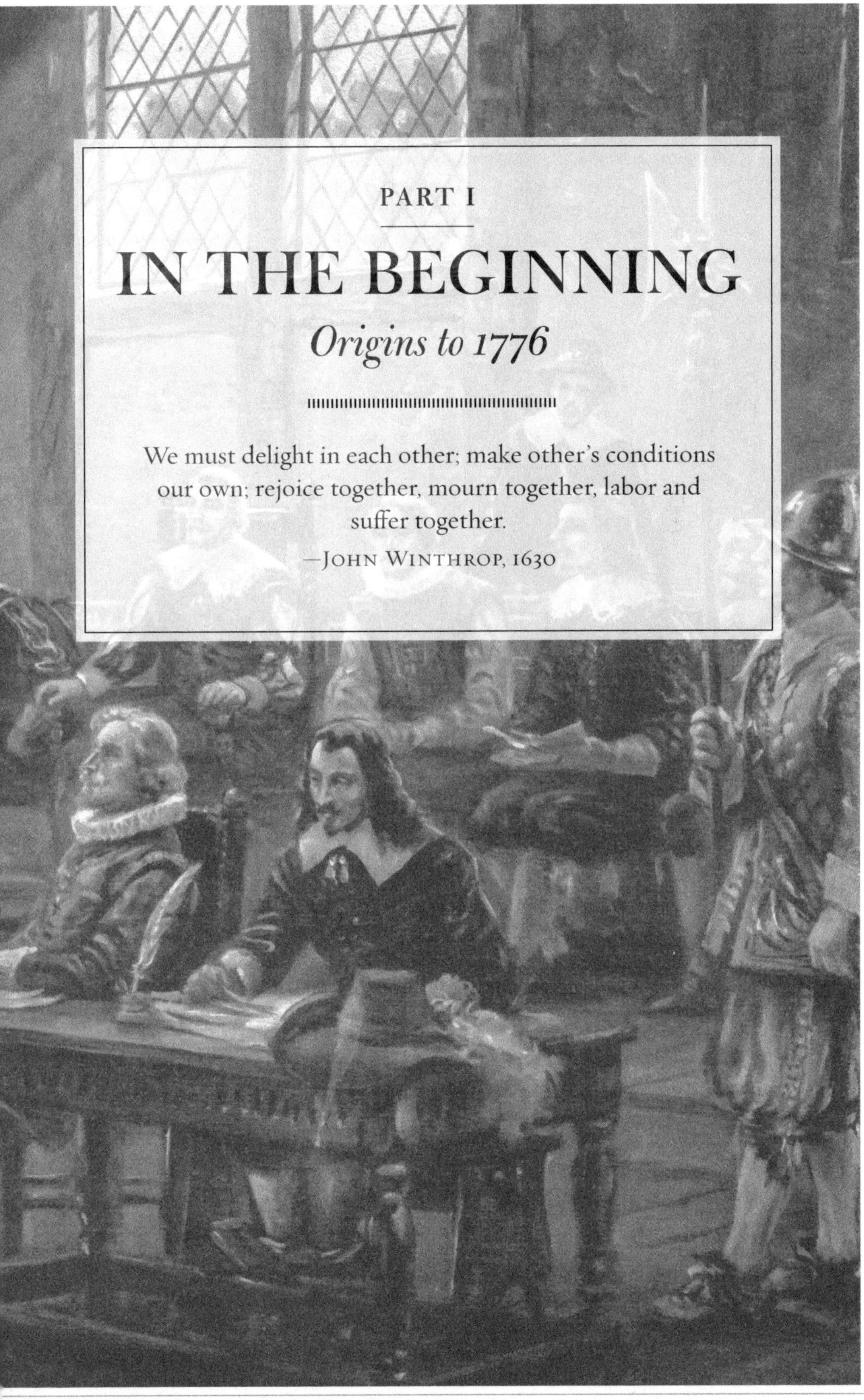

PREVIOUS SPREAD: *A rendering of the meeting of the first General Assembly of Virginia, held in the choir of the church at Jamestown in the summer of 1619. The gathering marked the beginning of representative government in English North America.*

---

IT WAS THE BOLDEST OF CLAIMS. "The cause of America," Thomas Paine would write in the winter of 1776, "is in a great measure the cause of all mankind. . . . Ye that dare oppose, not only the tyranny, but the tyrant, stand forth! Every spot of the old world is overrun with oppression. . . . O! receive the fugitive, and prepare in time an asylum for mankind." The words came from Paine's influential pamphlet *Common Sense,* a case for the burgeoning American Revolution so vivid and so transporting that the commander of the Continental Army, George Washington, ordered that it be read aloud to all of his troops. Though a noted religious skeptic—Paine would later turn his formidable pen to attacking traditional Christian faith in his sulfurous *The Age of Reason*—he framed the American bid for independence from Great Britain in moral terms, arguing that the colonists' fight against King George III and the onus of hereditary authority was a battle between good and evil. In this Paine was speaking in a familiar vernacular of the time. "We are engaged in a most important contest; not for power but freedom," the Reverend Samuel Stillman preached in Boston in 1779. "We mean not to change our masters, but to secure to ourselves, and to generations, yet unborn, the perpetual enjoyment of civil and religious liberty, in their fullest extent." Or, as John Dickinson, the author of *Letters from a Farmer in Pennsylvania,* wrote in *The Liberty Song:*

*By uniting we stand, by dividing we fall;*
*In so RIGHTEOUS a Cause let us hope to succeed,*
*For Heaven approves of each generous Deed.*

*For Heaven approves:* No understanding of American history is possible without a grasp of the sense of covenant and of mission that prevailed in British North America from the founding of Virginia and of the Massachusetts Bay Colony in the seventeenth century. As John Winthrop preached in a 1630 sermon, linking the New World to Jesus's Sermon on the Mount, America was to be "as a city upon a hill" whose temporal fortunes would wax or wane according to the virtues of the people, an understanding underscored in the Mayflower Compact drafted by dissenters arriving in Massachusetts in 1620. The continent was seen to be a special place in a providential universe—a universe that was not random but rather the conscious creation of the Lord God and an object of ongoing divine concern and judgment.

The colonists' emphasis on Scripture informed their view of their own political rights. If God had made all people equal, they held, then individuals were sacred and no man could arbitrarily rule over another. Unless, of course, the individuals were Black, or Native American, or women. Abigail Adams, for one, made the case for the male American authorities to "Remember the Ladies" in the months before the Declaration. The ideal of innate human equality was deeply felt but strictly limited; much of the unfolding national drama would be about bringing that ideal, which had been present in the American experience from the beginning, closer to a reality for all.

The selections that follow illustrate how liberty and enslavement coexisted from at least 1619. That was the year a roughly democratic general assembly met in Jamestown—and the first enslaved Black people were brought to Virginia. The case for emancipation was in (limited) circulation. Perhaps the first moral protest against slavery was published in 1688 by Quakers in Germantown, Pennsylvania. "There is a saying, that we should do to all men like as we will be done ourselves; making no difference of what generation, descent, or colour they are," read the Germantown document. "To bring men hither [to America], or to rob and sell them against their will, we stand against."

Such is evidence of the gap between the loftiness of John Winthrop's 1630 sermon and the world of human enslavement described in 1700 by Samuel Sewall in his antislavery tract *The Selling of Joseph*. In her poem "On Being Brought from Africa to America," published in 1773, Phillis Wheatley, who had been transported to Massachusetts in 1761 and sold into enslavement, summoned readers to see Black people as fellow creatures of God.

The tensions between the colonies and London in British North America in the middle of the eighteenth century rose around 1765 with the passage of the Stamp Act, which imposed wide-ranging taxes. Over the next decade revolutionary sentiment grew in proportion to London's attempts to exert a measure of control over colonial affairs. The conflict entered a new, violent phase with a clash at Lexington and

Concord in April 1775. To the south, in Virginia, the royal governor Lord Dunmore's November 1775 proclamation offering freedom to any enslaved person who joined the British cause helped unify white opinion against London and prompted the colony's assembly to threaten death to anyone who answered Dunmore's call.

In memory, of course, the American Revolution appears inevitable. Perhaps as many as a fifth of American colonists, however, remained loyal to Britain, which means the national experiment was forged amid division. The Thomas Paine view—that in America, as he put it, "the law is king"—prevailed. And the revolution went forward.

★ ★ ★

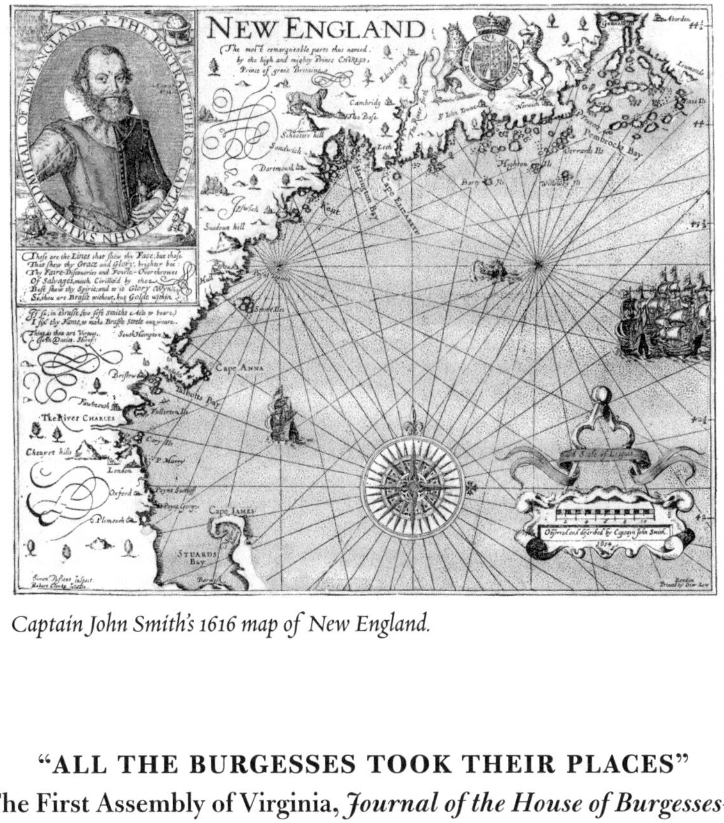

*Captain John Smith's 1616 map of New England.*

## "ALL THE BURGESSES TOOK THEIR PLACES"

### The First Assembly of Virginia, *Journal of the House of Burgesses*—July 30, 1619

A brief account of the opening moments of the first representative assembly to meet in British North America.

The most convenient place we could finde to sitt in was the Quire of the Churche, Where Sir *George Yeardley* the Governour being sett downe in his accustomed place, those of the Counsel of Estate sate next him on both handes excepte onely the Secretary then appointed Speaker, who sate right before him; *John Twine* clerke of the General Assembly being placed nexte the Speaker and *Thomas Pierse* the Sergeant standing at the barre, to be ready for any service the Assembly should command him. But for as muche as mens affaires doe little prosper where Gods service is neglected; all the Burgesses took their places in the Quire, till a Prayer was said by Mr *Bucke,* the Minister, that it would please God to guide us & sanctifie all our proceedings to his owne glory, and the good of his Plantation, Prayer being ended, to the intente that as wee had begun at God Almighty soe wee might proceed with awful and due respecte towards his Lieutenant, our most gratious & dread Soveraigne, all the Burgesses were intreated to retyre themselves into the body of the Churche; which being done, before they were fully admitted, they were called in order & by name, & so every man (none staggering at it) tooke the oathe of Supremacy, & then entered the Assembly.

⋆ ⋆ ⋆

## "20. AND ODD NEGROES"

### Letter of John Rolfe on the Coming of Slavery to Jamestown, Virginia—1619/1620

The English explorer and tobacco farmer John Rolfe (1585–1622), who had arrived in Virginia a decade earlier, describes the arrival of what are thought to be the first enslaved Black people in British North America.

About the latter end of August, a Dutch man of Warr of the burden of a 160 tunnes arrived at Point-Comfort, the Comandors name Capt Jope, his Pilott for the West Indies one Mr Marmaduke an Englishman. They mett with the Treasurer in the West Indyes, and determined to hold consort shipp hetherward, but in their passage lost one the other. He brought not any thing but 20. and odd Negroes, which the Governor and Cape Marchant bought for victualls (whereof he was in greate need as he pretended) at the best and easyest rates they could. He hadd a lardge and ample Commyssion from his Excellency to range and to take purchase in the West Indyes.

★ ★ ★

## "A CIVIL BODY POLITICK"
### The Mayflower Compact—1620

The first governing covenant of the Plymouth Colony was signed by Puritan men of the *Mayflower* as they arrived in the New World. Plymouth would become part of the Massachusetts Bay Colony in the last decade of the seventeenth century.

IN THE NAME OF GOD, AMEN. We, whose names are underwritten, the Loyal Subjects of our dread Sovereign Lord King James, by the Grace of God, of Great Britain, France, and Ireland, King, Defender of the Faith, &c. Having undertaken for the Glory of God, and Advancement of the Christian Faith, and the Honour of our King and Country, a Voyage to plant the first Colony in the northern Parts of Virginia; Do by these Presents, solemnly and mutually, in the Presence of God and one another, covenant and combine ourselves together into a civil Body Politick, for our better Ordering and Preservation, and Furtherance of the Ends aforesaid: And by Virtue hereof do enact, constitute, and frame, such just and equal Laws, Ordinances, Acts, Constitutions, and Officers, from time to time, as shall be thought most meet and convenient for the general Good of the Colony; unto which we promise all due Submission and Obedience.

★ ★ ★

## "A CITY UPON A HILL"
## John Winthrop, *A Model of Christian Charity*—1630

The layman and future Massachusetts Bay Colony governor John Winthrop (1588–1649) preached this sermon as Puritan settlers migrated to New England. The "shipwreck" he rhetorically feared was division within the colony. His hope was that Massachusetts would be united by religious principles and practices.

NOW THE ONLY way to avoid this shipwreck, and to provide for our posterity, is to follow the counsel of Micah, *to do justly, to love mercy, to walk humbly with our God.* For this end, we must be knit together, in this work, as one man. We must entertain each other in brotherly affection. We must be willing to abridge ourselves of our superfluities, for the supply of other's necessities. We must uphold a familiar commerce together in all meekness, gentleness, patience and liberality. We must delight in each other; make other's conditions our own; rejoice together, mourn together, labor and suffer together, always having before our eyes our commission and community in the work, as members of the same body. So shall we *keep the unity of the spirit in the bond of peace.* The Lord will be our God, and delight to dwell among us, as His own people, and will command a blessing upon us in all our ways. So that we shall see much more of His wisdom, power, goodness and truth, than formerly we have been acquainted with. We shall find that the God of Israel is among us, when ten of us shall be able to resist a thousand of our enemies; when He shall make us a praise and glory that men shall say of succeeding plantations, "may the Lord make it like that of *New* England." For we must consider that we shall be as a city upon a hill. The eyes of all people are upon us. So that if we shall deal falsely with our God in this work we have undertaken, and so cause Him to withdraw His present help from us, we shall be made a story and a by-word through the world.

★ ★ ★

## "OF ONE BLOOD"
### Samuel Sewall, *The Selling of Joseph*—1700

The English-born Samuel Sewall (1652–1730) was a Massachusetts merchant, clergyman, and judge.

FOR AS MUCH as Liberty is in real value next unto Life: None ought to part with it themselves, or deprive others of it, but upon most mature Consideration.

The Numerousness of Slaves at this day in the Province, and the Uneasiness of them under their Slavery, hath put many upon thinking whether the Foundation of it be firmly and well laid; so as to sustain the Vast Weight that is built upon it. It is most certain that all Men, as they are the Sons of *Adam,* are Coheirs; and have equal Right unto Liberty, and all other outward Comforts of Life. *GOD hath given the Earth* [with all its Commodities] *unto the Sons of* Adam. . . . *And hath made of One Blood, all Nations of Men, for to dwell on all the face of the Earth, and hath determined the Times before appointed, and the bounds of their habitation: That they should seek the Lord. Forasmuch then as we are the Offspring of* GOD &c. . . .

Inordinate Self love should likewise be demolished. GOD expects that Christians should be of a more Ingenuous and benign frame of spirit. Christians should carry it to all the World, as the *Israelites* were to carry it one towards another. And for men obstinately to persist in holding their Neighbours and Brethren under the Rigor of perpetual Bondage, seems to be no proper way of gaining Assurance that God ha's given them Spiritual Freedom. Our Blessed Saviour has altered the Measures of the ancient Love-Song, and set it to a most Excellent New Tune, which all ought to be ambitious of Learning. . . . These *Ethiopians,* as black as they are; seeing they are the Sons and Daughters of the First *Adam,* the Brethren and Sisters of the Last ADAM, and the Offspring of GOD; They ought to be treated with a Respect agreeable.

⋆ ⋆ ⋆

## "MY BENIGHTED SOUL"
### Phillis Wheatley, "On Being Brought from Africa to America," *Poems on Various Subjects, Religious and Moral*—1773

Born in Africa and sold into enslavement in Boston, Wheatley (c. 1753–1784) was a notable poet of the Revolutionary era. She corresponded with George Washington and was praised by Benjamin Rush, who thought her a "genius."

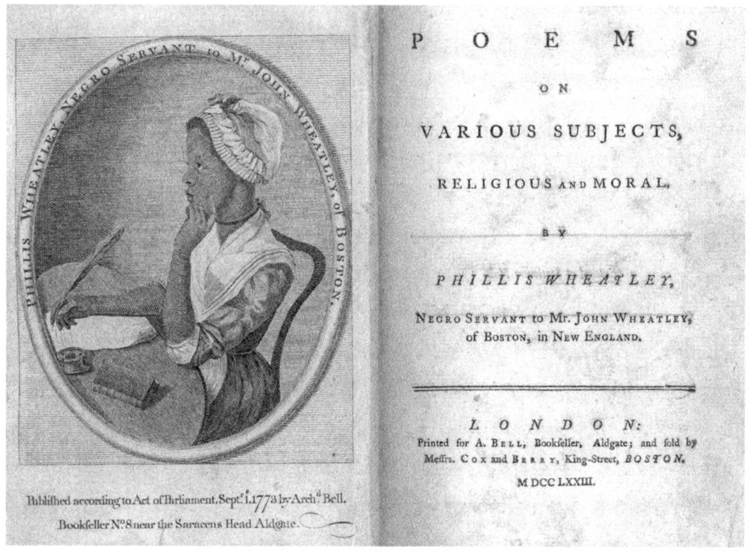
PHILLIS WHEATLEY, NEGRO SERVANT to Mr. JOHN WHEATLEY, of BOSTON.

Published according to Act of Parliament, Sept. 1, 1773 by Arch.d Bell, Bookseller N.o 8 near the Saracens Head Aldgate.

P O E M S
ON
VARIOUS SUBJECTS,
RELIGIOUS AND MORAL.
BY
*PHILLIS WHEATLEY*,
NEGRO SERVANT to Mr. JOHN WHEATLEY, of BOSTON, in NEW ENGLAND.

*L O N D O N:*
Printed for A. BELL, Bookseller, Aldgate; and sold by Messrs. COX and BERRY, King-Street, *BOSTON*.
M DCC LXXIII.

*'Twas mercy brought me from my* Pagan *land,*
*Taught my benighted soul to understand*
*That there's a God, that there's a* Saviour *too:*
*Once I redemption neither sought nor knew.*
*Some view our sable race with scornful eye,*
*"Their colour is a diabolic die."*
*Remember,* Christians, Negros, *black as* Cain,
*May be refin'd, and join th' angelic train.*

★ ★ ★

## "THIS MOST UNHAPPY COUNTRY"
### Lord Dunmore's Proclamation—November 7, 1775

The royal lieutenant governor of Virginia, Lord Dunmore (1730–1809), seeks to rally support for the Crown by promising liberty to enslaved people who take up arms against the rebelling colonists. The Virginia legislature's reply follows.

### A PROCLAMATION.

As I HAVE ever entertained hopes that an accommodation might have taken place between *Great-Britain* and this colony, without being compelled, *by my duty*, to this most disagreeable, but now absolutely necessary step, rendered so by a body of armed men, unlawfully assembled, firing on his Majesty's tenders, and the formation of an army, and that army now on their march to attack his Majesty's troops, and destroy the well disposed subjects of this colony: To defeat such treasonable purposes, and that all such traitors, and their abetters, may be brought to justice, and that the peace and good order of this colony may be again restored, which the ordinary course of the civil law is unable to effect, I have thought fit to issue this my proclamation, hereby declaring, that until the aforesaid good purposes can be obtained, I do, in virtue of the power and authority to me given, *by his Majesty*, determine to execute martial law, and cause the same to be executed throughout this colony; and to the end that *peace* and *good order* may the sooner be restored, I do require every person capable of bearing arms to

*Born in Scotland, John Murray, fourth earl of Dunmore, was the British crown's top official in New York in 1770 and then in Virginia from 1771 to 1775.*

resort to his Majesty's STANDARD, or be looked upon as traitors to his Majesty's crown and government, and thereby become liable to the penalty the law inflicts upon such offences, *such as forfeiture of life, confiscation of lands,* &c. &c. And I do hereby farther declare all *indented servants, Negroes,* or others (appertaining to rebels) *free,* that are able and willing to bear arms, they *joining his Majesty's troops,* as soon as may be, for the more speedily reducing this Colony to a *proper sense* of their duty, to his Majesty's crown and dignity. I do further order, and require all his Majesty's liege subjects to retain their quitrents, or any other taxes due, or that may become due, in their own custody, till such time as peace may be again restored to this at present most unhappy country, or demanded of them for their former salutary purposes, by officers properly authorized to receive the same.

*Given on board the ship* William, off Norfolk, *the 7th of* Nov.

★ ★ ★

## "UNLAWFUL AND WICKED STEP"

### Virginia Convention Response to Lord Dunmore's Proclamation—December 14, 1775

---

WHEREAS LORD DUNMORE, by his proclamation, dated on board the ship William, off Norfolk, the 7th day of November 1775, hath offered freedom to such able-bodied slaves as are willing to join him, and take up arms, against the good people of this colony, giving thereby encouragement to a general insurrection, which may induce a necessity of inflicting the severest punishments upon those unhappy people, already deluded by his base and insidious arts; and whereas, by an act of the General Assembly now in force in this colony, it is enacted, that all negro or other slaves, conspiring to rebel or make insurrection, shall suffer death, and be excluded all benefit of clergy: We think it proper to declare, that all slaves who have been, or shall be seduced, by his lordship's proclamation, or other arts, to desert their masters' service, and take up arms against the inhabitants of this colony, shall be liable to such punishment as shall hereafter be directed by the General Convention. And to that end all such, who have taken this unlawful and wicked step, may return in safety to their duty, and escape the punishment due to their crimes, we hereby promise pardon to them, they surrendering themselves to Col. William Woodford, or any other commander of our troops, and not appearing in arms after the publication hereof. And we do farther earnestly recommend it to all humane and benevolent persons in this colony to explain and make known this our offer of mercy to those unfortunate people.

★ ★ ★

## "IN AMERICA THE LAW IS KING"
### Thomas Paine, *Common Sense*—1776

Thomas Paine (1737–1809) produced hugely influential pamphlets arguing for the cause of independence and of democratic reform. *Common Sense* appeared in January 1776.

NO MAN WAS a warmer wisher for a reconciliation than myself, before the fatal nineteenth of April, 1775 [the day of the battles of Lexington and Concord], but the moment the event of that day was made known, I rejected the hardened, sullen-tempered Pharaoh of England forever; and disdain the wretch, that with the pretended title of FATHER OF HIS PEOPLE can unfeelingly hear of their slaughter, and composedly sleep with their blood upon his soul. . . .

Where, say some, is the king of America? I'll tell you, Friend, he reigns above, and doth not make havoc of mankind like the royal brute of Great Britain. . . . So far as we approve of monarchy . . . in America the law is king. . . .

A government of our own is our natural right. . . . Ye that oppose independence now, ye know not what ye do: ye are opening the door to eternal tyranny. . . . There are thousands and tens of thousands, who would think it glorious to expel from the Continent, that barbarous and hellish power, which hath stirred up the Indians and the Negroes to destroy us. . . .

O! ye that love mankind! Ye that dare oppose not only the tyranny but the tyrant, stand forth! Every spot of the old world is overrun with oppression. Freedom hath been hunted round the Globe. Asia and Africa have long expelled her. Europe regards her like a stranger, and England hath given her warning to depart. O! receive the fugitive, and prepare in time an asylum for mankind.

★ ★ ★

*Wise and well-read, Abigail Smith Adams was a steadfast counselor to her husband, John, through revolutionary tumult, diplomatic complexities, and ultimately the difficulties of the American presidency.*

## "REMEMBER THE LADIES"

### Abigail Adams to John Adams, Braintree, Massachusetts—March 31, 1776

Abigail Adams (1744–1818), wife of John Adams (1735–1826), urged her husband, then a delegate from Massachusetts to the Second Continental Congress, to make laws that would recognize at least some rights for women in the nascent United States.

I LONG TO HEAR that you have declared an independency—and by the way in the new Code of Laws which I suppose it will be necessary for you to make I desire you would Remember the Ladies, and be more generous and favorable to them than your ancestors. Do not put such unlimited power into the hands of the Husbands. Remember all Men would be tyrants if they could. If particular care and attention is not paid to the Ladies we are determined to foment a Rebellion, and will not hold ourselves bound by any Laws in which we have no voice, or Representation.

That your Sex are Naturally Tyrannical is a Truth so thoroughly established as to admit of no dispute, but such of you as wish to be happy willingly give up the harsh title of Master for the more tender and endearing one of Friend. Why then, not put it out of the power of the vicious and the Lawless to use us with cruelty and indignity with impunity. Men of Sense in all Ages abhor those customs which treat us only as the vassals of your Sex. Regard us then as Beings placed by providence under your protection and in imitation of the Supreme Being make use of that power only for our happiness.

## PART II

# REVOLUTION TO REPUBLIC

*1776–1815*

I believe this . . . the strongest government on earth. I believe it the only one, where every man, at the call of the law, would fly to the standard of the law, and would meet invasions of the public order as his own personal concern.

—Thomas Jefferson, 1801

Previous Spread: *Presided over by George Washington, the Constitutional Convention met in Philadelphia in the summer of 1787. This 1940 painting by the artist Howard Chandler Christy is in the House wing of the Capitol of the United States.*

Once independence had been won in the 1780s, John Adams indulged in a bit of cynical—and self-pitying—speculation. "The history of our Revolution will be one continued lie from one end to the other," Adams, now vice president of the United States, wrote to Dr. Benjamin Rush in 1790. "The essence of the whole will be that Dr. Franklin's electrical Rod smote the Earth and out sprung General Washington. That Franklin electrified him with his rod—and thence forward these two conducted all the Policy, Negotiations, Legislatures and War." It was a typical worry of the political man—that the few would be celebrated while the many were forgotten. "A desire to be observed, considered, esteemed, praised, beloved, and admired by his fellows," Adams wrote, "is one of the earliest, as well as the keenest, dispositions discovered in the heart of man."

Adams understood that heart, which was often dark, and he was an essential part of an American founding that recognized human failings and sought to create a government that took account of ambition and of sin. In this part, we move from the Declaration of Independence with its aspirational opening to the hard work of making a Constitution. George Washington provided a model of exemplary conduct; his resignation of his commission to the Continental Congress was singular for its humility, marking a moment in which a man who likely could have amassed great personal power chose to surrender his place for the good of the whole. King George III is said to have recognized the scale of Washington's sacrifice, remarking that the American officer would be "the greatest man in the world" if he were to "retire to a private situation" once victory was won.

The failure of the Articles of Confederation to establish a coherent national government led to a call for a convention to be held in Philadelphia, a grand assembly that met from May to September 1787 to construct a new order based on divided sovereignty. In a final speech to the gathering, Benjamin Franklin spoke of compromise, a vital element in any large-scale public undertaking. Alexander Hamilton, James Madison, and John Jay authored a series of pro-ratification essays to encourage the states to adopt the Constitution. As Patrick Henry's impassioned anti-Federalist speech in Virginia indicates, victory was far from assured and was won only once promises were made to add a Bill of Rights as soon as practicable.

Partisanship was coeval with the formation of the new government. "Where a constitution, like ours, wears a mixed aspect of monarchy and republicanism," Thomas Jefferson wrote a decade after the convention, "its citizens will naturally divide into two classes of sentiment, according as their tone of body or mind, their habits, connections, and callings induce them to wish to strengthen either the monarchial or the republican features of the constitution." Washington warned against the "spirit of party" in his Farewell Address, but that spirit was perennial, for the clash of interests was never-ending. "The essence of a free government consists in an effectual control of rivalries," John Adams wrote. "The executive and the legislative powers are natural rivals; and if each has not an effectual control over the other, the weaker will ever be the lamb in the paws of the wolf. The nation which will not adopt an equilibrium of power must adopt a despotism. There is no other alternative. Rivalries must be controlled, or they will throw all things into confusion; and there is nothing but despotism or a balance of power which can control them." In what Jefferson attacked as a "reign of witches" during Adams's 1797 to 1801 presidency, the Alien and Sedition Acts became law, giving the executive the power to target immigrants and to suppress dissent.

A dozen years of Federalist rule thus came to an end with Jefferson's inauguration in March 1801, when Jefferson defeated Adams. As president, Washington had tended to fall in with Alexander Hamilton's vision of a strong national government, and Adams had continued along that path. The election of Jefferson marked the first transfer of power under the Constitution, and in his inaugural address the new president tried to define an American political culture in which differences of opinion were expected and managed within the rule of law and some measure of personal civility.

At the same time, slavery and anti-Black racial prejudice remained a fact of American life. In 1813, amid the War of 1812, James Forten of Pennsylvania protested a law seeking to ban people of color from settling in the state. It was a reminder, if any were needed, that the national project of liberty was far from complete.

★ ★ ★

## "WE HOLD THESE TRUTHS"
### Thomas Jefferson et al., the Declaration of Independence—1776

As a delegate from Virginia to the Second Continental Congress, Thomas Jefferson (1743–1826) was asked to draft a declaration of independence from Great Britain in the early summer of 1776. He did so in Philadelphia as a member of a committee that included Benjamin Franklin of Pennsylvania, John Adams of Massachusetts, Robert R. Livingston of New York, and Roger Sherman of Connecticut.

### IN CONGRESS, JULY 4, 1776

The unanimous Declaration of the thirteen united States of America, When in the Course of human events, it becomes necessary for one people to dissolve the political bands which have connected them with another, and to assume among the powers of the earth, the separate and equal station to which the Laws of Nature and of Nature's God entitle them, a decent respect to the opinions of mankind requires that they should declare the causes which impel them to the separation.

We hold these truths to be self-evident, that all men are created equal, that they are endowed by their Creator with certain unalienable Rights, that among these are Life, Liberty and the pursuit of Happiness.—That to secure these rights, Governments are instituted among Men, deriving their just powers from the consent of the governed,—That whenever any Form of Government becomes destructive of these ends, it is the Right of the People to alter or to abolish it, and to institute new Government, laying its foundation on such principles and organizing its powers in such form, as to them shall seem most likely to effect their Safety and Happiness. Prudence, indeed, will dictate that Governments long established should not be changed for light and transient causes; and accordingly all experience hath shewn, that mankind are more disposed to suffer, while evils are sufferable, than to right themselves by abolishing the forms to which they are accustomed. But when a long train of abuses and usurpations, pursuing invariably the same Object evinces a design to reduce them under absolute Despotism, it is their right, it is their duty, to throw off such Government, and to provide new Guards for their future

*At once political and philosophical, Thomas Jefferson was only thirty-three years old when he was assigned the task of drafting the Declaration of Independence from Great Britain.*

security.—Such has been the patient sufferance of these Colonies; and such is now the necessity which constrains them to alter their former Systems of Government. . . .

We, therefore, the Representatives of the united States of America, in General Congress, Assembled, appealing to the Supreme Judge of the world for the rectitude of our intentions, do, in the Name, and by Authority of the good People of these Colonies, solemnly publish and declare, That these United Colonies are, and of Right ought to be Free and Independent States; that they are Absolved from all Allegiance to the British Crown, and that all political connection between them and the State of Great Britain, is and ought to be totally dissolved; and that as Free and Independent States, they have full Power to levy War, conclude Peace, contract Alliances, establish Commerce, and to do all other Acts and Things which Independent States may of right do. And for the support of this Declaration, with a firm reliance on the protection of divine Providence, we mutually pledge to each other our Lives, our Fortunes and our sacred Honor.

★ ★ ★

## "I RETIRE FROM THE GREAT THEATRE"
## George Washington, Address to Congress Resigning His Commission—December 23, 1783

George Washington (1732–1799), who had led the Continental Army as commander in chief since 1775, traveled to Annapolis in late 1783 to offer his resignation in the wake of victory over the British. There was, one delegate noted, a "copious shedding of tears" as the general did that most unusual of things: voluntarily surrender power.

*The artist John Trumbull's rendering of General Washington's resigning his commission to the Congress, which was then sitting in Annapolis, Maryland, at the conclusion of the Revolutionary War.*

THE GREAT EVENTS on which my resignation depended having at length taken place; I have now the honor of offering my sincere Congratulations to Congress and of presenting myself before them to surrender into their hands the trust committed to me, and to claim the indulgence of retiring from the Service of my Country.

Happy in the confirmation of our Independence and Sovereignty, and pleased with the opportunity afforded the United States of becoming a respectable Nation, I resign with satisfaction the Appointment I accepted with diffidence. A diffidence in my abilities to accomplish so arduous a task, which however was superseded by a confidence in the rectitude of our Cause, the support of the Supreme Power of the Union, and the patronage of Heaven.

The Successful termination of the War has verified the most sanguine expectations, and my gratitude for the interposition of Providence, and the assistance I have received from my Country-men, increases with every review of the momentous Contest. . . .

Having now finished the work assigned me, I retire from the great theatre of Action; and bidding an Affectionate farewell to this August body under whose orders I have so long acted, I here offer my Commission, and take my leave of all the employments of public life.

★ ★ ★

## "FOR THE SAKE OF OUR POSTERITY"

### Benjamin Franklin, Final Speech to the Constitutional Convention—September 17, 1787

---

It had been a long summer. As the Constitutional Convention came to a close, Benjamin Franklin (1706–1790) rose to offer a kind of benediction. A plea for proportion and for a willingness to live with ambiguity, Franklin's remarks encouraged the delegates to send the draft to the states for ratification with one voice.

I CONFESS THAT I do not entirely approve of this Constitution at present, but Sir, I am not sure I shall never approve it: For having lived long, I have experienced many Instances of being oblig'd, by better Information or fuller Consideration, to change Opinions even on important Subjects, which I once thought right, but found to be otherwise. It is therefore that the older I grow the more apt I am to doubt my own Judgment and to pay more Respect to the Judgment of others. . . .

In these Sentiments, Sir, I agree to this Constitution, with all its Faults, if they are such: because I think a General Government necessary for us, and there is no Form of Government but what may be a Blessing to the

*Wily and worldly, Benjamin Franklin brought decades of experience and a sense of balance to the often contentious debates over the Constitution in the summer of 1787.*

People if well administered; and I believe farther that this is likely to be well administered for a Course of Years, and can only end in Despotism as other Forms have done before it, when the People shall become so corrupted as to need Despotic Government, being incapable of any other. I doubt too whether any other Convention we can obtain, may be able to make a better Constitution: For when you assemble a Number of Men to have the Advantage of their joint Wisdom, you inevitably assemble with those Men all their Prejudices, their Passions, their Errors of Opinion, their local Interests, and their selfish Views. From such an Assembly can a perfect Production be expected? It therefore astonishes me, Sir, to find this System approaching so near to Perfection as it does; and I think it will astonish our Enemies, who are waiting with Confidence to hear that our Councils are confounded, like those of the Builders of Babel, and that our States are on the Point of Separation, only to meet hereafter for the Purpose of cutting one another's Throats. Thus I consent, Sir, to this Constitution because I expect no better, and because I am not sure that it is not the best. The Opinions I have had of its Errors, I sacrifice to the Public Good. I have never whisper'd a Syllable of them abroad. Within these Walls they were born, & here they shall die. If every one of us in returning to our Constituents were to report the Objections he has had to it, and endeavor to gain Partisans in support of them, we might prevent its being generally received, and thereby lose all the salutary Effects & great Advantages resulting naturally in our favor among foreign Nations, as well as among ourselves, from our real or apparent Unanimity. Much of the Strength and Efficiency of any Government, in procuring & securing Happiness to the People depends on Opinion, on the general Opinion of the Goodness of that Government as well as of the Wisdom & Integrity of its Governors. I hope therefore that for our own Sakes, as a Part of the People, and for the Sake of our Posterity, we shall act heartily & unanimously in recommending this Constitution, wherever our Influence may extend, and turn our future Thoughts and Endeavors to the Means of having it well administered.

On the whole, Sir, I cannot help expressing a Wish, that every Member of the Convention, who may still have Objections to it, would with me on this Occasion doubt a little of his own Infallibility, and to make manifest our Unanimity, put his Name to this Instrument.

★ ★ ★

## "WE THE PEOPLE"
### Preamble to the Constitution—1787

Edited by Pennsylvania delegate Gouverneur Morris (1752–1816), the final preamble was the product of the convention's Committee of Style, which received the draft document on Saturday, September 8, 1787.

WE THE PEOPLE of the United States, in Order to form a more perfect Union, establish Justice, insure domestic Tranquility, provide for the common defense, promote the general Welfare, and secure the Blessings of Liberty to ourselves and our Posterity, do ordain and establish this Constitution for the United States of America.

★ ★ ★

## "THE UTILITY OF THE UNION"
### Alexander Hamilton, *The Federalist No. 1*—October 27, 1787

Along with James Madison (1751–1836) and John Jay (1745–1829), Alexander Hamilton (1757?–1804) wrote a series of newspaper essays urging the adoption of the Constitution by the state ratifying conventions. Taken together, eighty-five pieces were published between October 1787 and May 1788.

AMONG THE MOST formidable of the obstacles which the new Constitution will have to encounter may readily be distinguished the obvious interest of a certain class of men in every State to resist all changes which may hazard a diminution of the power, emolument, and consequence of the offices they hold under the State establishments; and the perverted ambition of another class of men, who will either hope to aggrandize themselves by the confusions of their country, or will flatter themselves with fairer prospects of elevation from the subdivision of the empire into several partial confederacies than from its union under one government.

*The cosmopolitan Alexander Hamilton, who believed there was much in the British system of government to be admired and emulated, took the lead in defending the proposed Constitution during ratification.*

It is not, however, my design to dwell upon observations of this nature. I am well aware that it would be disingenuous to resolve indiscriminately the opposition of any set of men (merely because their situations might subject them to suspicion) into interested or ambitious views. Candor will oblige us to admit that even such men may be actuated by upright intentions; and it cannot be doubted that much of the opposition which has made its appearance, or may hereafter make its appearance, will spring from sources, blameless at least, if not respectable—the honest errors of minds led astray by preconceived jealousies and fears. So numerous indeed and so powerful are the causes which serve to give a false bias to the judgment, that we, upon many occasions, see wise and good men on the wrong as well as on the right side of questions of the first magnitude to society. This circumstance, if duly attended to, would furnish a lesson of moderation to those who are ever so much persuaded of their being in the right in any controversy. And a further reason for caution, in this respect, might be drawn from the reflection that we are not always sure that those who advocate the truth are influenced by purer principles than their antagonists. Ambition, avarice, personal animosity, party opposition, and many other motives not more laudable than these, are apt to operate as well upon those who support as those who oppose the right side of a question. Were there not even these inducements to moderation, nothing could be more ill-judged than that intolerant spirit which has, at all times, characterized political parties. For in politics, as in religion, it is equally absurd to aim at making proselytes by fire and sword. Heresies in either can rarely be cured by persecution.

And yet, however just these sentiments will be allowed to be, we have already sufficient indications that it will happen in this as in all former cases of great national discussion. A torrent of angry and malignant passions will be let loose. To judge from the conduct of the opposite parties, we shall be led to conclude that they will mutually hope to evince the justness of their opinions, and to increase the number of their converts by the loudness of their declamations and the bitterness of their invectives. An enlightened zeal for the energy and efficiency of government will be stigmatized as the offspring of a temper fond of despotic power and hostile to the principles of liberty. An over-scrupulous jealousy of danger to the rights of the people, which is more commonly the fault of the head than of the heart, will be represented as mere pretense and artifice, the stale bait for popularity at the expense of the public good. It will be forgotten, on the one hand, that jealousy is the usual concomitant of love, and that the noble enthusiasm of liberty is apt to be infected with a spirit of narrow and illiberal distrust. On the other hand, it will be equally forgotten that the vigor of government is essential to the security of liberty; that, in the contemplation of a sound and well-informed judgment, their interest can never be separated; and that a dangerous ambition more often lurks behind the specious mask of zeal for the rights of the people than under the forbidden appearance of zeal for the firmness and efficiency of government. History will teach us that the former has been found a much more certain road to the introduction of despotism than the latter, and that of those men who have overturned the liberties of republics, the greatest number have begun their career by paying an obsequious court to the people; commencing demagogues, and ending tyrants.

In the course of the preceding observations, I have had an eye, my fellow-citizens, to putting you upon your guard against all attempts, from whatever quarter, to influence your decision in a matter of the utmost moment to your welfare, by any impressions other than those which may result from the evidence of truth. You will, no doubt, at the same time, have collected from the general scope of them, that they proceed from a source not unfriendly to the new Constitution. Yes, my countrymen, I own to you that, after having given it an attentive consideration, I am clearly of opinion it is your interest to adopt it. I am convinced that this is the safest course for your liberty, your dignity, and your happiness. I affect not reserves which I do not feel. I will not amuse you with an appearance of deliberation when I have decided. I frankly acknowledge to you my convictions, and I will freely lay before you the reasons on which they are founded. The consciousness of good intentions disdains ambiguity. I shall not, however, multiply professions on this head. My motives must remain in the depository of my own breast. My arguments will be open to all, and may be judged of by all. They shall at least be offered in a spirit which will not disgrace the cause of truth.

I propose, in a series of papers, to discuss the following interesting particulars:

THE UTILITY OF THE UNION TO YOUR POLITICAL PROSPERITY

THE INSUFFICIENCY OF THE PRESENT CONFEDERATION TO PRESERVE THAT UNION

THE NECESSITY OF A GOVERNMENT AT LEAST EQUALLY ENERGETIC WITH THE ONE PROPOSED, TO THE ATTAINMENT OF THIS OBJECT

THE CONFORMITY OF THE PROPOSED CONSTITUTION TO THE TRUE PRINCIPLES OF REPUBLICAN GOVERNMENT

ITS ANALOGY TO YOUR OWN STATE CONSTITUTION

and lastly, THE ADDITIONAL SECURITY WHICH ITS ADOPTION WILL AFFORD TO THE PRESERVATION OF THAT SPECIES OF GOVERNMENT, TO LIBERTY, AND TO PROPERTY. . . .

It may perhaps be thought superfluous to offer arguments to prove the utility of the UNION, a point, no doubt, deeply engraved on the hearts of the great body of the people in every State, and one, which it may be imagined, has no adversaries. But the fact is, that we already hear it whispered in the private circles of those who oppose the new Constitution, that the thirteen States are of too great extent for any general system, and that we must of necessity resort to separate confederacies of distinct portions of the whole. This doctrine will, in all probability, be gradually propagated, till it has votaries enough to countenance an open avowal of it. For nothing can be more evident, to those who are able to take an enlarged view of the subject, than the alternative of an adoption of the new Constitution or a dismemberment of the Union. It will therefore be of use to begin by examining the advantages of that Union, the certain evils, and the probable dangers, to which every State will be exposed from its dissolution. This shall accordingly constitute the subject of my next address.

PUBLIUS.

★ ★ ★

## "ENLIGHTENED STATESMEN WILL NOT ALWAYS BE AT THE HELM"

### James Madison, *The Federalist No. 10*—November 22, 1787

Virginia's James Madison was perhaps the central architect of the Constitution. A quiet force, he had studied the history of republics with care and held a persistent view that human frailty and ambition required checks and balances in order to sustain an experiment in popular government.

BY A FACTION, I understand a number of citizens, whether amounting to a majority or a minority of the whole, who are united and actuated by some common impulse of passion, or of interest, adverse to the rights of other citizens, or to the permanent and aggregate interests of the community.

There are two methods of curing the mischiefs of faction: the one, by removing its causes; the other, by controlling its effects.

There are again two methods of removing the causes of faction: the one, by destroying the liberty which is essential to its existence; the other, by giving to every citizen the same opinions, the same passions, and the same interests.

It could never be more truly said than of the first remedy, that it was worse than the disease. Liberty is to faction what air is to fire, an aliment without which it instantly expires. But it could not be less folly to abolish liberty, which is essential to political life, because it nourishes faction, than it would be to wish the annihilation of air, which is essential to animal life, because it imparts to fire its destructive agency.

*James Madison—bookish, diminutive, and determined—was perhaps the crucial architect of the Constitution. His skepticism about human nature drove him to insist on a division of power to check the influence of any single interest.*

The second expedient is as impracticable as the first would be unwise. As long as the reason of man continues fallible, and he is at liberty to exercise it, different opinions will be formed. As long as the connection subsists between his reason and his self-love, his opinions and his passions will have a reciprocal influence on each other; and the former will be objects to which the latter will attach themselves. The diversity in the faculties of men, from which the rights of property originate, is not less an insuperable obstacle to a uniformity of interests. The protection of these faculties is the first object of government. From the protection of different and unequal faculties of acquiring property, the possession of different degrees and kinds of property immediately results; and from the influence of these on the sentiments and views of the respective proprietors, ensues a division of the society into different interests and parties.

The latent causes of faction are thus sown in the nature of man; and we see them everywhere brought into different degrees of activity, according to the different circumstances of civil society. A zeal for different opinions concerning religion, concerning government, and many other points, as well of speculation as of practice; an attachment to different leaders ambitiously contending for pre-eminence and power; or to persons of other descriptions whose fortunes have been interesting to the human passions, have, in turn, divided mankind into parties, inflamed them with mutual animosity, and rendered them much more disposed to vex and oppress each other than to co-operate for their common good. So strong is this propensity of mankind to fall into mutual animosities, that where no substantial occasion presents itself, the most frivolous and fanciful distinctions have been sufficient to kindle their unfriendly passions and excite their most violent conflicts. . . . But the most common and durable source of factions has been the various and unequal distribution of property. Those who hold and those who are without property have ever formed distinct interests in society. Those who are creditors, and those who are debtors, fall under a like discrimination. A landed interest, a manufacturing interest, a mercantile interest, a moneyed interest, with many lesser interests, grow up of necessity in civilized nations, and divide them into different classes, actuated by different sentiments and views. The regulation of these various and interfering interests forms the principal task of modern legislation, and involves the spirit of party and faction in the necessary and ordinary operations of the government. . . .

It is in vain to say that enlightened statesmen will be able to adjust these clashing interests, and render them all subservient to the public good. Enlightened statesmen will not always be at the helm. Nor, in many cases, can such an adjustment be made at all without taking into view indirect and remote considerations, which will rarely prevail over the immediate interest which one party may find in disregarding the rights of another or the good of the whole.

The inference to which we are brought is, that the CAUSES of faction cannot be removed, and that relief is only to be sought in the means of controlling its EFFECTS.

If a faction consists of less than a majority, relief is supplied by the republican principle, which enables the majority to defeat its sinister views by regular vote. It may clog the administration, it may convulse the society; but it will be unable to execute and mask its violence under the forms of the Constitution. When a majority is included in a faction, the form of popular government, on the other hand, enables it to sacrifice to its ruling passion or interest both the public good and the rights of other citizens. To secure the public good and private rights against the danger of such a faction, and at the same time to preserve the spirit and the form of popular government, is then the great object to which our inquiries are directed. Let me add that it is the great desideratum by which this form of government can be rescued from the opprobrium under which it has so long labored, and be recommended to the esteem and adoption of mankind.

By what means is this object attainable? Evidently by one of two only. Either the existence of the same passion or interest in a majority at the same time must be prevented, or the majority, having such coexistent passion or interest, must be rendered, by their number and local situation, unable to concert and carry into effect schemes of oppression. If the impulse and the opportunity be suffered to coincide, we well know that neither moral nor religious motives can be relied on as an adequate control. They are not found to be such on the injustice and violence of individuals, and lose their efficacy in proportion to the number combined together, that is, in proportion as their efficacy becomes needful.

From this view of the subject it may be concluded that a pure democracy, by which I mean a society consisting of a small number of citizens, who assemble and administer the government in person, can admit of no cure for the mischiefs of faction. A common passion or interest will, in almost every case, be felt by a majority of the whole; a communication and concert result from the form of government itself; and there is nothing to check the inducements to sacrifice the weaker party or an obnoxious individual. Hence it is that such democracies have ever been spectacles of turbulence and contention; have ever been found incompatible with personal security or the rights of property; and have in general been as short in their lives as they have been violent in their deaths. Theoretic politicians, who have patronized this species of government, have erroneously supposed that by reducing mankind to a perfect equality in their political rights, they would, at the same time, be perfectly equalized and assimilated in their possessions, their opinions, and their passions.

A republic, by which I mean a government in which the scheme of representation takes place, opens a different prospect, and promises the cure for which we are seeking.

★ ★ ★

## "IT IS NOT A DEMOCRACY"

### Patrick Henry, Antifederalist Speech to the Virginia Ratifying Convention—June 5, 1788

A fabled patriot in the Revolutionary cause, Patrick Henry (1736–1799) was a powerful and popular politician in Virginia who had twice served as governor. His opposition to the proposed federal Constitution helped bring about the Bill of Rights as part of the price of ratification.

I WISH I WAS possessed with talents, or possessed of anything that might enable me to elucidate this great subject. I am not free from suspicion: I am apt to entertain doubts. . . . The fate of this question and of America may depend on this. Have they said, We, the states? Have they made a proposal of a compact between states? If they had, this would be a confederation. It is otherwise most clearly a consolidated government. The question turns, sir, on that poor little thing—the expression, We, the people, instead of the states, of America. I need not take much pains to show that the principles of this system are extremely pernicious, impolitic, and dangerous. Is this a monarchy, like England—a compact between prince and people, with checks on the former to secure the liberty of the latter? Is this a confederacy, like Holland—an association of a number of independent states, each of which retains its individual sovereignty? It is not a democracy, wherein the people retain all their rights securely. Had these principles been adhered to, we should not have been brought to this alarming transition, from a confederacy to a consolidated government. . . . Here is a

*In the Virginia ratification debates, the eloquent Patrick Henry, the first and sixth governor, turned his formidable energies against the proposed Constitution—and very nearly prevailed.*

resolution as radical as that which separated us from Great Britain. It is radical in this transition; our rights and privileges are endangered, and the sovereignty of the states will be relinquished: and cannot we plainly see that this is actually the case? The rights of conscience, trial by jury, liberty of the press, all your immunities and franchises, all pretensions to human rights and privileges, are rendered insecure, if not lost, by this change, so loudly talked of by some, and inconsiderately by others. Is this tame relinquishment of rights worthy of freemen? Is it worthy of that manly fortitude that ought to characterize republicans? It is said eight states have adopted this plan. I declare that if twelve states and a half had adopted it, I would, with manly firmness, and in spite of an erring world, reject it. . . .

This Constitution is said to have beautiful features; but when I come to examine these features, sir, they appear to me horribly frightful. Among other deformities, it has an awful squinting; it squints towards monarchy; and does not this raise indignation in the breast of every true American?

Your President may easily become king. Your Senate is so imperfectly constructed that your dearest rights may be sacrificed by what may be a small minority; and a very small minority may continue forever unchangeably this government, although horridly defective. . . . Show me that age and country where the rights and liberties of the people were placed on the sole chance of their rulers being good men, without a consequent loss of liberty!

If your American chief be a man of ambition and abilities, how easy is it for him to render himself absolute! The army is in his hands, and if he be a man of address, it will be attached to him, and it will be the subject of long meditation with him to seize the first auspicious moment to accomplish his design; and, sir, will the American spirit solely relieve you when this happens? . . . Away with your President! we shall have a king: the army will salute him monarch: your militia will leave you, and assist in making him king, and fight against you: and what have you to oppose this force? What will then become of you and your rights? Will not absolute despotism ensue?

★ ★ ★

## "WE HAVE BECOME A NATION"

### Benjamin Rush, Observations on the Fourth of July Procession in Philadelphia, *Pennsylvania Mercury*—July 15, 1788

The Pennsylvania physician Benjamin Rush (1746–1813) had signed the Declaration of Independence and served as a delegate to the Constitutional Convention.

THE CLERGY FORMED a very agreeable part of the Procession—They manifested, by their attendance, their sense of the connection between religion and good government. They amounted to seventeen in number. Four and five of them marched arm in arm with each other, to exemplify the Union. Pains were taken to connect Ministers of the most dissimilar religious principles together, thereby to shew the influence of a free government in promoting christian charity. The Rabbi of the Jews, locked in the arms of two ministers of the gospel, was a most delightful sight. There could not have been a more happy emblem contrived, of that section of the new constitution, which opens all its power and offices alike, not only to every sect of christians, but to worthy men of *every* religion. . . .

I must not forget to mention that the weather proved uncommonly favourable to the entertainment. The sun was not to be seen till near two o'clock, at which time the procession was over. A pleasant and cooling breeze blew all day from the south, and in the evening the sky was illuminated by a beautiful Aurora Borealis. Under this head another fact is equally worthy of notice. Notwithstanding the haste with which the machines were made, and the manner in which they were drawn through the streets, and notwithstanding the great number of women and children that were assembled on fences, scaffolds and the roofs of houses, to see the procession, *no one* accident happened to any body. These circumstances gave occasion for hundreds to remark that "Heaven was on the federal side of the question."

'Tis done! We have become a nation.—America has ceased to be the only power in the world, that has derived no benefit from her declaration of independence. We are more than repaid for the distresses of the war, and the disappointments of the peace. The torpid resources of our country already discover signs of life and motion. We are no longer the scoff of our enemies. The reign of violence is over. Justice has descended from heaven to dwell in our land, and ample restitution has at last been made to human nature, by our New Constitution, for all the injuries she has sustained in the old world from arbitrary governments—false religions—and unlawful commerce.

★ ★ ★

## "SHARPENED BY THE SPIRIT OF REVENGE"
### George Washington, Farewell Address— Published September 19, 1796

---

Washington chose to retire from the presidency after two terms, setting a precedent that would endure until 1940. Written with the aid of both Alexander Hamilton and James Madison, Washington's Farewell Address called on the country to eschew reflexive partisanship and cultivate civic virtue.

LET ME NOW take a . . . comprehensive view, & warn you in the most solemn manner against the baneful effects of the Spirit of Party, generally.

This spirit, unfortunately, is inseparable from our nature, having its root in the strongest passions of the human Mind. It exists under different shapes in all Governments, more or less stifled, controlled, or repressed; but in those of the popular form it is seen in its greatest rankness and is truly their worst enemy.

The alternate domination of one faction over another, sharpened by the spirit of revenge natural to party dissension, which in different ages & countries has perpetrated the most horrid enormities, is itself a frightful despotism. But this leads at length to a more formal and permanent despotism. The disorders & miseries, which result, gradually incline the minds of men to seek security & repose in the absolute power of an Individual: and sooner or later the chief of some prevailing faction more able or more fortunate than his competitors, turns this disposition to the purposes of his own elevation, on the ruins of Public Liberty.

Without looking forward to an extremity of this kind (which nevertheless ought not to be entirely out of sight) the common & continual mischiefs of the spirit of Party are sufficient to make it the interest and the duty of a wise People to discourage and restrain it.

It serves always to distract the Public Councils and enfeeble the Public Administration. It agitates the Community with ill-founded jealousies and false alarms, kindles the animosity of one part against another, foments occasionally riot & insurrection. It opens the door to foreign influence & corruption, which find a facilitated access to the government itself through the channels of party passions. Thus the policy and the will of one country, are subjected to the policy and will of another.

There is an opinion that parties in free countries are useful checks upon the Administration of the Government and serve to keep alive the spirit of Liberty. This within certain limits is probably true—and in Governments of a Monarchical cast Patriotism may look with indulgence, if not with favor, upon the spirit of party. But in those of the popular character, in Governments purely elective, it is a spirit not to be encouraged. From their natural tendency, it is certain there will always be enough of that spirit for every salutary purpose. And there being constant danger of excess, the effort ought to be, by force of public opinion, to mitigate & assuage it. A fire not to be quenched; it demands a uniform vigilance to prevent its bursting into a flame, lest instead of warming it should consume. . . .

Of all the dispositions and habits which lead to political prosperity,

Religion and morality are indispensable supports. In vain would that man claim the tribute of Patriotism, who should labor to subvert these great Pillars of human happiness, these firmest props of the duties of Men & citizens. The mere Politician, equally with the pious man ought to respect & to cherish them. A volume could not trace all their connections with private & public felicity. Let it simply be asked where is the security for property, for reputation, for life, if the sense of religious obligation *desert* the oaths, which are the instruments of investigation in Courts of Justice? And let us with caution indulge the supposition, that morality can be maintained without religion. Whatever may be conceded to the influence of refined education on minds of peculiar structure—reason & experience both forbid us to expect that National morality can prevail in exclusion of religious principle.

★ ★ ★

## "WITH ONE HEART AND ONE MIND"

### Thomas Jefferson, First Inaugural Address—March 4, 1801

Jefferson's narrow election over John Adams in 1800 marked the first transfer of American power between competing parties.

ALL . . . will bear in mind this sacred principle, that though the will of the majority is in all cases to prevail, that will, to be rightful, must be reasonable; that the minority possess their equal rights, which equal laws must protect, and to violate would be oppression. Let us then, fellow citizens, unite with one heart and one mind, let us restore to social intercourse that harmony and affection without which liberty, and even life itself, are but dreary things. And let us reflect that having banished from our land that religious intolerance under which mankind so long bled and suffered, we have yet gained little if we countenance a political intolerance, as despotic, as wicked, and capable of as bitter and bloody persecutions. During the throes and convulsions of the ancient world, during the agonizing spasms of infuriated man, seeking through blood and slaughter his long lost liberty, it was not wonderful that the agitation of the billows should reach even this distant and peaceful shore; that this should be more felt and feared by some and less by others; and should divide opinions as to measures of safety; but every difference of opinion is not a difference of principle. We have called by different names brethren of the same principle. We are all republicans: we are all federalists. If there be any among us who would wish to dissolve this Union, or to change its republican form, let them stand undisturbed as monuments of the safety with which error of opinion may be tolerated, where reason is left free to combat it. I know indeed that some honest men fear that a republican government cannot be strong; that this government is not strong enough. But would the honest patriot, in the full tide of successful experiment, abandon a government which has so far kept us free and firm, on the theoretic and visionary fear, that this government, the world's best hope, may, by possibility, want energy to preserve itself? I trust not. I believe this, on the contrary, the strongest government on earth. I believe it the only one, where every man, at the call of the law, would fly to the standard of the law, and would meet invasions of the public order as his own personal concern.—Sometimes it is said that man cannot be trusted with the government of himself. Can he then be trusted with the government of others? Or have we found angels, in the form of kings, to govern him? Let history answer this question.

Let us then, with courage and confidence, pursue our own federal and republican principles; our attachment to union and representative government.

⋆ ⋆ ⋆

## "WITH SHAMEFUL STRIPES"

### James Forten, *Letters from a Man of Colour, on a Late Bill Before the Senate of Pennsylvania*—April 1813

A free Black man born in Philadelphia, James Forten (1766–1842) was a leading abolitionist. His *Letters from a Man of Colour* argued against a Pennsylvania law prohibiting the immigration of other free Black people into the state.

WE HOLD THIS truth to be self-evident that God created all men equal, and is one of the most prominent features in the Declaration of Independence and in that glorious fabrick of collected wisdom, our noble Constitution. This idea embraces the Indian and European, the Savage and the Saint, the Peruvian and the Laplander, the white Man and the African, and whatever measures are adopted subversive of this inestimable privilege, are in direct violation of the letter and spirit of our Constitution, and become subject to the animadversion of all, particularly those who are deeply interested in the measure.

These thoughts were suggested by the promulgation of a late bill, before the Senate of Pennsylvania, to prevent the emigration of people of colour into this state. It was not passed into law at this session and must in consequence lay over until the next, before when we sincerely hope, the white men, whom we should look upon as our protectors, will have become convinced of the inhumanity and impolicy of such a measure, and forbear to deprive us of those inestimable treasures, Liberty and Independence. This is almost the only state in the Union wherein the African race have justly boasted of rational liberty and the protection of the laws, and shall it now be said they have been deprived of that liberty, and publickly exposed for sale to the highest bidder? Shall colonial inhumanity that has marked many of us with shameful stripes, become the practice of the people of Pennsylvania, while Mercy stands weeping at the miserable spectacle?

People of Pennsylvania, descendants of the immortal Penn, doom us not to the unhappy fate of thousands of our countrymen in the Southern States and the West Indies; despise the traffick in blood, and the blessing of the African will forever be around you. Many of us are men of property, for the security of which, we have hitherto looked to the laws of our blessed state, but should this become a law, our property is jeopardized, since the same power which can expose to sale an unfortunate fellow creature, can wrest from him those estates, which years of honest industry have accumulated. Where shall the poor African look for protection, should the people of Pennsylvania consent to oppress him? We grant there are a number of worthless men belonging to our colour, but there are laws of sufficient rigour for their punishment, if properly and duly enforced. We wish not to screen the guilty from punishment, but with the guilty do not permit the innocent to suffer. If there are worthless men, there are also men of merit among the African race, who are useful members of Society. The truth of this let their benevolent institutions and the numbers clothed and fed by them witness. Punish the guilty man of colour to the utmost limit of the laws, but sell him not to slavery! If he is in danger of becoming a publick charge prevent him! If he is too indolent to labour for his own subsistence, compel him to do so; but sell him not to slavery. By selling him you do not make him better, but commit a wrong, without benefitting the object of it or society at large. Many of our ancestors were brought here more than one hundred years ago; many of our fathers, many of ourselves, have fought and bled for the Independence of our country. Do not then expose us to sale. Let not the spirit of the father behold the son robbed of that Liberty which he died to establish, but let the motto of our Legislators be: "The Law knows no distinction."

A MAN OF COLOUR.

PART III

# THE UNION AND ITS DISCONTENTS

## *1815–1860*

Education, then, beyond all other devices of human origin, is the great equalizer of the conditions of men—the balance-wheel of the social machinery.

—Horace Mann, 1848

PREVIOUS SPREAD: *This 1942 painting depicts the Trail of Tears—the forced 1838 removal of the Cherokees from their ancestral lands east of the Mississippi River to present-day Oklahoma.*

"I WAS BORN FOR A STORM," Andrew Jackson once remarked, "and a calm does not suit me." The lawyer, slave-owning Tennessee planter, legislator, and general came from the lowest rungs of white society in America, driving himself forward after an orphaned youth in the Carolinas. He came to national renown with his victory over the British in the Battle of New Orleans in the first days of January 1815—a military success that was seen as the capstone of the War of 1812, a clash of arms ending the fifty-year struggle for American sovereignty that had begun with the Stamp Act in 1765.

The decades of the 1820s through Fort Sumter were shaped by contradictory trends. One was the gradual democratization of American life for white men—the spread of suffrage, the creation of economic opportunities, and the rise of what scholars sometimes call the Market Revolution. "The principle of equality, which makes men independent of each other, gives them a habit and a taste for following in their private actions no other guide than their own will," Alexis de Tocqueville wrote in his 1831 *Democracy in America*. "This complete independence, which they constantly enjoy in regard to their equals and in the intercourse of private life, tends to make them look upon all authority with a jealous eye and speedily suggests to them the notion and the love of political freedom. Men living at such times have a natural bias towards free institutions."

Another vital force was the contest between pro- and antislavery opinion. Partly inspired by the successful abolition campaign in Britain—Parliament passed a gradual-emancipation bill in 1833—antislavery sentiment was gaining strength in America. William Lloyd Garrison founded the abolitionist newspaper *The Liberator* in 1831; by decade's end the American Anti-Slavery Society would publish *American Slavery as It Is: Testimony of a Thousand Witnesses,* compiled by Theodore Dwight Weld, Angelina Grimké, and Sarah Grimké. Reaction was swift: White Southerners began to question the utility of the Union if national sentiment was to run against the slave-owning interest. The long-standing defense of slavery as a "necessary evil" inflicted on the New World by Great Britain gave way to arguments that the institution was "a good—a positive good," as John C. Calhoun of South Carolina put it in 1837.

An early test of the relative strength of the white Southern interest came in battles over a federal protective tariff in the late 1820s and early 1830s. Calhoun offered a case for nullification, the alleged right of a state to choose which federal laws it would follow; as president, Andrew Jackson stood strong, arguing for the supremacy of the Union—a case made even more eloquently and passionately by Daniel Webster. The issue came to a crisis in 1832 and 1833, when Jackson threatened the use of troops to enforce federal authority in a resistant South Carolina before a compromise was reached. (The objectionable tariff was reduced.) The enduring legacy of the nullification drama was the articulation of the dispositive role of federal power—and everyone knew, or at least suspected, that the tariff had been but a proxy for coming battles over the future of slavery. By opposing Calhoun and the South Carolinians, Jackson gave his successors—notably Abraham Lincoln, who would consult both Jackson's Proclamation of December 1832 and Webster's Senate speech on liberty and union in drafting his own first inaugural—an example of presidential leadership in the cause of Union over secession.

The nature of liberty was ferociously debated in these decades. Advocates of suffrage for women met at Seneca Falls, New York; Frederick Douglass did all he could to fire what he called "the conscience of the Nation" in favor of emancipation; and defenders of the interests of Native Americans argued, unsuccessfully, in favor of the rights of indigenous peoples. Given the seeming intractability of the American system to address such questions, chiefly slavery, William Lloyd Garrison attacked the Constitution as "an agreement with death and a covenant with hell." Garrison's view was that the document was not commensurate with the moral challenges of the age. Frederick Douglass disagreed, arguing that the Union under the Constitution offered reformers the best chance to move forward.

★ ★ ★

## "TO INTERPOSE HER VETO"
## John C. Calhoun, *South Carolina Exposition and Protest*—December 19, 1828

John C. Calhoun (1782–1850) articulated a theory of states' rights that gave a philosophical framework to white Southern sectionalism. While the initial occasion for the doctrine of nullification was the federal tariff that the South found objectionable, it was clear to contemporaries that Calhoun's work would ultimately be of utility should the federal government move against slavery.

LOOKING TO FACTS and not mere hypothesis, the constitution has made us a community only to the extent of our common interest, leaving the states distinct and independent, as to their peculiar interests, and has drawn the line of separation with consummate skill. The great question however is, what means are provided by our system for the purpose of enforcing this fundamental provision: If we look to the practical operation of the system, we will find, on the side of the states, not a solitary constitutional means resorted to, in order to protect their reserved rights, against the encroachment of the general government. . . .

With these views the committee are solemnly of impression if the system be persevered in, after due forbearance on the part of the state, that it will be her sacred duty to interpose her veto; a duty to herself, to the Union, to present, and to future generations, and to the cause of liberty over the world, to arrest the progress of a power, which, if not arrested, must in its consequences, corrupt the public morals, and destroy the liberty of the country.

★ ★ ★

## "YOUR CRUELTIES AND MURDERS"
## David Walker, *Appeal to the Coloured Citizens of the World*—September 1829

Born to a free mother and an enslaved father in North Carolina, David Walker (1786–1830) settled in Boston and became a widely read advocate of abolition.

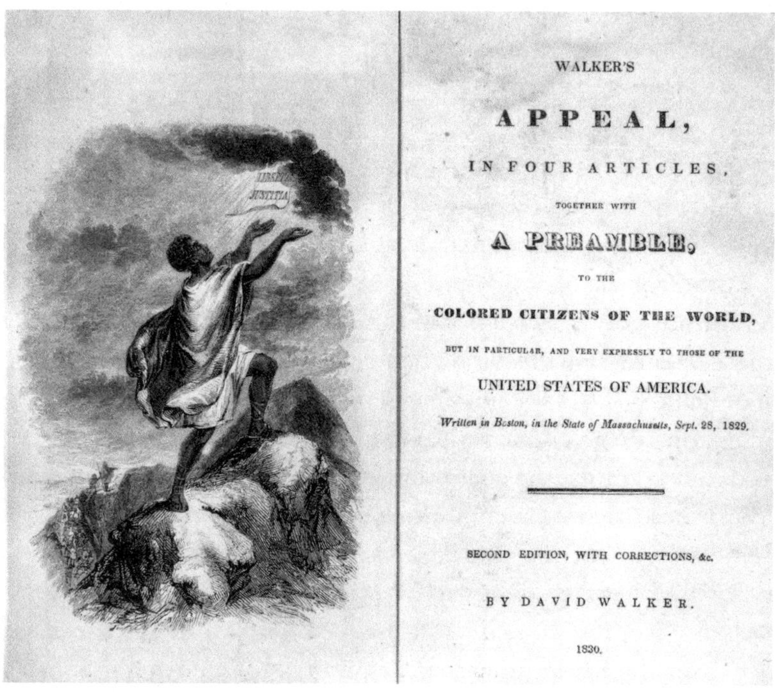

WALKER'S

APPEAL,

IN FOUR ARTICLES,

TOGETHER WITH

A PREAMBLE,

TO THE

COLORED CITIZENS OF THE WORLD,

BUT IN PARTICULAR, AND VERY EXPRESSLY TO THOSE OF THE

UNITED STATES OF AMERICA.

*Written in Boston, in the State of Massachusetts, Sept. 28, 1829.*

SECOND EDITION, WITH CORRECTIONS, &c.

BY DAVID WALKER.

1830.

MY DEARLY BELOVED *Brethren and Fellow Citizens.*

Having travelled over a considerable portion of these United States, and having, in the course of my travels, taken the most accurate observations of things as they exist—the result of my observations has warranted the full and unshaken conviction, that we, (coloured people of these United States,) are the most degraded, wretched, and abject set of beings that ever lived since the world began; and I pray God that none like us ever may live again until time shall be no more. They tell us of the Israelites in Egypt, the Helots in Sparta, and of the Roman Slaves, which last were made up from almost every nation under heaven, whose sufferings under those ancient and heathen nations, were, in comparison with ours, under this enlightened and Christian nation, no more than a cypher—or, in other words, those heathen nations of antiquity, had but little more among them than the name and form of slavery; while wretchedness and endless miseries were reserved, apparently in a phial, to be poured out upon our fathers ourselves and our children, by *Christian* Americans! . . .

I call upon the professing Christians, I call upon the philanthropist, I call upon the very tyrant himself, to show me a page of history, either sacred or profane, on which a verse can be found, which maintains, that the Egyptians heaped the *insupportable insult* upon the children of Israel, by telling them that they were not of the *human family*. Can the whites deny this charge? Have they not, after having reduced us to the deplorable condition of slaves under their feet, held us up as descending originally from the tribes of *Monkeys* or *Orang-Outangs*? O! my God! I appeal to every man of feeling—is not this insupportable? Is it not heaping the most gross insult upon our miseries, because they have got us under their feet and we cannot help ourselves? Oh! pity us we pray thee, Lord Jesus, Master. . . .

I must observe to my brethren that at the close of the first Revolution in this country, with Great Britain, there were but thirteen States in the Union, now there are twenty-four, most of which are slaveholding States, and the whites are dragging us around in chains and in handcuffs, to their new States and Territories to work their mines and farms, to enrich them and their children—and millions of them believing firmly that we being a little darker than they, were made by our Creator to be an inheritance to them and their children for ever—the same as a parcel of *brutes*.

Are we MEN! !—I ask you, O my brethren—are we MEN? Did our Creator make us to be slaves to dust and ashes like ourselves? Are they not dying worms as well as we? Have they not to make their appearance before the tribunal of Heaven, to answer for the deeds done in the body, as well as we? Have we any other Master but Jesus Christ alone? Is he not their Master as well as ours?—What right then, have we to obey and call any other Master, but Himself? How we could be so *submissive* to a gang of men, whom we cannot tell whether they are *as good* as ourselves or not, I never could conceive. . . .

America is more our country, than it is the whites—we have enriched it with our *blood and tears.* The greatest riches in all America have arisen from our blood and tears:—and will they drive us from our property and homes, which we have earned with our *blood*? They must look sharp or this very thing will bring swift destruction upon them. The Americans have got so fat on our blood and groans, that they have almost forgotten the God of armies. . . .

See your Declaration Americans! ! ! Do you understand your own language? Hear your languages, proclaimed to the world, July 4th, 1776—"We hold these truths to be self evident—that ALL MEN ARE CREATED EQUAL! ! that they *are endowed by their Creator with certain unalienable rights;* that among these are life, *liberty,* and the pursuit of happiness! !" Compare your own language above, extracted from your Declaration of Independence, with your cruelties and murders inflicted by your cruel and unmerciful fathers and yourselves on our fathers and on us—men who have never given your fathers or you the least provocation! ! ! ! ! !

* * *

## "LIBERTY AND UNION, NOW AND FOREVER"
### Daniel Webster's Second Reply to Hayne—January 26, 1830

Congressman, senator, and two-time secretary of state Daniel Webster (1782–1852) was a statesman who represented both New Hampshire and Massachusetts in Washington at different times. In this speech, delivered in a debate on nullification with Senator Robert Hayne of South Carolina, Webster rendered a prose poem to the virtues of the Union in a time of nascent sectionalism.

I HAVE NOT ALLOWED myself, sir, to look beyond the Union, to see what might be hidden in the dark recess behind. I have not coolly weighed the chances of preserving liberty when the bonds that unite us together shall be broken asunder. I have not accustomed myself to hang over the precipice of disunion, to see whether, with my short sight, I can fathom the depth of the abyss below; nor could I regard him as a safe counselor in the affairs in this government whose thoughts should be mainly bent on considering, not how the Union may be best preserved but how tolerable might be the condition of the people when it should be broken up and destroyed. While the Union lasts, we have high, exciting, gratifying prospects spread out before us, for us and our children. Beyond that I seek not to penetrate the veil.

God grant that in my day, at least, that curtain may not rise! God grant that on my vision never may be opened what lies behind! When my eyes shall be turned to behold for the last time the sun in heaven, may I not see him shining on the broken and dishonored fragments of a once glorious Union; on states dissevered, discordant, belligerent; on a land rent with civil feuds, or drenched, it may be, in fraternal blood! Let their last feeble and lingering glance rather behold the gorgeous ensign of the republic, now known and honored throughout the earth, still full high advanced, its arms and trophies streaming in their original luster, not a stripe erased or polluted, nor a single star obscured, bearing for its motto, no such miserable interrogatory as "What is all this worth?" nor those other words of delusion and folly, "Liberty first and Union afterwards"; but everywhere, spread all over in characters of living light, blazing on all its ample folds, as they float over the sea and over the land, and in every wind under the whole heavens, that other sentiment, dear to every true American heart—Liberty and Union, now and forever, one and inseparable!

★ ★ ★

## "A MUCH INJURED PEOPLE"

### Memorial of the Ladies of Steubenville, Ohio, Against the Forcible Removal of the Indians Without the Limits of the United States—February 15, 1830

In a sense, the perennially tragic mistreatment of the indigenous peoples on the American continent was codified in the Indian Removal Act of 1830, legislation whose enforcement led to the Trail of Tears. This protest was one of the few instances of resistance to the policy that

MEMORIAL.

To the Honorable the Senate and House of Representatives of the United States. The Memorial of the undersigned, Residents of the State of ~~Pennsylvania,~~ Ohio and Town of Steubenville

**Respectfully Sheweth:**

That your memorialists are deeply impressed with the belief that the present crisis in the affairs of the Indian nations, calls loudly on *all* who can feel for the woes of humanity, to solicit with earnestness, your honorable body, to bestow on this subject, involving as it does the prosperity and happiness of more than fifty thousand of our fellow christians; the immediate consideration, demanded by its interesting nature and pressing importance.

It is readily acknowledged, that the wise and venerated founders of our country's free institutions, have committed the powers of government to those whom nature and reason declare the best fitted to exercise them; and your memorialists would sincerely deprecate any presumptuous interference on the part of their own sex, with the ordinary political affairs of the country, as wholly unbecoming the character of American Females. Even in private life we may not presume to direct the general conduct, or control the acts of those who stand in the near and guardian relations of husbands and brothers, yet all admit that *there are times* when duty and affection call on us to *advise* and *persuade*, as well as to cheer or to console. And if we approach the public representatives of our husbands and brothers, only in the humble character of suppliants in the cause of mercy and humanity, may we not hope that even the small voice of *female* sympathy will be heard?

Compared with the estimate placed on Woman, and the attention paid to her in other nations, the generous and refined deference shown by all ranks and classes of men, in this country, to our sex, forms a striking contrast; and as an honorable and distinguishing trait in the American character, has often excited the admiration of intelligent foreigners. Nor is this general kindness lightly regarded or coldly appreciated, but with warm feelings of affectionate pride, and hearts swelling with gratitude, the mothers and daughters of America bear testimony to the generous nature of their countrymen.

When, therefore, injury and oppression threaten to crush a hapless people within our borders, we, the feeblest of the feeble, appeal with confidence to those who should be the representatives of national virtues as they are the depositories of national powers, and implore them to succor the weak & unfortunate.—In despite of the *undoubted natural right*, which the Indians have, to the land of their forefathers, and in the face of solemn treaties, pledging the faith of the nation for their secure possession of those lands, it is intended, we are told, to force them from their native soil, and to compel them to seek new homes in a distant and dreary wilderness. To you then, as the constitutional protectors of the Indians within our territory and as the peculiar guardians of our national character, and our country's welfare, we solemnly and earnestly appeal to save this remnant of a much injured people from annihilation, to shield our country from the curses denounced on the cruel and ungrateful, and to shelter the American character from lasting dishonor.

And your petitioners will ever pray.

The Steubenville Memorial

resulted in the removal of roughly fifty thousand native people to the west.

THAT YOUR MEMORIALISTS are deeply impressed with the belief, that the present crisis in the affairs of the Indian nations, calls loudly on *all* who can feel for the woes of humanity, to solicit, with earnestness, your honorable body to bestow on this subject, involving, as it does, the prosperity and happiness of more than fifty thousand of our fellow Christians, the immediate consideration demanded by its interesting nature and pressing importance.

It is readily acknowledged, that the wise and venerated founders of our country's free institutions have committed the powers of Government to those whom nature and reason declare the best fitted to exercise them; and your memorialists would sincerely deprecate any presumptuous interference on the part of their own sex with the ordinary political affairs of the country, as wholly unbecoming the character of the American females. Even in private life, we may not presume to direct the general conduct, or control the acts of those who stand in the near and guardian relations of husbands and brothers; yet all admit that *there are times* when duty and affection call on us to *advise* and *persuade,* as well as to cheer or to console. And if we approach the public Representatives of our husbands and brothers, only in the humble character of suppliants in the cause of mercy and humanity, may we not hope that even the small voice of *female* sympathy will be heard?

Compared with the estimate placed on woman, and the attention paid to her in other nations, the generous and refined deference shown by all ranks and classes of men, in this country, to our sex, forms a striking contrast; and as an honorable and distinguishing trait in the American character, has often excited the admiration of intelligent foreigners. Nor is this general kindness lightly regarded or coldly appreciated; but, with warm feelings of affectionate pride, and hearts swelling with gratitude, the mothers and daughters of America bear testimony to the generous nature of their countrymen.

When, therefore, injury and oppression threaten to crush a hapless people within our borders, we, the feeblest of the feeble, appeal with confidence to those who should be representatives of national virtues as they are the depositaries of national powers, and implore them to succor the weak and unfortunate. In despite of the *undoubted natural right* which the Indians have to the land of their forefathers, and in the face of solemn treaties, pledging the faith of the nation for their secure possession of those lands, it is intended, we are told, to force them from their native soil, and to compel them to seek new homes in a distant and dreary wilderness. To you, then, as the constitutional protectors of the Indians within our territory, and as the peculiar guardians of our national character, and our country's welfare, we solemnly and earnestly appeal, to save this remnant of a much injured people from annihilation, to shield our country from the curses denounced on the cruel and ungrateful, and to shelter the American character from lasting dishonor.

★ ★ ★

## "AND I WILL BE HEARD"

### William Lloyd Garrison, *The Liberator*—January 1, 1831

---

The abolitionist William Lloyd Garrison (1805–1879) founded *The Liberator* newspaper in Boston on the first day of 1831; his inaugural editorial would become one of the most-quoted pieces of antislavery literature in American history. The paper would be published until 1865, when the Thirteenth Amendment to the Constitution to abolish slavery was at last ratified in the final months of the Civil War.

ASSENTING TO THE "self-evident truth" maintained in the American Declaration of Independence, "that all men are created equal, and endowed by their Creator with certain inalienable rights—among which are life, liberty and the pursuit of happiness," I shall strenuously contend for the immediate enfranchisement of our slave population. . . .

I will be as harsh as truth, and as uncompromising as justice. On this subject, I do not wish to think, or to speak, or write, with moderation. No! no! Tell a man whose house is on fire to give a moderate alarm; tell him to moderately rescue his wife from the hands of the ravisher; tell the mother to gradually extricate her babe from the fire into which it

*Even after slavery was abolished in 1865, William Lloyd Garrison remained a radical reformer. "I am still for immediate, unconditional, everlasting emancipation from oppression of everyone on the face of the earth," he told a woman's suffrage gathering in 1873.*

has fallen;—but urge me not to use moderation in a cause like the present. I am in earnest—I will not equivocate—I will not excuse—I will not retreat a single inch—AND I WILL BE HEARD. The apathy of the people is enough to make every statue leap from its pedestal, and to hasten the resurrection of the dead.

It is pretended that I am retarding the cause of emancipation by the coarseness of my invective and the precipitancy of my measures. The charge is not true. On this question my influence,—humble as it is,—is felt at this moment to a considerable extent, and shall be felt in coming years—not perniciously, but beneficially—not as a curse, but as a blessing; and posterity will bear testimony that I was right. I desire to thank God, that he enables me to disregard "the fear of man which bringeth a snare," and to speak his truth in its simplicity and power.

★ ★ ★

## "ONE BOND OF COMMON INTEREST"

### Andrew Jackson, Proclamation to the People of South Carolina on Nullification—December 10, 1832

Elected president in 1828, Andrew Jackson (1767–1845) embodied the ambitions of a large element of white America. Born far from the highest echelons of power and wealth, Jackson rose in the world, becoming a lawyer, a politician, a general, a slaveowner, and a relentless enemy of indigenous people who held lands coveted by men like Jackson. Yet Jackson believed in the American Union and stood against nullification, a states'-rights movement that he believed was but prelude to secession.

*Devoted to the Union and to a powerful presidential office—particularly with himself in it—Andrew Jackson refused to give quarter to white Southern radicals who challenged the supremacy of the federal government.*

THE CONSTITUTION OF the United States . . . forms a government, not a league, and whether it be formed by compact between the States, or in any other manner, its character is the same. It is a government in which all the people are represented, which operates directly on the people individually, not upon the States; they retained all the power they did not grant. But each State having expressly parted with so many powers as to constitute jointly with the other States a single nation, cannot from that period possess any right to secede, because such secession does not break a league, but destroys the unity of a nation, and any injury to that unity is not only a breach which would result from the contravention of a compact, but it is an offense against the whole Union. To say that any State may at pleasure secede from the Union, is to say that the United States are not a nation because it would be a solecism to contend that any part of a nation might dissolve its connection with the other parts, to their injury or ruin, without committing any offense. Secession, like any other revolutionary act, may be morally justified by the extremity of oppression; but to call it a constitutional right, is confounding the meaning of terms, and can only be done through gross error, or to deceive those who are willing to assert a right, but would pause before they made a revolution, or incur the penalties consequent upon a failure. . . .

Fellow-citizens of my native State! let me not only admonish you, as the first magistrate of our common country, not to incur the penalty of its laws, but use the influence that a father would over his children whom he saw rushing to a certain ruin. In that paternal language, with that paternal feeling, let me tell you, my countrymen, that you are deluded by men who are either deceived themselves or wish to deceive you. . . .

Contemplate the condition of that country of which you still form an important part; consider its government uniting in one bond of common interest and general protection so many different States—giving to all their inhabitants the proud title of AMERICAN CITIZEN—protecting their commerce—securing their literature and arts—facilitating their intercommunication—defending their frontiers—and making their name respected in the remotest parts of the earth! Consider the extent of its territory its increasing and happy population, its advance in arts, which render life agreeable, and the sciences which elevate the mind! See education spreading the lights of religion, morality, and general information into every cottage in this wide extent of our Territories and States! Behold it as the asylum where the wretched and the oppressed find a refuge and support! Look on this picture of happiness and honor, and say, WE TOO, ARE CITIZENS OF AMERICA.

★ ★ ★

## "THE *POLITICAL RELIGION* OF THE NATION"
### Abraham Lincoln, Address Before the Young Men's Lyceum of Springfield, Illinois—January 27, 1838

As a young lawyer and state legislator in Illinois, Abraham Lincoln (1809–1865) was at once thoughtful and ambitious. In this, his first major speech, Lincoln spoke of the centrality of the insights of the Revolutionary generation—chiefly, that the nation should be dedicated to the preservation of individual liberty and to the rule of law.

AS A SUBJECT for the remarks of the evening, *the perpetuation of our political institutions,* is selected.

In the great journal of things happening under the sun, we, the American People, find our account running, under date of the nineteenth century of the Christian era.—We find ourselves in the peaceful possession, of the fairest portion of the earth, as regards extent of territory, fertility of soil, and salubrity of climate. We find ourselves under the government of a system of political institutions, conducing more essentially to the ends of civil and religious liberty, than any of which the history of former times tells us. We, when mounting the stage of existence, found ourselves the legal inheritors of these fundamental blessings. We toiled not in the acquirement or establishment of them—they are a legacy bequeathed us, by a *once* hardy, brave, and patriotic, but *now* lamented and departed race of ancestors. Theirs was the task (and nobly they performed it) to possess themselves, and through themselves, us, of this goodly land; and to uprear upon its hills and its valleys, a political edifice of liberty and equal rights; 'tis ours only, to transmit these, the former, unprofaned by the foot of an invader; the latter, undecayed by the lapse of time and untorn by usurpation, to the latest generation that fate shall permit the world to know. This task of gratitude to our fathers, justice to ourselves, duty to posterity, and love for our species in general, all imperatively require us faithfully to perform.

How then shall we perform it?—At what point shall we expect the approach of danger? By what means shall we fortify against it?—Shall we expect some transatlantic military giant, to step the Ocean, and crush us at a blow? Never!—All the armies of Europe, Asia and Africa combined, with all the treasure of the earth (our own excepted) in their military chest; with a Buonaparte for a commander, could not by force, take a drink from the Ohio, or make a track on the Blue Ridge, in a trial of a thousand years.

At what point then is the approach of danger to be expected? I answer, if it ever reach us, it must spring up amongst us. It cannot come from abroad. If destruction be our lot, we must ourselves be its author and finisher. As a nation of freemen, we must live through all time, or die by suicide. . . .

I know the American People are *much* attached to their government;—I know they would suffer *much* for its sake;—I know they would endure evils long and patiently, before they would ever think of exchanging it for another. Yet, notwithstanding all this, if the laws be continually despised and disregarded, if their rights to be secure in their persons and property, are held by no better tenure than the caprice of a mob, the alienation of their affections from the Government is the natural consequence; and to that, sooner or later, it must come.

Here then, is one point at which danger may be expected.

The question recurs, "how shall we fortify against it?" The answer is simple. Let every American, every lover of liberty, every well-wisher to his posterity, swear by the blood of the Revolution, never to violate in the least particular, the laws of the country; and never to tolerate their violation by others. As the patriots of seventy-six did to the support of the Declaration of Independence, so to the support of the Constitution and Laws, let every American pledge his life, his property, and his sacred honor;—let every man remember that to violate the law, is to trample on the blood of his father, and to tear the character of his own, and his children's liberty. Let reverence for the laws, be breathed by every American mother, to the lisping babe, that prattles on her lap—let it be taught in schools, in seminaries, and in colleges; let it be written in Primers, spelling books, and in Almanacs;—let it be preached from the pulpit, proclaimed in legislative halls, and enforced in courts of justice. And, in short, let it become the *political religion* of the nation; and let the old and the young, the rich and the poor, the grave and the gay, of all sexes and tongues, and colors and conditions, sacrifice unceasingly upon its altars.

While ever a state of feeling, such as this, shall universally, or even, very generally prevail throughout the nation, vain will be every effort, and fruitless every attempt, to subvert our national freedom.

When I so pressingly urge a strict observance of all the laws, let me not be understood as saying there are no bad laws, nor that grievances may not arise, for the redress of which, no legal provisions have been made.—I mean to say no such thing. But I do mean to say, that, although bad laws, if they exist, should be repealed as soon as possible, still while they continue in force, for the sake of example, they should be religiously observed. So also in unprovided cases. If such arise, let proper legal provisions be made for them with the least possible delay; but, till then, let them, if not too intolerable, be borne with.

There is no grievance that is a fit object of redress by mob law. In any case that arises, as for instance, the promulgation of abolitionism, one of two positions is necessarily true; that is, the thing is right within itself, and therefore deserves the protection of all law and all good citizens; or, it is wrong, and therefore proper to be prohibited by legal enactments; and in neither case, is the interposition of mob law, either necessary, justifiable, or excusable.

But, it may be asked, why suppose danger to our political institutions? Have we not preserved them for more than fifty years? And why may we not for fifty times as long?

We hope there is *no sufficient* reason. We hope all dangers may be overcome; but to conclude that no danger may ever arise, would itself be extremely dangerous. There are now, and will hereafter be, many causes, dangerous in their tendency, which have not existed heretofore; and which are not too insignificant to merit attention. That our government should have been maintained in its original form from its establishment until now, is not much to be wondered at. It had many props to support it through that period, which now are decayed, and crumbled away. Through that period, it was felt by all, to be an undecided experiment; now, it is understood to be a successful one.—Then, all that sought celebrity and fame, and distinction, expected to find them in the success of that experiment. Their *all* was staked upon it:—their destiny was *inseparably* linked with it. Their ambition aspired to display before an admiring world, a practical demonstration of the truth of a proposition, which had hitherto been considered, at best no better, than problematical; namely, *the capability of a people to govern themselves.* If they succeeded, they were to be immortalized; their names were to be transferred to counties and cities, and rivers and mountains; and to be revered and sung, and toasted through all time. If they failed, they were to be called knaves and fools, and fanatics for a fleeting hour; then to sink and be forgotten. They succeeded. The experiment is successful; and thousands have won their deathless names in making it so. But the game is caught; and I believe it is true, that with the catching, end the pleasures of the chase. This field of glory is harvested, and the crop is already appropriated. But new reapers will arise, and *they,* too, will seek a field. It is to deny, what the history of the world tells us is true, to suppose that men of ambition and talents will not continue to spring up amongst us. And, when they do, they will as naturally seek the gratification of their ruling passion, as others have so done before them. The question then, is, can that gratification be found in supporting and maintaining an edifice that has been erected by others? Most certainly it cannot. Many great and good men sufficiently qualified for any task they should undertake, may ever be found, whose ambition would inspire to nothing beyond a seat in Congress, a gubernatorial or a presidential chair; *but such belong not to the family of the lion, or the tribe of the eagle.* What! think you these places would satisfy an Alexander, a Caesar, or a Napoleon?—Never! Towering genius distains a beaten path. It seeks regions hitherto unexplored.—It sees *no distinction* in adding story to story, upon the monuments of fame, erected to the memory of others. It *denies* that it is glory enough to serve under any chief. It *scorns* to tread in the footsteps of *any* predecessor, however illustrious. It thirsts and burns for distinction; and, if possible, it will have it, whether at the expense of emancipating slaves, or enslaving freemen. Is it unreasonable then to expect, that some man possessed of the loftiest genius, coupled with ambition sufficient to push it to its utmost stretch, will at some time, spring up among us? And when such a one does, it will require the people to be united with each other, attached to the government and laws, and generally intelligent, to successfully frustrate his designs.

Distinction will be his paramount object, and although he would as willingly, perhaps more so, acquire it by doing good as harm; yet, that opportunity being past, and nothing left to be done in the way of building up, he would set boldly to the task of pulling down. . . .

Another reason which *once was;* but which, to the same extent, is *now no more,* has done much in maintaining our institutions thus far. I mean the powerful influence which the interesting scenes of the revolution had upon the *passions* of the people as distinguished from their judgment. By this influence, the jealousy, envy, and avarice, incident to our nature, and so common to a state of peace, prosperity, and conscious strength, were, for the time, in a great measure smothered and rendered inactive; while the deep-rooted principles of *hate,* and the powerful motive of *revenge,* instead of being turned against each other, were directed exclusively against the British nation. And thus, from the force of circumstances, the basest principles of our nature, were either made to lie dormant, or to become the active agents in the advancement of the noblest cause—that of establishing and maintaining civil and religious liberty.

But this state of feeling *must fade, is fading, has faded,* with the circumstances that produced it.

I do not mean to say, that the scenes of the revolution *are now* or *ever will* be entirely forgotten; but that like every thing else, they must fade upon the memory of the world, and grow more and more dim by the lapse of time. In history, we hope, they will be read of, and recounted, so long as the bible shall be read;—but even granting that they will, their influence *cannot be* what it heretofore has been. Even then, they *cannot be* so universally known, nor so vividly felt, as they were by the generation just gone to rest. At the close of that struggle, nearly every adult male had been a participator in some of its scenes. The consequence was, that of those scenes, in the form of a husband, a father, a son or brother, a *living history* was to be found in every family—a history bearing the indubitable testimonies of its own authenticity, in the limbs mangled, in the scars of wounds received, in the midst of the very scenes related—a history, too, that could be read and understood alike by all, the wise and the ignorant, the learned and the unlearned.—But *those* histories are gone. They *can* be read no more forever. They *were* a fortress of strength; but, what invading foeman could *never do,* the silent artillery of time *has done;* the leveling of its walls. They are gone.—They *were* a forest of giant oaks; but the all-resistless hurricane has swept over them, and left only, here and there, a lonely trunk, despoiled of its verdure, shorn of its foliage; unshading and unshaded, to murmur in a few gentle breezes, and to combat with its mutilated limbs, a few more ruder storms, then to sink, and be no more.

They *were* the pillars of the temple of liberty; and now, that they have crumbled away, that temple must fall, unless we, their descendants, supply their places with other pillars, hewn from the solid quarry of sober reason. Passion has helped us; but can do so no more. It will in future be our enemy. Reason, cold, calculating, unimpassioned reason, must furnish all the materials for our future support and defence.—Let those materials be moulded into *general intelligence, sound morality,* and in particular, *a reverence for the constitution and laws:* and, that we improved to the last; that we remained free to the last; that we revered his name to the last; that, during his long sleep, we permitted no hostile foot to pass over or desecrate his resting place; shall be that which to learn the last trump shall awaken our WASHINGTON.

Upon these let the proud fabric of freedom rest, as the rock of its basis; and as truly as has been said of the only greater institution, "*the gates of hell shall not prevail against it.*"

★ ★ ★

## "THE GREAT EQUALIZER OF THE CONDITIONS OF MEN"

### Horace Mann, *Twelfth Annual Report to the Secretary of the Massachusetts Board of Education*—1848

Horace Mann (1796–1859) was a lawyer, legislator, and secretary of the Massachusetts Board of Education. Founder of *The Common School Journal* in 1838, he campaigned for public schools in the conviction that an educated citizenry was central to the durability of democratic culture and government.

Under the providence of God, our means of education are the grand machinery by which the "raw material" of human nature can be worked up into inventors and discoverers, into skilled artisans and scientific farmers, into scholars and jurists, into the founders of benevolent institutions, and the great expounders of ethical and theological science. By means of early education, those embryos of talent may be quickened which will solve the difficult problems of political and economical law; and by them, too, the genius may be kindled which will blaze forth in the poets of humanity. Our schools, far more than they have done, may supply the presidents and professors of colleges, and superintendents of public instruction, all over the land; and send, not only into our sister States, but across the Atlantic, the men of practical science, to superintend the construction of the great works of art. Here, too, may those judicial powers be developed and invigorated, which will make legal principles so clear and convincing as to prevent appeals to force; and, should the clouds of war ever lower over our country, some hero may be found—the nursling of our schools, and ready to become the leader of our armies, that best of all heroes—who will secure the glories of a peace, unstained by the magnificent murders of the battle-field. . . .

*The versatile Horace Mann of Massachusetts served as secretary of the state's Board of Education, as a member of the U.S. House of Representatives, and as president of Antioch College.*

Without undervaluing any other human agency, it may be safely affirmed that the common school, improved and energized, as it can easily be, may become the most effective and benignant of all the forces of civilization. Two reasons sustain this position. In the first place, there is a universality in its operation, which can be affirmed of no other institution whatever. If administered in the spirit of justice and conciliation, all the rising generation may be brought within the circle of its reformatory and elevating influences. And, in the second place, the materials upon which it operates are so pliant and ductile as to be susceptible of assuming a greater variety of forms than any other earthly work of the Creator. The inflexibility and ruggedness of the oak, when compared with the lithe sapling or the tender germ, are but feeble emblems to typify the docility of childhood when contrasted with the obduracy and intractableness of man. It is these inherent advantages of the common school, which, in our own State, have produced results so striking, from a system so imperfect, and an administration so feeble. In teaching the blind and the deaf and dumb, in kindling the latent spark of intelligence that lurks in an idiot's mind, and in the more holy work of reforming abandoned and outcast children, education has proved what it can do by glorious experiments. These wonders it has done in its infancy, and with the lights of a limited experience; but when its faculties shall be fully developed, when it shall be trained to wield its mighty energies for the protection of society against the giant vices which now invade and torment it,—against intemperance, avarice, war, slavery, bigotry, the woes of want, and the wickedness of waste,—then there will not be a height to which these enemies of the race can escape which it will not scale, nor a Titan among them all whom it will not slay. . . .

NOW, SURELY NOTHING but universal education can counterwork this tendency to the domination of capital and the servility of labor. If one class possesses all the wealth and the education, while the residue of society is ignorant and poor, it matters not by what name the relation between them may be called: the latter, in fact and in truth, will be the servile dependents and subjects of the former. But, if education be equably diffused, it will draw property after it, by the strongest of all attractions; for such a thing never did happen, and never can happen, as that an intelligent and practical body of men should be permanently poor. Property and labor in different classes are essentially antagonistic; but property and labor, in the same class are essentially fraternal. The people of Massachusetts have, in some degree, appreciated the truth, that the unexampled prosperity of the State—its comfort, its competence, its general intelligence and virtue—is attributable to the education, more or less perfect, which all its people have received;

but are they sensible of a fact equally important?—namely, that it is to this same education that two-thirds of the people are indebted for not being, to-day, the vassals of as severe a tyranny, in the form of capital, as the lower classes of Europe are bound to in the form of brute force?

Education, then, beyond all other devices of human origin, is the great equalizer of the conditions of men,—the balance-wheel of the social machinery. . . . The spread of education, by enlarging the cultivated class or caste, will open a wider area over which the social feelings will expand; and, if this education should be universal and complete, it would do more than all things else to obliterate factitious distinctions in society. . . .

For the creation of wealth, then,—for the existence of a wealthy people and a wealthy nation,—intelligence is the grand condition. The number of improvers will increase as the intellectual constituency, if I may so call it, increases. In former times, and in most parts of the world even at the present day, not one man in a million has ever had such a development of mind as made it possible for him to become a contributor to art or science. Let this development precede, and contributions, numberless, and of inestimable value, will be sure to follow.

★ ★ ★

## "ALL MEN AND WOMEN ARE CREATED EQUAL"
### Declaration of Sentiments and Resolutions, Woman's Rights Convention, Seneca Falls, New York—July 19–20, 1848

The first national women's rights convention issued this Declaration of Sentiments in midsummer 1848 at a meeting held in the Wesleyan Methodist Chapel in Seneca Falls.

WHEN, IN THE course of human events, it becomes necessary for one portion of the family of man to assume among the people of the earth a position different from that which they have hitherto occupied, but one to which the laws of nature and of nature's God entitle them, a decent respect to the opinions of mankind requires that they should declare the causes that impel them to such a course.

We hold these truths to be self-evident: that all men and women are created equal; that they are endowed by their Creator with certain inalienable rights; that among these are life, liberty, and the pursuit of happiness; that to secure these rights governments are instituted, deriving their just powers from the consent of the governed. Whenever any form of Government becomes destructive of these ends, it is the right of those who suffer from it to refuse allegiance to it, and to insist upon the institution of a new government, laying its foundation on such principles, and organizing its powers in such form as to them shall seem most likely to effect their safety and happiness. Prudence, indeed, will dictate that governments long established should not be changed for light and transient causes; and accordingly, all experience hath shown that mankind are more disposed to suffer, while evils are sufferable, than to right themselves by abolishing the forms to which they are accustomed. But when a long train of abuses and usurpations, pursuing invariably the same object, evinces a design to reduce them under absolute despotism, it is their duty to throw off such government, and to provide new guards for their future security. Such has been the patient sufferance of the women under this government, and such is now the necessity which constrains them to demand the equal station to which they are entitled.

The history of mankind is a history of repeated injuries and usurpations on the part of man toward woman, having in direct object the establishment of an absolute tyranny over her. To prove this, let facts be submitted to a candid world.

He has never permitted her to exercise her inalienable right to the elective franchise.

He has compelled her to submit to laws, in the formation of which she had no voice.

He has withheld from her rights which are given to the most ignorant and degraded men—both natives and foreigners.

Having deprived her of this first right of a citizen, the elective franchise, thereby leaving her without representation in the halls of legislation, he has oppressed her on all sides.

He has made her, if married, in the eye of the law, civilly dead.

He has taken from her all right in property, even to the wages she earns.

He has made her, morally, an irresponsible being, as she can commit many crimes with impunity, provided they be done in the presence of her husband. In the covenant of marriage, she is compelled to promise obedience to her husband, he becoming, to all intents and purposes, her master—the law giving him power to deprive her of her liberty, and to administer chastisement.

He has so framed the laws of divorce, as to what shall be the proper causes of divorce; in case of separation, to whom the guardianship of the children shall be given; as to be wholly regardless of the happiness of women—the law, in all cases, going upon a false supposition of the supremacy of man, and giving all power into his hands.

After depriving her of all rights as a married woman, if single, and the owner of property, he has taxed her to support a government which recognizes her only when her property can be made profitable to it.

He has monopolized nearly all the profitable employments, and from those she is permitted to follow, she receives but a scanty remuneration.

He closes against her all the avenues to wealth and distinction, which he considers most honorable to himself. As a teacher of theology, medicine, or law, she is not known.

He has denied her the facilities for obtaining a thorough education—all colleges being closed against her.

He allows her in Church as well as State, but a subordinate position, claiming Apostolic authority for her exclusion from the ministry, and with some exceptions, from any public participation in the affairs of the Church.

He has created a false public sentiment, by giving to the world a different code of morals for man and woman, by which moral delinquencies which exclude women from society, are not only tolerated but deemed of little account in man.

He has usurped the prerogative of Jehovah himself, claiming it as his right to assign for her a sphere of action, when that belongs to her conscience and her God.

He has endeavored, in every way that he could to destroy her confidence in her own powers, to lessen her self-respect, and to make her willing to lead a dependent and abject life.

Now, in view of this entire disfranchisement of one-half the people of this country, their social and religious degradation,—in view of the unjust laws above mentioned, and because women do feel themselves aggrieved, oppressed, and fraudulently deprived of their most sacred rights, we insist that they have immediate admission to all the rights and privileges which belong to them as citizens of these United States.

In entering upon the great work before us, we anticipate no small amount of misconception, misrepresentation, and ridicule; but we shall use every instrumentality within our power to effect our object. We shall employ agents, circulate tracts, petition the State and national Legislatures, and endeavor to enlist the pulpit and the press in our behalf. We hope this Convention will be followed by a series of Conventions, embracing every part of the country.

Firmly relying upon the final triumph of the Right and the True, we do this day affix our signatures to this declaration.

★ ★ ★

## "THE FIAT OF THE ALMIGHTY"
### Frederick Douglass, Oration at Corinthian Hall, Rochester, New York—July 5, 1852

Born into enslavement in Maryland, Frederick Douglass (1818–1895) became one of the most influential Americans of the nineteenth century. Author, orator, and editor, he was based in Rochester, New York; advised President Lincoln; and became a global figure as an advocate of emancipation.

THE FACT IS, ladies and gentlemen, the distance between this platform and the slave plantation, from which I escaped, is considerable—and the difficulties to be overcome in getting from the latter to the former, are by no means slight. That I am here to-day, is, to me, a matter of astonishment as well as of gratitude. You will not, therefore, be surprised, if in what I have to say, I evince no elaborate preparation, nor grace my speech with any high sounding exordium. With little experience and with less learning, I have been able to throw my thoughts hastily and imperfectly together; and trusting to your patient and generous indulgence, I will proceed to lay them before you.

This, for the purpose of this celebration, is the 4th of July. It is the birthday of your National Independence, and of your political freedom. This, to you, is what the Passover was to the emancipated people of God. It carries your minds back to the day, and to the act of your great deliverance; and to the signs, and to the wonders, associated with that act that day. This celebration also marks the beginning of another year of your national life; and reminds you that the Republic of America is now 76 years old. I am glad, fellow-citizens, that your nation is so young. Seventy-six years, though a good old age for a man, is but a mere speck in the life of a nation. Three score years and ten is the allotted time for individual men; but nations number their years by thousands. According to this fact, you are, even now only in the beginning of your national career, still lingering in the period of childhood. I repeat, I am glad this is so. There is hope in the thought, and hope is much needed, under the dark clouds which lower above the horizon. The eye of the reformer is met with angry flashes, portending disastrous times; but his heart may well beat lighter at the thought that America is young, and that she is still in the impressible stage of her existence. May he not hope that high lessons of wisdom, of justice and of truth, will yet give direction to her destiny? Were the nation older, the patriot's heart might be sadder, and the reformer's brow heavier. Its future might be shrouded in gloom, and the hope of its prophets go out in sorrow. There is consolation in the

*Escaping enslavement in Maryland, Frederick Douglass was a figure of international renown. He met with President Lincoln in the White House during the Civil War and ultimately became the U.S. Marshal of the District of Columbia and the American minister to Haiti.*

thought, that America is young. Great streams are not easily turned from channels, worn deep in the course of ages. They may sometimes rise in quiet and stately majesty, and inundate the land, refreshing and fertilizing the earth with their mysterious properties. They may also rise in wrath and fury, and bear away, on their angry waves, the accumulated wealth of years of toil and hardship. They, however, gradually flow back to the same old channel, and flow on as serenely as ever. But, while the river may not be turned aside, it may dry up, and leave nothing behind but the withered branch, and the unsightly rock, to howl in the abyss-sweeping wind, the sad tale of departed glory. As with rivers so with nations. . . .

Feeling themselves harshly and unjustly treated, by the home government, your fathers, like men of honesty, and men of spirit, earnestly sought redress. They petitioned and remonstrated; they did so in a decorous, respectful, and loyal manner. Their conduct was wholly unexceptionable. This, however, did not answer the purpose. They saw themselves treated with sovereign indifference, coldness and scorn. Yet they persevered. They were not the men to look back.

As the sheet anchor takes a firmer hold, when the ship is tossed by the storm, so did the cause of your fathers grow stronger, as it breasted the chilling blasts of kingly displeasure. The greatest and best of British statesmen admitted its justice, and the loftiest eloquence of the British Senate came to its support. But, with that blindness which seems to be the unvarying characteristic of tyrants, since Pharoah and his hosts were drowned in the Red sea, the British Government persisted in the exactions complained of.

The madness of this course, we believe, is admitted now, even by England; but we fear the lesson is wholly lost on our present rulers.

Oppression makes a wise man mad. Your fathers were wise men, and if they did not go mad, they became restive under this treatment. They felt themselves the victims of grievous wrongs, wholly incurable in their colonial capacity. With brave men there is always a remedy for oppression. Just here, the idea of a total separation of the colonies from the crown was born! It was a startling idea, much more so, than we, at this distance of time, regard it. The timid and the prudent (as has been intimated) of that day, were, of course, shocked and alarmed by it. . . .

On the 2d of July, 1776, the old Continental Congress, to the dismay of the lovers of ease, and the worshippers of property, clothed that dreadful idea with all the authority of national sanction. They did so in the form of a resolution. . . .

Citizens, your fathers made good that resolution. They succeeded; and to-day you reap the fruits of their success. The freedom gained is yours; and you, therefore, may properly celebrate this anniversary. The 4th of July is the first great fact in your nation's history—the very ring-bolt in the chain of your yet undeveloped destiny.

Pride and patriotism, not less than gratitude, prompt you to celebrate and to hold it in perpetual remembrance. I have said that the Declaration of Independence is the RINGBOLT to the chain of your nation's destiny; so, indeed, I regard it. The principles contained in that instrument are saving principles. Stand by those principles, be true to them on all occasions, in all places, against all foes, and at whatever cost. . . .

Fellow Citizens, I am not wanting in respect for the fathers of this republic. The signers of the Declaration of Independence were brave men. They were great men too—great enough to give fame to a great age. It does not often happen to a nation to raise, at one time, such a number of truly great men. The point from which I am compelled to view them is not, certainly the most favorable; and yet I cannot contemplate their great deeds with less than admiration. They were statesmen, patriots and heroes, and for the good they did, and the principles they contended for, I will unite with you to honor their memory.

They loved their country better than their own private interests; and, though this is not the highest form of human excellence, all will concede that it is a rare virtue, and that when it is exhibited, it ought to command respect. He who will, intelligently, lay down his life for his country, is a man whom it is not in human nature to despise. Your fathers staked their lives, their fortunes, and their sacred honor, on the cause of their country. In their admiration of liberty, they lost sight of all other interests. . . .

How circumspect, exact and proportionate were all their movements! How unlike the politicians of an hour! Their statesmanship looked beyond the passing moment, and stretched away in strength into the distant future. They seized upon eternal principles, and set a glorious example in their defense. Mark them! . . .

Fellow-citizens, pardon me, allow me to ask, why am I called upon to speak here to-day? What have I, or those I represent, to do with your national independence? Are the great principles of political freedom and of natural justice, embodied in that Declaration of Independence, extended to us? and am I, therefore, called upon to bring our humble offering to the national altar, and to confess the benefits and express devout gratitude for the blessings resulting from your independence to us?

Would to God, both for your sakes and ours, that an affirmative answer could be truthfully returned to these questions! Then would my task be light, and my burden easy and delightful. For *who* is there so cold, that a nation's sympathy could not warm him? Who so obdurate and dead to the claims of gratitude, that would not thankfully acknowledge such priceless benefits? Who so stolid and selfish, that would not give his voice to swell the hallelujahs of a nation's jubilee, when the chains of servitude had been torn from his limbs? I am not that man. In a case like that, the dumb might eloquently speak, and the "lame man leap as an hart."

But, such is not the state of the case. I say it with a sad sense of the disparity between us. I am not included within the pale of this glorious anniversary! Your high independence only reveals the immeasurable distance between us. The blessings in which you, this day, rejoice, are not enjoyed in common. The rich inheritance of justice, liberty, prosperity and independence, bequeathed by your fathers, is shared by you, not by me. The sunlight that brought life and healing to you, has brought stripes and death to me. This Fourth July is *yours,* not *mine. You* may rejoice, *I* must mourn. To drag a man in fetters into the grand illuminated temple of liberty, and call upon him to join you in joyous anthems, were inhuman mockery and sacrilegious irony. Do you mean, citizens, to mock me, by asking me to speak to-day? If so, there is a parallel to your conduct. And let me warn you that it is dangerous to copy the example of a nation whose crimes, towering up to heaven, were thrown down by the breath of the Almighty, burying that nation in irrecoverable ruin! I can to-day take up the plaintive lament of a peeled and woe-smitten people! . . .

Fellow-citizens; above your national, tumultuous joy, I hear the mournful wail of millions! whose chains, heavy and grievous yesterday, are, to-day, rendered more intolerable by the jubilee shouts that reach them. If I do forget, if I do not faithfully remember those bleeding children of sorrow this day, "may my right hand forget her cunning, and may my tongue cleave to the roof of my mouth!" To forget them, to pass lightly over their wrongs, and to chime in with the popular theme, would be treason most scandalous and shocking, and would make me a reproach before God and the world.

My subject, then, fellow-citizens, is AMERICAN SLAVERY. I shall see, this day, and its popular characteristics, from the slave's point of view. Standing, there, identified with the American bondman, making his wrongs mine, I do not hesitate to declare, with all my soul, that the character and conduct of this nation never looked blacker to me than on this 4th of July! Whether we turn to the declarations of the past, or to the professions of the present, the conduct of the nation seems equally hideous and revolting. America is false to the past, false to the present, and solemnly binds herself to be false to the future. Standing with God and the crushed and bleeding slave on this occasion, I will, in the name of humanity which is outraged, in the name of liberty which is fettered, in the name of the constitution and the Bible, which are disregarded and trampled upon, dare to call in question and to denounce, with all the emphasis I can command, everything that serves to perpetuate slavery—the great sin and shame of America! "I will not equivocate; I will not excuse;" I will use the severest language I can command; and yet not one word shall escape me that any man, whose judgment is not blinded by prejudice, or who is not at heart a slaveholder, shall not confess to be right and just.

But I fancy I hear some one of my audience say, it is just in this circumstance that you and your brother abolitionists fail to make a favorable impression on the public mind. Would you argue more, and denounce less, would you persuade more, and rebuke less, your cause would be much more likely to succeed. But, I submit, where all is plain there is nothing to be argued. What point in the anti-slavery creed would you have me argue? On what branch of the subject do the people of this country need light? Must I undertake to prove that the slave is a man? That point is conceded already. Nobody doubts it. The slaveholders themselves acknowledge it in the enactment of laws for their government. They acknowledge it when they punish disobedience on the part of the slave. There are seventy-two crimes in the State of Virginia, which, if committed by a black man, (no matter how ignorant he be,) subject him to the punishment of death; while only two of the same crimes will subject a white man to the like punishment.—What is this but the acknowledgement that the slave is a moral, intellectual and responsible being. The manhood of the slave is conceded. It is admitted in the fact that Southern statute books are covered with enactments forbidding, under severe fines and penalties, the teaching of the slave to read or to write.—When you can point to any such laws, in reference to the beasts of the field, then I may consent to argue the manhood of the slave. When the dogs in your streets, when the fowls of the air, when the cattle on your hills, when the fish of the sea, and the reptiles that crawl, shall be unable to distinguish the slave from a brute, *then* will I argue with you that the slave is a man!

For the present, it is enough to affirm the equal manhood of the negro race. Is it not astonishing that, while we are ploughing, planting and reaping, using all kinds of mechanical tools, erecting houses, constructing bridges, building ships, working in metals of brass, iron, copper, silver and gold; that, while we are reading, writing and cyphering, acting as clerks, merchants and secretaries, having among us lawyers, doctors, ministers, poets, authors, editors, orators and teachers; that, while we are engaged in all manner of enterprises common to other men, digging gold in California, capturing the whale in the Pacific, feeding sheep and cattle on the hillside, living, moving, acting, thinking, planning, living in families as husbands, wives and children, and, above all, confessing and worshipping the Christian's God, and looking hopefully for life and immortality beyond the grave, we are called upon to prove that we are men!

Would you have me argue that man is entitled to liberty? that he is the rightful owner of his own body? You have already declared it. Must I argue the wrongfulness of slavery? Is that a question for Republicans? Is it to be settled by the rules of logic and argumentation, as a matter beset with great difficulty, involving a doubtful application of the principle of justice, hard to be understood? How should I look to-day, in the presence of Americans, dividing, and subdividing a discourse, to show that men have a natural right to freedom? speaking of it relatively, and positively, negatively, and affirmatively. To do so, would be to make myself ridiculous, and to offer an insult to your understanding.—There is not a man beneath the canopy of heaven, that does not know that slavery is wrong *for him.*

What, am I to argue that it is wrong to make men brutes, to rob them of their liberty, to work them without wages, to keep them ignorant of their relations to their fellow men, to beat them with sticks, to flay their flesh with the lash, to load their limbs with irons, to hunt them with dogs, to sell them at auction, to sunder their families, to knock out their teeth, to burn their flesh, to starve them into obedience and submission to their masters? Must I argue that a system thus marked with blood, and stained with pollution, is *wrong*? No I will not. I have better employment for my time and strength, than such arguments would imply.

What, then, remains to be argued? Is it that slavery is not divine; that God did not establish it; that our doctors of divinity are mistaken? There is blasphemy in the thought. That which is inhuman, cannot be divine! *Who* can reason on such a proposition? They that can, may; I cannot. The time for such argument is past.

At a time like this, scorching irony, not convincing argument, is needed. O! had I the ability, and could I reach the nation's ear, I would, today, pour out a fiery stream of biting ridicule, blasting reproach, withering sarcasm, and stern rebuke. For it is not light that is needed, but fire; it is not the gentle shower, but thunder. We need the storm, the whirlwind, and the earthquake. The feeling of the nation must be quickened; the conscience of the nation must be roused; the propriety of the nation must be startled; the hypocrisy of the nation must be exposed; and its crimes against God and man must be proclaimed and denounced.

What, to the American slave, is your 4th of July? I answer; a day that reveals to him, more than all other days in the year, the gross injustice and cruelty to which he is the constant victim. To him, your celebration is a sham; your boasted liberty, an unholy license; your national greatness, swelling vanity; your sounds of rejoicing are empty and heartless; your denunciations of tyrants, brass fronted impudence; your shouts of liberty and equality, hollow mockery; your prayers and hymns, your sermons and thanksgivings, with all your religious parade, and solemnity, are, to him, mere bombast, fraud, deception, impiety, and hypocrisy—a thin veil to cover up crimes which would disgrace a nation of savages. There is not a nation on the earth guilty of practices, more shocking and bloody, than are the people of these United States, at this very hour.

Go where you may, search where you will, roam through all the monarchies and despotisms of the old world, travel through South America, search out every abuse, and when you have found the last, lay your facts by the side of the every day practices of this nation, and you will say with me, that, for revolting barbarity and shameless hypocrisy, America reigns without a rival....

To me the American slave-trade is a terrible reality. When a child, my soul was often pierced with a sense of its horrors. I lived on Philpot Street, Fell's Point, Baltimore, and have watched from the wharves, the slave ships in the Basin, anchored from the shore, with their cargoes of human flesh, waiting for favorable winds to waft them down the Chesapeake....

The flesh-mongers gather up their victims by dozens, and drive them, chained, to the general depot at Baltimore. When a sufficient number have been collected here, a ship is chartered, for the purpose of conveying the forlorn crew to Mobile, or to New Orleans. From the slave prison to the ship, they are usually driven in the darkness of night; for since the anti-slavery agitation, a certain caution is observed.

In the deep still darkness of midnight, I have been often aroused by the dead heavy footsteps, and the piteous cries of the chained gangs that passed our door. The anguish of my boyish heart was intense; and I was often consoled, when speaking to my mistress in the morning, to hear her say that the custom was very wicked; that she hated to hear the rattle of the chains, and the heart-rending cries. I was glad to find one who sympathised with me in my horror.

Fellow-citizens, this murderous traffic is, to-day, in active operation in this boasted republic. In the solitude of my spirit, I see clouds of dust raised on the highways of the South; I see the bleeding footsteps; I hear the doleful wail of fettered humanity, on the way to the slave-markets, where the victims are to be sold like *horses, sheep,* and *swine,* knocked off to the highest bidder. There I see the tenderest ties ruthlessly broken, to gratify the lust, caprice and rapacity of the buyers and sellers of men. My soul sickens at the sight....

Fellow-citizens! I will not enlarge further on your national inconsistencies. The existence of slavery in this country brands your republicanism as a sham, your humanity as a base pretense, and your christianity as a lie. It destroys your moral power abroad; it corrupts your politicians at home. It saps the foundation of religion; it makes your name a hissing, and a by-word to a mocking earth. It is the antagonistic force in your government, the only thing that seriously disturbs and endangers your *Union.* It fetters your progress; it is the enemy of improvement, the deadly foe of education; it fosters pride; it breeds insolence; it promotes vice; it shelters crime; it is a curse to the earth that supports it; and yet, you cling to it, as if it were the sheet anchor of all your hopes. Oh! be warned! be warned! a horrible reptile is coiled up in your nation's bosom; the venomous creature is nursing at the tender breast of your youthful republic; *for the love of God, tear away,* and fling from you the hideous monster, and *let the weight of twenty millions, crush and destroy it forever!*

But it is answered in reply to all this, that precisely what I have now denounced is, in fact, guaranteed and sanctioned by the Constitution of the United States; that, the right to hold, and to hunt slaves is a part of that Constitution framed by the illustrious Fathers of this Republic.

*Then,* I dare to affirm, notwithstanding all I have said before, your fathers stooped, basely stooped. . . .

And instead of being the honest men I have before declared them to be, they were the veriest imposters that ever practised on mankind. *This* is the inevitable conclusion, and from it there is no escape; but I differ from those who charge this baseness on the framers of the Constitution of the United States. *It is a slander upon their memory,* at least, so I believe. . . .

Fellow-citizens! there is no matter in respect to which, the people of the North have allowed themselves to be so ruinously imposed upon, as that of the pro-slavery character of the Constitution. In *that* instrument I hold there is neither warrant, license, nor sanction of the hateful thing; but interpreted, as it *ought* to be interpreted, the Constitution is a GLORIOUS LIBERTY DOCUMENT. Read its preamble, consider its purposes. Is slavery among them? Is it at the gateway? or is it in the temple? it is neither. While I do not intend to argue this question on the present occasion, let me ask, if it be not somewhat singular that, if the Constitution were intended to be, by its framers and adopters, a slave-holding instrument, why neither *slavery, slaveholding,* nor *slave* can anywhere be found in it. . . .

Now, take the constitution according to its plain reading, and I defy the presentation of a single pro-slavery clause in it. On the other hand it will be found to contain principles and purposes, entirely hostile to the existence of slavery. . . .

Allow me to say, in conclusion, notwithstanding the dark picture I have this day presented, of the state of the nation, I do not despair of this country. There are forces in operation, which must inevitably, work the downfall of slavery. "*The arm of the Lord is not shortened,*" and the doom of slavery is certain.

I, therefore, leave off where I began, with *hope.* While drawing encouragement from "the Declaration of Independence," the great principles it contains, and the genius of American Institutions, my spirit is also cheered by the obvious tendencies of the age. Nations do not now stand in the same relation to each other that they did ages ago. No nation can now shut itself up, from the surrounding world, and trot round in the same old path of its fathers without interference. The time *was* when such could be done. Long established customs of hurtful character could formerly fence themselves in, and do their evil work with social impunity. Knowledge was then confined and enjoyed by the privileged few, and the multitude walked on in mental darkness. But a change has now come over the affairs of mankind. Walled cities and empires have become unfashionable. The arm of commerce has borne away the gates of the strong city. Intelligence is penetrating the darkest corners of the globe. It makes its pathway over and under the sea, as well as on the earth. Wind, steam, and lightning are its chartered agents. Oceans no longer divide, but link nations together. From Boston to London is now a holiday excursion. Space is comparatively annihilated. Thoughts expressed on one side of the Atlantic, are distinctly heard on the other.

The far off and almost fabulous Pacific rolls in grandeur at our feet. The Celestial Empire, the mystery of ages, is being solved. The fiat of the Almighty, "*Let there be Light,*" has not yet spent its force. No abuse, no outrage whether in taste, sport or avarice, can now hide itself from the all-pervading light.

⋆ ⋆ ⋆

## "THE ARC IS A LONG ONE"
### Theodore Parker, "Of Justice and the Conscience," *Ten Sermons of Religion*—1853

Educated at Harvard, Theodore Parker (1810–1860) was a Unitarian minister and abolitionist.

CONSCIENCE RESTS IN justice as an end, as the mind in truth. As truth is the side of God turned towards the intellect, so is justice the side of Him which conscience looks upon. Love of justice is the moral part of piety.

When I am a baby, in my undeveloped moral state, I do not love justice, nor conform to it; when I am sick, and have not complete control over this republic of nerves and muscles, I fail of justice, and heed it not; when I am stung with beastly rage, blinded by passion, or over attracted from my proper sphere of affection, another man briefly possessing me, I may not love the absolute and eternal right, private capillary attraction conflicting with the universal gravitation. But in my maturity, in my cool and personal hours, when I am most myself, and the accidents of my bodily temperament and local surroundings are controlled by the substance of my manhood, then I love justice with a firm, unwavering love. That is the natural fealty of my conscience to its liege-lord. Then I love justice, not for the consequences thereof, for bodily gain, but for itself, for the moral truth and loveliness thereof. Then if justice crown me I am glad, not merely with my personal feeling, because it is I who wear the crown, but because it is the crown of justice. . . .

What an ideal democracy now floats before the eyes of earnest and religious men,—fairer than the "Republic" of Plato, or More's "Utopia," or the golden age of fabled memory! It is justice that we want to organize—justice for all, for rich and poor. There the slave shall be free from his master. There shall be no want, no oppression, no fear of man, no fear of God, but only love. "There is a good time coming"—so we all believe when we are young and full of life and healthy hope.

God has made man with the instinctive love of justice in him, which gradually gets developed in the world. But in Himself justice is infinite.

This justice of God must appear in the world, and in the history of men; and, after all "the wrongs that patient merit of the unworthy takes," still you see that the ploughshare of justice is drawn through and through the field of the world, uprooting the savage plants. The proverbs of the nations tell us this: "The mills of the gods grind slow, but they grind to powder"; "Ill got ill spent"; "The triumphing of the wicked is but for a moment"; "What the Devil gives, he also takes"; "Honesty is the best policy"; "No butter will stick to a bad man's bread." Sometimes these sayings come from the instinct of justice in man, and have a little ethical exaggeration about them, but yet more often they represent the world's experience of facts more than its consciousness of ideas.

Look at the facts of the world. You see a continual and progressive triumph of the right. I do not pretend to understand the moral universe, the arc is a long one, my eye reaches but little ways. I cannot calculate the curve and complete the figure by the experience of sight; I can divine it by conscience. But from what I see I am sure it bends towards justice. Things refuse to be mismanaged long. Jefferson trembled when he thought of slavery and remembered that God is just. Ere long all America will tremble. . . .

[God's] justice, our morality working with that, shall one day create a unity amongst all men more fair than the face of nature, and add a wondrous beauty, wondrous happiness, to this great family of men. Will you fear lest a wrong should prove immortal? So far as anything is false, or wrong, it is weak; so far as true and right, is omnipotently strong. Never fear that a just thought shall fail to be a thing; the power of God, the wisdom of God, and the justice of God are on its side, and it cannot fail,—no more than God himself can perish. Wrong is the accident of human development. Right is of the substance of humanity, justice the goal we are to reach.

But in human affairs the justice of God must work by human means. Men are the measures of God's principles; our morality the instrument of his justice, which stilleth alike the waves of the sea, the tumult of the people, and the oppressor's brutal rage. Justice is the idea of God, the ideal of man, the rule of conduct writ in the nature of mankind. The ideal must become actual, God's thought a human thing, made real in a reign of righteousness, and a kingdom—no, a Commonwealth—of justice on the earth. You and I can help forward that work. God will not disdain to use our prayers, our self-denial, and the little atoms of justice that personally belong to us, to establish his mighty work,—the development of mankind.

You and I may work with Him, and, as on the floor of the Pacific Sea little insects lay the foundation of firm islands, slowly uprising from the tropic wave, so you and I in our daily life, in house, or field, or shop, obscurely faithful, may prepare the way for the republic of righteousness, the democracy of justice that is to come. Our own morality shall bless us here; not in our outward life alone, but in the inward and majestic life of conscience. All the justice we mature shall bless us here, yea, and hereafter; but at our death we leave it added to the common store of humankind. Even the crumbs that fall from our table may save a brother's life. You and I may help deepen the channel of human morality in which God's justice runs, and the wrecks of evil, which now check the stream, be borne off the sooner by the strong, all-conquering tide of right, the river of God that is full of blessing.

* * *

## "THE SLAVEHOLDING SPIRIT REJOICES"

### William Lloyd Garrison, Address at Framingham, Massachusetts— July 4, 1854

I AM A BELIEVER in that portion of the Declaration of American Independence in which it is set forth, as among self-evident truths, "that all men are created equal; that they are endowed by their Creator with certain inalienable rights; that among these are life, liberty, and the pursuit of happiness." Hence, I am an Abolitionist. Hence, I cannot but regard oppression in every form—and most of all, that which turns a man into a thing—with indignation and abhorrence. Not to cherish these feelings would be recreancy to principle. They who desire me to be dumb on the subject of Slavery, unless I will open my mouth in its defense, ask me to give the lie to my professions, to degrade my manhood, and to stain my soul. I will not be a liar, a poltroon, or a hypocrite, to accommodate any party, to gratify any sect, to escape any odium or peril, to save any interest, to preserve any institution, or to promote any object. Convince me that one man may rightfully make another man his slave, and I will no longer subscribe to the Declaration of Independence. Convince me that liberty is not the inalienable birthright of every human being, of whatever complexion or clime, and I will give that instrument to the consuming fire. I do not know how to espouse freedom and slavery together. I do not know how to worship God and Mammon at the same time. If other men choose to go upon all-fours, I choose to stand erect, as God designed every man to stand. If, practically falsifying its heaven-attested principles, this nation denounces me for refusing to imitate its example, then, adhering all the more tenaciously to those principles, I will not cease to rebuke it for its guilty inconsistency. Numerically, the contest may be an unequal one, for the time being; but the Author of liberty and the Source of justice, the adorable God, is more than multitudinous, and he will defend the right. My crime is, that I will not go with the multitude to do evil. My singularity is, that when I say that Freedom is of God, and Slavery is of the devil, I mean just what I say. My fanaticism is, that I insist on the American people abolishing Slavery, or ceasing to prate of the rights of man. My hardihood is, in measuring them by their own standard, and convicting them out of their own mouths. . . .

Notwithstanding the lessons taught us by Pilgrim Fathers and Revolutionary Sires, at Plymouth Rock, on Bunker Hill, at Lexington, Concord and Yorktown; notwithstanding our Fourth of July celebrations, and ostentatious displays of patriotism; in what European nation is personal liberty held in such contempt as in our own? Where are there such unbelievers in the natural equality and freedom of mankind? Our slaves outnumber the entire population of the country at the time of our revolutionary struggle. In vain do they clank their chains, and fill the air with their shrieks, and make their supplications for mercy. In vain are their sufferings portrayed, their wrongs rehearsed, their rights defended. As Nero fiddled while Rome was burning, so the slaveholding spirit of this nation rejoices, as one barrier of liberty after another is destroyed, and fresh victims are multiplied for the cotton-field and the auction-block. For one impeachment of the slave system, a thousand defenses are made. For one rebuke of the man-stealer, a thousand denunciations of the Abolitionists are heard. For one press that bears a faithful testimony against Slavery, a score are ready to be prostituted to its service. For one pulpit that is not "recreant to its trust," there are ten that openly defend slaveholding as compatible with Christianity, and scores that are dumb. For one church that excludes the human enslaver from its communion table, multitudes extend to him the right hand of religious fellowship. The wealth, the enterprise, the literature, the politics, the religion of the land, are all combined to give extension and perpetuity to the Slave Power. Everywhere to do homage to it, to avoid collision with it, to propitiate its favor, is deemed essential—nay, is essential to political preferment and ecclesiastical advancement. Nothing is so unpopular as impartial liberty. The two great parties which absorb nearly the whole voting strength of the Republic are pledged to be deaf, dumb and blind to whatever outrages the Slave Power may attempt to perpetrate. Cotton is in their ears—blinds are over their eyes—padlocks are upon their lips. They are as clay in the hands of the potter, and already molded into vessels of dishonor, to be used for the vilest purposes. The tremendous power of the Government is actively wielded to "crush out" the little Anti-Slavery life that remains in individual hearts, and to open new and boundless domains for the expansion of the Slave system. . . .

How has the slave system grown to its present enormous dimensions? Through compromise. How is it to be exterminated? Only by an uncompromising spirit. This is to be carried out in all the relations of life—social, political, religious. Put not on the list of your friends, nor allow admission to your domestic circle, the man who on principle defends Slavery, but treat him as a moral leper. . . .

While the present Union exists, I pronounce it hopeless to expect any repose, or that any barrier can be effectually raised against the extension of Slavery. With two thousand million dollars' worth of property in human flesh in its hands, to be watched and wielded as one vast interest for all the South—with forces never divided, and purposes never conflictive—with a spurious, negro hating religion universally diffused, and everywhere ready to shield it from harm—with a selfish, sordid, divided North, long since bereft of its manhood, to cajole, bribe and intimidate—with its foot planted on two-thirds of our vast national domains, and there unquestioned, absolute and bloody in its sway—with the terrible strength and boundless resources of the whole country at its command—it cannot be otherwise than that the Slave

Power will consummate its diabolical purposes to the uttermost. The Northwest Territory, Nebraska, Mexico, Cuba, Haiti, the Sandwich Islands, and colonial possessions in the tropics—to seize and subjugate these to its accursed reign, and ultimately to re-establish the foreign Slave Trade as a lawful commerce, are among its settled designs. It is not a question of probabilities, but of time. . . .

While, therefore, the Union is preserved, I see no end to the extension or perpetuity of Chattel Slavery—no hope for peaceful deliverance of the millions who are clanking their chains on our blood-red soil. Yet I know that God reigns, and that the slave system contains within itself the elements of destruction. But how long it is to curse the earth, and desecrate his image, he alone foresees. It is frightful to think of the capacity of a nation like this to commit sin, before the measure of its iniquities be filled, and the exterminating judgments of God overtake it. . . .

These are solemn times. It is not a struggle for national salvation; for the nation, as such, seems doomed beyond recovery. The reason why the South rules, and the North falls prostrate in servile terror, is simply this: With the South, the preservation of Slavery is paramount to all other considerations—above party success, denominational unity, pecuniary interest, legal integrity, and constitutional obligation. With the North, the preservation of the Union is placed above all other things—above honor, justice, freedom, integrity of soul, the Decalogue and the Golden Rule—the Infinite God himself. All these she is ready to discard for the Union. Her devotion to it is the latest and the most terrible form of idolatry. She has given to the Slave Power a *carte blanche,* to be filled as it may dictate—and if, at any time, she grows restive under the yoke, and shrinks back aghast at the new atrocity contemplated, it is only necessary for that Power to crack the whip of Disunion over her head, as it has done again and again, and she will cower and obey like a plantation slave—for has she not sworn that she will sacrifice everything in heaven and on earth, rather than the Union?

What then is to be done? Friends of the slave, the question is not whether by our efforts we can abolish Slavery, speedily or remotely—for duty is ours, the result is with God; but whether we will go with the multitude to do evil, sell our birthright for a mess of pottage, cease to cry aloud and spare not, and remain in Babylon when the command of

God is, "Come out of her, my people, that ye be not partakers of her sins, and that ye receive not of her plagues." Let us stand in our lot, "and having done all, to stand." At least, a remnant shall be saved. Living or dying, defeated or victorious, be it ours to exclaim, "No compromise with Slavery! Liberty for each, for all, forever! Man above all institutions! The supremacy of God over the whole earth!"

★ ★ ★

## "SLAVERY IS A DOOMED SYSTEM"

**Frederick Douglass, The *Dred Scott* Decision, Speech Delivered Before the American Anti-Slavery Society, New York City—May 14, 1857**

---

TO MANY, THE prospects of the struggle against slavery seem far from cheering. Eminent men, North and South, in Church and State, tell us that the omens are all against us. Emancipation, they tell us, is a wild, delusive idea; the price of human flesh was never higher than now; slavery was never more closely entwined about the hearts and affections of the southern people than now; that whatever of conscientious scruple, religious conviction, or public policy, which opposed the system of slavery forty or fifty years ago, has subsided; and that slavery never reposed upon a firmer basis than now. Completing this picture of the happy and prosperous condition of this system of wickedness, they tell us that this state of things is to be set to our account. Abolition agitation has done it all. How deep is the misfortune of my poor, bleeding people, if this be so! How lost their condition, if even the efforts of their friends but sink them deeper in ruin!

Without assenting to this strong representation of the increasing strength and stability of slavery, without denouncing what of untruth pervades it, I own myself not insensible to the many difficulties and discouragements that beset us on every hand. They fling their broad and gloomy shadows across the pathway of every thoughtful colored man in this country. For one, I see them clearly, and feel them sadly. With an earnest, aching heart, I have long looked for the realization of the hope of my people. Standing, as it were, barefoot, and treading upon the sharp and flinty rocks of the present, and looking out upon the boundless sea of the future, I have sought, in my humble way, to penetrate the intervening mists and clouds, and, perchance, to descry, in the dim and shadowy distance, the white flag of freedom, the precise speck of time at which the cruel bondage of my people should end, and the long entombed millions rise from the foul grave of slavery and death. But of that time I can know nothing, and you can know nothing. All is uncertain at that point. One thing, however, is certain; slaveholders are in earnest, and mean to cling to their slaves as long as they can, and to the bitter end. They show no sign of a wish to quit their iron grasp upon the sable throats of their victims. Their motto is, "a firmer hold and a tighter grip" for every new effort that is made to break their cruel power. The case is one of life or death with them, and they will give up only when they must do that or do worse.

In one view the slaveholders have a decided advantage over all opposition. It is well to notice this advantage—the advantage of complete organization. They are organized; and yet were not at the pains of creating their organizations. The State governments, where the system of slavery exists, are complete slavery organizations. The church organizations in those States are equally at the service of slavery; while the Federal Government, with its army and navy, from the chief magistracy in Washington, to the Supreme Court, and thence to the chief marshalship at New York, is pledged to support, defend, and propagate the crying curse of human bondage. The pen, the purse, and the sword, are united against the simple truth, preached by humble men in obscure places.

This is one view. It is, thank God, only one view; there is another, and a brighter view. David, you know, looked small and insignificant when going to meet Goliath, but looked larger when he had slain his foe. . . . Thus hath it ever been. Oppression, organized as ours is, will appear invincible up to the very hour of its fall. Sir, let us look at the other side, and see if there are not some things to cheer our heart and nerve us up anew in the good work of emancipation.

Take this fact—for it is a fact—the anti-slavery movement has, from first to last, suffered no abatement. It has gone forth in all directions, and is now felt in the remotest extremities of the Republic.

It started small, and was without capital either in men or money. The odds were all against it. It literally had nothing to lose, and everything to gain. There was ignorance to be enlightened, error to be combatted, conscience to be awakened, prejudice to be overcome, apathy to be aroused, the right of speech to be secured, mob violence to be subdued, and a deep, radical change to be inwrought in the mind and heart of the whole nation. This great work, under God, has gone on, and gone on gloriously.

Amid all changes, fluctuations, assaults, and adverses of every kind, it has remained firm in its purpose, steady in its aim, onward and upward, defying all opposition, and never losing a single battle. Our strength is in the growth of anti-slavery conviction, and this has never halted.

There is a significant vitality about this abolition movement. It has taken a deeper, broader, and more lasting hold upon the national heart than ordinary reform movements. Other subjects of much interest come and go, expand and contract, blaze and vanish, but the huge question of American Slavery, comprehending, as it does, not merely the weal or the woe of four millions, and their countless posterity, but the weal or the woe of this entire nation, must increase in magnitude and in majesty with every hour of its history. From a cloud not bigger than a man's hand, it has overspread the heavens. It has risen from a grain not bigger than a mustard seed. Yet see the fowls of the air, how they crowd its branches.

Politicians who cursed it, now defend it; ministers, once dumb, now speak in its praise; and presses, which once flamed with hot denunciations against it, now surround the sacred cause as by a wall of living fire. Politicians go with it as a pillar of cloud by day, and the press as a pillar of fire by night. With these ancient tokens of success, I, for one, will not despair of our cause.

Those who have undertaken to suppress and crush out this agitation for Liberty and humanity, have been most woefully disappointed. Many who have engaged to put it down, have found themselves put down. The agitation has pursued them in all their meanderings, broken in upon their seclusion, and, at the very moment of fancied security, it has settled down upon them like a mantle of unquenchable fire. Clay, Calhoun, and Webster each tried his hand at suppressing the agitation; and they went to their graves disappointed and defeated.

Loud and exultingly have we been told that the slavery question is settled, and settled forever. You remember it was settled thirty-seven years ago, when Missouri was admitted into the Union with a slaveholding constitution, and slavery prohibited in all territory north of thirty-six degrees of north latitude. Just fifteen years afterwards, it was settled again by voting down the right of petition, and gagging down free discussion in Congress. Ten years after this it was settled again by the annexation of Texas, and with it the war with Mexico. In 1850 it was again settled. This was called a final settlement. By it slavery was virtually declared to be the equal of Liberty, and should come into the Union on the same terms. By it the right and the power to hunt down men, women, and children, in every part of this country, was conceded to our southern brethren, in order to keep them in the Union. Four years after this settlement, the whole question was once more settled, and settled by a settlement which unsettled all the former settlements.

The fact is, the more the question has been settled, the more it has needed settling. The space between the different settlements has been strikingly on the decrease. The first stood longer than any of its successors.

There is a lesson in these decreasing spaces. The first stood fifteen years—the second, ten years—the third, five years—the fourth stood four years—and the fifth has stood the brief space of two years.

This last settlement must be called the Taney settlement. We are now told, in tones of lofty exultation, that the day is lost—all lost—and that we might as well give up the struggle. The highest authority has spoken. The voice of the Supreme Court has gone out over the troubled waves of the National Conscience, saying peace, be still.

This infamous decision of the Slaveholding wing of the Supreme Court maintains that slaves are within the contemplation of the Constitution of the United States, property; that slaves are property in the same sense that horses, sheep, and swine are property; that the old doctrine that slavery is a creature of local law is false; that the right of the slaveholder to his slave does not depend upon the local law, but is secured wherever the Constitution of the United States extends; that Congress has no right to prohibit slavery anywhere; that slavery may go in safety anywhere under the star-spangled banner; that colored persons of African descent have no rights that white men are bound to respect; that colored men of African descent are not and cannot be citizens of the United States.

You will readily ask me how I am affected by this devilish decision—this judicial incarnation of wolfishness? My answer is, and no thanks to the slaveholding wing of the Supreme Court, my hopes were never brighter than now.

I have no fear that the National Conscience will be put to sleep by such an open, glaring, and scandalous tissue of lies as that decision is, and has been, over and over, shown to be.

The Supreme Court of the United States is not the only power in this world. It is very great, but the Supreme Court of the Almighty is greater. Judge Taney can do many things, but he cannot perform impossibilities. He cannot bail out the ocean, annihilate the firm old earth, or pluck the silvery star of liberty from our Northern sky. He may decide, and decide again; but he cannot reverse the decision of the Most High. He cannot change the essential nature of things—making evil good, and good evil.

Happily for the whole human family, their rights have been defined, declared, and decided in a court higher than the Supreme Court. "There is a law," says [British abolitionist Henry Lord] Brougham, "above all the enactments of human codes, and by that law, unchangeable and eternal, man cannot hold property in man."

Your fathers have said that man's right to liberty is self-evident. There is no need of argument to make it clear. The voices of nature, of conscience, of reason, and of revelation, proclaim it as the right of all rights, the foundation of all trust, and of all responsibility. Man was born with it. It was his before he comprehended it. The *deed* conveying it to him is written in the center of his soul, and is recorded in Heaven. The sun in the sky is not more palpable to the sight than man's right to liberty is to the moral vision. To decide against this right in the person of Dred Scott, or the humblest and most whip-scarred bondman in the land, is to decide against God. It is an open rebellion against God's government. It is an attempt to undo what God has done, to blot out the broad distinction instituted by the *All-wise* between men and things, and to change the image and superscription of the ever-living God into a speechless piece of merchandise.

Such a decision cannot stand. God will be true though every man be a liar. We can appeal from this hell-black judgment of the Supreme Court, to the court of common sense and common humanity. We can appeal from man to God. If there is no justice on earth, there is yet justice in heaven. You may close your Supreme Court against the black man's cry for justice, but you cannot, thank God, close against him the ear of a sympathizing world, nor shut up the Court of Heaven. All that is merciful and just, on earth and in Heaven, will execrate and despise this edict of Taney.

If it were at all likely that the people of these free States would tamely submit to this demonical judgment, I might feel gloomy and sad over it, and possibly it might be necessary for my people to look for a home in some other country. But as the case stands, we have nothing to fear.

In one point of view, we, the abolitionists and colored people, should meet this decision, unlooked for and monstrous as it appears, in a cheerful spirit. This very attempt to blot out forever the hopes of an enslaved people may be one necessary link in the chain of events preparatory to the downfall and complete overthrow of the whole slave system.

The whole history of the anti-slavery movement is studded with proof that all measures devised and executed with a view to ally and diminish the anti-slavery agitation, have only served to increase, intensify, and embolden that agitation. This wisdom of the crafty has been confounded, and the counsels of the ungodly brought to nought. It was so with the Fugitive Slave Bill. It was so with the Kansas-Nebraska Bill; and it will be so with this last and most shocking of all pro-slavery devices, this Taney decision.

When great transactions are involved, where the fate of millions is concerned, where a long enslaved and suffering people are to be delivered, I am superstitious enough to believe that the finger of the Almighty may be seen bringing good out of evil, and making the wrath of man redound to his honor, hastening the triumph of righteousness.

The American people have been called upon, in a most striking manner, to abolish and put away forever the system of slavery. The subject has been pressed upon their attention in all earnestness and sincerity. The cries of the slave have gone forth to the world, and up to the throne of God. This decision, in my view, is a means of keeping the nation awake on the subject. It is another proof that God does not mean that we shall go to sleep, and forget that we are a slave-holding nation.

Step by step we have seen the slave power advancing; poisoning, corrupting, and perverting the institutions of the country; growing more and more haughty, imperious, and exacting. The white man's liberty has been marked out for the same grave with the black man's.

The ballot box is desecrated, God's law set at nought, armed legislators stalk the halls of Congress, freedom of speech is beaten down in the Senate. The rivers and highways are infested by border ruffians, and white men are made to feel the iron heel of slavery. This ought to arouse us to kill off the hateful thing. They are solemn warnings to which the white people, as well as the black people, should take heed.

If these shall fail, judgment, more fierce or terrible, may come. The lightning, whirlwind, and earthquake may come. Jefferson said that he trembled for his country when he reflected that God is just, and his justice cannot sleep forever. The time may come when even the crushed worm may turn under the tyrant's feet. Goaded by cruelty, stung by a burning sense of wrong, in an awful moment of depression and desperation, the bondman and bondwoman at the south may rush to one wild and deadly struggle for freedom. Already slaveholders go to bed with bowie knives, and apprehend death at their dinners. Those who enslave, rob, and torment their cooks, may well expect to find death in their dinner-pots. . . .

By all the laws of nature, civilization, and of progress, slavery is a doomed system. Not all the skill of politicians, North and South, not all the sophistries of Judges, not all the fulminations of a corrupt press, not all the hypocritical prayers, or the hypocritical refusals to pray of a hollow-hearted priesthood, not all the devices of sin and Satan, can save the vile thing from extermination. . . .

Come what will, I hold it to be morally certain that, sooner or later, by fair means or foul means, in quiet or in tumult, in peace or in blood, in judgment or in mercy, slavery is doomed to cease out of this otherwise goodly land, and liberty is destined to become the settled law of this Republic.

I base my sense of the certain overthrow of slavery, in part, upon the nature of the American Government, the Constitution, the tendencies of the age, and the character of the American people; and this, notwithstanding the important decision of Judge Taney.

I know of no soil better adapted to the growth of reform than American soil. I know of no country where the conditions for affecting great changes in the settled order of things, for the development of right ideas of liberty and humanity, are more favorable than here in these United States.

The very groundwork of this government is a good repository of Christian civilization. The Constitution, as well as the Declaration of Independence, and the sentiments of the founders of the Republic, give us a platform broad enough, and strong enough, to support the most comprehensive plans for the freedom and elevation of all the people of this country, without regard to color, class, or clime.

PART IV

# THE FIERY TRIAL

*1860–1865*

Our poor and forlorn brother whom thou hast labeled "slave," is also a man. He may be unfortunate, weak, helpless and despised and hated; nevertheless he is a man.

—Henry Highland Garnet, 1865

PREVIOUS SPREAD: *The white South greeted Abraham Lincoln's election to the presidency in 1860 with secession; the nation would be at war with itself after the Confederate attack on Fort Sumter in Charleston Harbor in April 1861.*

THE ISSUES WERE CLEAR to those with eyes to see and ears to hear. "We know what is coming in this Union," Senator Alfred Iverson of Georgia remarked in December 1860, the month after Abraham Lincoln's victory in the presidential election. "It is universal emancipation and the turning loose upon society in the Southern States of the mass of corruption which will be made by emancipation. We intend to avoid it if we can. . . . We are obliged to have African slavery to cultivate our cotton, our rice, and our sugar fields. African slavery is essential not only to our prosperity, but to our existence as a people." On Christmas Day in Nashville, Tennessee, a diarist wrote: "Lincoln has been elected President & the whole South is shaken from center to circumference." As state after state followed South Carolina out of the Union—delegates in Charleston had voted for secession in the third week of December—Alexander Stephens of Georgia, speaking in Savannah, was explicit about the mission of the newly formed Confederate States of America. "Our new government," Stephens said in March 1861, "is founded upon . . . the great truth that the negro is not equal to the white man; that slavery subordination to the superior race is his natural and normal condition. This, our new government, is the first, in the history of the world, based upon this great physical, philosophical, and moral truth."

Lincoln had sought—and barely won—the presidency with a moral antislavery argument. "Their thinking it right," he had said of the slave-owning South, "and our thinking it wrong, is the precise fact upon which depends the whole controversy." Lincoln frustrated abolitionists who wished to see him move further, faster, but it is striking that the white South resorted to secession not on the occasion of Lincoln's inauguration but on the mere fact of his election. The most virulent proslavery elements in the country, then, saw Lincoln as a fatal foe.

Beginning in September 1862 and then on January 1, 1863, Lincoln issued emancipation proclamations. In his 1864 reelection campaign, the president ran on a platform calling for an abolition amendment to the Constitution, refusing to put emancipation on the table for possible peace talks with the Confederacy even when he was in danger of losing the race. The organizing thought in Lincoln's political mind, first expressed in the address to the Springfield Lyceum, was the centrality of the promise of the Declaration. "Without the *Constitution* and the *Union,* we could not have attained [the creation and maintenance of the nation]: but even these are not the primary cause of our great prosperity," Lincoln once wrote. "There is something back of these, entwining itself more closely about the human heart. That something, is the principle of 'Liberty to all'—the principle that clears the *path* for all—gives *hope* to all—and, by consequence, *enterprise,* and *industry* to all."

Guided by such thinking, Lincoln waged the Civil War and prevailed in the 1864 election against George McClellan. At four o'clock on the afternoon of Tuesday, January 31, 1865, the Thirteenth Amendment abolishing slavery was approved by the Congress. It had been a long time coming. "In a great national crisis, like ours, unanimity of action among those seeking a common end is very desirable—almost indispensable," Lincoln had told the Congress in December 1864. "And yet no approach to such unanimity is attainable, unless some deference shall be paid to the will of the majority, simply because it is the will of the majority. In this case the common end is the maintenance of the Union; and, among the means to secure that end, such will, through the election, is most clearly declared in favor of such constitutional amendment."

In the wake of the amendment's passage—an event Lincoln hailed as a "great moral victory"—the Reverend Henry Highland Garnet, pastor of Washington's Fifteenth Street Presbyterian Church, became the first Black man to speak in the chamber of the United States House of Representatives. The invitation to preach in the House fulfilled a promise of House Chaplain William Henry Channing, who had pledged "that a colored minister should stand on the speaker's platform, and by that practical illustration, demonstrate that one central principle of the War for Freedom and Union was to prove that 'in Christ' all disciples are alike free, and that all God's children, black and white, are peers in the Father's House."

★ ★ ★

## "RIGHT MAKES MIGHT"
### Abraham Lincoln, Address at Cooper Union, New York City—February 27, 1860

A candidate for the Republican nomination for president, Lincoln came East, to New York, to address the slavery question in the months before the Republican National Convention. In this excerpt, he begins with words to the proslavery forces in the South.

YOUR PURPOSE, THEN, plainly stated, is that you will destroy the Government, unless you be allowed to construe and enforce the Constitution as you please, on all points in dispute between you and us. You will rule or ruin in all events. . . .

A few words now to Republicans. *It is exceedingly desirable that all parts of this great Confederacy shall be at peace, and in harmony, one with another. Let us Republicans do our part to have it so. Even though much provoked, let us do nothing through passion and ill temper. Even though the southern people will not so much as listen to us, let us calmly consider their demands, and yield to them if, in our deliberate view of our duty, we possibly can. . . .*

The question recurs, what will satisfy them? Simply this: We must not only let them alone, but we must somehow, convince them that we do let them alone. This, we know by experience, is no easy task. We have been so trying to convince them from the very beginning of our organization, but with no success. In all our platforms and speeches we have constantly protested our purpose to let them alone; but this has had no tendency to convince them. Alike unavailing to convince them, is the fact that they have never detected a man of us in any attempt to disturb them.

These natural, and apparently adequate means all failing, what will convince them? This, and this only: cease to call slavery *wrong*, and join them in calling it *right*. And this must be done thoroughly—done in *acts* as well as in *words*. Silence will not be tolerated—we must place ourselves avowedly with them. . . .

Holding, as they do, that slavery is morally right, and socially elevating, they cannot cease to demand a full national recognition of it, as a legal right, and a social blessing.

Nor can we justifiably withhold this, on any ground save our conviction that slavery is wrong. If slavery is right, all words, acts, laws, and constitutions against it, are themselves wrong, and should be silenced, and swept away. If it is right, we cannot justly object to its nationality—its universality; if it is wrong, they cannot justly insist upon its extension—its enlargement. All they ask, we could readily grant, if we thought slavery right; all we ask, they could as readily grant, if they thought it wrong. Their thinking it right, and our thinking it wrong, is the precise fact upon which depends the whole controversy. Thinking it right, as they do, they are not to blame for desiring its full recognition, as being right; but, thinking it wrong, as we do, can we yield to them? Can we cast our votes with their view, and against our own? In view of our moral, social, and political responsibilities, can we do this?

Wrong as we think slavery is, we can yet afford to let it alone where it is, because that much is due to the necessity arising from its actual presence in the nation; but can we, while our votes will prevent it, allow it to spread into the National Territories, and to overrun us here in these Free States? If our sense of duty forbids this, then let us stand by our duty, fearlessly and effectively. Let us be diverted by none of those sophistical contrivances wherewith we are so industriously plied and belabored—contrivances such as groping for some middle ground between the right and the wrong, vain as the search for a man who should be neither a living man nor a dead man—such as a policy of "don't care" on a question about which all true men do care—such as Union appeals beseeching true Union men to yield to Disunionists, reversing the divine rule, and calling, not the sinners, but the righteous to repentance—such as invocations to Washington, imploring men to unsay what Washington said, and undo what Washington did.

Neither let us be slandered from our duty by false accusations against us, nor frightened from it by menaces of destruction to the Government nor of dungeons to ourselves. LET US HAVE FAITH THAT RIGHT MAKES MIGHT, AND IN THAT FAITH, LET US, TO THE END, DARE TO DO OUR DUTY AS WE UNDERSTAND IT.

* * *

## "THE NEGRO IS NOT EQUAL TO THE WHITE MAN"
## Alexander Stephens, Corner-Stone Speech, Savannah, Georgia—March 21, 1861

Alexander Stephens (1812–1883) served in the U.S. House from Georgia and became vice president of the Confederate States of America. In these remarks he laid out the thinking behind the secessionist cause and argued for the virtues of the Confederate constitution. The Civil War would break out within a month of Stephens's address in Savannah.

THE NEW [CONFEDERATE] constitution has put at rest, *forever,* all the agitating questions relating to our peculiar institution—African slavery as it exists amongst us—[and] the proper status of the negro in our form of civilization. This was the immediate cause of the late rupture and present revolution. Jefferson in his forecast, had anticipated this, as the "rock upon which the old Union would split." He was right. What was conjecture with him, is now a realized fact. But whether he fully comprehended the great truth upon which that rock *stood* and *stands,* may be doubted. The prevailing ideas entertained by him and most of the leading statesmen at the time of the formation of the old constitution, were that the enslavement of the African was in violation of the laws of nature; that it was wrong in *principle,* socially, morally, and politically. It was an evil they knew not well how to deal with, but the general opin-

*Known as "Little Aleck," Alexander Stephens of Taliaferro County was a longtime U.S. congressman from Georgia; he returned to the House after the Civil War and died while serving as governor in 1883.*

ion of the men of that day was that, somehow or other in the order of Providence, the institution would be evanescent and pass away. This idea, though not incorporated in the constitution, was the prevailing idea at that time. The constitution, it is true, secured every essential guarantee to the institution while it should last, and hence no argument can be justly urged against the constitutional guarantees thus secured, because of the common sentiment of the day. Those ideas, however, were fundamentally wrong. They rested upon the assumption of the equality of races. This was an error. It was a sandy foundation, and the government built upon it fell when the "storm came and the wind blew."

Our new government is founded upon exactly the opposite idea; its foundations are laid, its corner-stone rests, upon the great truth that the negro is not equal to the white man; that slavery subordination to the superior race is his natural and normal condition. This, our new government, is the first, in the history of the world, based upon this great physical, philosophical, and moral truth. This truth has been slow in the process of its development, like all other truths in the various departments of science. It has been so even amongst us. Many who hear me, perhaps, can recollect well, that this truth was not generally admitted, even within their day. The errors of the past generation still clung to many as late as twenty years ago. Those at the North, who still cling to these errors, with a zeal above knowledge, we justly denominate fanatics. All fanaticism springs from an aberration of the mind from a defect in reasoning. It is a species of insanity. One of the most striking characteristics of insanity, in many instances, is forming correct conclusions from fancied or erroneous premises; so with the anti-slavery fanatics. Their conclusions are right if their premises were. They assume that the negro is equal, and hence conclude that he is entitled to equal privileges and rights with the white man. If their premises were correct, their conclusions would be logical and just but their premise being wrong, their whole argument fails. I recollect once of having heard a gentleman from one of the northern States, of great power and ability, announce in the House of Representatives, with imposing effect, that we of the South would be compelled, ultimately, to yield upon this subject of slavery, that it was as impossible to war successfully against a principle in politics, as it was in physics or mechanics. That the principle would ultimately prevail. That we, in maintaining slavery as it exists with us, were warring against a principle, a principle founded in nature, the principle of the equality of men. The reply I made to him was, that upon his own grounds, we should, ultimately, succeed, and that he and his associates, in this crusade against our institutions, would ultimately fail. The truth announced, that it was as impossible to war successfully against a principle in politics as it was in physics and mechanics, I admitted; but told him that it was he, and those acting with him, who were warring against a principle. They were attempting to make things equal which the Creator had made unequal.

In the conflict thus far, success has been on our side, complete throughout the length and breadth of the Confederate States. It is upon this, as I have stated, our social fabric is firmly planted; and I cannot permit myself to doubt the ultimate success of a full recognition of this principle throughout the civilized and enlightened world.

As I have stated, the truth of this principle may be slow in development, as all truths are and ever have been, in the various branches of science. It was so with the principles announced by Galileo. It was so with Adam Smith and his principles of political economy. It was so with [William] Harvey, and his theory of the circulation of the blood. It is stated that not a single one of the medical profession, living at the time of the announcement of the truths made by him, admitted them. Now, they are universally acknowledged. May we not, therefore, look with confidence to the ultimate universal acknowledgment of the truths upon which our system rests? It is the first government ever instituted upon the principles in strict conformity to nature, and the ordination of Providence, in furnishing the materials of human society. Many governments have been founded upon the principle of the subordination and serfdom of certain classes of the same race; such were and are in violation of the laws of nature. Our system commits no such violation of nature's laws. With us, all of the white race, however high or low, rich or poor, are equal in the eye of the law. Not so with the negro. Subordination is his place. He, by nature, or by the curse against Canaan, is fitted for that condition which he occupies in our system. The architect, in the construction of buildings, lays the foundation with the proper material—the granite; then comes the brick or the marble. The substratum of our society is made of the material fitted by nature for it, and by experience we know that it is best, not only for the superior, but for the inferior race, that it should be so. It is, indeed, in conformity with the ordinance of the Creator. It is not for us to inquire into the wisdom of His ordinances, or to question them. For His own purposes, He has made one race to differ from another, as He has made "one star to differ from another star in glory." The great objects of humanity are best attained when there is conformity to His laws and decrees, in the formation of governments as well as in all things else. Our confederacy is founded upon principles in strict conformity with these laws. This stone which was rejected by the first builders "is become the chief of the corner" the real "corner-stone" in our new edifice. I have been asked, what of the future? It has been apprehended by some that we would have arrayed against us the civilized world. I care not who or how many they may be against us, when we stand upon the eternal principles of truth, if we are true to ourselves and the principles for which we contend, we are obliged to, and must triumph.

★ ★ ★

## "A NEW BIRTH OF FREEDOM"

### Abraham Lincoln, Gettysburg Address—November 19, 1863

FOUR SCORE AND seven years ago our fathers brought forth on this continent, a new nation, conceived in Liberty, and dedicated to the proposition that all men are created equal.

Now we are engaged in a great civil war, testing whether that nation, or any nation so conceived and so dedicated, can long endure. We are met on a great battle-field of that war. We have come to dedicate a portion of that field, as a final resting place for those who here gave their lives that the nation might live. It is altogether fitting and proper that we should do this.

But, in a larger sense, we can not dedicate—we can not consecrate—we can not hallow—this ground. The brave men, living and dead, who struggled here, have consecrated it, far above our poor power to add or detract. The world will little note, nor long remember what we say here, but it can never forget what they did here. It is for us the living, rather, to be dedicated here to the unfinished work which they who fought here have thus far so nobly advanced. It is rather for us to be here dedicated to the great task remaining before us—that from these honored dead we take increased devotion to that cause for which they gave the last full measure of devotion—that we here highly resolve that these dead shall not have died in vain—that this nation, under God, shall have a new birth of freedom—and that government of the people, by the people, for the people, shall not perish from the earth.

★ ★ ★

## "EMANCIPATE, ENFRANCHISE, EDUCATE"
### Henry Highland Garnet, Sermon in the House of Representatives—February 12, 1865

The Reverend Henry Highland Garnet (1815–1882) was born into enslavement in Maryland. His family escaped and went to New York, where he became a minister and advocate of abolition. Garnet was serving as pastor of the Fifteenth Street Presbyterian Church in Washington, D.C., when he was invited to preach a Sunday sermon in the House of Representatives in the wake of the passage of the Thirteenth Amendment.

WHAT IS SLAVERY? Too well do I know what it is. I will present to you a bird's-eye view of it; and it shall be no fancy picture, but one that is sketched by painful experience. I was born among the cherished institutions of slavery. My earliest recollections of parents, friends, and the home of my childhood are clouded with its wrongs. The first sight that met my eyes was a Christian mother enslaved by professed Christians, but, thank God, now a saint in heaven. The first sounds that startled my ear and sent a shudder through my soul were the cracking of the whip, and the clanking of chains. These sad memories mar the beauties of my native shores and darken all the slave-land, which, but for the reign of despotism, had been a paradise. But those shores are fairer now. The mists have left my native valleys, and the clouds have

*In 1843, Henry Highland Garnet had called for a militant revolt against slaveowners.*

rolled away from the hills, and Maryland, the unhonored grave of my fathers, is now the free home of their liberated and happier children.

Let us view this demon, which the people have worshipped as a God. Come forth, thou grim monster, that thou mayest be critically examined! There he stands. Behold him, one and all. Its work is to chattelize man; to hold property in human beings. Great God! I would as soon attempt to enslave GABRIEL or MICHAEL as to enslave a man made in the image of God, and for whom Christ died. Slavery is snatching man from the high place to which he was lifted by the hand of God, and dragging him down to the level of the brute creation, where he is made to be the companion of the horse and the fellow of the ox.

It tears the crown of glory from his head and as far as possible obliterates the image of God that is in him. Slavery preys upon man, and man only. A brute cannot be made a slave. Why? Because a brute has not reason, faith, nor an undying spirit, nor conscience. It does not look forward to the future with joy or fear, nor reflect upon the past with satisfaction or regret. But who in this vast assembly, who in all this broad land, will say that the poorest and most unhappy brother in chains and servitude has not every one of these high endowments? Who denies it? Is there one? If so, let him speak. There is not one; no, not one.

But slavery attempts to make a man a brute. It treats him as a beast. . . .

Our poor and forlorn brother whom thou hast labelled "*slave,*" is also a man. He may be unfortunate, weak, helpless, and despised, and hated; nevertheless he is a man. His God and thine has stamped on his forehead his title to his inalienable rights in characters that can be read by every intelligent being. Pitiless storms of outrage may have beaten upon his defenseless head, and he may have descended through ages of oppression; yet he is a man. God made him such, and his brother cannot unmake him. Woe, woe to him who attempts to commit the accursed crime.

Slavery commenced its dreadful work in kidnaping unoffending men in a foreign and distant land, and in piracy on the seas. The plunderers were not the followers of Mahomet, nor the devotees of Hinduism, nor benighted pagans, nor idolaters, but people called Christians, and thus the ruthless traders in the souls and bodies of men fastened upon Christianity a crime and stain at the sight of which it shudders and shrieks.

It is guilty of the most heinous iniquities ever perpetrated upon helpless women and innocent children. Go to the shores of the land of my forefathers, poor bleeding Africa, which, although she has been bereaved and robbed for centuries, is nevertheless beloved by all her worthy descendants wherever dispersed. Behold a single scene that there meets your eyes. Turn not away either from shame, pity or indifference, but look and see the beginning of this cherished and petted institution. Behold a hundred youthful mothers seated on the ground, dropping their tears upon the hot sands, and filling the air with their lamentations. . . .

This commerce in human beings has been carried on until three hundred thousand have been dragged from their native land in a single year. While this foreign trade has been pursued, who can calculate the enormities and extent of the domestic traffic which has flourished in every slave State, while the whole country has been open to the hunters of men.

It is the highly concentrated essence of all conceivable wickedness. Theft, robbery, pollution, unbridled passion, incest, cruelty, cold-blooded murder, blasphemy, and defiance of the laws of God. It teaches children to disregard parental authority. It tears down the marriage altar and tramples its sacred ashes under its feet. It creates and nourishes polygamy. It feeds and pampers its hateful handmaid, prejudice.

It has divided our national councils. It has engendered deadly strife between brethren. It has wasted the treasure of the Commonwealth and the lives of thousands of brave men, and driven troops of helpless women and children into yawning tombs. It has caused the bloodiest civil war recorded in the book of time. It has shorn this nation of its locks of strength that was rising as a young lion in the Western world. It has offered us as a sacrifice to the jealousy and cupidity of tyrants, despots, and adventurers of foreign countries. It has opened a door through which a usurper, a perjured but powerful prince, might stealthily enter and build an empire on the golden borders of our southwestern frontier, and which is but a steppingstone to further and unlimited conquests on this continent. It has desolated the fairest portions of our land, "until the wolf long since driven back by the march of civilization returns after the lapse of a hundred years and howls amidst its ruins."

It seals up the Bible and mutilates its sacred truths, and flies into the face of the Almighty, and impiously asks, "*Who art thou that I should obey thee?*" Such are the outlines of this fearful national sin; and yet the condition to which it reduces man, it is affirmed, is the best that can possibly be devised for him. . . .

Let us here take up the golden rule, and adopt the self-application mode of reasoning to those who hold these erroneous views. Come, gird up thy loins and answer like a man, if thou canst. Is slavery, as it is seen in its origin, continuance and end, the best possible condition for thee? Oh, no! Wilt thou bear that burden on thy shoulders, which thou wouldst lay upon thy fellow man? No. Wilt thou bear a part of it, or remove a little of its weight with one of thy fingers? The sharp and indignant answer is no, no! Then how, and when, and where, shall we apply to thee the golden rule, which says, "*Therefore all things that ye would that others should do to you, do ye even so unto them, for this is the law of the prophets.*" . . .

The other day, when the light of Liberty streamed through this marble pile, and the hearts of the noble band of patriotic statesmen leaped for joy, and this our national capital shook from foundation to dome with the shouts of a ransomed people, then methinks the spirits of Washington, Jefferson, the Jays, the Adamses, and Franklin, and Lafayette, and Giddings, and Lovejoy, and those of all the mighty, and glorious dead, remembered by history, because they were faithful to truth, justice, and liberty, were hovering over the august assembly. Though unseen by mortal eyes, doubtless they joined the angelic choir, and said, Amen. . . .

It is often asked when and where will the demands of the reformers of this and coming ages end? It is a fair question, and I will answer.

When all unjust and heavy burdens shall be removed from every man in the land. When all invidious and proscriptive distinctions shall be blotted out from our laws, whether they be constitutional, statute or municipal laws. When emancipation shall be followed by enfranchisement, and all men holding allegiance to the government shall enjoy every right of American citizenship. When our brave and gallant soldiers shall have justice done unto them. When the men who endure the sufferings and perils of the battlefield in the defense of their country, and in order to keep our rulers in their places, shall enjoy the well-earned privilege of voting for them. When in the army and navy, and in every legitimate and honorable occupation, promotion shall smile upon merit without the slightest regard to the complexion of a man's face. When there shall be no more class legislation and no more trouble concerning the black man and his rights than there is in regard to other American citizens. When, in every respect, he shall be equal before the law, and shall be left to make his own way in the social walks of life. . . .

Let slavery die. It has had a long and fair trial. God himself has pleaded against it. The enlightened nations of the earth have condemned it. Its death warrant is signed by God and man. Do not commute its sentence. Give it no respite, but let it be ignominiously executed.

Honorable Senators and Representatives, illustrious rulers of this great nation, I cannot refrain this day from invoking upon you, in God's name, the blessings of millions who were ready to perish, but to whom a new and better life has been opened by your humanity, justice and patriotism. You have said, "Let the Constitution of the country be so amended that slavery and involuntary servitude shall no longer exist in the United States, except in punishment for crime." Surely, an act so sublime could not escape divine notice; and doubtless the deed has been recorded in the archives of heaven. Volumes may be appropriated to your praise and renown in the history of the world. Genius and art may perpetuate the glorious act on canvas and in marble, but certain and more lasting monuments in commemoration of your decision are already erected in the hearts and memories of a grateful people.

The nation has begun its exodus from worse than Egyptian bondage; and I beseech you that you say to the people that they go forward. With the assurance of God's favor in all things done in obedience to his righteous will, and guided by day and by night by the pillars of cloud and fire, let us not pause until we have reached the other and safe side of the stormy and crimson sea. Let freemen and patriots mete out complete and equal justice to all men and thus prove to mankind the superiority of our democratic, republican government.

Favored men, and honored of God as his instruments, speedily finish the work which he has given you to do. Emancipate, enfranchise, educate, and give the blessings of the gospel to every American citizen.

★ ★ ★

## "WITH MALICE TOWARD NONE"

### Abraham Lincoln, Second Inaugural Address—March 4, 1865

FELLOW COUNTRYMEN: AT this second appearing to take the oath of the presidential office there is less occasion for an extended address than there was at the first. Then a statement somewhat in detail of a course to be pursued seemed fitting and proper. Now, at the expiration of four years during which public declarations have been constantly called forth on every point and phase of the great contest which still absorbs the attention and engrosses the energies of the nation little that is new could be presented. The progress of our arms, upon which all else chiefly depends is as well known to the public as to myself and it is I trust reasonably satisfactory and encouraging to all. With high hope for the future no prediction in regard to it is ventured.

On the occasion corresponding to this four years ago all thoughts

*Lincoln's Second Inaugural on the East Front of the U.S. Capitol on Saturday, March 4, 1865; John Wilkes Booth was also in attendance that day.*

were anxiously directed to an impending civil war. All dreaded it—all sought to avert it. While the inaugural address was being delivered from this place devoted altogether to saving the Union without war insurgent agents were in the city seeking to destroy it without war—seeking to dissolve the Union and divide effects by negotiation. Both parties deprecated war but one of them would make war rather than let the nation survive, and the other would accept war rather than let it perish. And the war came.

One eighth of the whole population were colored slaves not distributed generally over the Union but localized in the southern part of it. These slaves constituted a peculiar and powerful interest. All knew that this interest was somehow the cause of the war. To strengthen, perpetuate and extend this interest was the object for which the insurgents would rend the Union even by war while the government claimed no right to do more than to restrict the territorial enlargement of it. Neither party expected for the war the magnitude or the duration which it has already attained. Neither anticipated that the cause of the conflict might cease with or even before the conflict itself should cease. Each looked for an easier triumph and a result less fundamental and astounding. Both read the same Bible and pray to the same God and each invokes His aid against the other. It may seem strange that any men should dare to ask a just God's assistance in wringing their bread from the sweat of other men's faces but let us judge not that we be not judged. The prayers of both could not be answered—that of neither has been answered fully. The Almighty has His own purposes. "Woe unto the world because of offenses! For it must needs be that offenses come; but woe to that man by whom the offense cometh." If we shall suppose that American slavery is one of those offenses which in the providence of God must needs come but which having continued through His appointed time He now wills to remove and that He gives to both North and South this terrible war as the woe due to those by whom the offense came shall we discern therein any departure from those divine attributes which the believers in a living God always ascribe to Him. Fondly do we hope—fervently do we pray—that this mighty scourge of war may speedily pass away. Yet, if God wills that it continue until all the wealth piled by the bondsman's two hundred and fifty years of unrequited toil shall be sunk and until every drop of blood drawn with the lash shall be paid by another drawn with the sword as was said three thousand years ago so still it must be said "the judgments of the Lord are true and righteous altogether."

With malice toward none; with charity for all; with firmness in the right, as God gives us to see the right, let us strive on to finish the work we are in; to bind up the nation's wounds; to care for him who shall have borne the battle, and for his widow, and his orphan—to do all which may achieve and cherish a just and lasting peace among ourselves and with all nations.

PRESIDENT
"This is the time to su

PART V

# A TROUBLED PEACE

*1865–1932*

The good citizen will demand liberty for himself, and as a matter of pride he will see to it that others receive liberty which he thus claims as his own.

—Theodore Roosevelt, 1910

PREVIOUS SPREAD: *The long battle for woman's suffrage ended in victory with the passage and the ratification of the Nineteenth Amendment in August 1920.*

THE .44-CALIBER PISTOL HAD BEEN DESIGNED by the Philadelphia gunsmith Henry Deringer, and the lead ball fired into the back of Abraham Lincoln's head by John Wilkes Booth would have been traveling at a speed of about 400 feet per second, or 273 miles per hour. The attack took place at Ford's Theatre in Washington at about a quarter past ten on the evening of April 14, 1865—Good Friday. The president was taken to a neighboring house and laid out on a bed, and he slipped away through the watches of the night. Attending surgeons declared Abraham Lincoln dead at twenty-two minutes past seven o'clock on the morning of Saturday, April 15. Three and a half hours later, at Kirkwood House, the establishment at Twelfth Street and Pennsylvania Avenue where he boarded, Vice President Andrew Johnson was sworn in as the seventeenth president of the United States.

It had been the most extraordinary of weeks. The previous Sunday, April 9, Robert E. Lee had surrendered to Ulysses S. Grant at Appomattox Court House in Virginia, effectively ending the Civil War, a conflict that claimed perhaps as many as 750,000 lives. Lincoln had lived to see the victory—a triumph he hoped would signal a "new birth of freedom"—but now he was gone. Racist and sympathetic to the interests of white Southerners, President Johnson would prove a disastrous steward of the postwar era, opposing the Freedmen's Bureau, civil-rights legislation, and the Fourteenth and Fifteenth Amendments. The durability of white supremacist ideology was manifest in the writings of Edward A. Pollard, who published two books on what he called the Lost Cause. The war, Pollard wrote, "did not decide negro equality; it did not decide negro suffrage; it did not decide States' Rights. . . . And these things which the war did not decide, the Southern people will still cling to, still claim, and still assert in them their rights and views."

And so they would. "It is by no means surprising," observed the Union general Carl Schurz in the months after Appomattox, "that prejudices and resentments, which for years were so assiduously cultivated and so violently inflamed, should not have been turned into affection by a defeat; nor are they likely to disappear as long as the southern people continue to brood over their losses and misfortunes." Jim Crow laws, Klan violence and terror, and prevailing white Southern opinion sought to repeal the verdict of the war. In 1867, President Johnson asserted that Black people were incapable of self-government. "No independent government of any form has ever been successful in their hands," Johnson wrote in his Annual Message to Congress. "On the contrary, wherever they have been left to their own devices they have shown a constant tendency to relapse into barbarism." It was, the historian Eric Foner noted, "probably the most blatantly racist pronouncement ever to appear in an official state paper of an American president."

As president, Ulysses S. Grant, who took office in 1869, tried to impose order on the unruly South, asking for—and receiving—federal authority to break the Ku Klux Klan. After Washington stemmed at least large-scale racist violence, the attorney general of the United States, Amos T. Akerman, captured the complexities of the age in a single remark. "Though rejoiced at the suppression of KuKluxery even in one neighborhood," he wrote, "I feel greatly saddened by this business. It has revealed a perversion of moral sentiment among the Southern whites which bodes ill to that part of the country for this generation."

Akerman was right. The withdrawal of federal troops from the Louisiana and South Carolina statehouses in 1877—a result of a compromise that gave Republican Rutherford B. Hayes the presidency over Democrat Samuel Tilden—essentially left the South to its own devices. "The whole South—every state in the South—had got into the hands of the very men who held us as slaves," a formerly enslaved person remarked. The nadir came two decades later, when the Supreme Court, in *Plessy v. Ferguson,* a case out of New Orleans, declared the racist principle of "separate but equal" to be constitutional.

White supremacy was not fueled only by anti-Black sentiment. Immigration patterns also led to virulent reaction, particularly against those of Jewish and of Roman Catholic backgrounds. It had been ever thus. John Adams's Alien and Sedition Acts had been exclusionary; there were nineteenth-century reactions to immigration, including the creation of the Know-Nothing party after the 1848 European revolutions and the 1882 Chinese Exclusion Act under President Chester A. Arthur. Writings such as Rudyard Kipling's 1899 "The White Man's Burden," Madison Grant's 1916 *The Passing of the Great Race,* and Lothrop

Stoddard's 1920 *The Rising Tide of Color: The Threat Against White World-Supremacy* argued for the superiority of the white race with an emphasis on the Anglo-Saxon peoples. Surveying the landscape, W.E.B. Du Bois wrote: "In 1918, in order to win the war, we had to make Germans into Huns. In order to win, the South had to make Negroes into thieves, monsters, and idiots. Tomorrow, we must make Latins, South-eastern Europeans, Turks and other Asiatics into actual 'lesser breeds without the law'"—a quotation from Kipling's 1897 poem "Recessional."

As Du Bois noted, many of these forces intersected in the years of the 1917 Bolshevik Revolution and of World War I to create a Red Scare in the United States—a time of exaggerated fears that immigrants could be subversive socialists. The crackdown on dissent pursued by the Woodrow Wilson administration led to test cases such as Eugene V. Debs's trial for speaking out against the war and to the founding of the American Civil Liberties Union in 1920.

The cause of women's suffrage at last triumphed with the 1920 ratification of the Nineteenth Amendment. "It was a great crusade, the world has seen none more wonderful," the suffrage leader Carrie Chapman Catt wrote on Thanksgiving Day 1920. "My admiration, love, and reverence go out to that band which fought and won a revolution."

The suffrage victory was a bright spot in a dim era of ongoing segregation, attacks on free speech, the birth of a second Ku Klux Klan, and, in Dayton, Tennessee, a 1925 trial that pitted religious fundamentalism against intellectual inquiry. Conformity seemed prevalent. "America is no longer a free country, in the old sense; and liberty is, increasingly, a mere rhetorical figure," Katharine Fullerton Gerould wrote in *Harper's*. "The only way in which an American citizen who is really interested in all the social and political problems of his country can preserve any freedom of expression, is to choose the mob that is most sympathetic to him, and abide under the shadow of that mob."

* * *

## "BITTER AND VINDICTIVE"

### Carl Schurz, *Report on the Condition of the South,* December 19, 1865

Born in Germany, Carl Schurz (1829–1906) moved to the United States in 1852. He became a lawyer in Wisconsin and an early member of the Republican Party, serving as a diplomat in Spain under President Lincoln and as a brigadier general in the Union army. After the Confederate surrender at Appomattox, Schurz was dispatched to the South to offer a firsthand account of the defeated region.

A BELIEF, CONVICTION, OR prejudice, or whatever you may call it, so widely spread and apparently so deeply rooted as this, that the negro will not work without physical compulsion, is certainly calculated to have a very serious influence upon the conduct of the people entertaining it. It naturally produced a desire to preserve slavery in its original form as much and as long as possible—and you may, perhaps, remember the admission made by one of the provisional governors, over two months after the close of the war, that the people of his State still indulged in a lingering hope slavery might yet be preserved—or to introduce into the new system that element of physical compulsion which would make the negro work. Efforts were, indeed, made to hold the negro in his old state of subjection, especially in such localities where our military forces had not yet penetrated, or where the country was not garrisoned in detail. Here and there planters succeeded for a limited period to keep their former slaves in ignorance, or at least doubt, about their new rights; but the main agency employed for that purpose was force and intimidation. In many instances negroes who walked away from the plantations, or were found upon the roads, were shot or otherwise severely punished, which was calculated to produce the impression among those remaining with their masters that an attempt to escape from slavery would result in certain destruction. A large proportion of the many acts of violence committed is undoubtedly attributable to this motive. . . . The documents attached to this report abound in testimony to this effect. For the sake of illustration I will give some instances:

Brigadier General Fessenden reported to Major General Gillmore from Winnsboro, South Carolina, July 19, as follows: "The spirit of the people, especially in those districts not subject to the salutary influence of General Sherman's army, is that of concealed and, in some instances, of open hostility, though there are some who strive with honorable good faith to promote a thorough reconciliation between the government and their people. A spirit of bitterness and persecution manifests itself towards the negroes. They are shot and abused outside the immediate protection of our forces *by men who announce their determination to take the law into their own hands, in defiance of our authority.* To protect the negro and punish these still rebellious individuals it will be necessary to have this country pretty thickly settled with soldiers." I received similar verbal reports from other parts of South Carolina. To show the hopes still indulged in by some, I may mention that one of the sub-district commanders, as he himself informed me, knew planters within the limits of his command who had made contracts with their former slaves *avowedly* for the object of keeping them together on their plantations, so that they might have them near at hand, and thus more easily reduce them to their former condition, when, after the restoration of the civil power, the "unconstitutional emancipation proclamation" would be set aside. . . .

At Atlanta, Georgia, I had an opportunity to examine some cases of the nature above described myself. While I was there, 9th and 10th of August, several negroes came into town with bullet and buckshot wounds in their bodies. From their statements, which, however, were only corroborating information previously received, it appeared that the reckless and restless characters of that region had combined to keep the negroes where they belonged. Several freedmen were shot in the attempt to escape, others succeeded in eluding the vigilance of their persecutors; large numbers, terrified by what they saw and heard, quietly remained under the restraint imposed upon them, waiting for better opportunities. . . .

A similar system was followed in Alabama, but enough has become known to indicate the condition of things in localities not immediately under the eye of the military. In that State the efforts made to hold the negro in a state of subjection appear to have been of a particularly atrocious nature. Rumors to that effect which reached me at Montgomery induced me to make inquiries at the post hospital. The records of that institution showed a number of rather startling cases which had occurred immediately after the close of the war, and some of a more recent date; all of which proved that negroes leaving the plantations, and found on the roads, were exposed to the savagest treatment. An extract from the records of the hospital is appended, . . . also a statement signed by the provost marshal at Selma, Alabama, Major J.P. Houston. He says: "There have come to my notice officially twelve cases, in which I am morally certain the trials have not been had yet, that negroes were killed by whites. In a majority of cases the provocation consisted in the negroes' trying to come to town or to return to the plantation after having been sent away. The cases above enumerated, I am convinced, are but a small part of those that have actually been perpetrated." . . .

The conviction . . . that slavery in the old form cannot be maintained has forced itself upon the minds of many of those who ardently desired its preservation. But while the necessity of a new system was recognized as far as the right of property in the individual negro is concerned, many attempts were made to introduce into that new system the element of physical compulsion, which, as above stated, is so generally considered indispensable. This was done by simply adhering, as to the treatment of the laborers, as much as possible to the traditions of the old system, even where the relations between employers and laborers had been fixed by contract. The practice of corporal punishment was still continued to a great extent, although, perhaps, not in so regular a manner as it was practiced in times gone by. . . . The habit is so inveterate with a great many persons as to render, on the least provocation, the impulse to whip a negro almost irresistible. It will continue to be so until the southern people will have learned, so as never to forget it, that a black man has rights which a white man is bound to respect.

Here I will insert some remarks on the general treatment of the blacks as a class, from the whites as a class. It is not on the plantations and at the hands of the planters themselves that the negroes have to suffer the greatest hardships. Not only the former slaveholders, but the non-slaveholding whites, who, even previous to the war, seemed to be more ardent in their pro-slavery feelings than the planters themselves, are possessed by a singularly bitter and vindictive feeling against the colored race since the negro has ceased to be property. The pecuniary value which the individual negro formerly represented having disappeared, the maiming and killing of colored men seems to be looked upon by many as one of those venial offences which must be forgiven to the outraged feelings of a wronged and robbed people. Besides, the services rendered by the negro to the national cause during the war, which make him an object of special interest to the loyal people, make him an object of particular vindictiveness to those whose hearts were set upon the success of the rebellion. The number of murders and assaults perpetrated upon negroes is very great; we can form only an approximative estimate of what is going on in those parts of the south which are not closely garrisoned, and from which no regular reports are received, by what occurs under the very eyes of our military authorities. As to my personal experience, I will only mention that during my two days sojourn at Atlanta, one negro was stabbed with fatal effect on the street, and three were poisoned, one of whom died. While I was at Montgomery, one negro was cut across the throat evidently with intent to kill, and another was shot, but both escaped with their lives. . . . It is a sad fact that the perpetration of those acts is not confined to that class of people which might be called the rabble. Several "gentlemen of standing" have been tried before military commissions for such offences.

* * *

## "THE WAR HAS NOT SWALLOWED UP EVERYTHING"
## Edward A. Pollard, *The Lost Cause: A New Southern History of the War of the Confederates*—1866

---

Edward Alfred Pollard (1831–1872) was the editor of the *Daily Richmond Examiner* and the author, in 1866, of *The Lost Cause: A New Southern History of the War of the Confederates.* In it and in a succeeding volume published in 1868, *The Lost Cause Regained,* Pollard argued that the Confederacy's military loss in the Civil War need not mean the defeat of white supremacy. There would be, he wrote, an unfolding "war of ideas" over the meaning and implications of the war.

THE WAR HAS left the South its own memories, its own heroes, its own tears, its own dead. Under these traditions, sons will grow to manhood, and lessons sink deep that are learned from the lips of widowed mothers.

*Edward A. Pollard's writings on the Civil War have longed shaped white Southern views about the conflict.*

It would be immeasurably the worst consequence of defeat in this war that the South should lose its moral and intellectual distinctiveness as a people, and cease to assert its well-known superiority in civilization, in political scholarship, and in all the standards of individual character over the people of the North. That superiority has been recognized by every foreign observer, and by the intelligent everywhere; for it is the South that in the past produced four-fifths of the political literature of America, and presented in its public men that list of American names best known in the Christian world. That superiority the war has not conquered or lowered; and the South will do right to claim and to cherish it.

The war has not swallowed up everything. There are great interests which stand out of the pale of the contest, which it is for the South still to cultivate and maintain. She must submit fairly and truthfully to *what the war has properly decided.* But the war properly decided only what was put in issue: the restoration of the Union and the excision of slavery; and to these two conditions the South submits. But the war did not decide negro equality; it did not decide negro suffrage; it did not decide State Rights, although it may have exploded their abuse; it did not decide the orthodoxy of the Democratic party; it did not decide the right of a people to show dignity in misfortune, and to maintain self-respect in the face of adversity. And these things which the war did not decide, the Southern people will still cling to, still claim, and still assert in them their rights and views.

This is not the language of insolence and faction. It is the stark letter of right, and the plain syllogism of common sense. It is not untimely or unreasonable to tell the South to cultivate her superiority as a people; to maintain her old schools of literature and scholarship; to assert, in the forms of her thought, and in the style of her manners, her peculiar civilization, and to convince the North that, instead of subjugating an inferior country, she has obtained the alliance of a noble and cultivated people, and secured a bond of association with those she may be proud to call brethren!

In such a condition there may possibly be a solid and honorable peace; and one in which the South may still preserve many things dear to her in the past. There may not be a political South. Yet there may be a social and intellectual South. But if, on the other hand, the South, mistaking the consequences of the war, accepts the position of the inferior, and gives up what was never claimed or conquered in the war; surrenders her schools of intellect and thought, and is left only with the brutal desire of the conquered for "bread and games"; then indeed to her people may be applied what Tacitus wrote of those who existed under the Roman Empire: "We cannot be said to have lived, but rather to have crawled in silence, the young towards the decrepitude of age and the old to dishonorable graves."

⋆ ⋆ ⋆

## "TO RELAPSE INTO BARBARISM"

### Andrew Johnson, Third Annual Message to Congress—December 3, 1867

A Tennessean selected by the 1864 Republican National Convention to replace Hannibal Hamlin of Maine as the vice presidential candidate in the year of Abraham Lincoln's reelection campaign, Andrew Johnson (1808–1875) succeeded to the presidency after Ford's Theatre in April 1865. In the White House Johnson frequently sought to repeal the verdict of the war and opposed measures to bring about equality of the races before the law.

THE BLACKS IN the South are entitled to be well and humanely governed, and to have the protection of just laws for all their rights of person and property. If it were practicable at this time to give them a Government exclusively their own, under which they might manage their own affairs in their own way, it would become a grave question whether we ought to do so, or whether common humanity would not require us to save them from themselves. But under the circumstances this is only a speculative point. It is not proposed merely that they shall govern themselves, but that they shall rule the white race, make and administer State laws, elect Presidents and members of Congress, and shape to a greater or less extent the future destiny of the whole country. Would such a trust and power be safe in such hands?

The peculiar qualities which should characterize any people who are fit to decide upon the management of public affairs for a great state have seldom been combined. It is the glory of white men to know that they have had these qualities in sufficient measure to build upon this continent a great political fabric and to preserve its stability for more than ninety years, while in every other part of the world all similar experiments have failed. But if anything can be proved by known facts, if all reasoning upon evidence is not abandoned, it must be acknowledged that in the progress of nations Negroes have shown less capacity for government than any other race of people. No independent government of any form has ever been successful in their hands. On the contrary, wherever they have been left to their own devices they have shown a constant tendency to relapse into barbarism. In the Southern States, however, Congress has undertaken to confer upon them the privilege of the ballot. Just released from slavery, it may be doubted whether as a class they know more than their ancestors how to organize and regulate civil society.

Indeed, it is admitted that the blacks of the South are not only regardless of the rights of property, but so utterly ignorant of public affairs that their voting can consist in nothing more than carrying a ballot to the place where they are directed to deposit it. I need not remind you that the exercise of the elective franchise is the highest attribute of an American citizen, and that when guided by virtue, intelligence, patriotism, and a proper appreciation of our free institutions it constitutes the true basis of a democratic form of government, in which the sovereign power is lodged in the body of the people. A trust artificially created, not for its own sake, but solely as a means of promoting the general welfare, its influence for good must necessarily depend upon the elevated character and true allegiance of the elector. It ought, therefore, to be reposed in none except those who are fitted morally and mentally to administer it well; for if conferred upon persons who do not justly estimate its value and who are indifferent as to its results, it will only serve as a means of placing power in the hands of the unprincipled and ambitious, and must eventuate in the complete destruction of that liberty of which it should be the most powerful conservator. I have therefore heretofore urged upon your attention the great danger—to be apprehended from an untimely extension of the elective franchise to any new class in our country, especially when the large majority of that class, in wielding the power thus placed in their hands, can not be expected correctly to comprehend the duties and responsibilities which pertain to suffrage. Yesterday, as it were, 4,000,000 persons were held in a condition of slavery that had existed for generations; to-day they are freemen and are assumed by law to be citizens.

It cannot be presumed, from their previous condition of servitude, that as a class they are as well informed as to the nature of our Government as the intelligent foreigner who makes our land the home of his choice. In the case of the latter neither a residence of five years and the knowledge of our institutions which it gives nor attachment to the principles of the Constitution are the only conditions upon which he can be admitted to citizenship; he must prove in addition a good moral character, and thus give reasonable ground for the belief that he will be faithful to the obligations which he assumes as a citizen of the Republic. Where a people—the source of all political power—speak by their suffrages through the instrumentality of the ballot box, it must be carefully guarded against the control of those who are corrupt in principle and enemies of free institutions, for it can only become to our political and social system a safe conductor of healthy popular sentiment when kept free from demoralizing influences. Controlled through fraud and usurpation by the designing, anarchy and despotism must inevitably follow. In the hands of the patriotic and worthy our Government will be preserved upon the principles of the Constitution inherited from our fathers. It follows, therefore, that in admitting to the ballot box a new class of voters not qualified for the exercise of the elective franchise we weaken our system of government instead of adding to its strength and durability.

★ ★ ★

## "THE HOUR AND THE MAN OF OUR REDEMPTION"
### Frederick Douglass, "Oration in Memory of Abraham Lincoln," Washington, D.C.—April 14, 1876

Douglass spoke at the dedication of the Emancipation Memorial, sometimes called the Freedmen's Monument, on Capitol Hill in Washington. Funded entirely by formerly enslaved people, the memorial tells its own history with a plaque that reads:

In Grateful Memory of
ABRAHAM LINCOLN
This monument was erected . . .
With funds contributed solely by
emancipated citizens of the United States
Declared free by his proclamation
January 1st A.D. 1863.
The first contribution of five dollars was made by Charlotte Scott a freed woman of Virginia
Being her first earnings in freedom
And consecrated
By her suggestion and request
On the day she heard of President Lincoln's death
To build a monument to his memory

The dedication was attended by President Ulysses S. Grant and other notable Washington figures.

We are here in the District of Columbia, here in the city of Washington, the most luminous point of American territory; a city recently transformed and made beautiful in its body and in its spirit; we are here in the place where the ablest and best men of the country are sent to devise the policy, enact the laws, and shape the destiny of the Republic; we are here, with the stately pillars and majestic dome of the Capitol of the nation looking down upon us; we are here, with the broad earth freshly adorned with the foliage and flowers of spring for our church, and all races, colors, and conditions of men for our congregation—in a word, we are here to express, as best we may, by appropriate forms and ceremonies, our grateful sense of the vast, high, and preeminent services rendered to ourselves, to our race, to our country, and to the whole world by Abraham Lincoln.

Truth is proper and beautiful at all times and in all places, and it is never more proper and beautiful in any case than when speaking of a great public man whose example is likely to be commended for honor and imitation long after his departure to the solemn shades, the silent continents of eternity. It must be admitted, truth compels me to admit, even here in the presence of the monument we have erected to his memory, Abraham Lincoln was not, in the fullest sense of the word, either our man or our model. In his interests, in his associations, in his habits of thought, and in his prejudices, he was a white man.

He was preeminently the white man's President, entirely devoted to the welfare of white men. He was ready and willing at any time during the first years of his administration to deny, postpone, and sacrifice the rights of humanity in the colored people to promote the welfare of the white people of this country. In all his education and feeling he was an American of the Americans. He came into the Presidential chair upon one principle alone, namely, opposition to the extension of slavery. His arguments in furtherance of this policy had their motive and mainspring in his patriotic devotion to the interests of his own race. To protect, defend, and perpetuate slavery in the states where it existed Abraham Lincoln was not less ready than any other President to draw the sword of the nation. He was ready to execute all the supposed guarantees of the United States Constitution in favor of the slave system anywhere inside the slave states. He was willing to pursue, recapture, and send back the fugitive slave to his master, and to suppress a slave rising for liberty, though his guilty master were already in arms against the Government. The race to which we belong were not the special objects of his consideration. Knowing this, I concede to you, my white fellow-citizens, a pre-eminence in this worship at once full and supreme. First, midst, and last, you and yours were the objects of his deepest affection and his most earnest solicitude. You are the children of Abraham Lincoln. We are at best only his step-children; children by adoption, children by forces of circumstances and necessity. To you it especially belongs to sound his praises, to preserve and perpetuate his memory, to multiply his statues, to hang his pictures high upon your walls, and commend his example, for to you he was a great and glorious friend and benefactor. Instead of supplanting you at his altar, we would exhort you to build high his monuments; let them be of the most costly material, of the most cunning workmanship; let their forms be symmetrical, beautiful, and perfect, let their bases be upon solid rocks, and their summits lean against the unchanging blue, overhanging sky, and let them endure forever! But while in the abundance of your wealth, and in the fullness of your just and patriotic devotion, you do all this, we entreat you to despise not the humble offering we this day unveil to view; for while Abraham Lincoln saved for you a country, he delivered us from a bondage, according to Jefferson, one hour of which was worse than ages of the oppression your fathers rose in rebellion to oppose.

Fellow-citizens, ours is no new-born zeal and devotion—merely a thing of this moment. The name of Abraham Lincoln was near and dear to our hearts in the darkest and most perilous hours of the Republic. We were no more ashamed of him when shrouded in clouds of darkness, of doubt, and defeat than when we saw him crowned with victory, honor, and glory. Our faith in him was often taxed and strained to the uttermost, but it never failed. When he tarried long in the mountain; when he strangely told us that we were the cause of the war; when he still more strangely told us that we were to leave the land in which we were born; when he refused to employ our arms in defense of the Union; when, after accepting our services as colored soldiers, he refused to retaliate our murder and torture as colored prisoners; when he told us he would save the Union if he could with slavery; when he revoked the Proclamation of Emancipation of General Fremont; when he refused to remove the popular commander of the Army of the Potomac, in the days of its inaction and defeat, who was more zealous in his efforts to protect slavery than to suppress rebellion; when we saw all this, and more, we were at times grieved, stunned, and greatly bewildered; but our hearts believed while they ached and bled. Nor was this, even at that time, a blind and unreasoning superstition. Despite the mist and haze that surrounded him; despite the tumult, the hurry, and confusion of the hour, we were able to take a comprehensive view of Abraham Lincoln, and to make reasonable allowance for the circumstances of his position. We saw him, measured him, and estimated him; not by stray utterances to injudicious and tedious delegations, who often tried his patience; not by isolated facts torn from their connection; not by any partial and imperfect glimpses, caught at inopportune moments; but by a broad survey, in the light of the stern logic of great events, and in view of that divinity which shapes our ends, rough hew them how we will, we came to the conclusion that the hour and the man of our redemption had somehow met in the person of Abraham Lincoln. It mattered little to us what language he might employ on special occasions; it mattered little to us, when we fully knew him, whether he was swift or slow in his movements; it was enough for us that Abraham Lincoln was at the head of a great movement, and was in living and earnest sympathy with that movement, which, in the nature of things, must go on until slavery should be utterly and forever abolished in the United States.

When, therefore, it shall be asked what we have to do with the memory of Abraham Lincoln, or what Abraham Lincoln had to do with us, the answer is ready, full, and complete. Though he loved Caesar less than Rome, though the Union was more to him than our freedom or our future, under his wise and beneficent rule we saw ourselves gradually lifted from the depths of slavery to the heights of liberty and manhood; under his wise and beneficent rule, and by measures approved and vigorously pressed by him, we saw that the handwriting of ages, in the form of prejudice and proscription, was rapidly fading away from the face of our whole country; under his rule, and in due time, about as soon after all as the country could tolerate the strange spectacle, we saw our brave sons and brothers laying off the rags of bondage, and being clothed all over in the blue uniforms of the soldiers of the United States; under his rule we saw two hundred thousand of our dark and dusky people responding to the call of Abraham Lincoln, and with muskets on their shoulders, and eagles on their buttons, timing their high footsteps to liberty and union under the national flag; under his rule we saw the independence of the black republic of Hayti, the special object of slave-holding aversion and horror, fully recognized, and her minister, a colored gentleman, duly received here in the city of Washington; under his rule we saw the internal slave-trade, which so long disgraced the nation, abolished, and slavery abolished in the District of Columbia; under his rule we saw for the first time the law enforced against the foreign slave trade, and the first slave-trader hanged like any other pirate or murderer; under his rule, assisted by the greatest captain of our age, and his inspiration, we saw the Confederate States, based upon the idea that our race must be slaves, and slaves forever, battered to pieces and scattered to the four winds; under his rule, and in the fullness of time, we saw Abraham Lincoln, after giving the slave-holders three months' grace in which to save their hateful slave system, penning the immortal paper, which, though special in its language, was general in its principles and effect, making slavery forever impossible in the United States. Though we waited long, we saw all this and more.

Can any colored man, or any white man friendly to the freedom of all men, ever forget the night which followed the first day of January, 1863, when the world was to see if Abraham Lincoln would prove to be as good as his word? I shall never forget that memorable night, when in a distant city I waited and watched at a public meeting, with three thousand others not less anxious than myself, for the word of deliverance which we have heard read today. Nor shall I ever forget the outburst of joy and thanksgiving that rent the air when the lightning brought to us the emancipation proclamation. In that happy hour we forgot all delay, and forgot all tardiness, forgot that the President had bribed the rebels to lay down their arms by a promise to withhold the bolt which would smite the slave-system with destruction; and we were thenceforward willing to allow the President all the latitude of time, phraseology, and every honorable device that statesmanship might require for the achievement of a great and beneficent measure of liberty and progress. . . .

Though deep, he was transparent; though strong, he was gentle; though decided and pronounced in his convictions, he was tolerant towards those who differed from him, and patient under reproaches. Even those who only knew him through his public utterance obtained a tolerably clear idea of his character and personality. The image of the man went out with his words, and those who read them knew him.

I have said that President Lincoln was a white man, and shared the prejudices common to his countrymen towards the colored race. Looking back to his times and to the condition of his country, we are compelled to admit that this unfriendly feeling on his part may be safely set down as one element of his wonderful success in organizing the loyal American people for the tremendous conflict before them, and bringing them safely through that conflict. His great mission was to accomplish two things: first, to save his country from dismemberment and ruin; and, second, to free his country from the great crime of slavery. To do one or the other, or both, he must have the earnest sympathy and the powerful cooperation of his loyal fellow-countrymen. Without this primary and essential condition to success his efforts must have been vain and utterly fruitless. Had he put the abolition of slavery before the salvation of the Union, he would have inevitably driven from him a powerful class of the American people and rendered resistance to rebellion impossible. Viewed from the genuine abolition ground, Mr. Lincoln seemed tardy, cold, dull, and indifferent; but measuring him by the sentiment of his country, a sentiment he was bound as a statesman to consult, he was swift, zealous, radical, and determined.

Though Mr. Lincoln shared the prejudices of his white fellow-countrymen against the negro, it is hardly necessary to say that in his heart of hearts he loathed and hated slavery. The man who could say, "Fondly do we hope, fervently do we pray, that this mighty scourge of war shall soon pass away, yet if God wills it continue till all the wealth piled by two hundred years of bondage shall have been wasted, and each drop of blood drawn by the lash shall have been paid for by one drawn by the sword, the judgments of the Lord are true and righteous altogether," gives all needed proof of his feeling on the subject of slavery. He was willing, while the South was loyal, that it should have its pound of flesh, because he thought that it was so nominated in the bond; but farther than this no earthly power could make him go.

Fellow-citizens, whatever else in this world may be partial, unjust, and uncertain, time, time! is impartial, just, and certain in its action. In the realm of mind, as well as in the realm of matter, it is a great worker, and often works wonders. The honest and comprehensive statesman, clearly discerning the needs of his country, and earnestly endeavoring to do his whole duty, though covered and blistered with reproaches, may safely leave his course to the silent judgment of time. Few great public men have ever been the victims of fiercer denunciation than Abraham Lincoln was during his administration. He was often wounded in the house of his friends. Reproaches came thick and fast upon him from within and from without, and from opposite quarters. He was assailed by Abolitionists; he was assailed by slave-holders; he was assailed by the men who were for peace at any price; he was assailed by those who were for a more vigorous prosecution of the war; he was assailed for not making the war an abolition war; and he was bitterly assailed for making the war an abolition war.

But now behold the change: the judgment of the present hour is, that taking him for all in all, measuring the tremendous magnitude of the work before him, considering the necessary means to ends, and surveying the end from the beginning, infinite wisdom has seldom sent any man into the world better fitted for his mission than Abraham Lincoln. His birth, his training, and his natural endowments, both mental and physical, were strongly in his favor. Born and reared among the lowly, a stranger to wealth and luxury, compelled to grapple single-handed with the flintiest hardships of life, from tender youth to sturdy manhood, he grew strong in the manly and heroic qualities demanded by the great mission to which he was called by the votes of his countrymen. The hard condition of his early life, which would have depressed and broken down weaker men, only gave greater life, vigor, and buoyancy to the heroic spirit of Abraham Lincoln. He was ready for any kind and any quality of work. What other young men dreaded in the shape of toil, he took hold of with the utmost cheerfulness. . . .

All day long he could split heavy rails in the woods, and half the night long he could study his English Grammar by the uncertain flare and glare of the light made by a pine-knot. He was at home in the land with his axe, with his maul, with gluts, and his wedges; and he was equally at home on water, with his oars, with his poles, with his planks, and with his boat-hooks. And whether in his flat-boat on the Mississippi River, or at the fireside of his frontier cabin, he was a man of work. A son of toil himself, he was linked in brotherly sympathy with the sons of toil in every loyal part of the Republic. This very fact gave him tremendous power with the American people, and materially contributed not only to selecting him to the Presidency, but in sustaining his administration of the Government.

Upon his inauguration as President of the United States, an office, even when assumed under the most favorable condition, fitted to tax and strain the largest abilities, Abraham Lincoln was met by a tremendous crisis. He was called upon not merely to administer the Government, but to decide, in the face of terrible odds, the fate of the Republic.

A formidable rebellion rose in his path before him; the Union was already practically dissolved; his country was torn and rent asunder at the center. Hostile armies were already organized against the Republic, armed with the munitions of war which the Republic had provided for its own defense. The tremendous question for him to decide was whether his country should survive the crisis and flourish, or be dismembered and perish. His predecessor in office had already decided the question in favor of national dismemberment, by denying to it the right of self-defense and self-preservation—a right which belongs to the meanest insect.

Happily for the country, happily for you and for me, the judgment of James Buchanan, the patrician, was not the judgment of Abraham Lincoln, the plebeian. He brought his strong common sense, sharpened in the school of adversity, to bear upon the question. He did not hesitate, he did not doubt, he did not falter; but at once resolved that at whatever peril, at whatever cost, the union of the States should be preserved. A patriot himself, his faith was strong and unwavering in the patriotism of his countrymen. Timid men said before Mr. Lincoln's inauguration, that we have seen the last President of the United States. A voice in influential quarters said, "Let the Union slide." Some said that a Union maintained by the sword was worthless. Others said a rebellion of 8,000,000 cannot be suppressed; but in the midst of all this tumult and timidity, and against all this, Abraham Lincoln was clear in his duty, and had an oath in heaven. He calmly and bravely heard the voice of doubt and fear all around him; but he had an oath in heaven, and there was not power enough on earth to make this honest boatman, backwoodsman, and broad-handed splitter of rails evade or violate that sacred oath. He had not been schooled in the ethics of slavery; his plain life had favored his love of truth. He had not been taught that treason and perjury were the proof of honor and honesty. His moral training was against his saying one thing when he meant another. The trust that Abraham Lincoln had in himself and in the people was surprising and grand, but it was also enlightened and well founded. He knew the American people better than they knew themselves, and his truth was based upon this knowledge.

Fellow-citizens, the fourteenth day of April, 1865, of which this is the eleventh anniversary, is now and will ever remain a memorable day in the annals of this Republic. It was on the evening of this day, while a fierce and sanguinary rebellion was in the last stages of its desolating power; while its armies were broken and scattered before the invincible armies of Grant and Sherman; while a great nation, torn and rent by war, was already beginning to raise to the skies loud anthems of joy at the dawn of peace, it was startled, amazed, and overwhelmed by the crowning crime of slavery—the assassination of Abraham Lincoln. It was a new crime, a pure act of malice. No purpose of the rebellion was to be served by it. It was the simple gratification of a hell-black spirit of revenge. But it has done good after all. It has filled the country with a deeper abhorrence of slavery and a deeper love for the great liberator.

Had Abraham Lincoln died from any of the numerous ills to which flesh is heir; had he reached that good old age of which his vigorous constitution and his temperate habits gave promise; had he been permitted to see the end of his great work; had the solemn curtain of death come down but gradually—we should still have been smitten with a heavy grief, and treasured his name lovingly. But dying as he did die, by the red hand of violence, killed, assassinated, taken off without warning, not because of personal hate—for no man who knew Abraham Lincoln could hate him—but because of his fidelity to union and liberty, he is doubly dear to us, and his memory will be precious forever.

Fellow-citizens, I end, as I began, with congratulations. We have done a good work for our race today. In doing honor to the memory of our friend and liberator, we have been doing highest honors to ourselves and those who come after us; we have been fastening ourselves to a name and fame imperishable and immortal; we have also been defending ourselves from a blighting scandal. When now it shall be said that the colored man is soulless, that he has no appreciation of benefits or benefactors; when the foul reproach of ingratitude is hurled at us, and it is attempted to scourge us beyond the range of human brotherhood, we may calmly point to the monument we have this day erected to the memory of Abraham Lincoln.

★ ★ ★

## "NATIONS REEL AND STAGGER ON THEIR WAY"
### W.E.B. Du Bois, "The Propaganda of History," *Black Reconstruction in America*—1935

William Edward Burghardt Du Bois (1868–1963) was a scholar, an editor, and a founder of the National Association for the Advancement of Colored People.

HOW THE FACTS of American history have in the last half century been falsified because the nation was ashamed. The South was ashamed because it fought to perpetuate human slavery. The North was ashamed because it had to call in the black men to save the Union, abolish slavery and establish democracy.

What are American children taught today about Reconstruction? . . . An American youth attending college today would learn from current textbooks of history that the Constitution recognized slavery; that the chance of getting rid of slavery by peaceful methods was ruined by the Abolitionists; that after the period of Andrew Jackson, the two sections of the United States "had become fully conscious of their conflicting interests. Two irreconcilable forms of civilization. . . ." He would read that Harriet Beecher Stowe brought on the Civil War; that the assault on Charles Sumner was due to his "coarse invective" against a South Carolina Senator; and that Negroes were the only people to achieve emancipation with no effort on their part. That Reconstruction was a disgraceful attempt to subject white people to ignorant Negro rule. . . .

In other words, he would in all probability complete his education without any idea of the part which the black race has played in America; of the tremendous moral problem of abolition; of the cause and meaning of the Civil War and the relation which Reconstruction had to democratic government and the labor movement today. . . .

War and especially civil strife leave terrible wounds. It is the duty of humanity to heal them. It was therefore soon conceived as neither wise nor patriotic to speak of all the causes of strife and the terrible results to which national differences in the United States had led. And so, first of all, we minimized the slavery controversy which convulsed the nation from the Missouri Compromise down to the Civil War. On top of that, we passed by Reconstruction with a phrase of regret or disgust.

But are these reasons of courtesy and philanthropy sufficient for denying Truth? If history is going to be scientific, if the record of human action is going to be set down with the accuracy and faithfulness of detail which will allow its use as a measuring rod and guidepost for the future of nations, there must be set some standards of ethics in research and interpretation.

If, on the other hand, we are going to use history for our pleasure and amusement, for inflating our national ego, and giving us a false but pleasurable sense of accomplishment, then we must give up the idea of history as a science or as an art using the results of science, and admit frankly that we are using a version of historic fact in order to influence and educate the new generation along the way we wish.

It is propaganda like this that has led men in the past to insist that history is "lies agreed upon"; and to point out the danger in such misinformation. It is indeed extremely doubtful if any permanent benefit comes to the world through such action. Nations reel and stagger on their way; they make hideous mistakes; they commit frightful wrongs; they do great and beautiful things. And shall we not best guide humanity by telling the truth about all this, so far as the truth is ascertainable?

★ ★ ★

## "WE ASK FOR WOMAN A VOICE"

### Elizabeth Cady Stanton, "Solitude of Self," Address Delivered Before the House Judiciary Committee—January 18, 1892

Elizabeth Cady Stanton (1815–1902) was an advocate of women's rights and suffrage. With Lucretia Mott and others, Stanton was an architect of the 1848 Seneca Falls convention; in this excerpt she addresses the Congress on her movement's ongoing struggles.

THE POINT I wish plainly to bring before you on this occasion is the individuality of each human soul; our Protestant idea, the right of individual conscience and judgment—our republican idea, individual citizenship. In discussing the rights of woman, we are to consider, first, what belongs to her as an individual, in a world of her own, the arbiter of her own destiny, an imaginary Robinson Crusoe with her woman Friday on a solitary island. Her rights under such circumstances are to use all her faculties for her own safety and happiness.

Secondly, if we consider her as a citizen, as a member of a great nation, she must have the same rights as all other members, according to the fundamental principles of our Government.

Thirdly, viewed as a woman, an equal factor in civilization, her rights and duties are still the same—individual happiness and development.

Fourthly, it is only the incidental relations of life, such as mother, wife, sister, daughter, that may involve some special duties and training. In the usual discussion in regard to woman's sphere, such men as Herbert Spencer, Frederic Harrison, and Grant Allen uniformly subordinate her rights and duties as an individual, as a citizen, as a woman, to the necessities of these incidental relations, some of which a large class of woman may never assume. In discussing the sphere of man we do not decide his rights as an individual, as a citizen, as a man by his duties as a father, a husband, a brother, or a son, relations some of which he may never fill. Moreover he would be better fitted for these very relations and whatever special work he might choose to do to earn his bread by the complete development of all his faculties as an individual.

Just so with woman. The education that will fit her to discharge the duties in the largest sphere of human usefulness will best fit her for whatever special work she may be compelled to do.

The isolation of every human soul and the necessity of self-dependence must give each individual the right to choose his own surroundings.

The strongest reason for giving woman all the opportunities for higher education, for the full development of her faculties, forces of mind and body; for giving her the most enlarged freedom of thought and action; a complete emancipation from all forms of bondage, of custom, dependence, superstition; from all the crippling influences of fear, is the solitude and personal responsibility of her own individual life. The strongest reason why we ask for woman a voice in the government under which she lives; in the religion she is asked to believe; equality in social life, where she is the chief factor; a place in the trades and professions, where she may earn her bread, is because of her birthright to self-sovereignty; because, as an individual, she must rely on herself. No matter how much women prefer to lean, to be protected and supported, nor how much men desire to have them do so, they must make the voyage of life alone, and for safety in an emergency they must know something of the laws of navigation. To guide our own craft, we must be captain, pilot, engineer; with chart and compass to stand at the wheel; to match the wind and waves and know when to take in the sail, and to read the signs in the firmament over all. It matters not whether the solitary voyager is man or woman.

Nature having endowed them equally, leaves them to their own skill and judgment in the hour of danger, and, if not equal to the occasion, alike they perish.

To appreciate the importance of fitting every human soul for independent action, think for a moment of the immeasurable solitude of self. We come into the world alone, unlike all who have gone before us; we leave it alone under circumstances peculiar to ourselves. No mortal ever has been, no mortal ever will be like the soul just launched on the sea of life. There can never again be just such a combination of prenatal influences; never again just such environments as make up the infancy, youth and manhood of this one. Nature never repeats herself, and the possibilities of one human soul will never be found in another. No one has ever found two blades of ribbon grass alike, and no one will ever find two human beings alike. Seeing, then, what must be the infinite diversity in human character, we can in a measure appreciate the loss to a nation when any large class of the people is uneducated and unrepresented in the government. We ask for the complete development of every individual, first, for his own benefit and happiness. In fitting out an army we give each soldier his own knapsack, arms, powder, his blanket, cup, knife, fork and spoon. We provide alike for all their individual necessities, then each man bears his own burden.

Again we ask complete individual development for the general good; for the consensus of the competent on the whole round of human interest; on all questions of national life, and here each man must bear his share of the general burden. It is sad to see how soon friendless children are left to bear their own burdens before they can analyze their feelings; before they can even tell their joys and sorrows, they are thrown on their own resources. The great lesson that nature seems to teach us at all ages is self-dependence, self-protection, self-support. What a touching instance of a child's solitude; of that hunger of the heart for love and recognition, in the case of the little girl who helped to dress a Christmas tree for the children of the family in which she served. On finding there was no present for herself she slipped away in the darkness and spent the night in an open field sitting on a stone, and when found in the morning was weeping as if her heart would break. No mortal will ever know the thoughts that passed through the mind of that friendless child in the long hours of that cold night, with only the silent stars to keep her company. The mention of her case in the daily papers moved many generous hearts to send her presents, but in the hours of her keenest sufferings she was thrown wholly on herself for consolation.

*Thoughtful and prolific, Elizabeth Cady Stanton founded, with Susan B. Anthony, the National Woman Suffrage Association in 1869.*

In youth our most bitter disappointments, our brightest hopes and ambitions are known only to ourselves; even our friendship and love we never fully share with another; there is something of every passion in every situation we conceal. Even so in our triumphs and our defeats. The successful candidate for Presidency and his opponent each have a solitude peculiarly his own, and good form forbids either to speak of his pleasure or regret. The solitude of the king on his throne and the prisoner in his cell differs in character and degree, but it is solitude nevertheless.

We ask no sympathy from others in the anxiety and agony of a broken friendship or shattered love. When death sunders our nearest ties, alone we sit in the shadows of our affliction. Alike mid the greatest triumphs and darkest tragedies of life we walk alone. On the divine heights of human attainments, eulogized and worshiped as a hero or saint, we stand alone. In ignorance, poverty, and vice, as a pauper or criminal, alone we starve or steal; alone we suffer the sneers and rebuffs of our fellows; alone we are hunted and hounded through dark courts and alleys, in by-ways and highways; alone we stand in the judgment seat; alone in the prison cell we lament our crimes and misfortunes; alone we expiate them on the gallows. In hours like these we realize the awful solitude of individual life, its pains, its penalties, its responsibilities; hours in which the youngest and most helpless are thrown on their own resources for guidance and consolation. Seeing then that life must ever be a march and a battle, that each soldier must be equipped for his own protection, it is the height of cruelty to rob the individual of a single natural right.

To throw obstacles in the way of a complete education is like putting out the eyes; to deny the rights of property, like cutting off the hands. To deny political equality is to rob the ostracised of all self-respect; of credit in the market place; of recompense in the world of work; of a voice among those who make and administer the law; a choice in the jury before whom they are tried, and in the judge who decides their punishment. Shakespeare's play of Titus and Andronicus contains a terrible satire on woman's position in the nineteenth century—"Rude men" (the play tells us) "seized the king's daughter, cut out her tongue, cut off her hands, and then bade her go call for water and wash her hands." What a picture of woman's position! Robbed of her natural rights, handicapped by law and custom at every turn, yet compelled to fight her own battles, and in the emergencies of life to fall back on herself for protection.

The girl of sixteen, thrown on the world to support herself, to make her own place in society, to resist the temptations that surround her and maintain a spotless integrity, must do all this by native force or superior education. She does not acquire this power by being trained to trust others and distrust herself. If she wearies of the struggle, finding it hard work to swim upstream, and allow herself to drift with the current, she will find plenty of company, but not one to share her misery in the hour of her deepest humiliation. If she tried to retrieve her position, to conceal the past, her life is hedged about with fears lest willing hands should tear the veil from what she fain would hide. Young and friendless, *she* knows the bitter solitude of self.

How the little courtesies of life on the surface of society, deemed so important from man towards woman, fade into utter insignificance in view of the deeper tragedies in which she must play her part alone, where no human aid is possible.

The young wife and mother, at the head of some establishment with a kind husband to shield her from the adverse winds of life, with wealth, fortune and position, has a certain harbor of safety, secure against the ordinary ills of life. But to manage a household, have a desirable influence in society, keep her friends and the affections of her husband, train her children and servants well, she must have rare common sense, wisdom, diplomacy, and a knowledge of human nature. To do all this she needs the cardinal virtues and the strong points of character that the most successful statesman possesses.

An uneducated woman, trained to dependence, with no resources in herself must make a failure of any position in life. But society says women do not need a knowledge of the world, the liberal training that experience in public life must give, all the advantages of collegiate education; but when for the lack of all this, the woman's happiness is wrecked, alone she bears her humiliation; and the solitude of the weak and the ignorant is indeed pitiable. In the wild chase for the prizes of life they are ground to powder.

In age, when the pleasures of youth are passed, children grown up, married and gone, the hurry and hustle of life in a measure over, when the hands are weary of active service, when the old armchair and the fireside are the chosen resorts, then men and women alike must fall back on their own resources. If they cannot find companionship in books, if they have no interest in the vital questions of the hour, no interest in watching the consummation of reforms, with which they might have been identified, they soon pass into their dotage. The more fully the faculties of the mind are developed and kept in use, the longer the period of vigor and active interest in all around us continues. If from a lifelong participation in public affairs a woman feels responsible for the laws regulating our system of education, the discipline of our jails and prisons, the sanitary conditions of our private homes, public buildings, and thoroughfares, an interest in commerce, finance, our foreign relations, in any or all of these questions, her solitude will at least be respectable, and she will not be driven to gossip or scandal for entertainment.

The chief reason for opening to every soul the doors to the whole round of human duties and pleasures is the individual development thus attained, the resources thus provided under all circumstances to mitigate the solitude that at times must come to everyone. I once asked Prince Kropotkin, the Russian nihilist, how he endured his long years in prison, deprived of books, pen, ink, and paper. "Ah," he said, "I thought out many questions in which I had a deep interest. In the pursuit of an idea I took no note of time. When tired of solving knotty problems I recited all the beautiful passages in prose or verse I had ever learned. I became acquainted with myself and my own resources. I had a world of my own, a vast empire, that no Russian jailor or Czar could invade." Such is the value of liberal thought and broad culture when shut off from all human companionship, bringing comfort and sunshine within even the four walls of a prison cell.

As women ofttimes share a similar fate, should they not have all the consolation that the most liberal education can give? Their suffering in the prisons of St. Petersburg; in the long, weary marches to Siberia, and in the mines, working side by side with men, surely call for all the self-support that the most exalted sentiments of heroism can give. When suddenly roused at midnight, with the startling cry of "fire! fire!" to find the house over their heads in flames, do women wait for men to point the way to safety? And are the men, equally bewildered and half suffocated with smoke, in a position to do more than try to save themselves?

At such times the most timid women have shown a courage and heroism in saving their husbands and children that has surprised everybody. Inasmuch, then, as woman shares equally the joys and sorrows of time and eternity, is it not the height of presumption in man to propose to represent her at the ballot box and the throne of grace, to do her voting in the state, her praying in the church, and to assume the position of priest at the family altar.

Nothing strengthens the judgment and quickens the conscience like individual responsibility. Nothing adds such dignity to character as the recognition of one's self-sovereignty; the right to an equal place, everywhere conceded; a place earned by personal merit, not an artificial attainment, by inheritance, wealth, family, and position. Seeing, then, that the responsibilities of life rest equally on man and woman, that their destiny is the same, they need the same preparation for time and eternity. The talk of sheltering woman from the fierce storms of life is the sheerest mockery, for they beat on her from every point of the compass, just as they do on man, and with more fatal results, for he has been trained to protect himself, to resist, to conquer. Such are the facts in human experience, the responsibilities of individual sovereignty. Rich and poor, intelligent and ignorant, wise and foolish, virtuous and vicious, man and woman, it is ever the same, each soul must depend wholly on itself.

Whatever the theories may be of woman's dependence on man, in the supreme moments of her life he cannot bear her burdens. Alone she goes to the gates of death to give life to every man that is born into the world. No one can share her fears, no one mitigate her pangs; and if her sorrow is greater than she can bear, alone she passes beyond the gates into the vast unknown.

From the mountain tops of Judea, long ago, a heavenly voice bade His disciples, "Bear ye one another's burdens," but humanity has not yet risen to that point of self-sacrifice, and if ever so willing, how few the burdens are that one soul can bear for another. In the highways of Palestine; in prayer and fasting on the solitary mountain top; in the Garden of Gethsemane; before the judgment seat of Pilate; betrayed by one of His trusted disciples at His last supper; in His agonies on the cross, even Jesus of Nazareth, in these last sad days on earth, felt the awful solitude of self. Deserted by man, in agony he cries, "My God! My God! why hast Thou forsaken me?" And so it ever must be in the conflicting scenes of life, on the long weary march, each one walks alone. We may have many friends, love, kindness, sympathy, and charity to smooth our pathway in everyday life, but in the tragedies and triumphs of human experience each mortal stands alone.

But when all artificial trammels are removed, and women are recognized as individuals, responsible for their own environments, thoroughly educated for all the positions in life they may be called to fill; with all the resources in themselves that liberal thought and broad culture can give; guided by their own conscience and judgment; trained to self-protection by a healthy development of the muscular system and skill in the use of weapons of defense, and stimulated to self-support by the knowledge of the business world and the pleasure that pecuniary independence must ever give; when women are trained in this way they will, in a measure, be fitted for those hours of solitude that come alike to all, whether prepared or otherwise. As in our extremity we must depend on ourselves, the dictates of wisdom point to complete individual development.

In talking of education how shallow the argument, that each class must be educated for the special work it proposes to do, and all those faculties not needed in this special walk must lie dormant and utterly wither for want of use, when, perhaps, these will be the very faculties needed in life's greatest emergencies. Some say, Where is the use of drilling girls in the languages, the sciences, in law, medicine, theology? As wives, mothers, housekeepers, cooks, they need a different curriculum from boys who are to fill all positions. The chief cooks in our great hotels and ocean steamers are men. In large cities men run the bakeries; they make our bread, cake and pies. They manage the laundries; they are now considered our best milliners and dressmakers. Because some men fill these departments of usefulness, shall we regulate the curriculum in Harvard and Yale to their present necessities? If not, why this talk in our best colleges of a curriculum for girls who are crowding into the trades and professions; teachers in all our public schools, rapidly filling many lucrative and honorable positions in life? They are showing too, their calmness and courage in the most trying hours of human experience.

You have probably all read in the daily papers of the terrible storm in the Bay of Biscay when a tidal wave made such havoc on the shore, wrecking vessels, unroofing houses and carrying destruction everywhere. Among other buildings the woman's prison was demolished. Those who escaped saw men struggling to reach the shore. They promptly by clasping hands made a chain of themselves and pushed out into the sea, again and again, at the risk of their lives until they had brought six men to shore, carried them to a shelter, and did all in their power for their comfort and protection.

What special school of training could have prepared these women for this sublime moment of their lives? In times like this humanity rises above all college curriculums and recognizes Nature as the greatest of all teachers in the hour of danger and death. Women are already the equals of men in the whole of realm of thought, in art, science, literature, and government. With telescopic vision they explore the starry firmament and bring back the history of the planetary world. With chart and compass they pilot ships across the mighty deep, and with skillful finger send electric messages around the globe. In galleries of art the beauties of nature and the virtues of humanity are immortalized by them on canvas and by their inspired touch dull blocks of marble are transformed into angels of light.

In music [women] speak again the language of Mendelssohn, Beethoven, Chopin, Schumann, and are worthy interpreters of their great thoughts. The poetry and novels of the century are theirs, and they have touched the keynote of reform in religion, politics, and social life. They fill the editor's and professor's chair, and plead at the bar of justice, walk the wards of the hospital, and speak from the pulpit and the platform; such is the type of womanhood that an enlightened public sentiment welcomes to-day, and such the triumph of the facts of life over the false theories of the past.

Is it, then, consistent to hold the developed woman of this day within the same narrow political limits as the dame with the spinning wheel and knitting needle occupied in the past? No, no! Machinery has taken the labors of woman as well as man on its tireless shoulders; the loom and the spinning wheel are but dreams of the past; the pen, the brush, the easel, the chisel, have taken their places, while the hopes and ambitions of women are essentially changed.

We see reason sufficient in the outer conditions of human beings for individual liberty and development, but when we consider the self-dependence of every human soul we see the need of courage, judgment, and the exercise of every faculty of mind and body, strengthened and developed by use, in woman as well as man.

Whatever may be said of man's protecting power in ordinary conditions, mid all the terrible disasters by land and sea, in the supreme moments of danger, alone, woman must ever meet the horrors of the situation; the Angel of Death even makes no royal pathway for her. Man's love and sympathy enter only into the sunshine of our lives. In that solemn solitude of self, that links us with the immeasurable and the eternal, each soul lives alone forever. . . .

Such is individual life. Who, I ask you, can take, dare take, on himself the rights, the duties, the responsibilities of another human soul?

* * *

## "GIVE ME YOUR TIRED, YOUR POOR"
### Emma Lazarus, "The New Colossus"—1883

The poet Emma Lazarus (1849–1887) wrote these verses in 1883 to help fund construction of a pedestal for the Statue of Liberty. The poem was affixed in 1903 to the pedestal on a cast bronze plaque.

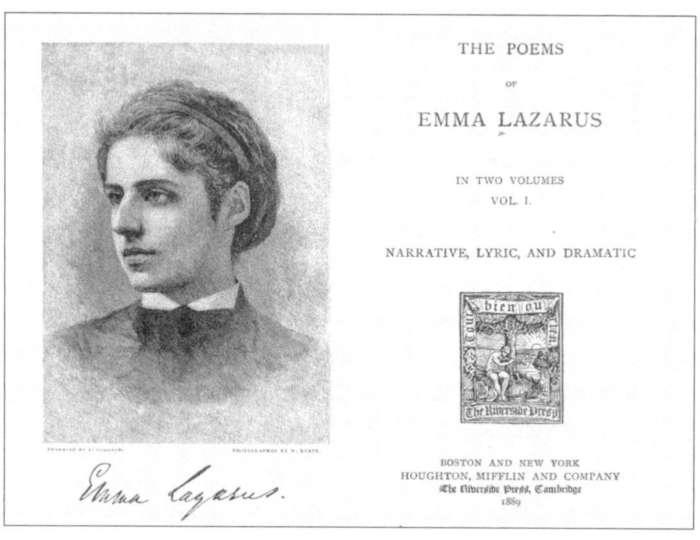

Emma Lazarus.

THE POEMS

OF

EMMA LAZARUS

IN TWO VOLUMES

VOL. I.

NARRATIVE, LYRIC, AND DRAMATIC

BOSTON AND NEW YORK

HOUGHTON, MIFFLIN AND COMPANY

The Riverside Press, Cambridge

1889

*Not like the brazen giant of Greek fame*
*With conquering limbs astride from land to land;*
*Here at our sea-washed, sunset gates shall stand*
*A mighty woman with a torch, whose flame*
*Is the imprisoned lightning, and her name*
*Mother of Exiles. From her beacon-hand*
*Glows world-wide welcome; her mild eyes command*
*The air-bridged harbor that twin cities frame.*
*"Keep, ancient lands, your storied pomp!" cries she*
*With silent lips. "Give me your tired, your poor,*
*Your huddled masses yearning to breathe free,*
*The wretched refuse of your teeming shore,*
*Send these, the homeless, tempest-tost to me,*
*I lift my lamp beside the golden door!"*

★ ★ ★

## "WHAT DOES LABOR WANT?"
### Samuel Gompers, A Paper Read Before the International Labor Conference, Columbian Exposition, Chicago, Illinois—August 28, 1893

Born in London, the labor leader Samuel Gompers (1850–1924) founded and led the American Federation of Labor.

MY FRIENDS, WE have met here today to celebrate the idea that has prompted thousands of working-people of Louisville and New Albany to parade the streets of your city; that prompts the toilers of Chicago to turn out by their fifty or hundred thousand of men; that prompts the vast army of wage-workers in New York to demonstrate their enthusiasm and appreciation of the importance of this idea; that prompts the toilers of England, Ireland, Germany, France, Italy, Spain, and Austria to defy the manifestos of the autocrats of the world and say that on May the first, 1890, the wage-workers of the world will lay down their tools in sympathy with the wage-workers of America, to establish a principle of limitations of hours of labor to eight hours for sleep, eight hours for work, and eight hours for what we will.

It has been charged time and again that were we to have more hours of leisure we would merely devote it to debauchery, to the cultivation of vicious habits—in other words, that we would get drunk. I desire to say this in answer to that charge: As a rule, there are two classes in society who get drunk. One is the class who has no work to do in consequence of too much money; the other class, who also has no work to do, because it can't get any, and gets drunk on its face. I maintain that that class in our social life that exhibits the greatest degree of sobriety is that class who are able, by a fair number of hours of day's work to earn fair wages—not overworked. The man who works twelve, fourteen, and sixteen hours a day requires some artificial stimulant to restore the life ground out of him in the drudgery of the day.

You have heard frequently this charge of drunkenness against the laboring class. Now, say there are a hundred men employed in a factory; and when the factory closes down at night ninety-five of these will go home to their wives and families, while the other five will go from the shop, and get drunk at the neighboring saloon. The modern moralist, looking at this factory closed down, will exclaim: "All of them drunk," while the fact is that ninety-five out of the hundred have gone to their homes, but are counted in with the five who have spent their money for liquor. Now, this modern moralist does not contemplate the other class that gets drunk. When they are ready to send him home an electric button is touched, a carriage arrives, and he is driven home; he is undressed and put to bed, and no one has seen him except those who are paid to keep quiet. The modern moralist gets up on the following Sunday morning, casts his eyes to heaven, and prays for the poor drunken devil that he saw yesterday.

Now, I don't want to see drunkenness on the part of any one, nor is it my intention to make a temperance speech, but we have outlived the charge made against us that we have devoted our leisure time to drunkenness and debauchery. I ask you where you find your tradesmen and mechanics and other workmen working more hours a day, is it not a fact that there is a larger degree of drunkenness in the community than where they work nine, ten or eight hours? And where the shorter hours have ruled, you find there is a greater degree of sobriety, far surpassing anything that has ever been seen before.

We ought to be able to discuss this question on a higher ground, and I am pleased to say that the movement in which we are engaged will stimulate us to it. They tell us that the eight-hour movement cannot be enforced, for the reason that it must check industrial and commercial progress. I say that the history of this country, in its industrial and commercial relations, shows the reverse. I say that is the plane on which this question ought to be discussed—that is the social question. As long as they make this question an economic one, I am willing to discuss it with them. I would retrace every step I have taken to advance this movement did it mean industrial and commercial stagnation. But it does not mean that. It means greater prosperity; it means a greater degree of progress for the whole people; it means more advancement and intelligence, and a nobler race of people. I would not unsay one word I have said, except to make it stronger. I would not retrace one step I have taken in my connection with this movement for the eight-hour law. I call on the wage-workers of Louisville and New Albany and the whole world to enforce it.

They say they can't afford it. Is that true? Let us see for one moment. If a reduction in the hours of labor causes industrial and commercial ruination, it would naturally follow increased hours of labor would increase the prosperity, commercial and industrial. If that were true, England and America ought to be at the tail end, and China at the head of civilization.

Is it not a fact that we find laborers in England and the United States, where the hours are eight, nine and ten hours a day—do we not find that the employers and laborers are more successful? Don't we find them selling articles cheaper? We do not need to trust the modern moralist to tell us those things. In all industries where the hours of labor are long, there you will find the least development of the power of invention. Where the hours of labor are long, men are cheap, and where men are cheap there is no necessity for invention. How can you expect a man to work ten or twelve or fourteen hours at his calling and then devote any time to the invention of a machine or discovery of a new principle or force? If he be so fortunate as to be able to read a paper he will fall asleep before he has read through the second or third line.

Why, when you reduce the hours of labor, say an hour a day, just think what it means. Suppose men who work ten hours a day had the time lessened to nine, or men who work nine hours a day have it reduced to eight hours; what does it mean? It means millions of golden hours and opportunities for thought. Some men might say you will go to sleep. Well, some men might sleep sixteen hours a day; the ordinary man might try that, but he would soon find he could not do it long. He would have to do something. He would probably go to the theater one night, to a concert another night, but he could not do that every night. He would probably become interested in some study and the hours that have been taken from manual labor are devoted to mental labor, and the mental labor of one hour produce for him more wealth than the physical labor of a dozen hours.

I maintain that this is a true proposition—that men under the short-hour system not only have opportunity to improve themselves, but to make a greater degree of prosperity for their employers. Why, my friends, how is it in China, how is it in Spain, how is it in India and Russia, how is it in Italy? Cast your eye throughout the universe and observe the industry that forces nature to yield up its fruits to man's necessities, and you will find that where the hours of labor are the shortest the progress of invention in machinery and the prosperity of the people are the greatest. It is the greatest impediment to progress to hire men cheaply. Wherever men are cheap, there you find the least degree of progress. It has only been under the great influence of our great republic, where our people have exhibited their great senses, that we can move forward, upward and onward, and are watched with interest in our movements of progress and reform.

I have said this much about the employers and their interest as connected with this question of the reduction of the hours of labor. Now I want to say a word as to the workingman. There are many people who believe that when the hours of labor are shortened wages necessarily fall. There is no more unsound proposition, politically or socially. We notice that in any country where the hours of labor are longest, not only are the employers the poorest, but the wage-workers are the poorest. It applies not only to countries, but it applies with the same force to States and cities, to different shops in cities, and affects the different industries of any one city. You notice in any of the establishments of Louisville or New Albany, or any other place you have been in, that the people who enter the factory or establishment the earliest in the morning and leave it the latest at night always receive the lowest wages in that establishment. And you notice that those who come latest in the morning and leave earliest in the evening are the best paid. This is no dream; it is a truth. I have another thought to express, if you have the patience to listen. First: A man who works eight hours a day can't afford to work as cheap as the man who works sixteen or eighteen hours a day. I will tell you why: The man who works eight hours a day has sixteen hours a day left. He must do something with them. He will go to the theater, read a magazine, or visit a friend at home and when he does he must have decent clothes.

He may take his wife or his best girl to a friend's. If he happens to be married, he takes his wife, and he wants her to be neat and clean and dressed fairly well. When his friend visits him he wants to have, probably, a pretty picture on the wall, or perhaps a piano or organ in his parlor; and he wishes everything about him to be bright and attractive. Take the other working man; he has no necessity for decent clothes—nobody comes to see him; he simply comes home to go to bed. He does not see his wife except when he returns from his work, and he is too tired to think about pictures and pianos. When he comes home the lamp is turned down ready for him to go to bed. For books and the study of political economy, or books treating of the condition of the people, or the current news in the newspapers, he has no time. Why, if it depended on him, you would not see the boasting publications of the papers claiming to have the largest circulation in the world. You will always find that the wage-worker who works the longest hours in the day has the least. Take, for example, China. There you will find that he receives six or eight cents a day—enough to pay for his rice and an occasional rat, as a luxury. You will find in the foreign countries people receiving in wages about as much as will supply them with those degrees of comfort that they are willing to live upon. In France they get enough to buy a square meal and a little wine. In America, workingmen can have a beefsteak much oftener, and perhaps a little better beefsteak, because they demand it. Whenever a man finds that he can live on just so much, he generally finds also that he doesn't get a cent more than what is necessary to get it. If a workingman thinks he can live on a sandwich and a herring, he is pretty apt to find that his employer is going to pay him enough to get that sandwich and herring.

The man who works the long hours has no necessities except the barest to keep body and soul together, so he can work. He goes to sleep and dreams of work; he rises in the morning to go to work; he takes his frugal lunch to work; he comes home again to throw himself down on a miserable apology for a bed so that he can get that little rest that he may be able to go to work again. He is nothing but a veritable machine. He lives to work instead of working to live.

My friends, the only thing the working people need besides the necessities of life, is time. Time. Time with which our lives begin; time with which our lives close; time to cultivate the better nature within us; time to brighten our homes. Time, which brings us from the lowest condition up to the highest civilization; time, so that we can raise men to a higher plane.

My friends, you will find that it has been ascertained that there is more than a million of our brothers and sisters—able-bodied men and women—on the streets, and on the highways and byways of our country willing to work but who cannot find it. You know that it is the theory of our government that we can work or cease to work at will. It is only a theory. You know that it is only a theory and not a fact. It is true that we can cease to work when we want to, but I deny that we can work when we will, so long as there are a million idle men and women tramping the streets of our cities, searching for work. The theory that we can work or cease to work when we will is a delusion and a snare. It is a lie.

What we want to consider is, first, to make our employment more secure, and, secondly, to make wages more permanent, and, thirdly, to give these poor people a chance to work. The laborer has been regarded as a mere producing machine . . . but back of labor is the soul of man and honesty of purpose and aspiration. Now you cannot, as the political economists and college professors, say that labor is a commodity to be bought and sold. I say we are American citizens with the heritage of all the great men who have stood before us; men who have sacrificed all in the cause except honor. Our enemies would like to see this movement thrust into hades, they would like to see it in a warmer climate, but I say to you that this movement has come to stay. Like Banquo's ghost, it will not stay down. I say the labor movement is a fixed fact. It has grown out of the necessities of the people, and, although some may desire to see it fail, still the labor movement will be found to have a strong lodgment in the hearts of the people, and we will go on until success has been achieved.

We want eight hours and nothing less. We have been accused of being selfish, and it has been said that we will want more; that last year we got an advance of ten cents and now we want more. We do want more. You will find that a man generally wants more. Go and ask a tramp what he wants, and if he doesn't want a drink he will want a good, square meal. You ask a workingman, who is getting two dollars a day, and he will say that he wants ten cents more. Ask a man who gets five dollars a day and he will want fifty cents more. The man who receives five thousand dollars a year wants six thousand a year, and the man who owns eight or nine hundred thousand dollars will want a hundred thousand dollars to make it a million, while the man who has his millions will want everything he can lay his hands on and then raise his voice against the poor devil who wants ten cents more a day. We live in the latter part of the nineteenth century. In the age of electricity and steam that has produced wealth a hundred fold, we insist that it has been brought about by the intelligence and the energy of the workingmen, and while we find that it is now easier to produce it is harder to live. We do want more, and when it becomes more, we shall still want more. And we shall never cease to demand more until we have received the results of our labor.

★ ★ ★

## "A WILD MOTLEY THRONG"
### Thomas Bailey Aldrich, "Unguarded Gates"—1895

The writer and editor Thomas Bailey Aldrich (1836–1907) captured the anti-immigrant sentiment of the era in these verses.

*WIDE open and unguarded stand our gates,*
*Named of the four winds, North, South, East, and West;*
*Portals that lead to an enchanted land*
*Of cities, forests, fields of living gold,*
*Vast prairies, lordly summits touched with snow,*
*Majestic rivers sweeping proudly past*
*The Arab's date-palm and the Norseman's pine—*
*A realm wherein are fruits of every zone,*
*Airs of all climes, for, lo! throughout the year*
*The red rose blossoms somewhere—a rich land,*
*A later Eden planted in the wilds,*
*With not an inch of earth within its bound*
*But if a slave's foot press it sets him free.*
*Here, it is written, Toil shall have its wage,*
*And Honor honor, and the humblest man*
*Stand level with the highest in the law.*
*Of such a land have men in dungeons dreamed,*
*And with the vision brightening in their eyes*
*Gone smiling to the fagot and the sword.*

*Wide open and unguarded stand our gates,*
*And through them presses a wild motley throng—*
*Men from the Volga and the Tartar steppes,*
*Featureless figures of the Hoang-Ho,*
*Malayan, Scythian, Teuton, Kelt, and Slav,*
*Flying the Old World's poverty and scorn;*
*These bringing with them unknown gods and rites,—*
*Those, tiger passions, here to stretch their claws.*
*In street and alley what strange tongues are loud,*
*Accents of menace alien to our air,*
*Voices that once the Tower of Babel knew!*

*O Liberty, white Goddess! is it well*
*To leave the gates unguarded? On thy breast*
*Fold Sorrow's children, soothe the hurts of fate,*
*Lift the down-trodden, but with hand of steel*
*Stay those who to thy sacred portals come*
*To waste the gifts of freedom. Have a care*
*Lest from thy brow the clustered stars be torn*
*And trampled in the dust. For so of old*
*The thronging Goth and Vandal trampled Rome,*
*And where the temples of the Cæsars stood*
*The lean wolf unmolested made her lair.*

★ ★ ★

## "DISTINCTIONS BASED UPON COLOR"
### Opinion of the Court, *Plessy v. Ferguson*—1896

In a challenge to a Louisiana law mandating racially segregated railcars, Homer A. Plessy brought suit on the grounds that segregation violated the equal-protection provisions of the Fourteenth Amendment. In a seven-to-one decision (one justice was away from Washington and did not participate), the United States Supreme Court, in an opinion authored by Justice Henry Billings Brown (1836–1913), ruled that "separate but equal" facilities were constitutional.

THE OBJECT OF the [Fourteenth] amendment was undoubtedly to enforce the absolute equality of the two races before the law, but, in the nature of things, it could not have been intended to abolish distinctions based upon color, or to enforce social, as distinguished from political, equality, or a commingling of the two races upon terms unsatisfactory to either. Laws permitting, and even requiring, their separation in places where they are liable to be brought into contact do not necessarily imply the inferiority of either race to the other, and have been generally, if not universally, recognized as within the competency of the state legislatures in the exercise of their police power. The most common instance of this is connected with the establishment of separate schools for white and colored children, which have been held to be a valid exercise of the legislative power even by courts of States where the political rights of the colored race have been longest and most earnestly enforced. . . .

So far, then, as a conflict with the Fourteenth Amendment is concerned, the case reduces itself to the question whether the statute of Louisiana is a reasonable regulation, and, with respect to this, there must necessarily be a large discretion on the part of the legislature. In determining the question of reasonableness, it is at liberty to act with reference to the established usages, customs, and traditions of the people, and with a view to the promotion of their comfort and the preservation of the public peace and good order. Gauged by this standard, we cannot say that a law which authorizes or even requires the separation of the two races in public conveyances is unreasonable, or more obnoxious to the Fourteenth Amendment than the acts of Congress requiring separate schools for colored children in the District of Columbia, the constitutionality of which does not seem to have been questioned, or the corresponding acts of state legislatures.

We consider the underlying fallacy of [Plessy's] argument to consist in the assumption that the enforced separation of the two races stamps the colored race with a badge of inferiority. If this be so, it is not by reason of anything found in the act, but solely because the colored race chooses to put that construction upon it. The argument necessarily assumes that if, as has been more than once the case and is not unlikely to be so again, the colored race should become the dominant power in the state legislature, and should enact a law in precisely similar terms, it would thereby relegate the white race to an inferior position. We imagine that the white race, at least, would not acquiesce in this assumption. The argument also assumes that social prejudices may be overcome by legislation, and that equal rights cannot be secured . . . except by an enforced commingling of the two races. We cannot accept this proposition. If the two races are to meet upon terms of social equality, it must be the result of natural affinities, a mutual appreciation of each other's merits, and a voluntary consent of individuals. . . .

Legislation is powerless to eradicate racial instincts or to abolish distinctions based upon physical differences, and the attempt to do so can only result in accentuating the difficulties of the present situation.

★ ★ ★

## "OUR CONSTITUTION IS COLOR-BLIND"

### John Marshall Harlan, Dissenting Opinion, *Plessy v. Ferguson*—1896

Born in Kentucky, John Marshall Harlan (1833–1911), known as the Great Dissenter, was appointed to the Supreme Court by President Rutherford B. Hayes in 1877. His was the lone vote against the *Plessy* majority.

THE WHITE RACE deems itself to be the dominant race in this country. And so it is in prestige, in achievements, in education, in wealth and in power. So, I doubt not, it will continue to be for all time if it remains true to its great heritage and holds fast to the principles of constitutional liberty. But in view of the Constitution, in the eye of the law, there is in this country no superior, dominant, ruling class of citizens. There is no caste here. Our Constitution is color-blind, and neither knows nor tolerates classes among citizens. In respect of civil rights, all citizens are equal before the law. The humblest is the peer of the most powerful. The law regards man as man, and takes no account of his surroundings or of his color when his civil rights as guaranteed by the supreme law of the land are involved. It is therefore to be regretted that this high tribunal, the final expositor of the fundamental law of the land, has reached the conclusion that it is competent for a State to regulate the enjoyment by citizens of their civil rights solely upon the basis of race.

In my opinion, the judgment this day rendered will, in time, prove to be quite as pernicious as the decision made by this tribunal in the *Dred Scott Case.* It was adjudged in that case that the descendants of Africans who were imported into this country and sold as slaves were not included nor intended to be included under the word "citizens" in the Constitution, and could not claim any of the rights and privileges which that instrument provided for and secured to citizens of the United States; that, at the time of the adoption of the Constitution, they were "considered as a subordinate and inferior class of beings, who had been subjugated by the dominant race, and, whether emancipated or not, yet remained subject to their authority, and had no rights or privileges but such as those who held the power and the government might choose to grant them." The recent amendments of the Constitution, it was supposed, had eradicated these principles from our institutions. But it seems that we have yet, in some of the States, a dominant race—a superior class of citizens, which assumes to regulate the enjoyment of civil rights, common to all citizens, upon the basis of race. The present decision, it may well be apprehended, will not only stimulate aggressions, more or less brutal and irritating, upon the admitted rights of colored citizens, but will encourage the belief that it is possible, by means of state enactments, to defeat the beneficent purposes which the people of the United States had in view when they adopted the recent amendments to the Constitution. . . .

The destinies of the two races in this country are indissolubly linked together, and the interests of both require that the common government of all shall not permit the seeds of race hate to be planted under the sanction of law. What can more certainly arouse race hate, what more certainly create and perpetuate a feeling of distrust between these races, than state enactments which, in fact, proceed on the ground that colored citizens are so inferior and degraded that they cannot be allowed to sit in public coaches occupied by white citizens. That, as all will admit, is the real meaning of such legislation as was enacted in Louisiana.

The sure guarantee of the peace and security of each race is the clear, distinct, unconditional recognition by our governments, National and State, of every right that inheres in civil freedom, and of the equality before the law of all citizens of the United States, without regard to race. State enactments regulating the enjoyment of civil rights upon the basis of race, and cunningly devised to defeat the legitimate results of the [Civil War] under the pretense of recognizing equality of rights, can have no other result than to render permanent peace impossible and to keep alive a conflict of races the continuance of which must do harm to all concerned.

★ ★ ★

## "SO LONG AS AMERICA IS UNJUST"
### Declaration of Principles, the Niagara Movement—1905

Founded in 1905 by W.E.B. Du Bois, William Monroe Trotter (1872–1934), and Mary Burnett Talbert (1866–1923), the Niagara Movement was an early civil-rights organization that called for racial equality before the law.

PROGRESS: The members of the conference, known as the Niagara Movement, assembled in annual meeting at Buffalo, July 11th, 12th and 13th, 1905, congratulate the Negro-Americans on certain undoubted evidences of progress in the last decade, particularly the increase of intelligence, the buying of property, the checking of crime, the uplift in home life, the advance in literature and art, and the demonstration of constructive and executive ability in the conduct of great religious, economic and educational institutions.

SUFFRAGE: At the same time, we believe that this class of American citizens should protest emphatically and continually against the curtailment of their political rights. We believe in manhood suffrage; we believe that no man is so good, intelligent or wealthy as to be entrusted wholly with the welfare of his neighbor.

CIVIL LIBERTY: We believe also in protest against the curtailment of our civil rights. All American citizens have the right to equal treatment in places of public entertainment according to their behavior and deserts.

ECONOMIC OPPORTUNITY: We especially complain against the denial of equal opportunities to us in economic life; in the rural districts of the South this amounts to peonage and virtual slavery; all over the South it tends to crush labor and small business enterprises; and everywhere American prejudice, helped often by iniquitous laws, is making it more difficult for Negro-Americans to earn a decent living.

EDUCATION: Common school education should be free to all American children and compulsory. High school training should be adequately provided for all, and college training should be the monopoly of no class or race in any section of our common country. We believe that, in defense of our own institutions, the United States should aid common school education, particularly in the South, and we especially recommend concerted agitation to this end. We urge an increase in public high school facilities in the South, where the Negro-Americans are almost wholly without such provisions. We favor well-equipped trade and technical schools for the training of artisans, and the need of adequate and liberal endowment for a few institutions of higher education must be patent to sincere well-wishers of the race.

COURTS: We demand upright judges in courts, juries selected without discrimination on account of color and the same measure of punishment and the same efforts at reformation for black as for white offenders. We need orphanages and farm schools for dependent children, juvenile reformatories for delinquents, and the abolition of the dehumanizing convict-lease system.

PUBLIC OPINION: We note with alarm the evident retrogression in this land of sound public opinion on the subject of manhood rights, republican government and human brotherhood, and we pray God that this nation will not degenerate into a mob of boasters and oppressors, but rather will return to the faith of the fathers, that all men were created free and equal, with certain unalienable rights.

HEALTH: We plead for health—for an opportunity to live in decent houses and localities, for a chance to rear our children in physical and moral cleanliness.

EMPLOYERS AND LABOR UNIONS: We hold up for public execration the conduct of two opposite classes of men: The practice among employers of importing ignorant Negro-American laborers in emergencies, and then affording them neither protection nor permanent employment; and the practice of labor unions in proscribing and boycotting and oppressing thousands of their fellow-toilers, simply because they are black. These methods have accentuated and will accentuate the war of labor and capital, and they are disgraceful to both sides.

PROTEST: We refuse to allow the impression to remain that the Negro-American assents to inferiority, is submissive under oppression and apologetic before insults. Through helplessness we may submit, but the voice of protest of ten million Americans must never cease to assail the ears of their fellows, so long as America is unjust.

COLOR-LINE: Any discrimination based simply on race or color is barbarous, we care not how hallowed it be by custom, expediency or prejudice. Differences made on account of ignorance, immorality, or disease are legitimate methods of fighting evil, and against them we have no word of protest; but discriminations based simply and solely on physical peculiarities, place of birth, color of skin, are relics of that unreasoning human savagery of which the world is and ought to be thoroughly ashamed.

"JIM CROW" CARS: We protest against the "Jim Crow" car, since its effect is and must be to make us pay first-class fare for third-class accommodations, render us open to insults and discomfort and to crucify wantonly our manhood, womanhood and self-respect.

SOLDIERS: We regret that this nation has never seen fit adequately to reward the black soldiers who, in its five wars, have defended their country with their blood, and yet have been systematically denied the promotions which their abilities deserve. And we regard as unjust, the exclusion of black boys from the military and naval training schools.

WAR AMENDMENTS: We urge upon Congress the enactment of appropriate legislation for securing the proper enforcement of those articles of freedom, the thirteenth, fourteenth and fifteenth amendments of the Constitution of the United States.

OPPRESSION: We repudiate the monstrous doctrine that the oppressor should be the sole authority as to the rights of the oppressed. The Negro race in America stolen, ravished and degraded, struggling up through difficulties and oppression, needs sympathy and receives criticism; needs help and is given hindrance, needs protection and is given mob-violence, needs justice and is given charity, needs leadership and is given cowardice and apology, needs bread and is given a stone. This nation will never stand justified before God until these things are changed.

THE CHURCH: Especially are we surprised and astonished at the recent attitude of the church of Christ—of an increase of a desire to bow to racial prejudice, to narrow the bounds of human brotherhood, and to segregate black men to some outer sanctuary. This is wrong, unchristian and disgraceful to the twentieth century civilization.

AGITATION: Of the above grievances we do not hesitate to complain, and to complain loudly and insistently. To ignore, overlook, or apologize for these wrongs is to prove ourselves unworthy of freedom.

Persistent manly agitation is the way to liberty, and toward this goal the Niagara Movement has started and asks the cooperation of all men of all races.

HELP: At the same time we want to acknowledge with deep thankfulness the help of our fellowmen from the Abolitionist down to those who today still stand for equal opportunity and who have given and still give of their wealth and of their poverty for our advancement.

DUTIES: And while we are demanding, and ought to demand, and will continue to demand the rights enumerated above, God forbid that we should ever forget to urge corresponding duties upon our people:

The duty to vote.

The duty to respect the rights of others.

The duty to work.

The duty to obey the laws.

The duty to be clean and orderly.

The duty to send our children to school.

The duty to respect ourselves, even as we respect others.

This statement, complaint and prayer we submit to the American people, and Almighty God.

★ ★ ★

## "A BLIGHT UPON OUR NATION"

### Ida B. Wells, "Lynching: Our National Crime," Address in New York City—1909

Ida B. Wells-Barnett (1862–1931) was born into enslavement in Holly Springs, Mississippi. She began her journalism career in Memphis (where she also taught school) and ultimately moved to Chicago. In these remarks she explored the scourge of lynching, the extrajudicial attacks on Black Americans.

THE LYNCHING RECORD for a quarter of a century merits the thoughtful study of the American people. It presents three salient facts: First, lynching is color-line murder. Second, crimes against women is the excuse, not the cause. Third, it is a national crime and requires a national remedy. Proof that lynching follows the color line is to be found in the statistics which have been kept for the past twenty-five years. During the few years preceding this period and while frontier law existed, the executions showed a majority of white victims. Later, however, as law courts and authorized judiciary extended into the far West, lynch law rapidly abated, and its white victims became few and far between. Just as the lynch-law regime came to a close in the West, a new mob movement started in the South.

This was wholly political, its purpose being to suppress the colored vote by intimidation and murder. Thousands of assassins banded together under the name of Ku Klux Klans, "Midnight Raiders," "Knights of the Golden Circle," et cetera, et cetera, spread a reign of terror, by beating, shooting and killing colored people by the thousands. In a few years, the purpose was accomplished, and the black vote was suppressed. But mob murder continued.

From 1882, in which year 52 were lynched, down to the present, lynching has been along the color line. Mob murder increased yearly until in 1892 more than 200 victims were lynched and statistics show that 3,284 men, women and children have been put to death in this quarter of a century. During the last ten years from 1899 to 1908 inclusive the number lynched was 959. Of this number 102 were white, while the colored victims numbered 857. No other nation, civilized or savage, burns its criminals; only under that Stars and Stripes is the human holocaust possible. Twenty-eight human beings burned at the stake, one of them a woman and two of them children, is the awful indictment against American civilization—the gruesome tribute which the nation pays to the color line.

Why is mob murder permitted by a Christian nation? What is the cause of this awful slaughter? This question is answered almost daily—always the same shameless falsehood that "Negroes are lynched to protect womanhood." Standing before a Chautauqua assemblage, John Temple Graves, at once champion of lynching and apologist for lynchers, said: "The mob stands today as the most potential bulwark between the women of the South and such a carnival of crime as would infuriate the world and precipitate the annihilation of the Negro race." This is the never-varying answer of lynchers and their apologists. All know

*The pioneering journalist Ida B. Wells-Barnett.*

that it is untrue. The cowardly lyncher revels in murder, then seeks to shield himself from public execration by claiming devotion to woman. But truth is mighty and the lynching record discloses the hypocrisy of the lyncher as well as his crime.

The Springfield, Illinois, mob rioted for two days, the militia of the entire state was called out, two men were lynched, hundreds of people driven from their homes, all because a white woman said a Negro assaulted her. A mad mob went to the jail, tried to lynch the victim of her charge and, not being able to find him, proceeded to pillage and burn the town and to lynch two innocent men. Later, after the police had found that the woman's charge was false, she published a retraction, the indictment was dismissed and the intended victim discharged. But the lynched victims were dead. Hundreds were homeless and Illinois was disgraced. . . .

Is there a remedy, or will the nation confess that it cannot protect its protectors at home as well as abroad? Various remedies have been suggested to abolish the lynching infamy, but year after year, the butchery of men, women and children continues in spite of plea and protest. . . .

Agitation, though helpful, will not alone stop the crime. Year after year statistics are published, meetings are held, resolutions are adopted and yet lynchings go on. Public sentiment does measurably decrease the sway of mob law, but the irresponsible bloodthirsty criminals who swept through the streets of Springfield, beating an inoffensive law-abiding citizen to death in one part of the town, and in another torturing and shooting to death a man who for threescore years had made a reputation for honesty, integrity and sobriety, had raised a family and had accumulated property, were not deterred from their heinous crimes by either education or agitation.

The only certain remedy is an appeal to law. Lawbreakers must be made to know that human life is sacred and that every citizen of this country is first a citizen of the United States and secondly a citizen of the state in which he belongs. This nation must assert itself and protect its federal citizenship at home as well as abroad. The strong arm of the government must reach across state lines whenever unbridled lawlessness defies state laws and must give to the individual under the Stars and Stripes the same measure of protection it gives to him when he travels in foreign lands. . . .

As a final word, it would be a beginning in the right direction if this conference can see its way clear to establish a bureau for the investigation and publication of the details of every lynching, so that the public could know that an influential body of citizens has made it a duty to give the widest publicity to the facts in each case; that it will make an effort to secure expressions of opinion all over the country against lynching for the sake of the country's fair name; and lastly, but by no means least, to try to influence the daily papers of the country to refuse to become accessory to mobs either before or after the fact. Several of the greatest riots and most brutal burnt offerings of the mobs have been suggested and incited by the daily papers of the offending community. If the newspaper which suggests lynching in its accounts of an alleged crime, could be held legally as well as morally responsible for reporting that "threats of lynching were heard"; or, "it is feared that if the guilty one is caught, he will be lynched"; or, "there were cries of 'lynch him,' and the only reason the threat was not carried out was because no leader appeared," a long step toward a remedy will have been taken.

In a multitude of counsel there is wisdom. Upon the grave question presented by the slaughter of innocent men, women and children there should be an honest, courageous conference of patriotic, law-abiding citizens anxious to punish crime promptly, impartially and by due process of law, also to make life, liberty and property secure against mob rule.

Time was when lynching appeared to be sectional, but now it is national—a blight upon our nation, mocking our laws and disgracing our Christianity. "With malice toward none but with charity for all" let us undertake the work of making the "law of the land" effective and supreme upon every foot of American soil—a shield to the innocent; and to the guilty, punishment swift and sure.

★ ★ ★

## "IT IS NOT THE CRITIC WHO COUNTS"
### Theodore Roosevelt, "Citizenship in a Republic," Address at the Sorbonne, Paris, France—April 23, 1910

Theodore Roosevelt (1858–1919) succeeded to the presidency in 1901 upon the assassination of William McKinley, then served until 1909.

*Ebullient and indefatigable, Theodore Roosevelt was a great believer in what he called "the life of strenuous endeavor."*

TO-DAY I SHALL speak to you on the subject of individual citizenship, the one subject of vital importance to you, my hearers, and to me and my countrymen, because you and we are great citizens of great democratic republics. A democratic republic such as ours—an effort to realize in its full sense government by, of, and for the people—represents the most gigantic of all possible social experiments, the one fraught with great responsibilities alike for good and evil. The success of republics like yours and like ours means the glory, and our failure the despair, of mankind; and for you and for us the question of the quality of the individual citizen is supreme. Under other forms of government, under the rule of one man or very few men, the quality of the leaders is all-important. If, under such governments, the quality of the rulers is high enough, then the nations for generations lead a brilliant career, and add substantially to the sum of world achievement, no matter how low the quality of the average citizen; because the average citizen is an almost negligible quantity in working out the final results of that type of national greatness.

But with you and us the case is different. With you here, and with us in my own home, in the long run, success or failure will be conditioned upon the way in which the average man, the average woman, does his or her duty, first in the ordinary, every-day affairs of life, and next in those great occasional crises which call for the heroic virtues. The average citizen must be a good citizen if our republics are to succeed. . . .

The poorest way to face life is to face it with a sneer. There are many men who feel a kind of twisted pride in cynicism; there are many who confine themselves to criticism of the way others do what they themselves dare not even attempt. There is no more unhealthy being, no man less worthy of respect, than he who either really holds, or feigns to hold, an attitude of sneering disbelief toward all that is great and lofty, whether in achievement or in that noble effort which, even if it fails, comes second to achievement. A cynical habit of thought and speech, a readiness to criticize work which the critic himself never tries to perform, an intellectual aloofness which will not accept contact with life's realities—all these are marks, not as the possessor would fain to think, of superiority, but of weakness. They mark the men unfit to bear their part manfully in the stern strife of living, who seek, in the affectation of contempt for the achievement of others, to hide from others and from themselves their own weakness. The role is easy; there is none easier, save only the role of the man who sneers alike at both criticism and performance.

It is not the critic who counts; not the man who points out how the strong man stumbles or where the doer of deeds could have done them better. The credit belongs to the man who is actually in the arena, whose face is marred by dust and sweat and blood; who strives valiantly; who errs, who comes short again and again, because there is no effort without error and shortcoming; but who does actually strive to do the deeds; who knows the great enthusiasms, the great devotions; who spends himself in a worthy cause; who at the best knows in the end the triumph of high achievement, and who at the worst, if he fails, at least fails while daring greatly, so that his place shall never be with those cold and timid souls who neither know victory nor defeat. Shame on the man of cultivated taste who permits refinement to develop into fastidiousness that unfits him for doing the rough work of a workaday world! Among the free peoples who govern themselves there is but a small field of usefulness open for the men of cloistered life who shrink from contact with their fellows. Still less room is there for those who deride or slight what is done by those who actually bear the brunt of the day; nor yet for those others who always profess that they would like to take action, if only the conditions of life were not exactly what they actually are. The man who does nothing cuts the same sordid figure in the pages of history, whether he be cynic, or fop, or voluptuary. There is little use for the being whose tepid soul knows nothing of the great and generous emotion, of the high pride, the stern belief, the lofty enthusiasm, of the men who quell the storm and ride the thunder. Well for these men if they succeed; well also, though not so well, if they fail, given only that they have nobly ventured, and have put forth all their heart and strength. It is warworn Hotspur, spent with hard fighting, he of the many errors and the valiant end, over whose memory we love to linger, not over the memory of the young lord who "but for the vile guns would have been a soldier." . . .

Perhaps the most important thing the ordinary citizen, and, above all, the leader of ordinary citizens, has to remember in political life is that he must not be a sheer doctrinaire. The closet philosopher, the refined and cultured individual who from his library tells how men ought to be governed under ideal conditions, is of no use in actual governmental work; and the one-sided fanatic, and still more the mob-leader, and the insincere man who to achieve power promises what by no possibility can be performed, are not merely useless but noxious. . . .

The good citizen will demand liberty for himself, and as a matter of pride he will see to it that others receive the liberty which he thus claims as his own. Probably the best test of true love of liberty in any country is the way in which minorities are treated in that country. Not only should there be complete liberty in matters of religion and opinion, but complete liberty for each man to lead his life as he desires, provided only that in so doing he does not wrong his neighbor. Persecution is bad because it is persecution, and without reference to which side happens at the moment to be the persecutor and which the persecuted. . . .

Of one man in especial, beyond anyone else, the citizens of a republic should beware, and that is of the man who appeals to them to support him on the ground that he is hostile to other citizens of the republic, that he will secure for those who elect him, in one shape or another, profit at the expense of other citizens of the republic. It makes no difference whether he appeals to class hatred or class interest, to religious or anti-religious prejudice. The man who makes such an appeal should always be presumed to make it for the sake of furthering his own interest. The very last thing an intelligent and self-respecting member of a democratic community should do is to reward any public man because that public man says that he will get the private citizen something to which this private citizen is not entitled, or will gratify some emotion or animosity which this private citizen ought not to possess. . . .

If a public man tries to get your vote by saying that he will do something wrong in your interest, you can be absolutely certain that if ever it becomes worth his while he will do something wrong against your interest.

⋆ ⋆ ⋆

## "A PROGRAM OF HUMAN WELFARE"
### Jane Addams, Nominating Speech for Theodore Roosevelt, Chicago, Illinois—August 7, 1912

In 1912, Theodore Roosevelt sought to return to the White House on a Progressive Party ticket in a race against the Republican William Howard Taft and the Democrat Woodrow Wilson. The activist Jane Addams (1860–1935) spoke for TR's nomination at the party's convention in Chicago.

A GREAT PARTY HAS pledged itself to the protection of children, to the care of the aged, to the relief of overworked girls, to the safeguarding of burdened men. Committed to these humane undertakings, it is inevitable that such a party should appeal to women, should seek to draw upon the great reservoir of their moral energy so long undesired and unutilized in practical politics—one is the corollary of the other; a program of human welfare on the one side, the necessity for women's participation on the other; one meets and completes the others.

*A native of Illinois, Jane Addams co-founded Hull-House, a settlement house in Chicago; she opposed American intervention in the First World War, and received a Nobel Peace Prize in 1931.*

We ratify this platform not only because it represents our earnest convictions and formulates our high hopes, but because it pulls upon our faculties and calls us to definite action. We find it a prophesy that democracy shall not be actually realized until no group of our people—certainly not ten million of them so sadly in need of reassurance—shall fail to bear the responsibilities of self-government, and that no class of evils shall lie beyond redress.

The new party is for the moment and will be [forever] more the American exponent of a worldwide movement towards juster social conditions, a movement which the United States, lagging behind other great nations, has been unaccountably slow to embody in political action. But finally the hour has come and the men and women assembled in this hall from all parts of this continent have crystallized a program and united on a common purpose.

I should like, therefore, to second the nomination of Theodore Roosevelt, because he is one of the few men in our public life who has been responsive to the social appeal and who has caught the significance of the modern movement. Because of that, because the program will require a leader of invincible courage, of open mind, of democratic sympathies, one endowed with power . . . to identify himself with the common lot, I heartily second the nomination so eloquently made by the gentleman from New York.

* * *

## "THE PEOPLE ARE AWAKENING"

### Eugene V. Debs, Statement to the Court upon Being Convicted of Violating the Sedition Act, Cleveland, Ohio—September 18, 1918

The longtime Socialist Party leader Eugene V. Debs (1855–1926) tested a World War I–era law banning dissent with an anti-war speech in Canton, Ohio. Tried and convicted, he was sentenced to ten years' imprisonment. President Warren G. Harding ultimately commuted the sentence.

IN THIS COUNTRY—the most favored beneath the bending skies—we have vast areas of the richest and most fertile soil, material resources in inexhaustible abundance, the most marvelous productive machinery on earth, and millions of eager workers ready to apply their labor to that machinery to produce in abundance for every man, woman, and child—and if there are still vast numbers of our people who are the victims of poverty and whose lives are an unceasing struggle all the way from youth to old age, until at last death comes to their rescue and lulls these hapless victims to dreamless sleep, it is not the fault of the Almighty: it cannot be charged to nature, but it is due entirely to the outgrown social system in which we live that ought to be abolished not only in the interest of the toiling masses but in the higher interest of all humanity. . . .

I believe, Your Honor, in common with all Socialists, that this nation ought to own and control its own industries. I believe, as all Socialists do, that all things that are jointly needed and used ought to be jointly owned—that industry, the basis of our social life, instead of being the private property of a few and operated for their enrichment, ought to be the common property of all, democratically administered in the interest of all. . . .

I am opposing a social order in which it is possible for one man who does absolutely nothing that is useful to amass a fortune of hundreds of millions of dollars, while millions of men and women who work all the days of their lives secure barely enough for a wretched existence.

This order of things cannot always endure. I have registered my protest against it. I recognize the feebleness of my effort, but, fortunately, I am not alone. There are multiplied thousands of others who, like myself, have come to realize that before we may truly enjoy the blessings of civilized life, we must reorganize society upon a mutual and cooperative basis; and to this end we have organized a great economic and political movement that spreads over the face of all the earth.

There are today upwards of sixty millions of Socialists, loyal, devoted adherents to this cause, regardless of nationality, race, creed, color, or sex. They are all making common cause. They are spreading with tireless energy the propaganda of the new social order. They are waiting, watching, and working hopefully through all the hours of the day and the night. They are still in a minority. But they have learned how to be patient and to bide their time. They feel—they know, indeed—that the time is coming, in spite of all opposition, all persecution, when this emancipating gospel will spread among all the peoples, and when this minority will become the triumphant majority and, sweeping into power, inaugurate the greatest social and economic change in history.

In that day we shall have the universal commonwealth—the harmonious cooperation of every nation with every other nation on earth. . . .

Your Honor, I ask no mercy and I plead for no immunity. I realize that finally the right must prevail. I never so clearly comprehended as now the great struggle between the powers of greed and exploitation on the one hand and upon the other the rising hosts of industrial freedom and social justice.

I can see the dawn of the better day for humanity. The people are awakening. In due time they will and must come to their own.

When the mariner, sailing over tropic seas, looks for relief from his weary watch, he turns his eyes toward the southern cross, burning luridly above the tempest-vexed ocean. As the midnight approaches, the southern cross begins to bend, the whirling worlds change their places, and with starry finger-points the Almighty marks the passage of time upon the dial of the universe, and though no bell may beat the glad tidings, the lookout knows that the midnight is passing and that relief and rest are close at hand. Let the people everywhere take heart of hope, for the cross is bending, the midnight is passing, and joy cometh with the morning.

* * *

## "CONTRARY TO THE SPIRIT OF THE CONSTITUTION"

### Anti-Klan Democratic National Convention Platform Plank—1924

---

**The second Ku Klux Klan was an important cultural and political force after its founding in 1915. By 1924, the anti-Black, anti-immigrant, anti-Semitic, anti-Catholic movement was sufficiently strong within the national Democratic Party that the party's convention at Madison Square Garden featured a battle over this excerpted proposed plank, which was defeated.**

WE CONDEMN POLITICAL secret societies of all kinds as opposed to the exercise of free government and contrary to the spirit of the Constitution of the United States. We pledge the Democratic Party to oppose any effort on the part of the Ku Klux Klan or any organization to interfere with the religious liberty or political freedom of any citizens, or to limit the civic rights of any citizen or body of citizens because of religion, birthplace, or racial origin.

* * *

## "WITHOUT DISCRIMINATION"

### Calvin Coolidge, "Cal Coolidge Tells Kluxers When to Stop," Letter on Black Candidate in *The Chicago Defender*—August 9, 1924

On learning of racist attacks being made against a Black man running as a Republican for a U.S. House seat, President Calvin Coolidge (1872–1933) defended the candidate.

THE SUGGESTION OF denying any measure of their full political rights to such a great group of our population as the colored people is one which, however it might be received in some other quarter, could not possibly be permitted by one who feels a responsibility for living up to the traditions and maintaining the principles of the Republican Party. Our Constitution guarantees equal rights to all our citizens, without discrimination on account of race or color. I have taken my oath to support that Constitution. It is the source of your rights and my rights. I propose to regard it, and administer it, as the source of the rights of all the people, whatever their belief or race.

★ ★ ★

*The Second Ku Klux Klan was a highly public phenomenon, openly marching in Washington, D.C., as it pursued a racist and nativist agenda in the 1920s.*

## "YOUR FOOL RELIGION"

### Clarence Darrow Examines William Jennings Bryan in *Tennessee v. Scopes* Trial, Dayton, Tennessee—July 20, 1925

In the summer of 1925, in Dayton, Tennessee, Clarence Darrow (1857–1938) defended John T. Scopes against a charge that he had violated state law by teaching the theory of evolution. The state was represented by William Jennings Bryan (1860–1925), a three-time presidential candidate and former secretary of state. Darrow put Bryan on the stand.

Judge—Do you want Mr. Bryan sworn?

Darrow—No.

Bryan—I can make affirmation; I can say "So help me God, I will tell the truth."

Darrow—No, I take it you will tell the truth, Mr. Bryan. You have given considerable study to the Bible, haven't you, Mr. Bryan?

Bryan—Yes, sir, I have tried to.

Darrow—Then you have made a general study of it?

Bryan—Yes, I have; I have studied the Bible for about 50 years, or sometime more than that, but, of course, I have studied it more as I have become older than when I was but a boy.

Darrow—You claim that everything in the Bible should be literally interpreted?

Bryan—I believe everything in the Bible should be accepted as it is given there: some of the Bible is given illustratively. For instance: "Ye are the salt of the earth." I would not insist that man was actually salt, or that he had flesh of salt, but it is used in the sense of salt as saving God's people.

Darrow—But when you read that Jonah swallowed the whale—or that the whale swallowed Jonah—excuse me please—how do you literally interpret that?

Bryan—When I read that a "big fish" swallowed Jonah—it does not say whale. That is my recollection of it. A big fish, and I believe it, and I believe in a God who can make a whale and can make a man and make both what He pleases.

Darrow—Now, you say, the big fish swallowed Jonah, and he there remained how long—three days—and then he spewed him upon the land. You believe that the big fish was made to swallow Jonah?

Bryan—I am not prepared to say that; the Bible merely says it was done.

Darrow—You don't know whether it was the ordinary run of fish, or made for that purpose?

Bryan—You may guess; you evolutionists guess. . . .

Darrow—You are not prepared to say whether that fish was made especially to swallow a man or not?

Bryan—The Bible doesn't say, so I am not prepared to say.

Darrow—But do you believe He made them—that He made such a fish and that it was big enough to swallow Jonah?

Bryan—Yes, sir. Let me add: One miracle is just as easy to believe as another.

Darrow—Just as hard?

Bryan—It is hard to believe for you, but easy for me. A miracle is a thing performed beyond what man can perform. When you get within the realm of miracles; and it is just as easy to believe the miracle of Jonah as any other miracle in the Bible.

Darrow—Perfectly easy to believe that Jonah swallowed the whale?

Bryan—If the Bible said so; the Bible doesn't make as extreme statements as evolutionists do.

Darrow—The Bible says Joshua commanded the sun to stand still for the purpose of lengthening the day, doesn't it, and you believe it?

Bryan—I do.

Darrow—Do you believe at that time the entire sun went around the earth?

Bryan—No, I believe that the earth goes around the sun.

Darrow—Do you believe that the men who wrote it thought that the day could be lengthened or that the sun could be stopped?

Bryan—I don't know what they thought.

Darrow—You don't know?

Bryan—I think they wrote the fact without expressing their own thoughts.

Darrow—Have you an opinion as to whether or not the men who wrote that thought—

Thomas Stewart [a prosecution lawyer]—I want to object, your honor. It has gone beyond the pale of any issue that could possibly be injected into this lawsuit, except by imagination. I do not think the defendant has a right to conduct the examination any further and I ask your honor to exclude it.

Bryan—It seems to me it would be too exacting to confine the defense to the facts. If they are not allowed to get away from the facts, what have they to deal with?

Judge—Mr. Bryan is willing to be examined. Go ahead.

Darrow—Can you answer my question directly? If the day was lengthened by stopping either the earth or the sun, it must have been the earth?

Bryan—Well, I should say so.

Darrow—Now, Mr. Bryan, have you ever pondered what would have happened to the earth if it had stood still?

Bryan—No.

Darrow—You have not?

Bryan—No; the God I believe in could have taken care of that, Mr. Darrow.

Darrow—I see. Have you ever pondered what would naturally happen to the earth if it stood still suddenly?

Bryan—No.

Darrow—Don't you know it would have been converted into molten mass of matter?

Bryan—You testify to that when you get on the stand, I will give you a chance.

Darrow—Don't you believe it?

Bryan—I would want to hear expert testimony on that.

Darrow—You have never investigated that subject?

Bryan—I don't think I have ever had the question asked.

Darrow—Or ever thought of it?

Bryan—I have been too busy on things that I thought were of more importance than that.

Darrow—You believe the story of the flood to be a literal interpretation?

Bryan—Yes, sir.

Darrow—When was that flood?

Bryan—I would not attempt to fix the date. The date is fixed, as suggested this morning.

Darrow—About 4004 B.C.?

Bryan—That has been the estimate of a man that is accepted today. [A witness had testified on Bishop James Ussher's theory that the earth was formed in 4004 B.C.] I would not say it is accurate.

Darrow—That estimate is printed in the Bible?

Bryan—Everybody knows, at least, I think most of the people know, that was the estimate given.

Darrow—But what do you think that the Bible itself says? Don't you know how it was arrived at?

Bryan—I never made a calculation.

Darrow—A calculation from what?

Bryan—I could not say.

Darrow—From the generations of man?

Bryan—I would not want to say that.

Darrow—What do you think?

Bryan—I do not think about things I don't think about.

Darrow—Do you think about things you do think about?

Bryan—Well, sometimes. (Laughter.)

Policeman—Let us have order. . . .

Thomas Stewart [prosecution attorney]—Your honor, he is perfectly able to take care of this, but we are attaining no evidence. This is not competent evidence.

Bryan—These gentlemen have not had much chance—they did not come here to try this case. They came here to try revealed religion. I am here to defend it and they can ask me any question they please.

Judge—All right. (Applause.)

Darrow—Great applause from the bleachers.

Bryan—From those whom you call "yokels."

Darrow—I have never called them yokels.

Bryan—That is the ignorance of Tennessee, the bigotry.

Darrow—You mean who are applauding you? (Applause.)

Bryan—Those are the people whom you insult.

Darrow—You insult every man of science and learning in the world because he does believe in your fool religion.

Judge—I will not stand for that.

Darrow—For what he is doing?

Judge—I am talking to both of you.

Darrow—Do you know anything about how many people there were in Egypt 3,500 years ago, or how many people there were in China 5,000 years ago?
Bryan—No.
Darrow—Have you ever tried to find out?
Bryan—No, sir. You are the first man I ever heard of who has been interested in it. (Laughter.)
Darrow—Mr. Bryan, am I the first man you ever heard of who has been interested in the age of human societies and primitive man?
Bryan—You are the first man I ever heard speak of the number of people at those different periods.
Darrow—Where have you lived all your life?
Bryan—Not near you. (Laughter and applause.)
Darrow—Nor near anybody of learning?
Bryan—Oh, don't assume you know it all.
Darrow—Do you know there are thousands of books in our libraries on all those subjects I have been asking you about?
Bryan—I couldn't say, but I will take your word for it. . . .
Darrow—Have you any idea how old the earth is?
Bryan—No.
Darrow—The book you have introduced in evidence tells you, doesn't it?
Bryan—I don't think it does, Mr. Darrow.
Darrow—Let's see whether it does; is this the one?
Bryan—That is the one, I think.
Darrow—It says B.C. 4004?
Bryan—That is Bishop Ussher's calculation.
Darrow—That is printed in the Bible you introduced?
Bryan—Yes, sir.
Darrow—Would you say that the earth was only 4,000 years old?
Bryan—Oh, no; I think it is much older than that.
Darrow—How much?
Bryan—I couldn't say.
Darrow—Do you say whether the Bible itself says it is older than that?
Bryan—I don't think it is older or not.
Darrow—Do you think the earth was made in six days?
Bryan—Not six days of 24 hours.
Darrow—Doesn't it say so?

Bryan—No, sir.

Judge—Are you about through, Mr. Darrow?

Darrow—I want to ask a few more questions about the creation.

Judge—I know. We are going to adjourn when Mr. Bryan comes off the stand for the day. Be very brief, Mr. Darrow. Of course, I believe I will make myself clearer. Of course, it is incompetent testimony before the jury. The only reason I am allowing this to go in at all is that they may have it in the appellate court as showing what the affidavit would be.

Bryan—The reason I am answering is not for the benefit of the superior court. It is to keep these gentlemen from saying I was afraid to meet them and let them question me, and I want the Christian world to know that any atheist, agnostic, unbeliever, can question me anytime as to my belief in God, and I will answer him.

Darrow—I want to take an exception to this conduct of this witness. He may be very popular down here in the hills—

Bryan—Your honor, they have not asked a question legally and the only reason they have asked any question is for the purpose, as the question about Jonah was asked, for a chance to give this agnostic an opportunity to criticize a believer in the word of God; and I answered the question in order to shut his mouth so that he cannot go out and tell his atheistic friends that I would not answer his questions. That is the only reason, no more reason in the world. . . .

Darrow—Mr. Bryan, do you believe that the first woman was Eve?

Bryan—Yes.

Darrow—Do you believe she was literally made out of Adam's rib?

Bryan—I do.

Darrow—Did you ever discover where Cain got his wife?

Bryan—No, sir. I leave the agnostics to hunt for her.

Darrow—You have never found out?

Bryan—I have never tried to find out.

Darrow—You have never tried to find out?

Bryan—No.

Darrow—The Bible says he got one, doesn't it? Were there other people on the earth at that time?

Bryan—I cannot say.

Darrow—You cannot say. Did that ever enter your consideration?

Bryan—Never bothered me.

Darrow—There were no others recorded, but Cain got a wife.

Bryan—That is what the Bible says.

Darrow—Where she came from you do not know. All right. Does the statement, "The morning and the evening were the first day," and "The morning and the evening were the second day," mean anything to you?

Bryan—I do not think it necessarily means a 24-hour day.

Darrow—You do not?

Bryan—No.

Darrow—What do you consider it to be?

Bryan—I have not attempted to explain it. If you will take the second chapter—let me have the book. [Reaches for a Bible.] The fourth verse of the second chapter says: "These are the generations of the heavens and of the earth, when they were created in the day that the Lord God made the earth and the heavens," the word "day" there in the very next chapter is used to describe a period. I do not see that there is any necessity for construing the words, "the evening and the morning," as meaning necessarily a 24-hour day, "in the day when the Lord made the heaven and the earth."

Darrow—Then, when the Bible said, for instance, "and God called the firmament heaven. And the evening and the morning were the second day," that does not necessarily mean twenty-four hours?

Bryan—I do not think it necessarily does.

Darrow—Do you think it does or does not?

Bryan—I know a great many think so.

Darrow—What do you think?

Bryan—I do not think it does.

Darrow—You think those were not literal days?

Bryan—I do not think they were twenty-four-hour days.

Darrow—What do you think about it?

Bryan—That is my opinion—I do not know that my opinion is better on that subject than those who think it does.

Darrow—You do not think that?

Bryan—No. But I think it would be just as easy for the kind of God we believe in to make the earth in six days as in six years or in 6 million years or in 600 million years. I do not think it important whether we believe one or the other.

Darrow—Do you think those were literal days?

Bryan—My impression is they were periods, but I would not attempt to argue against anybody who wanted to believe in literal days.

Darrow—I will read it to you from the Bible: "And the Lord God said unto the serpent, because thou hast done this, thou art cursed above all cattle, and above every beast of the field; upon thy belly shalt thou go and dust shalt thou eat all the days of thy life." Do you think that is why the serpent is compelled to crawl upon its belly?

Bryan—I believe that.

Darrow—Have you any idea how the snake went before that time?

Bryan—No, sir.

Darrow—Do you know whether he walked on his tail or not?

Bryan—No, sir. I have no way to know. (Laughter.)

Darrow—Now, you refer to the cloud that was put in heaven after the flood, the rainbow. Do you believe in that?

Bryan—Read it.

Darrow—All right, Mr. Bryan, I will read it for you.

Bryan—Your Honor, I think I can shorten this testimony. The only purpose Mr. Darrow has is to slur at the Bible, but I will answer his question. I will answer it all at once, and I have no objection in the world. I want the world to know that this man, who does not believe in a God, is trying to use a court in Tennessee to slur at it, and while it will require time, I am willing to take it.

Darrow—I object to your statement. I am examining you on your fool ideas that no intelligent Christian on earth believes.

Judge—Court is adjourned until 9 o'clock tomorrow morning.

* * *

## "NATIVE, WHITE, PROTESTANT SUPREMACY"

### Hiram Evans, "The Klan's Fight for Americanism," *North American Review*—March 1926

---

Born in Alabama, Hiram Evans (1881–1966) practiced dentistry in Texas and was Imperial Wizard of the Ku Klux Klan from 1922 until 1939.

There are three . . . great racial instincts, vital elements in both the historic and the present attempts to build an America which shall fulfill the aspirations and justify the heroism of the men who made the nation. These are the instincts of loyalty to the white race, to the traditions of America, and to the spirit of Protestantism, which has been an essential part of Americanism ever since the days of Roanoke and Plymouth Rock. They are condensed into the Klan slogan: "Native, white, Protestant supremacy."

First in the Klansman's mind is patriotism—America for Americans. He believes religiously that a betrayal of Americanism or the American race is treason to the most sacred trusts, a trust from his fathers and a trust from God. He believes too that Americanism can only be achieved if the pioneer stock is kept pure. There is more than race pride in this. Mongrelization has been proven bad. It is only between closely related stocks of the same race that interbreeding has improved men; the kind of interbreeding that went on in the early days of America between English, Dutch, German, Huguenot, Irish, and Scotch.

Racial integrity is a very definite thing to a Klansman. It means even more than good citizenship, for a man may be in all ways a good citizen and yet a poor American, unless he has racial understanding of Americanism, and instinctive loyalty to it. . . .

Americanism, to the Klansman, is a thing of the spirit, a purpose and a point of view, that can only come through instinctive racial understanding. It has, to be sure, certain defined principles, but he does not believe that many aliens understand those principles, even when they use our words in talking about them. . . . In short, the Klansman believes in the greatest possible diversity and individualism within the limits of the American spirit. But he believes also that few aliens can understand that spirit, that fewer try to, and that there must be resistance, intolerance even, toward anything that threatens it, or the fundamental national unity based upon it.

The second word in the Klansman's trilogy is "white." The white race must be supreme, not only in America but in the world. This is equally undebatable, except on the ground that the races might live together, each with full regard for the rights and interests of others, and that those rights and interests would never conflict. Such an idea, of course, is absurd; the colored races today, such as Japan, are clamoring not for equality but for their supremacy. The whole history of the world, on its broader lines, has been one of race conflicts, wars, subjugation or extinction. This is not pretty and certainly disagrees with the maudlin theories of cosmopolitanism, but it is truth. The world has been so made that each race must fight for its life, must conquer, accept slavery or die. The Klansman believes that the whites will not become slaves, and he does not intend to die before his time. . . .

The third of the Klan principles is that Protestantism must be supreme; that Rome shall not rule America. The Klansman believes this is not merely because he is a Protestant, nor even because the Colonies that are now our nation were settled for the purpose of wresting America from the control of Rome and establishing a land free of conscience. He believes it also because Protestantism is an essential part of Americanism; without it America could never have been created and without it she cannot go forward. Roman rule would kill it. . . .

Let it be clear what is meant by "supremacy." It is nothing more than power of control, under just laws. It is not imperialism, far less is it autocracy or even aristocracy of a race or stock of men. What it does mean is that we insist on our inherited right to insure our own safety, individually and as a race, to secure the future of our children, to maintain and develop our racial heritage in our own, white, Protestant, American way, without interference.

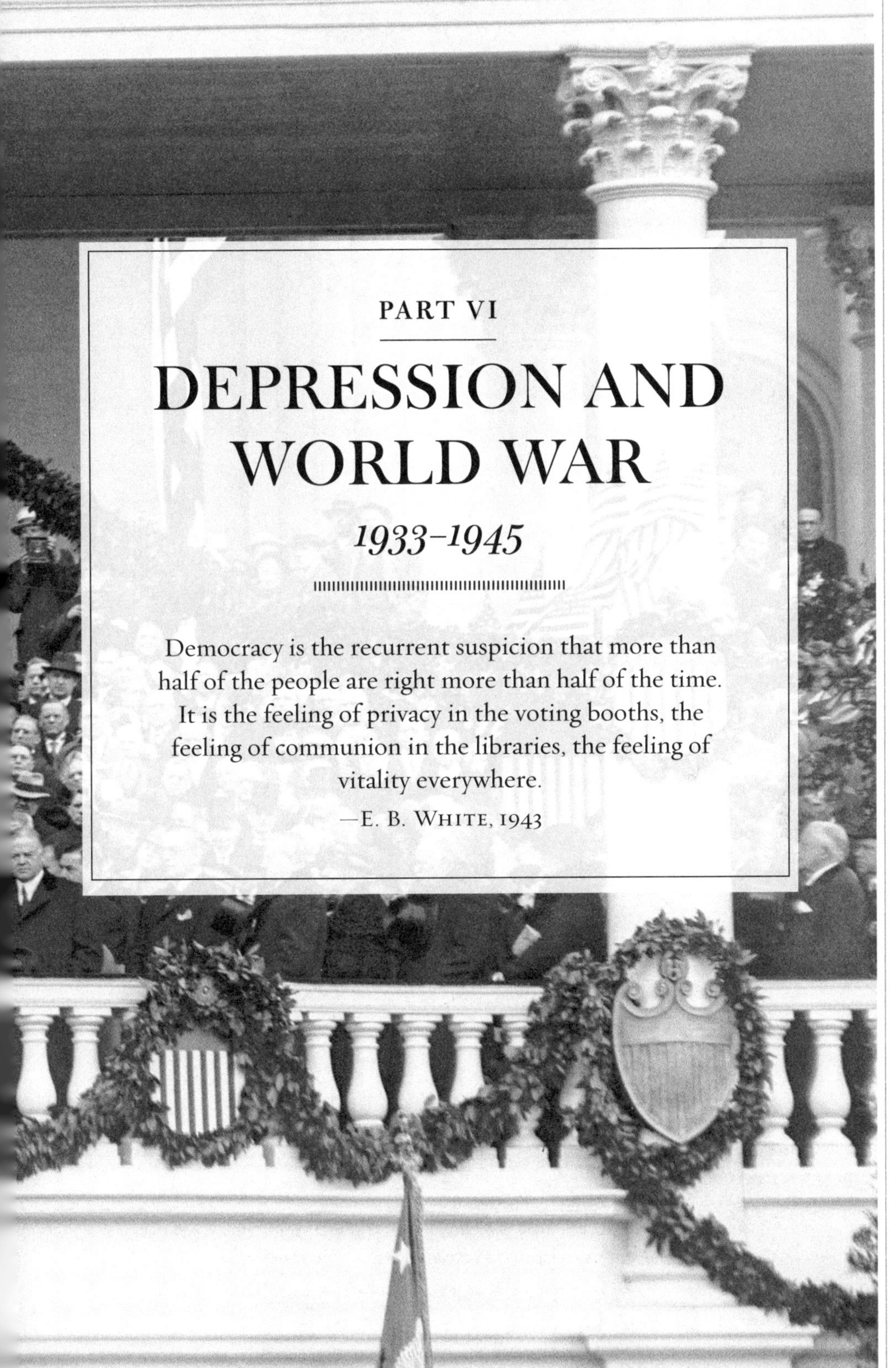

PART VI

# DEPRESSION AND WORLD WAR

## *1933–1945*

Democracy is the recurrent suspicion that more than half of the people are right more than half of the time. It is the feeling of privacy in the voting booths, the feeling of communion in the libraries, the feeling of vitality everywhere.

—E. B. White, 1943

PREVIOUS SPREAD: *"The only thing we have to fear," Franklin D. Roosevelt told the nation in his first inaugural address, delivered on Saturday, March 4, 1933, "is fear itself—nameless, unreasoning, unjustified terror which paralyzes needed efforts to convert retreat into advance."*

---

NO ONE WAS SURE WHAT WOULD HAPPEN. By 1932–33, the Great Depression consumed the United States, affecting every aspect of life. The financier Bernard Baruch said the country was facing a crisis "worse than war." As many as one out of every five American workers was out of a job. "There are many signs that if the lawfully constituted leadership does not soon substitute action for words," a Senate committee was told, "a new leadership, perhaps unlawfully constituted, will arise and act."

Into this sulfurous atmosphere came Franklin D. Roosevelt, who defeated Republican Herbert Hoover in the 1932 election on a promise of offering a "New Deal" to the American people. An adviser told FDR that solving the problem of the Depression would make him the nation's greatest president, but failure would make him the worst. "If I fail," Roosevelt replied, "I shall be the last one."

He faced twin threats—one from the left, the other from the right. Roosevelt remarked that the two most dangerous men in America were Huey Long, the populist "Kingfish" from Louisiana, who could lead a revolt from the left, and Douglas MacArthur, the army chief of staff who might mount a challenge to the constitutional order from the right. "There is incipient revolution in the air," MacArthur said as he led an attack on veterans gathered in Washington seeking their bonus. Further from the public eye, a group of Wall Street bankers attempted to bribe the Marine general Smedley Butler to raise an army to depose the president and install a fascist government.

Through trial and error, Roosevelt marshaled the federal government to bring relief to millions and keep democratic capitalism alive. With dictatorship on the march in Europe and imperial militarists in power in Japan, the threat to liberal democracy was not only national but global. As World War II came, Roosevelt carefully maneuvered between a largely isolationist United States and the exigencies of possible intervention. Pearl Harbor and Adolf Hitler's subsequent declaration of war on the United States brought the country fully into the conflict, which was to last four long years—a period in which the American government ordered the internment of Americans of Japanese descent and maintained racially segregated armed forces.

Amid the war in Europe came reports of Nazi atrocities as the Third Reich pursued a relentless policy of genocide against the Jewish people—a horrific crime against humanity that was discussed but less understood in real time than it would be when Allied forces liberated the camps in 1945. As the historian Gerhard L. Weinberg would write in 1998: "Every single life counts, and every individual saved counts. There cannot be the slightest doubt that more efforts could have been made by an earlier establishment of the War Refugee Board and by any number of other steps and actions. The general picture in terms of overall statistics would not have been very different; the record of the Allies would have been brighter, and each person saved could have lived out a decent life. The exertions of the Allies in World War II saved not only themselves but also the majority of the world's Jews. But the shadow of doubt whether enough was done will always remain, even if there really were not many things that could have been done."

World War II, therefore, was an instance of great nobility and of miserable tragedy. The United States largely rose to the occasion, but only after being forced into action by a direct attack. One need not sentimentalize the struggle to appreciate the sacrifice and the courage of the nation and its people. Nor, given the complexities of the war, should we seek comfort in such sentiment. The facts are bracing—and illuminating—enough.

★ ★ ★

## "FEAR ITSELF"

### Franklin D. Roosevelt, First Inaugural Address—March 4, 1933

Franklin D. Roosevelt (1882–1945) came to office in the grimmest of hours. He put the finishing touches on his inaugural address in his suite at the Mayflower Hotel in the days before the ceremony.

THIS IS A day of national consecration. And I am certain that on this day my fellow Americans expect that on my induction into the Presidency I will address them with a candor and a decision which the present situation of our people impels. This is preeminently the time to speak the truth, the whole truth, frankly and boldly. Nor need we shrink from honestly facing conditions in our country today. This great Nation will endure as it has endured, will revive and will prosper. So, first of all, let me assert my firm belief that the only thing we have to fear is fear itself—nameless, unreasoning, unjustified terror which paralyzes needed efforts to convert retreat into advance. In every dark hour of our national life a leadership of frankness and vigor has met with that understanding and support of the people themselves which is essential to victory. I am convinced that you will again give that support to leadership in these critical days.

In such a spirit on my part and on yours we face our common difficulties. They concern, thank God, only material things. Values have shrunken to fantastic levels; taxes have risen; our ability to pay has fallen; government of all kinds is faced by serious curtailment of income; the means of exchange are frozen in the currents of trade; the withered leaves of industrial enterprise lie on every side; farmers find no markets for their produce; the savings of many years in thousands of families are gone.

More important, a host of unemployed citizens face the grim problem of existence, and an equally great number toil with little return. Only a foolish optimist can deny the dark realities of the moment.

Yet our distress comes from no failure of substance. We are stricken by no plague of locusts. Compared with the perils which our forefathers conquered because they believed and were not afraid, we have still much to be thankful for. Nature still offers her bounty and human efforts have multiplied it. Plenty is at our doorstep, but a generous use of it languishes in the very sight of the supply. Primarily this is because rulers of the exchange of mankind's goods have failed through their own stubbornness and their own incompetence, have admitted their failure, and have abdicated. Practices of the unscrupulous money changers stand indicted in the court of public opinion, rejected by the hearts and minds of men.

True, they have tried, but their efforts have been cast in the pattern of an outworn tradition. Faced by failure of credit they have proposed only the lending of more money. Stripped of the lure of profit by which to induce our people to follow their false leadership, they have resorted to exhortations, pleading tearfully for restored confidence. They know only the rules of a generation of self-seekers. They have no vision, and when there is no vision the people perish.

The money changers have fled from their high seats in the temple of our civilization. We may now restore that temple to the ancient truths. The measure of the restoration lies in the extent to which we apply social values more noble than mere monetary profit.

Happiness lies not in the mere possession of money; it lies in the joy of achievement, in the thrill of creative effort. The joy and moral stimulation of work no longer must be forgotten in the mad chase of evanescent profits. These dark days will be worth all they cost us if they teach us that our true destiny is not to be ministered unto but to minister to ourselves and to our fellow men.

Recognition of the falsity of material wealth as the standard of success goes hand in hand with the abandonment of the false belief that public office and high political position are to be valued only by the standards of pride of place and personal profit; and there must be an end to a conduct in banking and in business which too often has given to a sacred trust the likeness of callous and selfish wrongdoing. Small wonder that confidence languishes, for it thrives only on honesty, on honor, on the sacredness of obligations, on faithful protection, on unselfish performance; without them it cannot live. Restoration calls, however, not for changes in ethics alone. This Nation asks for action, and action now.

Our greatest primary task is to put people to work. This is no unsolvable problem if we face it wisely and courageously. It can be accomplished in part by direct recruiting by the Government itself, treating the task as we would treat the emergency of a war, but at the same time, through this employment, accomplishing greatly needed projects to stimulate and reorganize the use of our natural resources.

Hand in hand with this we must frankly recognize the overbalance of population in our industrial centers and, by engaging on a national scale in a redistribution, endeavor to provide a better use of the land for those best fitted for the land. The task can be helped by definite efforts to raise the values of agricultural products and with this the power to purchase the output of our cities. It can be helped by preventing realistically the tragedy of the growing loss through foreclosure of our small homes and our farms. It can be helped by insistence that the Federal, State, and local governments act forthwith on the demand that their cost be drastically reduced. It can be helped by the unifying of relief activities which today are often scattered, uneconomical, and unequal. It can be helped by national planning for and supervision of all forms of transportation and of communications and other utilities which have a definitely public character. There are many ways in which it can be helped, but it can never be helped by merely talking about it. We must act. We must act quickly.

Finally, in our progress toward a resumption of work we require two safeguards against a return of the evils of the old order: there must be a strict supervision of all banking and credits and investments, so that there will be an end to speculation with other people's money; and there must be provision for an adequate but sound currency.

These are the lines of attack. I shall presently urge upon a new Congress, in special session, detailed measures for their fulfillment, and I shall seek the immediate assistance of the several States.

Through this program of action we address ourselves to putting our own national house in order and making income balance outgo. Our international trade relations, though vastly important, are in point of time and necessity secondary to the establishment of a sound national economy. I favor as a practical policy the putting of first things first. I shall spare no effort to restore world trade by international economic readjustment, but the emergency at home cannot wait on that accomplishment.

The basic thought that guides these specific means of national recovery is not narrowly nationalistic. It is the insistence, as a first consideration, upon the interdependence of the various elements in and parts of the United States—a recognition of the old and permanently important manifestation of the American spirit of the pioneer. It is the way to recovery. It is the immediate way. It is the strongest assurance that the recovery will endure.

In the field of world policy I would dedicate this Nation to the policy of the good neighbor—the neighbor who resolutely respects himself and, because he does so, respects the rights of others—the neighbor who respects his obligations and respects the sanctity of his agreements in and with a world of neighbors.

If I read the temper of our people correctly, we now realize as we have never realized before our interdependence on each other; that we cannot merely take but we must give as well; that if we are to go forward, we must move as a trained and loyal army willing to sacrifice for the good of a common discipline, because without such discipline no progress is made, no leadership becomes effective. We are, I know, ready and willing to submit our lives and property to such discipline, because it makes possible a leadership which aims at a larger good. This I propose to offer, pledging that the larger purposes will bind upon us all as a sacred obligation with a unity of duty hitherto evoked only in time of armed strife.

With this pledge taken, I assume unhesitatingly the leadership of this great army of our people dedicated to a disciplined attack upon our common problems.

Action in this image and to this end is feasible under the form of government which we have inherited from our ancestors. Our Constitution is so simple and practical that it is possible always to meet extraordinary needs by changes in emphasis and arrangement without loss of essential form. That is why our constitutional system has proved itself the most superbly enduring political mechanism the modern world has produced. It has met every stress of vast expansion of territory, of foreign wars, of bitter internal strife, of world relations.

It is to be hoped that the normal balance of executive and legislative authority may be wholly adequate to meet the unprecedented task before us. But it may be that an unprecedented demand and need for undelayed action may call for temporary departure from that normal balance of public procedure.

I am prepared under my constitutional duty to recommend the measures that a stricken Nation in the midst of a stricken world may require. These measures, or such other measures as the Congress may build out of its experience and wisdom, I shall seek, within my constitutional authority, to bring to speedy adoption.

But in the event that the Congress shall fail to take one of these two courses, and in the event that the national emergency is still critical, I shall not evade the clear course of duty that will then confront me. I shall ask the Congress for the one remaining instrument to meet the crisis—broad executive power to wage a war against the emergency, as great as the power that would be given to me if we were in fact invaded by a foreign foe.

For the trust reposed in me I will return the courage and the devotion that befit the time. I can do no less.

We face the arduous days that lie before us in the warm courage of national unity; with the clear consciousness of seeking old and precious moral values; with the clean satisfaction that comes from the stern performance of duty by old and young alike. We aim at the assurance of a rounded and permanent national life.

We do not distrust the future of essential democracy. The people of the United States have not failed. In their need they have registered a mandate that they want direct, vigorous action. They have asked for discipline and direction under leadership. They have made me the present instrument of their wishes. In the spirit of the gift I take it.

In this dedication of a Nation we humbly ask the blessing of God. May He protect each and every one of us. May He guide me in the days to come.

★ ★ ★

## "I MEAN THE SUPER-RICH"

### Huey P. Long, "Every Man a King" Radio Address—February 23, 1934

The charismatic Huey Long (1893–1935) rose from obscurity to dominate Louisiana politics as governor and, beginning in 1932, as a U.S. senator. He thought FDR's New Deal too timid and staked out a political position to Roosevelt's left, arguing for the redistribution of wealth amid the Great Depression. Long was planning a 1936 presidential campaign when he was assassinated in the state capitol in Baton Rouge.

I CONTEND, MY FRIENDS, that we have no difficult problem to solve in America, and that is the view of nearly everyone with whom I have discussed the matter here in Washington and elsewhere throughout the United States—that we have no very difficult problem to solve.

It is not the difficulty of the problem which we have; it is the fact that the rich people of this country—and by rich people I mean the super-rich—will not allow us to solve the problems, or rather the one little problem that is afflicting this country, because in order to cure all of our woes it is necessary to scale down the big fortunes, that we may scatter the wealth to be shared by all of the people.

We have a marvelous love for this Government of ours; in fact, it is almost a religion, and it is well that it should be, because we have a splendid form of government and we have a splendid set of laws. We have everything here that we need, except that we have neglected the fundamentals upon which the American Government was principally predicated.

How many of you remember the first thing that the Declaration of Independence said? It said, "We hold these truths to be self-evident, that there are certain inalienable rights of the people, and among them are life, liberty, and the pursuit of happiness"; and it said, further, "We hold the view that all men are created equal."

Now, what did they mean by that? Did they mean, my friends, to say that all men were created equal and that that meant that any one man was born to inherit $10,000,000,000 and that another child was to be born to inherit nothing?

Did that mean, my friends, that someone would come into this world without having had an opportunity, of course, to have hit one lick of work, should be born with more than it and all of its children and children's children could ever dispose of, but that another one would have to be born into a life of starvation?

That was not the meaning of the Declaration of Independence when it said that all men are created equal or "That we hold that all men are created equal."

Nor was it the meaning of the Declaration of Independence when it said that they held that there were certain rights that were inalienable—the right of life, liberty, and the pursuit of happiness. Is that right of life, my friends, when the young children of this country are being reared into a sphere which is more owned by 12 men than it is by 120 million people?

Is that, my friends, giving them a fair shake of the dice or anything like the inalienable right of life, liberty, and the pursuit of happiness, or anything resembling the fact that all people are created equal; when we have today in America thousands and hundreds of thousands and millions of children on the verge of starvation in a land that is overflowing with too much to eat and too much to wear?

I do not think you will contend that, and I do not think for a moment that they will contend it.

Now let us see if we cannot return this Government to the Declaration of Independence and see if we are going to do anything regarding it. Why should we hesitate or why should we quibble or why should we quarrel with one another to find out what the difficulty is, when we know what the Lord told us what the difficulty is, and Moses wrote it out so a blind man could see it, then Jesus told us all about it, and it was later written in the Book of James, where everyone could read it?

I refer to the Scriptures, now, my friends, and give you what it says not for the purpose of convincing you of the wisdom of myself, not for the purpose, ladies and gentlemen, of convincing you of the fact that I am quoting the Scripture means that I am to be more believed than someone else; but I quote you the Scripture, rather refer you to the Scripture, because whatever you see there you may rely upon will never be disproved so long as you or your children or anyone may live; and you may further depend upon the fact that not one historical fact that the Bible has ever contained has ever yet been disproved by any scientific discovery or by reason of anything that has been disclosed to man through his own individual mind or through the wisdom of the Lord which the Lord has allowed him to have.

But the Scripture says, ladies and gentlemen, that no country can survive, or for a country to survive it is necessary that we keep the wealth scattered among the people, that nothing should be held permanently by any one person, and that 50 years seems to be the year of jubilee in which all property would be scattered about and returned to the sources from which it originally came, and every seventh year debt should be remitted.

Those two things the Almighty said to be necessary—I should say He knew to be necessary, or else He would not have so prescribed that the property would be kept among the general run of the people and that everyone would continue to share in it; so that no one man would get half of it and hand it down to a son, who takes half of what was left, and that son hand it down to another one, who would take half of what was left, until, like a snowball going downhill, all of the snow was off of the ground except what the snowball had.

I believe that was the judgment and the view and the law of the Lord, that we would have to distribute wealth every so often, in order that there could not be people starving to death in a land of plenty, as there is in America today.

We have in America today more wealth, more goods, more food, more clothing, more houses than we have ever had. We have everything in abundance here. We have the farm problem, my friends, because we have too much cotton, because we have too much wheat, and have too much corn, and too much potatoes.

We have a home-loan problem because we have too many houses, and yet nobody can buy them and live in them. . . .

Now, my friends, if you were off on an island where there were 100 lunches, you could not let one man eat up the hundred lunches, or take the hundred lunches and not let anybody else eat any of them. If you did, there would not be anything else for the balance of the people to consume.

So, we have in America today, my friends, a condition by which about ten men dominate the means of activity in at least 85 percent of the activities that you own. They either own directly everything or they have got some kind of mortgage on it, with a very small percentage to be excepted. They own the banks, they own the steel mills, they own the railroads, they own the bonds, they own the mortgages, they own the stores, and they have chained the country from one end to the other, until there is not any kind of business that a small, independent man could go into today and make a living, and there is not any kind of business that an independent man can go into and make any money to buy an automobile with; and they have finally and gradually and steadily eliminated everybody from the fields in which there is a living to be made, and still they have got little enough sense to think they ought to be able to get more business out of it anyway.

If you reduce a man to the point where he is starving to death and bleeding and dying, how do you expect that man to get hold of any money to spend with you? It is not possible.

Then, ladies and gentlemen, how do you expect people to live, when the wherewith cannot be had by the people? . . .

It is necessary to save the Government of the country, but is much more necessary to save the people of America. We love this country. We love this Government. It is a religion, I say. It is a kind of religion people have read of when women, in the name of religion, would take their infant babes and throw them into the burning flame, where they would be instantly devoured by the all-consuming fire, in days gone by; and there probably are some people of the world even today, who, in the name of religion, throw their own babes to destruction; but in the name of our good government people today are seeing their own children hungry, tired, half naked, lifting their tear-dimmed eyes into the sad faces of their fathers and mothers, who cannot give them food and clothing they both needed, and which is necessary to sustain them, and that goes on day after day, and night after night, when day gets into darkness and blackness, knowing those children would arise in the morning without being fed, and probably go to bed at night without being fed.

Yet in the name of our government, and all alone, those people undertake and strive as hard as they can to keep a good government alive, and how long they can stand that no one knows. If I were in their place tonight, the place where millions are, I hope that I would have what I might say—I cannot give you the word to express the kind of fortitude they have; that is the word—hope that I might have the fortitude to praise and honor my government that had allowed me here in this land, where there is too much to eat and too much to wear, to starve in order that a handful of men can have so much more than they can ever eat or they can ever wear.

Now, we have organized a society, and we call it "Share Our Wealth Society," a society with the motto "every man a king."

Every man a king, so there would be no such thing as a man or woman who did not have the necessities of life, who would not be dependent upon the whims and caprices and *ipse dixit* of the financial martyrs for a living. What do we propose by this society? We propose to limit the wealth of big men in the country. There is an average of $15,000 in wealth to every family in America. That is right here today.

We do not propose to divide it up equally. We do not propose a division of wealth, but we propose to limit poverty that we will allow to be inflicted upon any man's family. We will not say we are going to try to guarantee any equality, or $15,000 to families. No; but we do say that one third of the average is low enough for any one family to hold, that there should be a guaranty of a family wealth of around $5,000; enough for a home, an automobile, a radio, and the ordinary conveniences, and the opportunity to educate their children; a fair share of the income of this land thereafter to that family so there will be no such thing as merely the select to have those things, and so there will be no such thing as a family living in poverty and distress.

We have to limit fortunes. Our present plan is that we will allow no one man to own more than $50 million. We think that with that limit we will be able to carry out the balance of the program. It may be necessary that we limit it to less than $50 million. It may be necessary, in working out of the plans, that no man's fortune would be more than $10 million or $15 million. But be that as it may, it will still be more than any one man, or any one man and his children and their children, will be able to spend in their lifetimes; and it is not necessary or reasonable to have wealth piled up beyond that point where we cannot prevent poverty among the masses.

Another thing we propose is old-age pension of $30 a month for everyone that is sixty years old. Now, we do not give this pension to a man making $1,000 a year, and we do not give it to him if he has $10,000 in property, but outside of that we do.

We will limit hours of work. There is not any necessity of having overproduction. I think all you have got to do, ladies and gentlemen, is just limit the hours of work to such an extent as people will work only so long as is necessary to produce enough for all of the people to have what they need. Why, ladies and gentlemen, let us say that all of these labor-saving devices reduce hours down to where you do not have to work but four hours a day; that is enough for these people, and then praise be the name of the Lord, if it gets that good. Let it be good and not a curse, and then we will have five hours a day and five days a week, or even less than that, and we might give a man a whole month off during a year, or give him two months; and we might do what other countries have seen fit to do, and what I did in Louisiana, by having schools by which adults could go back and learn the things that have been discovered since they went to school.

We will not have any trouble taking care of the agricultural situation. All you have to do is balance your production with your consumption. You simply have to abandon a particular crop that you have too much of, and all you have to do is store the surplus for the next year, and the government will take it over. When you have good crops in the area in which the crops that have been planted are sufficient for another year, put in your public works in the particular year when you do not need to raise any more, and by that means you get everybody employed. When the government has enough of any particular crop to take care of all of the people, that will be all that is necessary; and in order to do all of this, our taxation is going to be to take the billion-dollar fortunes and strip them down to frying size, not to exceed $50,000,000, and if it is necessary to come to $10,000,000, we will come to $10,000,000. We have worked the proposition out to guarantee a limit upon property (and no man will own less than one third the average), and guarantee a reduction of fortunes and a reduction of hours to spread wealth throughout this country. We would care for the old people above 60 and take them away from this thriving industry and give them a chance to enjoy the necessities and live in ease, and thereby lift from the market the labor which would probably create a surplus of commodities.

Those are the things we propose to do. "Every man a king." Every man to eat when there is something to eat; all to wear something when there is something to wear. That makes us all sovereign. . . .

Get together in your community tonight or tomorrow and organize one of our Share Our Wealth societies. If you do not understand it, write me and let me send you the platform; let me give you the proof of it.

This is Huey P. Long talking, United States Senator, Washington, D.C. Write me and let me send you the data on this proposition. Enroll with us. Let us make known to the people what we are going to do. I will send you a button, if I have got enough of them left. We have got a little button that some of our friends designed, with our message around the rim of the button, and in the center "Every man a king." Many thousands of them are meeting through the United States, and every day we are getting hundreds and hundreds of letters. Share Our Wealth societies are now being organized, and people have it within their power to relieve themselves from this terrible situation.

★ ★ ★

## "TO OVERTHROW PRESIDENT ROOSEVELT"

**"Gen. Butler Bares 'Fascist Plot' to Seize Government by Force,"**
***The New York Times*—November 21, 1934**

In the tumult of the time, Marine General Smedley Butler was approached by figures claiming to represent significant businessmen who wanted to fund a takeover of the federal government. Known as the "Wall Street Putsch" and the "Business Plot," the effort alarmed Butler, who told FBI director J. Edgar Hoover about the overtures and testified before Congress. "If General Butler had not been the patriot he was, and if they had been able to maintain secrecy, the plot certainly might very well have succeeded, having in mind the conditions existing at that time," recalled Representative John McCormack, Democrat of Massachusetts. "No one can say for sure, of course, but when times are desperate and people are frustrated, anything like that could happen."

A PLOT OF WALL Street interests to overthrow President Roosevelt and establish a Fascist dictatorship, backed by a private army of 500,000 ex-soldiers and others, was charged by Major Gen. Smedley D. Butler, retired Marine Corps officer, who appeared yesterday before the House of Representatives Committee on Un-American Activities, which began hearings on the charges.

Meeting in executive session at the Bar Association, it heard testimony from General Butler and Gerald P. MacGuire, a bond salesman in the Stock Exchange firm of Grayson M.-P. Murphy & Co., 52 Broadway, named by General Butler as having urged him to head the proposed Fascist army.

There were immediate emphatic denials by the purported plotters.

From Philadelphia came word that General Butler had told friends there that General Hugh S. Johnson, former [National Recovery Administration] administrator, was scheduled for the role of dictator, and that J. P. Morgan & Co. as well as Murphy & Co. were behind the plot.

General Johnson led the chorus of denials. Told of General Butler's charges, he barked:

"He had better be pretty damn careful. Nobody said a word to me about anything of this kind, and if they did I'd throw them out the window. I know nothing about it."

Thomas W. Lamont, partner in the firm of J. P. Morgan & Co., said: "Perfect moonshine! Too unutterably ridiculous to comment upon!"

Said Colonel Grayson M.-P. Murphy:

"A fantasy! I can't imagine how anyone could produce it or any sane person believe it. It is absolutely false so far as it relates to me and my firm, and I don't believe there is a word of truth in it with respect to Mr. MacGuire."

Mr. MacGuire, the alleged intermediary, said: "It's a joke—a publicity stunt. I know nothing about it. The matter is made out of whole cloth. I deny the story completely."

In Washington, aides of General Douglas MacArthur, Chief of Staff, who was confined to his quarters with a heavy cold, expressed amazement and amusement when told that the "plotters," according to General Butler, had used General MacArthur's name as an alternate for head of the Fascist army if General Butler did not accept.

*The highly decorated Smedley D. Butler.*

Another alternate as "the man on the white horse" to head the army, General Butler said, was Hanford MacNider, former national commander of the American Legion.

General Butler's story was that MacGuire approached him first with the Fascist army proposition last Summer, and then arranged for Robert Sterling Clark, a wealthy New Yorker with offices in the Stock Exchange Building, to visit him at Butler's home in Newtown Square, Pa.

MacGuire told him that the financial backers of the movement had subscribed $3,000,000, according to General Butler. He added that he was to assemble his 500,000 men in Washington, probably a year from now, with the expectation that such a show of force would enable it to take over the government peacefully in a few days.

It was hoped that President Roosevelt would "go along" as the King of Italy did with Mussolini, according to the story, but if he did not he, the Vice President and the Secretary of State would be forced to resign after appointing the proposed "dictator" as a new Secretary of State, who under the Constitution would then succeed to the Presidency.

General Butler was quoted as saying that Mr. MacGuire had tossed $18,000 in thousand-dollar bills on the bed of General Butler's hotel room in Newark, N.J., on one occasion, "to pay his expenses" in an unsuccessful effort to persuade him to make a speech in favor of the gold standard before the American Legion in Chicago. He also said that Mr. MacGuire showed him a bank book with deposits of $64,000 to "take care of his [Butler's] expenses" at Chicago and several checks drawn for large amounts by Mr. Clark, Colonel Murphy and John Mills to be placed to Butler's account for expenses at Chicago. Later, General Butler added, Mr. MacGuire told him that the same people who financed "the Chicago propaganda" were going to finance the Fascist "march on Washington."

Representative John W. McCormack of Massachusetts, chairman, and Representative Samuel Dickstein of New York, vice chairman, were the only members of the House committee at yesterday's session. They heard General Butler for about two hours in the morning, Mr. MacGuire an equal period in the afternoon. They also heard Captain Samuel Glazier, in charge of the [Civilian Conservation Corps] camp at Elkridge, Md.

According to Representative Dickstein, General Butler in his testimony substantiated most of the statements attributed to him and denied none. Both members said that General Butler made it clear that he had flatly rejected all proposals from the Fascist group.

Mr. McCormack announced that the committee would make a thorough investigation of General Butler's charges.

"We have been in possession of certain information for about five weeks and have been investigating it. We will call all the men mentioned in the story, although Mr. Clark is reported to be in Europe."

"From present indications," said Mr. Dickstein, "Butler has the evidence. He's not going to make any serious charges unless he has something to back them up. We'll have men here with bigger names than his."

Mr. Dickstein said that about sixteen persons mentioned by General Butler to the committee would be subpoenaed, and that a public hearing might be held next Monday. Mr. MacGuire was directed to reappear before the committee at 2 o'clock this afternoon.

After testifying before the committee, Mr. MacGuire told reports that he was a personal friend of General Butler, and had last seen him about six months ago when he went to Philadelphia to sell some bonds. They talked about an adequate military force for the nation and world affairs in general, he said, and never discussed a Fascist army or movement.

Colonel Murphy specifically denied to reporters that he had financed any Fascist plot, and characterized the statement that he had made out a check for General Butler's Chicago expenses as "an absolute lie." He said that he did not know General Butler and had never heard of the reputed Fascist movement until yesterday's charges were published.

Colonel Murphy said that he voted for President Roosevelt in 1932. Newspaper clippings show that the Mr. Clark named by General Butler made a cash contribution of $10,000 to the Democratic National Committee last year.

★ ★ ★

## "A DREAM SO STRONG"

### Langston Hughes, "Let America Be America Again," *Esquire*—July 1936

---

The poet Langston Hughes (1901–1967), a key figure in the Harlem Renaissance, published these verses in *Esquire* in July 1936.

*Let America be America again.*
*Let it be the dream it used to be.*
*Let it be the pioneer on the plain*
*Seeking a home where he himself is free.*

*(America never was America to me.)*

*Let America be the dream the dreamers dreamed—*
*Let it be that great strong land of love*
*Where never kings connive nor tyrants scheme*
*That any man be crushed by one above.*

*(It never was America to me.)*

*O, let my land be a land where Liberty*
*Is crowned with no false patriotic wreath,*
*But opportunity is real, and life is free,*
*Equality is in the air we breathe.*

*(There's never been equality for me,*
*Nor freedom in this "homeland of the free.")*

Say, who are you that mumbles in the dark?
And who are you that draws your veil across the stars?

*I am the poor white, fooled and pushed apart,*
*I am the Negro bearing slavery's scars.*
*I am the red man driven from the land,*
*I am the immigrant clutching the hope I seek—*
*And finding only the same old stupid plan*
*Of dog eat dog, of mighty crush the weak.*

*I am the young man, full of strength and hope,*
*Tangled in that ancient endless chain*
*Of profit, power, gain, of grab the land!*
*Of grab the gold! Of grab the ways of satisfying need!*
*Of work the men! Of take the pay!*
*Of owning everything for one's own greed!*

*I am the farmer, bondsman to the soil.*
*I am the worker sold to the machine.*
*I am the Negro, servant to you all.*
*I am the people, humble, hungry, mean—*
*Hungry yet today despite the dream.*
*Beaten yet today—O, Pioneers!*

*I am the man who never got ahead,*
*The poorest worker bartered through the years.*

*Yet I'm the one who dreamt our basic dream*
*In the Old World while still a serf of kings,*
*Who dreamt a dream so strong, so brave, so true,*
*That even yet its mighty daring sings*
*In every brick and stone, in every furrow turned*
*That's made America the land it has become.*
*O, I'm the man who sailed those early seas*
*In search of what I meant to be my home—*
*For I'm the one who left dark Ireland's shore,*
*And Poland's plain, and England's grassy lea,*
*And torn from Black Africa's strand I came*
*To build a "homeland of the free."*

*The free?*

*Who said the free? Not me?*
*Surely not me? The millions on relief today?*
*The millions shot down when we strike?*
*The millions who have nothing for our pay?*
*For all the dreams we've dreamed*
*And all the songs we've sung*
*And all the hopes we've held*
*And all the flags we've hung,*
*The millions who have nothing for our pay—*
*Except the dream that's almost dead today.*

*O, let America be America again—*
*The land that never has been yet—*
*And yet must be—the land where every man is free.*
*The land that's mine—the poor man's, Indian's, Negro's, ME—*
*Who made America,*
*Whose sweat and blood, whose faith and pain,*
*Whose hand at the foundry, whose plow in the rain,*
*Must bring back our mighty dream again.*

*Sure, call me any ugly name you choose—*
*The steel of freedom does not stain.*
*From those who live like leeches on the people's lives,*
*We must take back our land again,*
*America!*

*O, yes,*
*I say it plain,*
*America never was America to me,*
*And yet I swear this oath—*
*America will be!*

*Out of the rack and ruin of our gangster death,*
*The rape and rot of graft, and stealth, and lies,*
*We, the people, must redeem*
*The land, the mines, the plants, the rivers.*
*The mountains and the endless plain—*
*All, all the stretch of these great green states—*
*And make America again!*

★ ★ ★

## "THE AMERICAN FUTURE"

### Franklin D. Roosevelt, Fireside Chat—September 3, 1939

Roosevelt addressed the nation two days after Nazi Germany invaded Poland.

TONIGHT MY SINGLE duty is to speak to the whole of America.

Until four-thirty this morning I had hoped against hope that some miracle would prevent a devastating war in Europe and bring to an end the invasion of Poland by Germany.

For four long years a succession of actual wars and constant crises have shaken the entire world and have threatened in each case to bring on the gigantic conflict which is today unhappily a fact.

It is right that I should recall to your minds the consistent and at times successful efforts of your Government in these crises to throw the full weight of the United States into the cause of peace. In spite of spreading wars I think that we have every right and every reason to maintain as a national policy the fundamental moralities, the teachings of religion [and] the continuation of efforts to restore peace, because some day, though the time may be distant, we can be of even greater help to a crippled humanity. . . .

You must master at the outset a simple but unalterable fact in modern foreign relations between nations. When peace has been broken anywhere, the peace of all countries everywhere is in danger.

It is easy for you and for me to shrug our shoulders and to say that conflicts taking place thousands of miles from the continental United States, and, indeed, thousands of miles from the whole American Hemisphere, do not seriously affect the Americas—and that all the United States has to do is to ignore them and go about its own business. Passionately though we may desire detachment, we are forced to realize that every word that comes through the air, every ship that sails the sea, every battle that is fought does affect the American future. . . .

This nation will remain a neutral nation, but I cannot ask that every American remain neutral in thought as well. Even a neutral has a right

*A brilliant communicator, FDR mastered the art of what became famously known as his fireside chats, an innovation that brought the presidency closer to the people.*

to take account of facts. Even a neutral cannot be asked to close his mind or close his conscience.

I have said not once but many times that I have seen war and that I hate war. I say that again and again.

I hope the United States will keep out of this war. I believe that it will. And I give you assurance and reassurance that every effort of your Government will be directed toward that end.

As long as it remains within my power to prevent, there will be no blackout of peace in the United States.

⋆ ⋆ ⋆

## "WE ARE ON THE VERGE OF WAR"
## Charles Lindbergh, Radio Address from Des Moines, Iowa—September 11, 1941

Charles Lindbergh (1902–1974), who became a global celebrity after a solo flight across the Atlantic in 1927, was a leader of the America First Committee, an isolationist movement that sought to keep the United States from intervening in World War II.

IT IS NOW two years since this latest European war began. From that day in September, 1939, until the present moment, there has been an ever-increasing effort to force the United States into the conflict.

That effort has been carried on by foreign interests, and by a small minority of our own people; but it has been so successful that, today, our country stands on the verge of war.

At this time, as the war is about to enter its third winter, it seems appropriate to review the circumstances that have led us to our present position. Why are we on the verge of war? Was it necessary for us to become so deeply involved? Who is responsible for changing our national policy from one of neutrality and independence to one of entanglement in European affairs?

Personally, I believe there is no better argument against our intervention than a study of the causes and developments of the present war.

*A national hero, Charles Lindbergh used his fame to argue against American involvement in what Winston Churchill later called "the gathering storm."*

I have often said that if the true facts and issues were placed before the American people, there would be no danger of our involvement.

Here, I would like to point out to you a fundamental difference between the groups who advocate foreign war, and those who believe in an independent destiny for America.

If you will look back over the record, you will find that those of us who oppose intervention have constantly tried to clarify facts and issues; while the interventionists have tried to hide facts and confuse issues.

We ask you to read what we said last month, last year, and even before the war began. Our record is open and clear, and we are proud of it.

We have not led you on by subterfuge and propaganda. We have not resorted to "steps short of" anything, in order to take the American people where they did not want to go.

What we said before the elections, we say "again, and again, and again" today. And we will not tell you tomorrow that it was "just campaign oratory." Have you ever heard an interventionist, or a British agent, or a member of the administration in Washington, ask you to go back and study a record of what they have said since the war started?

Are these self-styled defenders of democracy willing to put the issue of war to a vote of our people? Do you find these crusaders for foreign freedoms advocating the freedom of speech, or the removal of censorship here in our own country?

The subterfuge and propaganda that exists in our country is obvious on every side. Tonight, I shall try to pierce through a portion of it, to the naked facts which lie beneath.

When this war started in Europe, it was clear that the American people were solidly opposed to entering it. Why shouldn't we be? We had the best defensive position in the world; we had a tradition of independence from Europe; and the one time we did take part in a European war left European problems unsolved, and debts to America unpaid.

National polls showed that when England and France declared war on Germany, in 1939, less than 10 percent of our population favored a similar course for America.

But there were various groups of people, here and abroad, whose interests and beliefs necessitated the involvement of the United States in the war. I shall point out some of these groups tonight, and outline their methods of procedure. In doing this, I must speak with the utmost frankness, for in order to counteract their efforts, we must know exactly who they are.

The three most important groups who have been pressing this country toward war are the British, the Jewish, and the Roosevelt administration. . . .

First, the British: It is obvious and perfectly understandable, that Great Britain wants the United States in the war on her side.

England is now in a desperate position.

Her population is not large enough and her armies are not strong enough to invade the continent of Europe and win the war she declared against Germany.

Her geographical position is such that she cannot win the war by the use of aviation alone, regardless of how many planes we send her. Even if America entered the war, it is improbable that the Allied armies could invade Europe and overwhelm the Axis powers.

But one thing is certain. If England can draw this country into the war, she can shift to our shoulders a large portion of the responsibility for waging it, and for paying its cost.

As you all know, we were left with the debts of the last European war; and unless we are more cautious in the future than we have been in the past, we will be left with the debts of the present one. If it were not for her hope that she can make us responsible for the war financially, as well as militarily, I believe England would have negotiated a peace in Europe many months ago, and be better off for doing so.

England has devoted, and will continue to devote every effort to get us into the war. We know that she spent huge sums of money in this country during the last war in order to involve us. Englishmen have written books about the cleverness of its use.

We know that England is spending great sums of money for propaganda in America during the present war. If we were Englishmen, we would do the same.

But our interest is first in America; and, as Americans, it is essential for us to realize the effort that British interests are making to draw us into their war.

The second major group I mentioned is the Jewish.

It is not difficult to understand why Jewish people desire the overthrow of Nazi Germany. The persecution they suffered in Germany would be sufficient to make bitter enemies of any race.

No person with a sense of the dignity of mankind can condone the persecution of the Jewish race in Germany. But no person of honesty and vision can look on their pro-war policy here today without seeing the dangers involved in such a policy, both for us and for them.

Instead of agitating for war, the Jewish groups in this country should be opposing it in every possible way, for they will be among the first to feel its consequences.

Tolerance is a virtue that depends upon peace and strength. History shows that it cannot survive war and devastation.

A few far-sighted Jewish people realize this, and stand opposed to intervention. But the majority still do not.

Their greatest danger to this country lies in their large ownership and influence in our motion pictures, our press, our radio and our government.

I am not attacking either the Jewish or the British people. Both races, I admire.

But I am saying that the leaders of both the British and the Jewish races, for reasons which are as understandable from their viewpoint as they are inadvisable from ours, for reasons which are not American, wish to involve us in the war.

We cannot blame them for looking out for what they believe to be their own interests, but we also must look out for ours. We cannot allow the natural passions and prejudices of other peoples to lead our country to destruction.

The Roosevelt administration is the third powerful group which has been carrying this country toward war.

Its members have used the war emergency to obtain a third presidential term for the first time in American history. They have used the war to add unlimited billions to a debt which was already the highest we have ever known.

And they have used the war to justify the restriction of congressional power, and the assumption of dictatorial procedures on the part of the president and his appointees.

The power of the Roosevelt administration depends upon the maintenance of a wartime emergency.

The prestige of the Roosevelt administration depends upon the success of Great Britain to whom the president attached his political future at a time when most people thought that England and France would easily win the war.

The danger of the Roosevelt administration lies in its subterfuge.

While its members have promised us peace, they have led us to war—heedless of the platform upon which they were elected. . . .

We are on the verge of a war for which we are still unprepared, and for which no one has offered a feasible plan for victory—a war which cannot be won without sending our soldiers across the ocean to force a landing on a hostile coast against armies stronger than our own.

We are on the verge of war, but it is not yet too late to stay out.

It is not yet too late to show that no amount of money, or propaganda, or patronage can force a free and independent people into war against its will. It is not yet too late to retrieve and to maintain the independent American destiny that our forefathers established in this new world.

The entire future of America rests upon our shoulders. It depends upon our action, our courage, and our intelligence. If you oppose our intervention in the war, now is the time to make your voice heard.

★ ★ ★

**WESTERN DEFENSE COMMAND AND FOURTH ARMY**
**WARTIME CIVIL CONTROL ADMINISTRATION**

**Presidio of San Francisco, California**
**April 30, 1942**

# INSTRUCTIONS TO ALL PERSONS OF JAPANESE ANCESTRY

## Living in the Following Area:

All that portion of the County of Los Angeles, State of California, within the boundary beginning at the intersection of Western Avenue and Redondo Beach Boulevard, northwest of Gardena; thence easterly on Redondo Beach Boulevard and Compton Boulevard to Atlantic Boulevard; thence southerly on Atlantic Boulevard to Artesia Street; thence westerly on Artesia Street to Alameda Street; thence southerly on Alameda to Carson Street; thence westerly on Carson Street to a point at which a north-south line established by Western Avenue intersects Carson Street; thence northerly on said line and Western Avenue to the point of beginning.

Pursuant to the provisions of Civilian Exclusion Order No. 29, this Headquarters, dated April 30, 1942, all persons of Japanese ancestry, both alien and non-alien, will be evacuated from the above area by 12 o'clock noon, P. W. T., Thursday, May 7, 1942.

No Japanese person living in the above area will be permitted to change residence after 12 o'clock noon, P. W. T., Thursday, April 30, 1942, without obtaining special permission from the representative of the Commanding General, Southern California Sector, at the Civil Control Station located at:

16522 South Western Avenue,
Torrance, California.

Such permits will only be granted for the purpose of uniting members of a family, or in cases of grave emergency.

The Civil Control Station is equipped to assist the Japanese population affected by this evacuation in the following ways:

1. Give advice and instructions on the evacuation.
2. Provide services with respect to the management, leasing, sale, storage or other disposition of most kinds of property, such as real estate, business and professional equipment, household goods, boats, automobiles and livestock.
3. Provide temporary residence elsewhere for all Japanese in family groups.
4. Transport persons and a limited amount of clothing and equipment to their new residence.

**The Following Instructions Must Be Observed:**

1. A responsible member of each family, preferably the head of the family, or the person in whose name most of the property is held, and each individual living alone, will report to the Civil Control Station to receive further instructions. This must be done between 8:00 A. M. and 5:00 P. M. on Friday, May 1, 1942, or between 8:00 A. M. and 5:00 P. M. on Saturday, May 2, 1942.
2. Evacuees must carry with them on departure for the Assembly Center, the following property:
(a) Bedding and linens (no mattress) for each member of the family;
(b) Toilet articles for each member of the family;
(c) Extra clothing for each member of the family;
(d) Sufficient knives, forks, spoons, plates, bowls and cups for each member of the family;
(e) Essential personal effects for each member of the family.

All items carried will be securely packaged, tied and plainly marked with the name of the owner and numbered in accordance with instructions obtained at the Civil Control Station.

The size and number of packages is limited to that which can be carried by the individual or family group.

3. No pets of any kind will be permitted.
4. No personal items and no household goods will be shipped to the Assembly Center.
5. The United States Government through its agencies will provide for the storage at the sole risk of the owner of the more substantial household items, such as iceboxes, washing machines, pianos and other heavy furniture. Cooking utensils and other small items will be accepted for storage if crated, packed and plainly marked with the name and address of the owner. Only one name and address will be used by a given family.
6. Each family, and individual living alone, will be furnished transportation to the Assembly Center. Private means of transportation will not be utilized. All instructions pertaining to the movement will be obtained at the Civil Control Station.

**Go to the Civil Control Station between the hours of 8:00 A. M. and 5:00 P. M., Friday, May 1, 1942, or between the hours of 8:00 A. M. and 5:00 P. M., Saturday, May 2, 1942, to receive further instructions.**

J. L. DeWITT
Lieutenant General, U. S. Army
Commanding

SEE CIVILIAN EXCLUSION ORDER NO. 29.

*A directive pursuant to President Roosevelt's Executive Order 9066, a wartime measure to intern Americans of Japanese descent. In 1988, President Ronald Reagan would sign the Civil Liberties Act, a formal apology for the internment program, which, the law said, was the result of "racial prejudice, war hysteria, and a failure of political leadership."*

## "COLD-BLOODED EXTERMINATION"
## Joint Declaration by Members of the United Nations on Nazi Atrocities—December 17, 1942

In a statement, the Allied forces arrayed against Nazi Germany denounced the systematic persecution and wholesale murder of captured Jewish people in Europe.

THE ATTENTION OF the Belgian, Czechoslovak, Greek, Jugoslav, Luxembourg, Netherlands, Norwegian, Polish, Soviet, United Kingdom and United States Governments and also of the French National Committee has been drawn to numerous reports from Europe that the German authorities, not content with denying to persons of Jewish race in all the territories over which their barbarous rule has been extended, the most elementary human rights, are now carrying into effect Hitler's oft-repeated intention to exterminate the Jewish people in Europe.

From all the occupied countries Jews are being transported in conditions of appalling horror and brutality to Eastern Europe. In Poland, which has been made the principal Nazi slaughterhouse, the ghettos established by the German invader are being systematically emptied of all Jews except a few highly skilled workers required for war industries. None of those taken away are ever heard of again. The able-bodied are slowly worked to death in labour camps. The infirm are left to die of exposure and starvation or are deliberately massacred in mass executions. The number of victims of these bloody cruelties is reckoned in many hundreds of thousands of entirely innocent men, women and children.

The above-mentioned governments and the French National Committee condemn in the strongest possible terms this bestial policy of cold-blooded extermination. They declare that such events can only strengthen the resolve of all freedom-loving peoples to overthrow the barbarous Hitlerite tyranny. They reaffirm their solemn resolution to insure that those responsible for these crimes shall not escape retribution, and to press on with the necessary practical measures to this end.

★ ★ ★

## "DEMOCRACY IS A LETTER TO THE EDITOR"

### E. B. White, "The Meaning of Democracy," *The New Yorker*—July 3, 1943

Elwyn Brooks White (1899–1985) was a longtime staff writer for *The New Yorker* magazine as well as an essayist for *Harper's*.

We received a letter from the Writers' War Board the other day asking for a statement on "The Meaning of Democracy." It presumably is our duty to comply with such a request, and it is certainly our pleasure.

Surely the Board knows what democracy is. It is the line that forms on the right. It is the don't in don't shove. It is the hole in the stuffed shirt through which the sawdust slowly trickles; it is the dent in the high hat. Democracy is the recurrent suspicion that more than half of the people are right more than half of the time. It is the feeling of privacy in the voting booths, the feeling of communion in the libraries, the feeling of vitality everywhere. Democracy is a letter to the editor. Democracy is the score at the beginning of the ninth. It is an idea which hasn't been disproved yet, a song the words of which have not gone bad. It's the mustard on the hot dog and the cream in the rationed coffee. Democracy is a request from a War Board, in the middle of a morning in the middle of a war, wanting to know what democracy is.

* * *

## "LET OUR HEARTS BE STOUT"

### Franklin D. Roosevelt, Prayer on D-Day Delivered by Radio from the White House—June 6, 1944

Roosevelt wrote this prayer the weekend before the launch of Operation Overlord, the Allied attack on the northern coast of France. These were the only words he spoke in public on the day of the invasion.

Almighty God: Our sons, pride of our nation, this day have set upon a mighty endeavor, a struggle to preserve our Republic, our religion, and our civilization, and to set free a suffering humanity.

Lead them straight and true; give strength to their arms, stoutness to their hearts, steadfastness in their faith.

They will need Thy blessings. Their road will be long and hard. For the enemy is strong. He may hurl back our forces. Success may not come with rushing speed, but we shall return again and again; and we know that by Thy grace, and by the righteousness of our cause, our sons will triumph.

They will be sore tried, by night and by day, without rest—until the victory is won. The darkness will be rent by noise and flame. Men's souls will be shaken with the violences of war.

For these men are lately drawn from the ways of peace. They fight not for the lust of conquest. They fight to end conquest. They fight to liberate. They fight to let justice arise, and tolerance and good will among all Thy people. They yearn but for the end of battle, for their return to the haven of home.

Some will never return. Embrace these, Father, and receive them, Thy heroic servants, into Thy kingdom.

And for us at home—fathers, mothers, children, wives, sisters, and brothers of brave men overseas, whose thoughts and prayers are ever with them—help us, Almighty God, to rededicate ourselves in renewed faith in Thee in this hour of great sacrifice.

Many people have urged that I call the nation into a single day of special prayer. But because the road is long and the desire is great, I ask that our people devote themselves in a continuance of prayer. As we rise to each new day, and again when each day is spent, let words of prayer be on our lips, invoking Thy help to our efforts.

Give us strength, too—strength in our daily tasks, to redouble the contributions we make in the physical and the material support of our armed forces.

And let our hearts be stout, to wait out the long travail, to bear sorrows that may come, to impart our courage unto our sons wheresoever they may be.

And, O Lord, give us faith. Give us faith in Thee; faith in our sons; faith in each other; faith in our united crusade. Let not the keenness of our spirit ever be dulled. Let not the impacts of temporary events, of

*On Tuesday, June 6, 1944, Allied forces struck the beaches of Normandy in what General Eisenhower called "the Great Crusade" to liberate Europe from Nazi tyranny.*

temporal matters of but fleeting moment—let not these deter us in our unconquerable purpose.

With Thy blessing, we shall prevail over the unholy forces of our enemy. Help us to conquer the apostles of greed and racial arrogancies. Lead us to the saving of our country, and with our sister nations into a world unity that will spell a sure peace—a peace invulnerable to the schemings of unworthy men. And a peace that will let all of men live in freedom, reaping the just rewards of their honest toil.

Thy will be done, Almighty God.

Amen.

★ ★ ★

## "THE THINGS I SAW BEGGAR DESCRIPTION"
## Dwight D. Eisenhower to George C. Marshall, Jr., on a Nazi Concentration Camp—April 15, 1945

As supreme commander of the Allied Expeditionary Force in Europe, General Dwight D. Eisenhower (1890–1969) toured a satellite camp of the Buchenwald death complex in the weeks before the German surrender.

*On Thursday, April 12, 1945—the same day FDR died in Warm Springs, Georgia—Eisenhower, along with Generals George Patton and Omar Bradley, toured Ohrdruf, a Nazi concentration camp that had been liberated by American forces.*

THE MOST INTERESTING—although horrible—sight that I encountered during the trip was a visit to a German internment camp near Gotha. The things I saw beggar description. While I was touring the camp I encountered three men who had been inmates and by one ruse or another had made their escape. I interviewed them through an interpreter. The visual evidence and the verbal testimony of starvation, cruelty and bestiality were so overpowering as to leave me a bit sick. In one room, where they were piled up twenty or thirty naked men, killed by starvation, George Patton would not even enter. He said he would get sick if he did so. I made the visit deliberately, in order to be in position to give first-hand evidence of these things if ever, in the future, there develops a tendency to charge these allegations merely to "propaganda."

If you could see your way clear to do it, I think you should make a visit here at the earliest possible moment, while we are still conducting a general offensive. You would be proud of the Army you have produced.

★ ★ ★

## "A GRAVE RESPONSIBILITY"

### U.S. Supreme Court Justice Robert H. Jackson, Opening Statement Before the International Military Tribunal at Nuremberg, Germany—November 21, 1945

Dispatched by President Harry S. Truman to the International Military Tribunal in Nuremberg, Germany, to try the leaders of the Nazi regime, Robert H. Jackson (1892–1954), an FDR-appointed associate justice of the Supreme Court, articulated a new vision of international law, including "crimes against humanity."

MAY IT PLEASE Your Honors: The privilege of opening the first trial in history for crimes against the peace of the world imposes a grave responsibility. The wrongs which we seek to condemn and punish have been so calculated, so malignant, and so devastating, that civilization cannot tolerate their being ignored, because it cannot survive their being repeated. That four great nations, flushed with victory and stung with injury stay the hand of vengeance and voluntarily submit their captive enemies to the judgment of the law is one of the most significant tributes that Power has ever paid to Reason.

In the prisoners' dock sit twenty-odd broken men. Reproached by the humiliation of those they have led almost as bitterly as by the desolation of those they have attacked, their personal capacity for evil is forever past. It is hard now to perceive in these men as captives the

*Defendants in the dock at Nuremberg, Germany; judges from the United States, the Soviet Union, Great Britain, and France presided over the trials.*

power by which as Nazi leaders they once dominated much of the world and terrified most of it. Merely as individuals their fate is of little consequence to the world.

What makes this inquest significant is that these prisoners represent sinister influences that will lurk in the world long after their bodies have returned to dust. We will show them to be living symbols of racial hatreds, of terrorism and violence, and of the arrogance and cruelty of power. They are symbols of fierce nationalisms and of militarism, of intrigue and war-making which have embroiled Europe generation after generation, crushing its manhood, destroying its homes, and impoverishing its life. They have so identified themselves with the philosophies they conceived and with the forces they directed that any tenderness to them is a victory and an encouragement to all the evils which are attached to their names. Civilization can afford no compromise with the social forces which would gain renewed strength if we deal ambiguously or indecisively with the men in whom those forces now precariously survive.

What these men stand for we will patiently and temperately disclose. We will give you undeniable proofs of incredible events. The catalog of crimes will omit nothing that could be conceived by a pathological pride, cruelty, and lust for power. These men created in Germany, under the "Führerprinzip," a National Socialist despotism equaled only by the dynasties of the ancient East. They took from the German people all those dignities and freedoms that we hold natural and inalienable rights in every human being. The people were compensated by inflaming and gratifying hatreds towards those who were marked as "scapegoats." Against their opponents, including Jews, Catholics, and free labor, the Nazis directed such a campaign of arrogance, brutality, and annihilation as the world has not witnessed since the pre-Christian ages. They excited the German ambition to be a "master race," which of course implies serfdom for others. They led their people on a mad gamble for domination. They diverted social energies and resources to the creation of what they thought to be an invincible war machine. They overran their neighbors. To sustain the "master race" in its war-making, they enslaved millions of human beings and brought them into Germany, where these hapless creatures now wander as "displaced persons." At length bestiality and bad faith reached such excess that they aroused the sleeping strength of imperiled Civilization. Its united efforts have ground the German war machine to fragments. But the struggle has left Europe a liberated yet prostrate land where a demoralized society struggles to survive. These are the fruits of the sinister forces that sit with these defendants in the prisoners' dock. . . .

We would also make clear that we have no purpose to incriminate the whole German people. We know that the Nazi Party was not put in power by a majority of the German vote. We know it came to power by an evil alliance between the most extreme of the Nazi revolutionists, the most unrestrained of the German reactionaries, and the most aggressive of the German militarists. If the German populace had willingly accepted the Nazi program, no Storm-troopers would have been needed in the early days of the Party and there would have been no need for concentration camps or the Gestapo, both of which institutions were inaugurated as soon as the Nazis gained control of the German State. Only after these lawless innovations proved successful at home were they taken abroad.

The German people should know by now that the people of the United States hold them in no fear, and in no hate. It is true that the

Germans have taught us the horrors of modern warfare, but the ruin that lies from the Rhine to the Danube shows that we, like our Allies, have not been dull pupils. If we are not awed by German fortitude and proficiency in war, and if we are not persuaded of their political maturity, we do respect their skill in the arts of peace, their technical competence, and the sober, industrious, and self-disciplined character of the masses of the German people. In 1933 we saw the German people recovering prestige in the commercial, industrial, and artistic world after the set-back of the last war. We beheld their progress neither with envy nor malice. The Nazi regime interrupted this advance. The recoil of the Nazi aggression has left Germany in ruins. The Nazi readiness to pledge the German word without hesitation and to break it without shame has fastened upon German diplomacy a reputation for duplicity that will handicap it for years. Nazi arrogance has made the boast of the "master race" a taunt that will be thrown at Germans the world over for generations. The Nazi nightmare has given the German name a new and sinister significance throughout the world which will retard Germany a century. The German, no less than the non-German world, has accounts to settle with these defendants.

The fact of the war and the course of the war, which is the central theme of our case, is history. From September 1st, 1939, when the German armies crossed the Polish frontier, until September 1942, when they met epic resistance at Stalingrad, German arms seemed invincible. Denmark and Norway, the Netherlands and France, Belgium and Luxembourg, the Balkans and Africa, Poland and the Baltic States, and parts of Russia, all had been overrun and conquered by swift, powerful, well-aimed blows. That attack on the peace of the world is the crime against international society which brings into international cognizance crimes in its aid and preparation which otherwise might be only internal concerns. It was aggressive war, which the nations of the world had renounced. It was war in violation of treaties, by which the peace of the world was sought to be safe-guarded.

This war did not just happen—it was planned and prepared for over a long period of time and with no small skill and cunning. The world has perhaps never seen such a concentration and stimulation of the energies of any people as that which enabled Germany 20 years after it was defeated, disarmed, and dismembered to come so near carrying out its plan to dominate Europe. Whatever else we may say of those who were the authors of this war, they did achieve a stupendous work in organization, and our first task is to examine the means by which these defendants and their fellow conspirators prepared and incited Germany to go to war. . . .

The chief instrumentality of cohesion in plan and action was the National Socialist German Workers Party, known as the Nazi Party. Some of the defendants were with it from the beginning. Others joined only after success seemed to have validated its lawlessness or power had invested it with immunity from the processes of the law. Adolf Hitler became its supreme leader or "Führer" in 1921.

On the 24th of February 1920, at Munich, it publicly had proclaimed its program. Some of its purposes would commend themselves to many good citizens, such as the demands for "profit-sharing in the great industries," "generous development of provision for old age," "creation and maintenance of a healthy middle class," "a land reform suitable to our national requirements," and "raising the standard of health." It also made a strong appeal to that sort of nationalism which in ourselves we call patriotism and in our rivals chauvinism. It demanded "equality of rights for the German people in its dealing with other nations, and the abolition of the peace treaties of Versailles and St. Germain." It demanded the "union of all Germans on the basis of the right of self-determination of peoples to form a Great Germany." It demanded "land and territory (colonies) for the enrichment of our people and the settlement of our surplus population." All of these, of course, were legitimate objectives if they were to be attained without resort to aggressive warfare.

The Nazi Party from its inception, however, contemplated war. It demanded the "abolition of mercenary troops and the formation of a national army." . . .

The Nazi Party declaration also committed its members to an anti-Semitic program. It declared that no Jew or any person of non-German blood could be a member of the nation. Such persons to be disfranchised, disqualified for office, subject to the alien laws, and entitled to nourishment only after the German population had first been provided for. All who had entered Germany after August 2, 1914, were to be required forthwith to depart, and all non-German immigration was to be prohibited. . . .

The forecast of religious persecution was clothed in the language of religious liberty, for the Nazi program stated, "We demand liberty for all religious denominations in the State." But, it continues with the limitation, "so far as they are not a danger to it and do not militate against the morality and moral sense of the German race."

The Party program foreshadowed the campaign of terrorism. It announced, "We demand ruthless war upon those whose activities are injurious to the common interests," and it demanded that such offenses be punished with death. . . .

The most savage and numerous crimes planned and committed by the Nazis were those against the Jews. Those in Germany in 1933 numbered about 500,000. In the aggregate, they had made for themselves positions which excited envy, and had accumulated properties which excited the avarice of the Nazis. They were few enough to be helpless and numerous enough to be held up as a menace.

Let there be no misunderstanding about the charge of persecuting Jews. What we charge against these defendants is not those arrogances and pretensions which frequently accompany the intermingling of different peoples and which are likely, despite the honest efforts of government, to produce regrettable crimes and convulsions. It is my purpose to show a plan and design, to which all Nazis were fanatically committed, to annihilate all Jewish people. . . .

Anti-Semitism also has been aptly credited with being a "spearhead of terror." The ghetto was the laboratory for testing repressive measures. Jewish property was the first to be expropriated, but the custom grew and included similar measures against anti-Nazi Germans, Poles, Czechs, Frenchmen, and Belgians. Extermination of the Jews enabled the Nazis to bring a practiced hand to similar measures against Poles, Serbs, and Greeks. The plight of the Jew was a constant threat to opposition or discontent among other elements of Europe's population—pacifists, conservatives, Communists, Catholics, Protestants, Socialists. . . .

On December 7th, 1941, a day which the late President Roosevelt declared "will live in infamy," victory for German aggression seemed certain. The Wehrmacht was at the gates of Moscow. Taking advantage of the situation, and while her plenipotentiaries were creating a diplomatic diversion in Washington, Japan without declaration of war treacherously attacked the United States at Pearl Harbor and the Philippines. Attacks followed swiftly on the British Commonwealth, and The Netherlands in the Southwest Pacific. These aggressions were met in the only way that they could be met, with instant declarations of war and with armed resistance which mounted slowly through many long months of reverses until finally the Axis was crushed to earth and deliverance for its victims was won.

SECU
FORT MO
SUSP
RESTOR
FULL SEC
NO. OF C
DISCIPL
ESTIMAT
NO. OF
FROM
ESTIM

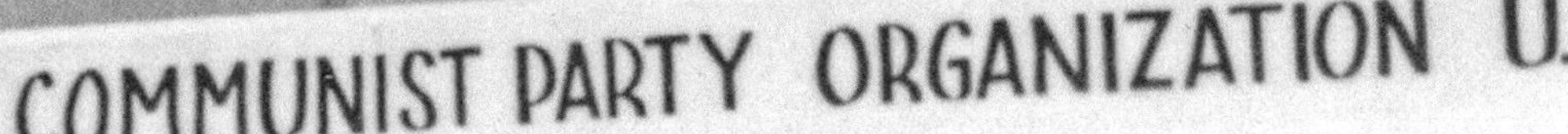


PART VII

# VICTORY AND CONSPIRACY

## *1945–1962*

No one race and no one people can claim to have done all the work to achieve greater dignity for human beings and great freedom to develop human personality. In each generation and in each country there must be a continuation of the struggle and new steps forward must be taken since this is preeminently a field in which to stand still is to retreat.

—Eleanor Roosevelt, 1948

PREVIOUS SPREAD: *The Red-hunting led by Senator Joseph R. McCarthy, Republican of Wisconsin, defined an era; he was a dominant factor in American politics from 1950 until 1954, when he was censured by a vote of his Senate colleagues.*

THE REPORTS WERE SHOCKING. On Friday, April 12, 1945, while staying at his cottage in Warm Springs, Georgia, Franklin Roosevelt died after being stricken by a cerebral hemorrhage. He had been president for a dozen years. "I couldn't believe it when somebody told me he was dead," the Roosevelt adviser Robert E. Sherwood recalled. "Like everybody else, I listened and listened to the radio, waiting for the announcement—probably in his own gaily reassuring voice—that it had all been a big mistake . . . and everything was going to be 'fine—grand—perfectly bully.'" But there would be no such announcement. A new era had begun.

Roosevelt left the stage at a perilous moment. The Allied forces were nearing victory over Germany, and the war in Europe would be over in a matter of weeks. Japan remained a live and formidable combatant, however, and the tensions that would soon define the Cold War with the Soviet Union were already evident. Conservatives in the United States believed Roosevelt had been overly accommodating to Joseph Stalin in the February 1945 summit meeting at Yalta—a feeling that helped drive the anti-Communist fervor of the ensuing years.

Roosevelt's successor, Harry Truman, was an architect of a new international order that rallied Western nations against Soviet aggression. From the Marshall Plan to the North Atlantic Treaty Organization (NATO), the United States would not repeat the mistakes of the isolationist 1920s. Truman was also forward-leaning on civil rights at home as Black Americans took the lead in campaigning for full inclusion in the life of the nation.

The Communist threat, the specter of nuclear war, and the shifting landscape at home fed a climate of fear and distrust. On returning to the United States from Europe, William L. Shirer of CBS, who had covered the rise of Nazi Germany, observed: "There was an atmosphere throughout the land [in the America of the early 1950s] of suspicion, intolerance, and fear that puzzled me. I had seen these poisons grow into ugly witch hunting and worse in the totalitarian lands abroad, but I was not prepared to find them taking root in our own splendid democracy." Conspiracy theories swept the country. From Robert Welch's right-wing John Birch Society to Senator Joseph McCarthy's campaign of innuendo, a sizable number of Americans chose to believe that their government itself was corrupt and rife with Communists.

President Dwight D. Eisenhower was often a target of such fevered and baseless charges, as was General George C. Marshall, Jr., who had served as secretary of state under President Truman. McCarthy was a master of the means of mass media, making headline-grabbing allegations and rarely following them up with facts. The headlines, he believed, were enough to accomplish his ends—ends that included possibly becoming president in 1956. An early opponent was Senator Margaret Chase Smith, Republican of Maine, who issued a courageous "Declaration of Conscience" as early as June 1950—four years before the Senate would at last vote to censure McCarthy, ending his reign of terror. Roy Cohn, McCarthy's counsel, later recalled a number of the reasons for the senator's fall. "He was impatient, overly aggressive, overly dramatic," Cohn wrote. "He acted on impulse. He tended to sensationalize the evidence he had—in order to draw attention to the rock-bottom seriousness of the situation. He would neglect to do important homework and consequently would, on occasion, make challengeable statements."

McCarthy and Welch were clear emblems of what the historian Richard Hofstadter would call "pseudo-conservatism," a collection of beliefs and impulses that ranged far beyond the classical conservative tradition of skepticism about large-scale public enterprises. "We have, at all times," Hofstadter observed in 1954, "two kinds of processes going on in inextricable connection with each other: *interest politics,* the clash of material aims and needs among various groups and blocs; and *status politics,* the clash of various projective rationalizations arising from status aspirations and other personal motives." The placid postwar years, then, were anything but.

★ ★ ★

## "AGAINST HUNGER, POVERTY, DESPERATION AND CHAOS"

### George C. Marshall, Jr., Commencement Address, Harvard University—June 5, 1947

George Marshall (1880–1959) had served as the chief of staff of the U.S. Army during World War II and become secretary of state in early 1947. Faced with a starving and desolate Europe, the Truman administration proposed a generous plan of aid—not least to build support for the Western democracies against the threat of Communist domination.

I NEED NOT TELL you gentlemen that the world situation is very serious. That must be apparent to all intelligent people. I think one difficulty is that the problem is one of such enormous complexity that the very mass of facts presented to the public by press and radio make it exceedingly difficult for the man in the street to reach a clear appraisement of the situation. Furthermore, the people of this country are distant from the troubled areas of the earth and it is hard for them to comprehend the plight and consequent reactions of the long-suffering peoples, and the effect of those reactions on their governments in connection with our efforts to promote peace in the world.

In considering the requirements for the rehabilitation of Europe, the physical loss of life, the visible destruction of cities, factories, mines and railroads was correctly estimated, but it has become obvious during recent months that this visible destruction was probably less serious than the dislocation of the entire fabric of European economy. For the past ten years conditions have been highly abnormal. The feverish preparation for war and the more feverish maintenance of the war effort engulfed all aspects of national economies. Machinery has fallen into disrepair or is entirely obsolete. Under the arbitrary and destructive Nazi rule, virtually every possible enterprise was geared into the German war machine. Long-standing commercial ties, private institutions, banks, insurance companies and shipping companies disappeared, through loss of capital, absorption through nationalization or by simple destruction. In many countries, confidence in the local currency has been severely shaken. The breakdown of the business structure of Europe during the war was complete. Recovery has been seriously retarded by the fact that two years after the close of hostilities a peace settlement with Germany and Austria has not been agreed upon. But even given a more prompt solution of these difficult problems, the rehabilitation of the economic structure of Europe quite evidently will require a much longer time and greater effort than had been foreseen.

There is a phase of this matter which is both interesting and serious. The farmer has always produced the foodstuffs to exchange with the city dweller for the other necessities of life. This division of labor is the basis of modern civilization. At the present time it is threatened with breakdown. The town and city industries are not producing adequate goods to exchange with the food-producing farmer. Raw materials and fuel are in short supply. Machinery is lacking or worn out. The farmer or the peasant cannot find the goods for sale which he desires to purchase. So the sale of his farm produce for money which he cannot use seems to him an unprofitable transaction. He, therefore, has withdrawn many fields from crop cultivation and is using them for grazing. He feeds more grain to stock and finds for himself and his family an ample supply of food, however short he may be on clothing and the other ordinary gadgets of civilization. Meanwhile people in the cities are short of food and fuel. So the governments are forced to use their foreign money and credits to procure these necessities abroad. This process exhausts funds which are urgently needed for reconstruction. This is a very serious situation [which] is rapidly developing which bodes no good for the world. The modern system of the division of labor upon which the exchange of products is based is in danger of breaking down.

The truth of the matter is that Europe's requirements for the next three or four years of foreign food and other essential products—principally from America—are so much greater than her present ability to pay that she must have substantial additional help, or face economic, social and political deterioration of a very grave character.

The remedy lies in breaking the vicious circle and restoring the confidence of the European people in the economic future of their own countries and of Europe as a whole. The manufacturer and the farmer throughout wide areas must be able and willing to exchange their products for currencies the continuing value of which is not open to question.

Aside from the demoralizing effect on the world at large and the possibilities of disturbances arising as a result of the desperation of the people concerned, the consequences to the economy of the United States should be apparent to all. It is logical that the United States should do whatever it is able to do to assist in the return of normal economic health in the world, without which there can be no political stability and no assured peace. Our policy is directed not against any country or doctrine but against hunger, poverty, desperation and chaos. Its purpose should be the revival of a working economy in the world so as to permit the emergence of political and social conditions in which free institutions can exist. Such assistance, I am convinced, must not be on a piecemeal basis as various crises develop. Any assistance that this Government may render in the future should provide a cure rather than a mere palliative. Any government that is willing to assist in the task of recovery will find full cooperation, I am sure, on the part of the United States Government. Any government which maneuvers to block the recovery of other countries cannot expect help from us. Furthermore, governments, political parties or groups which seek to perpetuate human misery in order to profit therefrom politically or otherwise will encounter the opposition of the United States.

It is already evident that, before the United States Government can proceed much further in its efforts to alleviate the situation and help start the European world on its way to recovery, there must be some agreement among the countries of Europe as to the requirements of the situation and the part those countries themselves will take in order to give proper effect to whatever action might be undertaken by this Government. It would be neither fitting nor efficacious for this Government to undertake to draw up unilaterally a program designed to place Europe on its feet economically. This is the business of the Europeans. The initiative, I think, must come from Europe. The role of this country should consist of friendly aid in the drafting of a European program and of later support of such a program so far as it may be practical for us to do so. The program should be a joint one, agreed to by a number, if not all European nations.

An essential part of any successful action on the part of the United States is an understanding on the part of the people of America of the character of the problem and the remedies to be applied. Political passion and prejudice should have no part. With foresight, and a willingness on the part of our people to face up to the vast responsibility which history has clearly placed upon our country, the difficulties I have outlined can and will be overcome.

★ ★ ★

## "I MEAN ALL AMERICANS"

### Harry S. Truman, Remarks to the National Association for the Advancement of Colored People, the Lincoln Memorial, Washington, D.C.—June 29, 1947

In 1944, Harry S. Truman (1884–1972), a senator from Missouri, joined the Democratic ticket as FDR's third (and final) vice presidential running mate. After succeeding to the presidency upon Roosevelt's death the next year, Truman desegregated the U.S. military, proposed wide-ranging civil-rights measures, and, in 1947, became the first president to address the NAACP.

I SHOULD LIKE TO talk to you briefly about civil rights and human freedom. It is my deep conviction that we have reached a turning point in the long history of our country's efforts to guarantee a freedom and equality to all our citizens. Recent events in the United States and abroad have made us realize that it is more important today than ever before to insure that all Americans enjoy these rights.

And when I say all Americans—I mean all Americans.

The civil rights laws written in the early years of our republic, and the traditions which have been built upon them, are precious to us. Those laws were drawn up with the memory still fresh in men's minds of the tyranny of an absentee government. They were written to protect the citizen against any possible tyrannical act by the new government in this country.

But we cannot be content with a civil liberties program, which emphasizes only the need of protection against the possibility of tyranny by the Government.

*President Truman speaks to the National Association for the Advancement of Colored People from the steps of the Lincoln Memorial in Washington, D.C., in June 1947.*

We cannot stop there.

We must keep moving forward, with new concepts of civil rights to safeguard our heritage. The extension of civil rights today means, not protection of the people against the Government, but protection of the people by the Government.

We must make the Federal Government a friendly, vigilant defender of the rights and equalities of all Americans. And again I mean all Americans.

As Americans, we believe that every man should be free to live his life as he wishes. He should be limited only by his responsibility to his fellow countrymen. If this freedom is to be more than a dream, each man must be guaranteed equality of opportunity. The only limit to an American's achievement should be his ability, his industry and his character. The rewards for his effort should be determined only by these truly relevant qualities.

Our immediate task is to remove the last remnants of the barriers which stand between millions of our citizens and their birthright. There is no justifiable reason for discrimination because of ancestry, or religion, or race, or color.

We must not tolerate such limitations on the freedom of any of our people and on their enjoyment of the basic rights, which every citizen in a truly democratic society must possess.

Every man should have the right to a decent home, the right to an education, the right to adequate medical care, the right to a worthwhile job, the right to an equal share in the making of public decisions through the ballot, and the right to a fair trial in a fair court.

We must insure that these rights—on equal terms—are enjoyed by every citizen.

To these principles I pledge my full and continued support.

Many of our people still suffer the indignity of insult, the harrowing fear of intimidation, and, I regret to say, the threat of physical injury and mob violence. The prejudice and intolerance in which these evils are rooted still exist. The conscience of our nation, and the legal machinery which enforces it, have not yet secured to each citizen full freedom from fear.

We cannot wait another decade or another generation to remedy those evils. We must work, as never before, to cure them now. The aftermath of war and the desire to keep faith with our nation's historic principles make the need a pressing one.

The support of desperate populations of battle-ravaged countries must be won for the free way of life. We must have them as allies in our continuing struggle for the peaceful solution of the world's problems. Freedom is not an easy lesson to teach, nor an easy cause to sell, to peoples beset by every kind of privation. They may surrender to the false security offered so temptingly by totalitarian regimes unless we can prove the superiority of democracy.

Our case for democracy should be as strong as we can make it. It should rest on practical evidence that we have been able to put our house in order.

For these compelling reasons, we can no longer afford the luxury of a leisurely attack upon prejudice and discrimination. There is much that State and local governments can do in providing positive safeguards for civil rights. But we cannot, any longer, await the growth of a will to action in the slowest state of the most backward community.

Our National Government must show the way.

This is a difficult and complex undertaking. Federal laws and administrative machineries must be improved and expanded. We must provide the government with better tools to do the job. As a first step, I appointed an Advisory Committee on Civil Rights last December. Its members, fifteen distinguished private citizens, have been surveying our civil rights difficulties and needs for several months. I am confident that the product of their work will be a sensible and vigorous program for action by all of us.

We must strive to advance civil rights wherever it lies within our power. For example, I have asked the Congress to pass legislation extending basic civil rights to the people of Guam and American Samoa so that these people can share our ideals of freedom and self-government. This step, with others which will follow, is evidence to the rest of the world of our confidence in the ability of all men to build free institutions.

The way ahead is not easy. We shall need all the wisdom, imagination and courage we can muster. We must and shall guarantee the civil rights of all our citizens. Never before has the need been so urgent for skillful and vigorous action to bring us closer to our ideal.

We can reach the goal. When past difficulties faced our Nation, we met the challenge with inspiring charters of human rights—the Declaration of Independence, the Constitution, the Bill of Rights and the Emancipation Proclamation. . . .

With these noble charters to guide us, and with faith in our hearts, we shall make our land a happier home for our people, a symbol of hope for all men, and a rock of security in a troubled world.

★ ★ ★

## "WE STAND FOR THE SEGREGATION OF THE RACES"
## Platform of the States' Rights Democratic (Dixiecrat) Party—August 14, 1948

Led by South Carolina governor Strom Thurmond (1902–2003), a group of Southern Democrats left the party's national convention in 1948 to protest President Truman's pro-civil-rights platform plank. The rebels formed what was popularly known as the Dixiecrat party; the ticket of Thurmond and Mississippi governor Fielding Wright (1895–1956) carried Alabama, Louisiana, Mississippi, and South Carolina in the general election that fall.

(1) We believe that the Constitution of the United States is the greatest charter of human liberty ever conceived by the mind of man.

(2) We oppose all efforts to invade or destroy the rights guaranteed by it to every citizen of this republic.

(3) We stand for social and economic justice, which, we believe can be guaranteed to all citizens only by a strict adherence to our Constitution and the avoidance of any invasion or destruction of the constitutional rights of the states and individuals. We oppose the totalitarian, centralized bureaucratic government and the police nation called for by the platforms adopted by the Democratic and Republican Conventions.

(4) We stand for the segregation of the races and the racial integrity of each race; the constitutional right to choose one's associates; to accept private employment without governmental interference, and to earn one's living in any lawful way. We oppose the elimination of segregation, the repeal of miscegenation statutes, the control of private employment by Federal bureaucrats called for by the misnamed civil rights program. We favor home-rule, local self-government and a minimum interference with individual rights.

(5) We oppose and condemn the action of the Democratic Convention in sponsoring a civil rights program calling for the elimination of segregation, social equality by Federal fiat, regulations of private employment practices, voting, and local law enforcement.

(6) We affirm that the effective enforcement of such a program

*The beginning of the end of Jim Crow segregation in the American South after World War II prompted a ferocious white backlash that often deployed Confederate symbolism.*

would be utterly destructive of the social, economic and political life of the Southern people, and of other localities in which there may be differences in race, creed or national origin in appreciable numbers.

(7) We stand for the checks and balances provided by the three departments of our government. We oppose the usurpation of legislative functions by the executive and judicial departments. We unreservedly condemn the effort to establish in the United States a police nation that would destroy the last vestige of liberty enjoyed by a citizen.

(8) We demand that there be returned to the people to whom of right they belong, those powers needed for the preservation of human rights and the discharge of our responsibility as democrats for human welfare. We oppose a denial of those by political parties, a barter or sale of those rights by a political convention, as well as any invasion or violation of those rights by the Federal Government. We call upon all Democrats and upon all other loyal Americans who are opposed to totalitarianism at home and abroad to unite with us in ignominiously defeating Harry S. Truman, Thomas E. Dewey and every other candidate for public office who would establish a Police Nation in the United States of America.

(9) We, therefore, urge that this Convention endorse the candidacies of J. Strom Thurmond and Fielding H. Wright for the President and Vice-president, respectively, of the United States of America.

★ ★ ★

## "WHAT FREEDOM IS"
### Eleanor Roosevelt, "The Struggle for Human Rights," Address at the Sorbonne, Paris, France—September 28, 1948

Eleanor Roosevelt (1884–1962) chaired the United Nations Commission on Human Rights and served as its first U.S. representative from 1947 to 1953.

*"The story," Eleanor Roosevelt told reporters after FDR's death, "is over." But it wasn't: The former First Lady remained in the arena for the rest of her life.*

I HAVE COME THIS evening to talk with you on one of the greatest issues of our time—that is the preservation of human freedom. I have chosen to discuss it here in France, at the Sorbonne, because here in this soil the roots of human freedom have long ago struck deep and here they have been richly nourished. It was here the Declaration of the Rights of Man was proclaimed, and the great slogans of the French Revolution—liberty, equality, fraternity—fired the imagination of men. I have chosen to discuss this issue in Europe because this has been the scene of the greatest historic battles between freedom and tyranny. I have chosen to discuss it in the early days of the General Assembly because the issue of human liberty is decisive for the settlement of outstanding political differences and for the future of the United Nations.

The decisive importance of this issue was fully recognized by the founders of the United Nations at San Francisco. Concern for the preservation and promotion of human rights and fundamental freedoms stands at the heart of the United Nations. Its Charter is distinguished by its preoccupation with the rights and welfare of individual men and women. The United Nations has made it clear that it intends to uphold human rights and to protect the dignity of the human personality. In the preamble to the Charter the keynote is set when it declares: "We the people of the United Nations determined . . . to reaffirm faith in fundamental human rights, in the dignity and worth of the human person, in the equal rights of men and women and of nations large and small, and . . . to promote social progress and better standards of life in larger freedom." This reflects the basic premise of the Charter that the peace and security of mankind are dependent on mutual respect for the rights and freedoms of all. . . .

We must not be confused about what freedom is. Basic human rights are simple and easily understood: freedom of speech and a free press; freedom of religion and worship; freedom of assembly and the right of petition; the right of men to be secure in their homes and free from unreasonable search and seizure and from arbitrary arrest and punishment.

We must not be deluded by the efforts of the forces of reaction to prostitute the great words of our free tradition and thereby to confuse the struggle. Democracy, freedom, human rights have come to have a definite meaning to the people of the world which we must not allow any nation to so change that they are made synonymous with suppression and dictatorship. . . .

Freedom for our peoples is not only a right, but also a tool. Freedom of speech, freedom of the press, freedom of information, freedom of assembly—these are not just abstract ideals to us; they are tools with which we create a way of life, a way of life in which we can enjoy freedom.

Sometimes the processes of democracy are slow, and I have known some of our leaders to say that a benevolent dictatorship would accomplish the ends desired in a much shorter time than it takes to go through the democratic processes of discussion and the slow formation of public opinion. But there is no way of insuring that a dictatorship will remain benevolent or that power once in the hands of a few will be returned to the people without struggle or revolution. This we have learned by experience and we accept the slow processes of democracy because we know that shortcuts compromise principles on which no compromise is possible.

The final expression of the opinion of the people with us is through free and honest elections, with valid choices on basic issues and candidates. The secret ballot is an essential to free elections but you must have a choice before you. I have heard my husband say many times that a people need never lose their freedom if they kept their right to a secret ballot and if they used that secret ballot to the full. Basic decisions of our society are made through the expressed will of the people. That is why when we see these liberties threatened, instead of falling apart, our nation becomes unified and our democracies come together as a unified group in spite of our varied backgrounds and many racial strains. . . .

In the United States we are old enough not to claim perfection. We recognize that we have some problems of discrimination but we find steady progress being made in the solution of these problems. Through normal democratic processes we are coming to understand our needs and how we can attain full equality for all our people. Free discussion on the subject is permitted. Our Supreme Court has recently rendered decisions to clarify a number of our laws to guarantee the rights of all. . . .

It is my belief, and I am sure it is also yours, that the struggle for democracy and freedom is a critical struggle, for their preservation is essential to the great objective of the United Nations to maintain international peace and security. Among free men the end cannot justify the means. We know the patterns of totalitarianism—the single political party, the control of schools, press, radio, the arts, the sciences, and the church to support autocratic authority; these are the age-old patterns against which men have struggled for three thousand years. These are the signs of reaction, retreat, and retrogression. The United Nations must hold fast to the heritage of freedom won by the struggle of its people; it must help us to pass it on to generations to come.

The development of the ideal of freedom and its translation into the everyday life of the people in great areas of the earth is the product of the efforts of many peoples. It is the fruit of a long tradition of vigorous thinking and courageous action. No one race and no one people can claim to have done all the work to achieve greater dignity for human beings and great freedom to develop human personality. In each generation and in each country there must be a continuation of the struggle and new steps forward must be taken since this is preeminently a field in which to stand still is to retreat. . . .

The future must see the broadening of human rights throughout the world. People who have glimpsed freedom will never be content until they have secured it for themselves. In a truest sense, human rights are a fundamental object of law and government in a just society.

★ ★ ★

## "A FINAL, ALL-OUT BATTLE"
## Joseph R. McCarthy, Lincoln's Birthday Address, Wheeling, West Virginia—February 9, 1950

---

A veteran of World War II, Joseph McCarthy (1908–1957) was elected as a Republican to the U.S. Senate in 1946. Nearly four years later he launched an anticommunist crusade with this speech in West Virginia. He would ultimately be condemned by his Senate colleagues in 1954.

LADIES AND GENTLEMEN, tonight as we celebrate the one hundred forty-first birthday of one of the greatest men in American history, I would like to be able to talk about what a glorious day today is in the

*The ruthless New York lawyer Roy Cohn served as Senator McCarthy's chief counsel.*

history of the world. As we celebrate the birth of this man who with his whole heart and soul hated war, I would like to be able to speak of peace in our time—of war being outlawed—and of world-wide disarmament. These would be truly appropriate things to be able to mention as we celebrate the birthday of Abraham Lincoln.

Five years after a world war has been won, men's hearts should anticipate a long peace—and men's minds should be free from the heavy weight that comes with war. But this is not such a period—for this is not a period of peace. This is a time of "the cold war." This is a time when all the world is split into two vast, increasingly hostile armed camps—a time of a great armament race.

Today we can almost physically hear the mutterings and rumblings of an invigorated god of war. You can see it, feel it, and hear it all the way from the Indochina hills, from the shores of Formosa, right over into the very heart of Europe itself.

The one encouraging thing is that the "mad moment" has not yet arrived for the firing of the gun or the exploding of the bomb which will set civilization about the final task of destroying itself. There is still a hope for peace if we finally decide that no longer can we safely blind our eyes and close our ears to those facts which are shaping up more and more clearly . . . and that is that we are now engaged in a showdown fight . . . not the usual war between nations for land areas or other material gains, but a war between two diametrically opposed ideologies.

The great difference between our western Christian world and the atheistic Communist world is not political, gentlemen, it is moral. For instance, the Marxian idea of confiscating the land and factories and running the entire economy as a single enterprise is momentous. Likewise, Lenin's invention of the one-party police state as a way to make Marx's idea work is hardly less momentous.

Stalin's resolute putting across of these two ideas, of course, did much to divide the world. With only these differences, however, the east and the west could most certainly still live in peace.

The real, basic difference, however, lies in the religion of immoralism invented by Marx, preached feverishly by Lenin, and carried to unimaginable extremes by Stalin. This religion of immoralism, if the Red half of the world triumphs—and well it may, gentlemen—this religion of immoralism will more deeply wound and damage mankind than any conceivable economic or political system.

Karl Marx dismissed God as a hoax, and Lenin and Stalin have added in clear-cut, unmistakable language their resolve that no nation, no people who believe in a god, can exist side by side with their communistic state.

Karl Marx, for example, expelled people from his Communist Party for mentioning such things as love, justice, humanity or morality. He called this "soulful ravings" and "sloppy sentimentality." . . .

Today we are engaged in a final, all-out battle between communistic atheism and Christianity. The modern champions of communism have selected this as the time, and ladies and gentlemen, the chips are down—they are truly down.

Lest there be any doubt that the time has been chosen, let us go directly to the leader of communism today—Joseph Stalin. Here is what he said—not back in 1928, not before the war, not during the war—but two years after the last war was ended: "To think that the Communist revolution can be carried out peacefully, within the framework of a Christian democracy, means one has either gone out of one's mind and lost all normal understanding, or has grossly and openly repudiated the Communist revolution."

Ladies and gentlemen, can there be anyone tonight who is so blind as to say that the war is not on? Can there be anyone who fails to realize that the Communist world has said the time is now? That this is the time for the show-down between the democratic Christian world and the communistic atheistic world?

The reason why we find ourselves in a position of impotency is not because our only powerful potential enemy has sent men to invade our shores but rather because of the traitorous actions of those who have been treated so well by this Nation. It has not been the less fortunate, or members of minority groups who have been traitorous to this Nation, but rather those who have had all the benefits that the wealthiest Nation on earth has had to offer . . . the finest homes, the finest college education and the finest jobs in government we can give.

This is glaringly true in the State Department. There the bright young men who are born with silver spoons in their mouths are the ones who have been most traitorous. . . .

I have here in my hand a list of 205 . . . names that were made known to the Secretary of State as being members of the Communist Party and who nevertheless are still working and shaping policy in the State Department.

★ ★ ★

## "THE SELFISH POLITICAL EXPLOITATION OF FEAR"

### Margaret Chase Smith, Declaration of Conscience, United States Senate—June 1, 1950

The first woman to serve in both the U.S. House and the U.S. Senate, the Maine Republican Margaret Chase Smith (1897–1995) was one of the earliest figures to take a stand against Joe McCarthy's tactics of hyperbole and smear.

I WOULD LIKE TO speak briefly and simply about a serious national condition. It is a national feeling of fear and frustration that could result in national suicide and the end of everything that we Americans hold dear. It is a condition that comes from the lack of effective leadership in either the Legislative Branch or the Executive Branch of our Government.

That leadership is so lacking that serious and responsible proposals are being made that national advisory commissions be appointed to provide such critically needed leadership.

I speak as briefly as possible because too much harm has already been done with irresponsible words of bitterness and selfish political opportunism.

I speak as simply as possible because the issue is too great to be obscured by eloquence. I speak simply and briefly in the hope that my words will be taken to heart.

I speak as a Republican, I speak as a woman.

I speak as a United States Senator.

I speak as an American.

The United States Senate has long enjoyed worldwide respect as the greatest deliberative body in the world. But recently that deliberative character has too often been debased to the level of a forum of hate and character assassination sheltered by the shield of congressional immunity.

It is ironical that we Senators can in debate in the Senate, directly or indirectly, by any form of words, impute to any American, who is not a Senator, any conduct or motive unworthy or unbecoming an American—and without that non-Senator American having any legal redress against us—yet if we say the same thing in the Senate about our colleagues we can be stopped on the grounds of being out of order. It is strange that we can verbally attack anyone else without restraint and with full protection and yet we hold ourselves above the same type of criticism here on the Senate Floor.

Surely the United States Senate is big enough to take self-criticism and self-appraisal. Surely we should be able to take the same kind of character attacks that we dish out to outsiders. I think that it is high time for the United States Senate and its members to do some soul searching—for us to weigh our consciences—on the manner in which we are performing our duty to the people of America—on the manner in which we are using or abusing our individual powers and privileges.

I think that it is high time that we remembered that we have sworn to uphold and defend the Constitution.

I think that it is high time that we remembered that the Constitution, as amended, speaks not only of the freedom of speech but also of trial by jury instead of trial by accusation. Whether it be a criminal prosecution in court or a character prosecution in the Senate, there is little practical distinction when the life of a person has been ruined.

Those of us who shout the loudest about Americanism in making character assassinations are all too frequently those who, by our own

*Senator Margaret Chase Smith, Republican of Maine, took the lead against McCarthyism not long after his initial Lincoln Day broadside in 1950.*

words and acts, ignore some of the basic principles of Americanism—the right to criticize; the right to hold unpopular beliefs; the right to protest; the right of independent thought.

The exercise of these rights should not cost one single American citizen his reputation or his right to a livelihood nor should he be in danger of losing his reputation or livelihood merely because he happens to know someone who holds unpopular beliefs.

Who of us doesn't? Otherwise none of us could call our souls our own. Otherwise thought control would have set in. The American people are sick and tired of being afraid to speak their minds lest they be politically smeared as "Communists" or "Fascists" by their opponents. Freedom of speech is not what it used to be in America.

It has been so abused by some that it is not exercised by others. The American people are sick and tired of seeing innocent people smeared and guilty people whitewashed. But there have been enough proved cases to cause nationwide distrust and strong suspicion that there may be something to the unproved, sensational accusations.

As a Republican, I say to my colleagues on this side of the aisle that the Republican Party faces a challenge today that is not unlike the challenge that it faced back in Lincoln's day.

The Republican Party so successfully met that challenge that it emerged from the Civil War as the champion of a united nation—in addition to being a Party that unrelentingly fought loose spending and loose programs.

Today our country is being psychologically divided by the confusion and the suspicions that are bred in the United States Senate to spread like cancerous tentacles of "know nothing, suspect everything" attitudes.

Today we have a Democratic Administration that has developed a mania for loose spending and loose programs. History is repeating itself—and the Republican Party again has the opportunity to emerge as the champion of unity and prudence.

The record of the present Democratic Administration has provided us with sufficient campaign issues without the necessity of resorting to political smears. America is rapidly losing its position as leader of the world simply because the Democratic Administration has pitifully failed to provide effective leadership.

The Democratic Administration has completely confused the American people by its daily contradictory grave warnings and optimistic assurances—that show the people that our Democratic Administration has no idea of where it is going.

The Democratic Administration has greatly lost the confidence of the American people by its complacency to the threat of communism here at home and the leak of vital secrets to Russia through key officials of the Democratic Administration.

There are enough proved cases to make this point without diluting our criticism with unproved charges. Surely these are sufficient reasons to make it clear to the American people that it is time for a change and that a Republican victory is necessary to the security of this country. Surely it is clear that this nation will continue to suffer as long as it is governed by the present ineffective Democratic Administration.

Yet to displace it with a Republican regime embracing a philosophy that lacks political integrity or intellectual honesty would prove equally disastrous to this nation. The nation sorely needs a Republican victory.

But I don't want to see the Republican Party ride to political victory on the Four Horsemen of Calumny—Fear, Ignorance, Bigotry and Smear.

I doubt if the Republican Party could—simply because I don't believe the American people will uphold any political party that puts political exploitation above national interest. Surely we Republicans aren't that desperate for victory.

I don't want to see the Republican Party win that way. While it might be a fleeting victory for the Republican Party, it would be a more lasting defeat for the American people. Surely it would ultimately be suicide for the Republican Party and the two-party system that has protected our American liberties from the dictatorship of a one-party system.

As members of the Minority Party, we do not have the primary authority to formulate the policy of our Government. But we do have the responsibility of rendering constructive criticism, of clarifying issues, of allaying fears by acting as responsible citizens.

As a woman, I wonder how the mothers, wives, sisters and daughters feel about the way in which members of their families have been politically mangled in Senate debate—and I use the word "debate" advisedly.

As a United States Senator, I am not proud of the way in which the Senate has been made a publicity platform for irresponsible sensationalism. I am not proud of the reckless abandon in which unproved charges have been hurled from this side of the aisle. I am not proud of the obviously staged, undignified countercharges that have been attempted in retaliation from the other side of the aisle.

I don't like the way the Senate has been made a rendezvous for vilification, for selfish political gain at the sacrifice of individual reputations and national unity. I am not proud of the way we smear outsiders from the Floor of the Senate and hide behind the cloak of congressional immunity and still place ourselves beyond criticism on the Floor of the Senate.

As an American, I am shocked at the way Republicans and Democrats alike are playing directly into the Communist design of "confuse, divide and conquer."

As an American, I don't want a Democratic Administration "white wash" or "cover up" any more than I want a Republican smear or witch hunt. As an American, I condemn a Republican "Fascist" just as much as I condemn a Democrat "Communist." I condemn a Democrat "Fascist" just as much as I condemn a Republican "Communist." They are equally dangerous to you and me and to our country.

As an American, I want to see our nation recapture the strength and unity it once had when we fought the enemy instead of ourselves. It is with these thoughts I have drafted what I call a "Declaration of Conscience." I am gratified that Senator Tobey, Senator Aiken, Senator Morse, Senator Ives, Senator Thye and Senator Hendrickson, have concurred in that declaration and have authorized me to announce their concurrence.

The declaration reads as follows:

### Statement of Seven Republican Senators

1. We are Republicans. But we are Americans first. It is as Americans that we express our concern with the growing confusion that threatens the security and stability of our country. Democrats and Republicans alike have contributed to that confusion.
2. The Democratic Administration has initially created the confusion by its lack of effective leadership, by its contradictory grave warnings and optimistic assurances, by its complacency to the threat of communism here at home, by its oversensitiveness to rightful criticism, by its petty bitterness against its critics.
3. Certain elements of the Republican party have materially added to this confusion in the hopes of riding the Republican party to victory through the selfish political exploitation of fear, bigotry, ignorance, and intolerance. There are enough mistakes of the Democrats' for Republicans to criticize constructively without resorting to political smears.
4. To this extent, Democrats and Republicans alike have unwittingly, but undeniably, played directly into the Communist design of "confuse, divide, and conquer."
5. It is high time that we stopped thinking politically as Republicans and Democrats about elections and started thinking patriotically as Americans about national security based on individual freedom. It is high time that we all stopped being

tools and victims of totalitarian techniques—techniques that, if continued here unchecked, will surely end what we have come to cherish as the American way of life.

★ ★ ★

## "WE MUST NOT CONFUSE DISSENT WITH DISLOYALTY"

**Edward R. Murrow, *See It Now,* CBS—March 9, 1954**

After rising to fame as a reporter for CBS radio in London during World War II, Edward R. Murrow (1908–1965) became an anchor in the early days of network television. In this broadcast—coming about four years after Senator Smith's remarks—Murrow made the case against Joe McCarthy.

No one familiar with the history of this country can deny that congressional committees are useful. It is necessary to investigate before legislating, but the line between investigating and persecuting is a very fine one and the junior Senator from Wisconsin has stepped over it repeatedly. His primary achievement has been in confusing the public mind, as between the internal and the external threats of Communism. We must not confuse dissent with disloyalty. We must remember always that accusation is not proof and that conviction depends upon evidence and due process of law. We will not walk in fear, one of another. We will not be driven by fear into an age of unreason, if we dig deep in our history and our doctrine, and remember that we are not descended from fearful men—not from men who feared to write, to speak, to associate and to defend causes that were, for the moment, unpopular.

This is no time for men who oppose Senator McCarthy's methods to keep silent, or for those who approve. We can deny our heritage and our history, but we cannot escape responsibility for the result. There is no way for a citizen of a republic to abdicate his responsibilities. As a nation we have come into our full inheritance at a tender age. We proclaim ourselves, as indeed we are, the defenders of freedom, wherever it continues to exist in the world, but we cannot defend freedom abroad by deserting it at home.

The actions of the junior Senator from Wisconsin have caused alarm and dismay amongst our allies abroad and given considerable comfort to our enemies. And whose fault is that? Not really his. He didn't create this situation of fear; he merely exploited it—and rather successfully. Cassius was right. "The fault, dear Brutus, is not in our stars, but in ourselves."

Good night and good luck.

★ ★ ★

## "AN ETERNAL CHAIN OF RIGHT AND DUTY"

### Russell Kirk, *The Conservative Mind*—1953

One of the most influential conservative writers and thinkers of the twentieth century, Russell Kirk (1918–1994) brought an eloquent pen and a scholarly sensibility to post–World War II American life and politics. Headquartered at his rural home, Piety Hill, in Mecosta, Michigan, Kirk was a historian of ideas, a literary critic, and an important popularizer of the work of figures ranging from Edmund Burke to T. S. Eliot. His 1953 book, *The Conservative Mind: From Burke to Eliot,* published by Henry Regnery, was a foundational text for conservatives seeking the political, moral, and philosophical origins of the American right. This excerpt is from the volume's 1960 edition.

"THE STUPID PARTY": this is John Stuart Mill's description of conservatives. Like certain other summary dicta which nineteenth-century liberals thought to be forever triumphant, this judgment needs review in our age of disintegrating liberal and radical theories. Certainly many dull and unreflecting people have lent their inertia to the cause of conservatism: "It is commonly sufficient for practical purposes if conservatives, without saying anything, just sit and think, or even if they merely sit," F.J.C. Hearnshaw observed. Edmund Burke, the greatest of modern conservative thinkers, was not ashamed to acknowledge the allegiance of humble men whose sureties are prejudice and prescription; for, with affection, he likened them to cattle under the English oaks, deaf to the insects of radical innovation. Yet the conservative principle has been defended, these past hundred and fifty years, by men of learning and genius. To review conservative ideas, examining their validity for this perplexed age, is the purpose of this book, which does not pretend to be a history of conservative parties. This study is a prolonged essay in definition. What is the essence of British and American conservatism? What system of ideas, common to England and the United States, has sustained men of conservative instincts in their resistance against radical theories and social transformation ever since the beginning of the French Revolution?

Walk beside the Liffey in Dublin, a little way west of the dome of the Four Courts, and you come to an old doorway in a blank wall. This is the roofless wreck of an eighteenth-century house, and until recently the house still was here, inhabited although condemned: Number 12, Arran Quay, formerly a brick building of three stories, which began as a gentleman's residence, sank to the condition of a shop, presently was used as a governmental office of the meaner sort, and was demolished in 1950—a history suggestive of changes on a mightier scale since 1729, in Irish society. For in that year, Edmund Burke, the greatest native of Ireland, was born here. Modern Dublin's memories do not extend much beyond the era of O'Connell, and the annihilation of Burke's birthplace seems to have stirred up no protest. Across the river you see what was once the town house of the Earls of Moira and is now the office of a society for suppressing mendicity; and beyond that, the gigantic Guinness brewery. Behind Burke's house (or the sad scrap of it that remains), toward the old church of St. Michan in which, they say, he was baptized, stretch tottering brick slums where barefoot children scramble over broken walls. If you turn toward O'Connell Street, an easy stroll takes you to the noble façade of Trinity College and the statues of Burke and Goldsmith; northward, near Parnell Square, you may hear living Irish orators proclaiming through amplifiers that they have succeeded in increasing sevenfold the pensions of widows, a mere earnest of their intent. And you may reflect, with Burke, "What shadows we are, and what shadows we pursue!"

Since Burke's day, there have been alterations aplenty in Dublin. Yet to the visitor, Ireland sometimes seems a refuge of tradition amidst the flux of our age, and Dublin a conservative old city; and so they are. A world that damns tradition, exalts equality, and welcomes change; a world that has clutched at Rousseau, swallowed him whole, and demanded prophets yet more radical; a world smudged by industrialism, standardized by the masses, consolidated by government; a world crippled by war, trembling between the colossi of East and West, and peering over a smashed barricade into the gulf of dissolution: this, our era, is the society Burke foretold, with all the burning energy of his rhetoric, in 1790. By and large, radical thinkers have won the day. For a century and a half, conservatives have yielded ground in a manner which, except for occasionally successful rear-guard actions, must be described as a rout.

As yet the causes of their shattering defeat are not wholly clear. Two general explanations are possible, however: first, that throughout the modern world "*things* are in the saddle," and conservative ideas, however sound, cannot resist the unreasoning forces of industrialism, centralization, secularism, and the levelling impulse; second, that conservative thinkers have lacked perspicacity sufficient to meet the conundrums of modern times. And either explanation has some foundation.

This book is a criticism of conservative thought; and space does not allow any very thorough discussion of the material forces and political currents which have been at once the forcing-bed and the harvest of conservative ideas. For similar reasons, one can deal only laconically with the radical adversaries of conservatism. But there are good political histories of the years since 1790, and the doctrines of liberalism and radicalism are sufficiently established in the popular mind; while conservatism has had few historians. Although the study of French and German conservative ideas (linked with British and American thought by the debt to Burke of Maistre, Bonald, Guizot, Gentz, Metternich, and a dozen other men of high talents) is full of interest, that subject is too intricate for treatment here; only Tocqueville, out of all the Continental men of ideas, has been properly recognized in this volume, and he chiefly because of his enduring influence upon Americans and Englishmen.

*The Conservative Mind,* then, is limited to British and American thinkers who have stood by tradition and old establishments. Only Britain and America, among the great nations, have escaped revolution since 1790, which seems attestation that their conservatism is a sturdy growth and that investigation of it may be rewarding. To confine the field more narrowly still, this book is an analysis of thinkers in the line of Burke. Convinced that Burke's is the true school of conservative principle, I have left out of consideration most anti-democratic liberals like Lowe, most anti-governmental individualists like Spencer, most anti-parliamentary writers like Carlyle.

Every conservative thinker discussed in the following chapters—even the Federalists who were Burke's contemporaries—felt the influence of the great Whig, although sometimes the ideas of Burke penetrated to them only through a species of intellectual filter. Conscious conservatism, in the modern sense, did not manifest itself until 1790, with the publication of *Reflections on the Revolution in France.* In that year the prophetic powers of Burke defined in the public consciousness, for the first time, the opposing poles of conservation and innovation. "The Carmagnole" announced the opening of our era, and the smoky energy of coal and steam in the north of England was the signal for another revolution. If one attempts to trace conservative ideas back to an earlier time in Britain, soon he is enmeshed in Whiggery, Toryism, and intellectual antiquarianism; for the modern issues, though earlier taking substance, were not yet distinct. Nor does the American struggle between conservatives and radicals become intense until Citizen Genêt and Tom Paine transport across the Atlantic enthusiasm for French liberty: the American Revolution, substantially, had Tocqueville, out of all the Continental men of ideas, tradition, against royal innovation. If one really must find a preceptor for conservatism who is older than Burke, he cannot rest satisfied with Bolingbroke, whose skepticism in religion disqualifies him, or with the Machiavellian Hobbes, or that old-fangled absolutist Filmer. Falkland, indeed, and Clarendon and Halifax and Strafford, deserve study; still more, in Richard Hooker one discovers profound conservative observations which Burke inherited with his Anglicanism and which Hooker drew in part from the Schoolmen and their authorities; but already one is back in the sixteenth century, and then in the thirteenth, and this book is concerned with modern problems. In any practical sense, Burke is the founder of our conservatism.

Canning and Coleridge and Scott and Southey and Wordsworth owed their political principles to the imagination of Burke; Hamilton and John Adams read Burke in America, and Randolph promulgated Burke's ideas in the Southern states. Burke's French disciples coined the word "conservative," which Croker, Canning, and Peel clapped to the great party that no longer was Tory or Whig, once the followers of Pitt and Portland had joined forces. Tocqueville applied the wisdom of Burke to his own liberal ends; Macaulay copied the reforming talents of his model. And these men passed on the tradition of Burke to succeeding generations. With such a roster of pupils, Burke's claim to speak for the real conservative genius should be difficult to deny. Yet scholars of some eminence have endeavored to establish Hegel as a kind of coadjutor to Burke. "Sir," said Samuel Johnson concerning Hume, "the fellow is a Tory by chance." Hegel's conservatism is similarly accidental, as Tocqueville remarks: "Hegel exacted submission to the ancient established powers of his own time; which he held to be legitimate, not only from existence, but from their origin. His scholars wished to establish powers of another kind.... From this Pandora's box have escaped all sorts of moral diseases from which the people [are] still suffering. But I have remarked that a general reaction is taking place against this sensual and socialist philosophy." Schlegel, Görres, and Stolberg—and Taine's school, in France—were admirers of both Hegel and Burke, which perhaps explains the confounding of their superficial resemblance with their fundamental inimicality. Hegel's metaphysics would have been as abhorrent to Burke as his style; Hegel himself does not seem to have read Burke; and people who think that these two men represent different facets of the same system are in danger of confusing authoritarianism (in the political sense) with conservatism. Marx could draw upon Hegel's magazine; he could find nothing to suit him in Burke.

But such distinctions are more appropriate in a concluding chapter than in a preface. Just now, a preliminary definition of the conservative idea is required.

Any informed conservative is reluctant to condense profound and intricate intellectual systems to a few pretentious phrases; he prefers to leave that technique to the enthusiasm of radicals. Conservatism is not a fixed and immutable body of dogma, and conservatives inherit from Burke a talent for re-expressing their convictions to fit the time. As a working premise, nevertheless, one can observe here that the essence of social conservatism is preservation of the ancient moral traditions of humanity. Conservatives respect the wisdom of their ancestors (this phrase was Strafford's, and Hooker's, before Burke illuminated it); they are dubious of wholesale alteration. They think society is a spiritual reality, possessing an eternal life but a delicate constitution: it cannot be scrapped and recast as if it were a machine. "What is conservatism?" Abraham Lincoln inquired once. "Is it not adherence to the old and tried, against the new and untried?" It is that, but it is more. Professor Hearnshaw, in his *Conservatism in England,* lists a dozen principles of conservatives, but possibly these may be comprehended in a briefer catalogue. I think that there are six canons of conservative thought:

(1) Belief that a divine intent rules society as well as conscience, forging an eternal chain of right and duty which links great and obscure, living and dead. Political problems, at bottom, are religious and moral problems. A narrow rationality, what Coleridge calls the Understanding, cannot of itself satisfy human needs. "Every Tory is a realist," says Keith Feiling: "he knows that there are great forces in heaven and earth that man's philosophy cannot plumb or fathom. We do wrong to deny it, when we are told that we do not trust human reason: we do not and we may not. Human reason set up a cross on Calvary, human reason set up the cup of hemlock, human reason was canonized in Nôtre Dame." Politics is the art of apprehending and applying the Justice which is above nature.

(2) Affection for the proliferating variety and mystery of traditional life, as distinguished from the narrowing uniformity and equalitarianism and utilitarian aims of most radical systems. This is why Quintin Hogg (Lord Hailsham) and R. J. White describe conservatism as "enjoyment." It is this buoyant view of life which Walter Bagehot called "the proper source of an animated Conservatism."

(3) Conviction that civilized society requires orders and classes. The only true equality is moral equality; all other attempts at levelling lead to despair, if enforced by positive legislation. Society longs for leadership, and if a people destroy natural distinctions among men, presently Buonaparte fills the vacuum.

(4) Persuasion that property and freedom are inseparably connected, and that economic levelling is not economic progress. Separate property from private possession, and liberty is erased.

(5) Faith in prescription and distrust of "sophisters and calculators."

Man must put a control upon his will and his appetite, for conservatives know man to be governed more by emotion than by reason. Tradition and sound prejudice provide checks upon man's anarchic impulse.

(6) Recognition that change and reform are not identical, and that innovation is a devouring conflagration more often than it is a torch of progress. Society must alter, for slow change is the means of its conservation, like the human body's perpetual renewal; but Providence is the proper instrument for change, and the test of a statesman is his cognizance of the real tendency of Providential social forces.

Various deviations from this system of ideas have occurred, and there are numerous appendages to it; but in general conservatives have adhered to these articles of belief with a consistency rare in political history. To catalogue the principles of their opponents is more difficult. At least five major schools of radical thought have competed for public favor since Burke entered politics: the rationalism of the philosophies, the romantic emancipation of Rousseau and his allies, the utilitarianism of the Benthamites, the positivism of Comte's school, and the collectivistic materialism of Marx and other socialists. This list leaves out of account those scientific doctrines, Darwinism chief among them, which have done so much to undermine the first principles of a conservative order. To express these several radicalisms in terms of a common denominator probably is presumptuous, foreign to the philosophical tenets of conservatism. All the same, in a hastily generalizing fashion one may say that radicalism since 1790 has tended to attack the prescriptive arrangement of society on the following grounds:

(1) The perfectibility of man and the illimitable progress of society: meliorism. Radicals believe that education, positive legislation, and alteration of environment can produce men like gods; they deny that humanity has a natural proclivity toward violence and sin.

(2) Contempt for tradition. Reason, impulse, and materialistic determinism are severally preferred as guides to social welfare, trustier than the wisdom of our ancestors. Formal religion is rejected and a variety of anti-Christian systems are offered as substitutes.

(3) Political levelling. Order and privilege are condemned; total democracy, as direct as practicable, is the professed radical

ideal. Allied with this spirit, generally, is a dislike of old parliamentary arrangements and an eagerness for centralization and consolidation.

(4) Economic levelling. The ancient rights of property, especially property in land, are suspect to almost all radicals; and collectivistic reformers hack at the institution of private property root and branch.

As a fifth point, one might try to define a common radical view of the state's function; but here the chasm of opinion between the chief schools of innovation is too deep for any satisfactory generalization. One can only remark that radicals unite in detesting Burke's description of the state as divinely ordained moral essence, a spiritual union of the dead, the living, and those yet unborn.

So much for preliminary delineation. The radical, when all is said, is a neoterist, in love with change; the conservative, a man who says with Joubert, *Ce sont les crampons qui unissent une génération à une autre*—these ancient institutions of politics and religion. *Conservez ce qu'ont vu vos pères.* If one seeks by way of definition more than this, the sooner he turns to particular thinkers, the safer ground he is on. In the following chapters, the conservative is described as statesman, as critic, as metaphysician, as man of letters. Men of ideas, rather than party leaders, determine the ultimate course of things, as Napoleon knew; and I have chosen my conservatives accordingly. There are some conservative thinkers—Lord Salisbury and Justice Story, for instance—about whom I would have liked to write more; some interesting disciples of Burke, among them Arnold, Morley, and Bryce, I have omitted because they were not regular conservatives. But the mainstream of conservative ideas is followed from 1790 to 1960.

In a revolutionary epoch, sometimes men taste every novelty, sicken of them all, and return to ancient principles so long disused that they seem refreshingly hearty when they are rediscovered. History often appears to resemble a roulette wheel; there is truth in the old Greek idea of cycles, and round again may come the number which signifies a conservative order. One of those flaming clouds which we deny to the Deity but arrogate to our own employment may erase our present elaborate constructions as abruptly as the tocsin in the Faubourg St. Germain terminated an age equally tired of itself. Yet this roulette-wheel simile would be repugnant to Burke (or to John Adams), who knew history to be the unfolding of a Design. The true conservative thinks of this process, which looks like chance or fate, as, rather, the Providential operation of a moral law of polarity. And Burke, could he see our century, never would concede that a consumption-society, so near to suicide, is the end for which Providence has prepared man. If a conservative order is indeed to return, we ought to know the tradition which is attached to it, so that we may rebuild society; if it is not to be restored, still we ought to understand Conservative ideas so that we may rake from the ashes what scorched fragments of civilization escape the conflagration of unchecked will and appetite.

* * *

## "RESTLESSNESS, SUSPICION, AND FEAR"

**Richard Hofstadter, "The Pseudo-Conservative Revolt—1954,"**
***The Paranoid Style in American Politics and Other Essays,* 1965**

---

An insightful and prolific historian of American politics, Richard Hofstadter (1916–1970) detected a troubling shift in traditional conservatism in the decade after World War II.

In the spring of 1954 I was invited by the directors of the American Civilization Program of Barnard College to speak on some aspect of American dissent. Since the McCarthist [*sic*] movement was then at its peak, I chose to speak on right-wing or, as I called it, pseudo-conservative dissent. In defining the right-wing movement, which was so fond of designating itself "conservative," as being in some sense of movement of dissent, I tried to pose the problem around which my argument was built. The lecture was later published in the Winter 1954–5 issue of *The American Scholar*. I have written nothing else of comparable brevity that aroused more attention or drew more requests for quotation on reprinting.

It soon became apparent that several writers, working independently and simultaneously, were arriving at roughly similar approaches to McCarthyism and related phenomena. Daniel Bell, in *The New American Right* (1955), collected and introduced the relevant pieces, which had been written by David Riesman and Nathan Glazer, Seymour M. Lipset, Talcott Parsons, and Peter Viereck; these essays are now most conveniently available, along with the editor's and authors' afterthoughts and new essays by Alan F. Westin and Herbert H. Hyman, in *The Radical Right* (1963), which puts the earlier analysis into the context of the 1960s. Inevitably the authors, despite significant differences in their political and social views, have come to be regarded as a school; but in commenting on our convergent ideas in the subsequent essays, I can speak only for myself.

On some counts I no longer hold with what I wrote in 1954. But it proved impossible to take adequate account of the limitations of this essay merely by revising it; and since it serves as a record of how things looked to some of us in 1954 and as a useful way of opening up a dialogue between the present and the recent past, it still seemed desirable to include it here. I therefore reprint it with only minor textual changes and a few added monitory footnotes. The task of correcting and extending it I have left to the two subsequent essays. The first of these restates the issues, and the second shows how pseudo-conservative politics were exemplified in the Goldwater campaign of 1964.

TWENTY YEARS AGO the dynamic force in American political life came from the side of liberal dissent, from the impulse to reform the inequities of our economic and social system and to change our ways of doing things, to the end that the sufferings of the Great Depression would never be repeated. Today the dynamic force in our political life no longer comes from the liberals who made the New Deal possible. By 1952 the liberals had had at least the trappings of power for twenty years. They could look back to a brief, exciting period in the mid 1930s when they had held power itself and had been able to transform the economic and administrative life of the nation. After twenty years the New Deal liberals have quite unconsciously taken on the psychology of those who have entered into possession. Moreover, a large part of the New Deal public, the jobless, distracted and bewildered men of 1933, have in the course of the years found substantial places in society for themselves, have become home-owners, suburbanites and solid citizens. Many of them still have the emotional commitments to the liberal dissent with which they grew up politically, but their social position is one of solid comfort. Among them the dominant tone has become one of satisfaction, even of a kind of conservatism. Insofar as Adlai Stevenson stirred their enthusiasm in 1952, it was not in spite of, but in part because of the air of poised and reliable conservatism that he brought to the Democratic convention. By comparison, Harry Truman's impassioned rhetoric, with its occasional thrusts at "Wall Street," seemed passé and rather embarrassing. The change did not escape Stevenson himself. "The strange alchemy of time," he said in a speech at Columbus, "has somehow converted the Democrats into the truly conservative party of this country—the party dedicated to conserving all that is best, and building solidly and safely on these foundations." What most that the old liberals now hope for is not to carry on with some ambitious new program, but simply to defend as much as possible of the old achievements and to try to keep traditional liberties of expression that are threatened.

There is, however, a dynamic of dissent in America today. Representing no more than a modest fraction of the electorate, it is not so powerful as the liberal dissent of the New Deal era, but it is powerful enough to set the tone of our political life and to establish throughout the country a kind of punitive reaction. The new dissent is certainly not radical—there are hardly any radicals of any sort left—nor is it precisely conservative. Unlike most of the liberal dissent of the past, the new dissent not only has no respect for nonconformism, but is based upon a relentless demand for conformity. It can most accurately be called pseudo-conservative—I borrow the term from the study of *The Authoritarian Personality* published in 1950 by Theodore W. Adorno and his associates—because its exponents, although they believe themselves to be conservatives and usually employ the rhetoric of conservatism, show signs of a serious and restless dissatisfaction with American life, traditions, and institutions. They have little in common with the temperate and compromising spirit of true conservatism in the classical sense of the word, and they are far from pleased with the dominant practical conservatism of the moment as it is represented by the Eisenhower administration. Their political reactions express rather a profound if largely unconscious hatred of our society and its ways—a hatred which one would hesitate to impute to them if one did not have suggestive evidence both from clinical techniques and from their own modes of expression.

From clinical interviews and thematic apperception tests, Adorno and his co-workers found that their pseudo-conservative subjects, although given to a form of political expression that combines a curious mixture of largely conservative with occasional radical notions, succeed in concealing from themselves impulsive tendencies that, if released in action, would be very far from conservative. The pseudo-conservative, Adorno writes, shows "conventionality and authoritarian submissiveness" in his conscious thinking and "violence, anarchic impulses, and chaotic destructiveness in the unconscious sphere. . . . The pseudo conservative is a man who, in the name of upholding traditional American values and institutions and defending them against more or less fictitious dangers, consciously or unconsciously aims at their abolition."*

Who is the pseudo-conservative, and what does he want? It is impossible to identify him by class, for the pseudo-conservative impulse can be found in practically all classes in society, although its power probably rests largely upon its appeal to the less educated members of the middle classes. The ideology of pseudo-conservatism can be characterized but not defined, because the pseudo-conservative tends to be more than ordinarily incoherent about politics. The lady who, when General Eisenhower's victory over Senator Taft had finally become official in 1952, stalked out of the Hilton Hotel declaiming, "This means eight more years of socialism" was probably a fairly good representative of the pseudo-conservative mentality. So also were the gentlemen who, at the Freedom Congress held at Omaha over a year ago by some "patriotic" organizations, objected to Earl Warren's appointment to the Supreme Court with the assertion: "Middle-of-the-road thinking can and will destroy us"; the general who spoke to the same group, demand-

* Theodor W. Adorno et al., *The Authoritarian Personality* (New York, 1950), pp. 675–76. While I have drawn heavily upon this enlightening study, I have some reservations about its methods and conclusions. For a critical review, see Richard Christie and Marie Jahoda, eds., *Studies in the Scope and Method of "The Authoritarian Personality"* (Glencoe, Illinois, 1954), particularly the penetrating comments by Edward Shils.

ing "an Air Force capable of wiping out the Russian Air Force and industry in one sweep," but also "a material reduction in military expenditures";* the people who a few years ago believed simultaneously that we had no business to be fighting communism in Korea and that the war should immediately be extended to an Asia-wide crusade against communism; and the most ardent supporters of the Bricker Amendment. Many of the most zealous followers of Senator McCarthy are also pseudo-conservatives, although his appeal clearly embraces a wider public.

The restlessness, suspicion and fear shown in various phases of the pseudo-conservative revolt give evidence of the real anguish which the pseudo-conservative experiences in his capacity as a citizen. He believes himself to be living in a world in which he is spied upon, plotted against, betrayed, and very likely destined for total ruin. He feels that his liberties have been arbitrarily and outrageously invaded. He is opposed to almost everything that has happened in American politics for the past twenty years. He hates the very thought of Franklin D. Roosevelt. He is disturbed deeply by American participation in the United Nations, which he can see only as a sinister organization. He sees his own country as being so weak that it is constantly about to fall victim to subversion; and yet he feels that it is so all-powerful that any failure it may experience in getting its way in the world—for instance, in the Orient—cannot possibly be due to its limitations but must be attributed to its having been betrayed.† He is the most bitter of all our citizens about our involvement in the wars of the past, but seems the least concerned about avoiding the next one. While he naturally does not like Soviet communism, what distinguishes him from the rest of us who also dislike it is that he shows little interest in, is often indeed bitterly hostile to such realistic measures as might actually strengthen the United States vis-à-vis Russia. He would much rather concern himself with the domestic scene, where communism is weak, than with those areas of the world where it is really strong and threatening. He wants to

* On the Omaha Freedom Congress see Leonard Boasberg, "Radical Reactionaries," *The Progressive,* December, 1953.

† See the comments of D. W. Brogan in "The Illusion of American Omnipotence," *Harper's,* December, 1952.

have nothing to do with the democratic nations of Western Europe, which seem to draw more of his ire than the Soviet Communists, and he is opposed to all "giveaway programs" designed to aid and strengthen these nations. Indeed, he is likely to be antagonistic to most of the operations of our federal government except congressional investigations, and to almost all of its expenditures. Not always, however, does he go so far as the speaker at the Freedom Congress who attributed the greater part of our national difficulties to "this nasty, stinking 16th [income tax] Amendment."

A great deal of pseudo-conservative thinking takes the form of trying to devise means of absolute protection against that betrayal by our own officialdom which the pseudo-conservative feels is always imminent. The Bricker Amendment, indeed, might be taken as one of the primary symptoms of pseudo-conservatism. Every dissenting movement brings its demand for constitutional changes; and the pseudo-conservative revolt, far from being an exception to this principle, seems to specialize in constitutional revision, at least as a speculative enterprise. The widespread latent hostility toward American institutions takes the form, among other things, of a flood of proposals to write drastic changes into the body of our fundamental law. In June 1954, Richard Rovere pointed out in a characteristically astute piece that Constitution-amending had become almost a major diversion in the Eighty-third Congress.* About a hundred amendments were introduced and referred to committee. Several of these called for the repeal of the income tax. Several embodied formulas of various kinds to limit non-military expenditures to some fixed portion of the national income. One proposed to bar all federal expenditures on "the general welfare"; another, to prohibit American troops from serving in any foreign country except on the soil of the potential enemy; another, to redefine treason to embrace not only persons trying to overthrow the government but also those trying to "weaken" it, even by peaceful means. The last proposal might bring the pseudo-conservative rebels themselves under the ban of treason: for the sum total of these amendments could easily serve to send the whole structure of American society crashing to the ground.

* Richard Rovere, "Letter from Washington," *New Yorker,* June 19, 1954, pp. 67–72.

As Mr. Rovere points out, it is not unusual for a large number of constitutional amendments to be lying about somewhere in the congressional hoppers. What is unusual is the readiness the Senate has shown to give them respectful consideration, and the peculiar populistic arguments some of its leading members have used to justify referring them to the state legislatures. While the ordinary Congress hardly ever has occasion to consider more than one amendment, the Eighty-third Congress saw six constitutional amendments brought to the floor of the Senate, all summoning simple majorities, and four winning the two-thirds majority necessary before they can be sent to the House and ultimately to the state legislatures. It must be added that, with the possible exception of the Bricker Amendment itself, none of the six amendments so honored can be classed with the most extreme proposals. But the pliability of the senators, the eagerness of some of them to pass the buck and defer to "the people of the country," suggests how strong they feel the pressure to be for some kind of change that will give expression to the vague desire to repudiate the past which underlies the pseudo-conservative revolt.

One of the most urgent questions we can ask about the United States in our time is: Where did all this sentiment arise? The readiest answer is that the new pseudo-conservatism is simply the old ultra-conservatism and the old isolationism heightened by the extraordinary pressures of the contemporary world. This answer, true though it may be, gives a deceptive sense of familiarity without much deepening our understanding, for the particular patterns of American isolationism and extreme right-wing thinking have themselves not been very satisfactorily explored. It will not do, to take but one example, to say that some people want the income tax amendment repealed because taxes have become very heavy in the past twenty years: for this will not explain why, of three people in the same tax bracket, one will grin and bear it and continue to support social welfare legislation as well as an adequate military establishment, while another responds by supporting in a matter-of-fact way the practical conservative leadership of the moment, and the third finds his feelings satisfied only by the angry conspiratorial accusations of conspiracy and extreme demands of the pseudo-conservative.

No doubt the circumstances determining the political style of any individual are complex. Although I am concerned here to discuss some of the neglected social-psychological elements in pseudo-conservatism, I do not wish to appear to deny the presence of important economic and political causes. I am aware, for instance, that wealthy reactionaries try to use pseudo-conservative organizers, spokesmen and groups to propagate their notions of public policy, and that some organizers of pseudo-conservative and "patriotic" groups often find in this work a means of making a living—thus turning a tendency toward paranoia into a vocational asset, probably one of the most perverse forms of occupational therapy known to man. A number of other circumstances—the drastic inflation and heavy taxes of our time, the imbalance in our party system, the deterioration of American urban life, considerations of partisan political expediency—also play a part. But none of these things seems to explain the broad appeal of pseudo-conservatism, its emotional intensity, its dense and massive irrationality, or some of the peculiar ideas it generates. Nor will they explain why those who profit by the organized movements find such a ready following among a large number of people, and why the rank-and-file janizaries of pseudo-conservatism are so eager to hurl accusations, write letters to congressmen and editors, and expend so much emotional energy and crusading idealism upon causes that plainly bring them no material reward.

Elmer Davis, seeking to account for such sentiment in his recent book *But We Were Born Free,* ventures a psychological hypothesis. He concludes, if I understand him correctly, that the genuine difficulties of our situation in the face of the power of international communism have inspired a widespread feeling of fear and frustration, and that those who cannot face these problems in a more rational way "take it out on their less influential neighbors, in the mood of a man who, being afraid to stand up to his wife in a domestic argument, relieves his feelings by kicking the cat."* This suggestion has the merit of both simplicity and plausibility, and it may begin to account for a portion of the pseudo-conservative public. But while we may dismiss our curiosity about the man who kicks the cat by remarking that some idiosyncrasy in his personal development has brought him to this pass, we can hardly help but

* Elmer Davis, *But We Were Born Free* (New York, 1954), pp. 35–36; cf. pp. 21–22 and *passim*.

wonder whether there are not, in the backgrounds of the hundreds of thousands of persons who are moved by the pseudo-conservative impulse, some commonly shared circumstances that will help to account for their all kicking the cat in unison.

All of us have reason to fear the power of international communism, and all our lives are profoundly affected by it. Why do some Americans try to face this threat for what it is, a problem that exists in a world-wide theater of action, while others try to reduce it largely to a matter of domestic conformity? Why do some of us prefer to look for allies in the democratic world, while others seem to prefer authoritarian allies or none at all? Why do the pseudo-conservatives express such a persistent fear and suspicion of *their own government,* whether its leadership rests in the hands of Roosevelt, Truman or Eisenhower? Why is the pseudo-conservative impelled to go beyond the more or less routine partisan argument that we have been the victims of considerable misgovernment during the past twenty years to the disquieting accusation that we have actually been the victims of persistent conspiracy and betrayal—"twenty years of treason"? Is it not true, moreover, that political types very similar to the pseudo-conservative have had a long history in the United States, and that this history goes back to a time when the Soviet power did not loom nearly so large on our mental horizons? Was the Ku Klux Klan, for instance, which was responsibly estimated to have had a membership of from 4,000,000 to 4,500,000 persons at its peak in the 1920's, a phenomenon totally dissimilar to the pseudo-conservative revolt?

What I wish to suggest—and I do so in the spirit of one setting forth nothing more than a speculative hypothesis—is that pseudo-conservatism is in good part a product of the rootlessness and heterogeneity of American life, and above all, of its peculiar scramble for status and its peculiar search for secure identity. Normally there is a world of difference between one's sense of national identity or cultural belonging and one's social status. However, in American historical development, these two things, so easily distinguishable in analysis, have been jumbled together in reality, and it is precisely this that has given such a special poignancy and urgency to our status-strivings. In this country a person's status—that is, his relative place in the prestige hierarchy of his community—and his rudimentary sense of belonging to the community—that is, what we call his "Americanism"—have been intimately joined. Because, as a people extremely democratic in our social institutions, we have had no clear, consistent and recognizable system of status, our personal status problems have an unusual intensity. Because we no longer have the relative ethnic homogeneity we had up to about eighty years ago, our sense of belonging has long had about it a high degree of uncertainty. We boast of "the melting pot," but we are not quite sure what it is that will remain when we have been melted down.

We have always been proud of the high degree of occupational mobility in our country—of the greater readiness, as compared with other countries, with which a person starting in a very humble place in our social structure could rise to a position of moderate wealth and status, and with which a person starting with a middling position could rise to great eminence. We have looked upon this as laudable in principle, for it is democratic, and as pragmatically desirable, for it has served many a man as a stimulus to effort and has, no doubt, a great deal to do with the energetic and effectual tone of our economic life. The American pattern of occupational mobility, while often much exaggerated, as in the Horatio Alger stories and a great deal of the rest of our mythology, may properly be credited with many of the virtues and beneficial effects that are usually attributed to it. But this occupational and social mobility, compounded by our extraordinary mobility from place to place, has also had its less frequently recognized drawbacks. Not the least of them is that this has become a country in which so many people do not know who they are or what they are or what they belong to or what belongs to them. It is a country of people whose status expectations are random and uncertain, and yet whose status aspirations have been whipped up to a high pitch by our democratic ethos and our rags-to-riches mythology.*

In a country where physical needs have been, by the scale of the

* The observation of Tocqueville: "It cannot be denied that democratic institutions strongly tend to promote the feeling of envy in the human heart; not so much because they afford to everyone the means of rising to the same level with others as because these means perpetually disappoint the persons who employ them. Democratic institutions awaken and foster a passion for equality which they can never entirely satisfy." Alexis de Tocqueville, *Democracy in America,* ed. by Phillips Bradley (New York, 1945), Vol. I, p. 201.

world's living standards, on the whole well met, the luxury of questing after status has assumed an unusually prominent place in our civic consciousness. Political life is not simply an arena in which the conflicting interests of various social groups in concrete material gains are fought out; it is also an arena into which status aspirations and frustrations are, as the psychologists would say, projected. It is at this point that the issues of politics, or the pretended issues of politics, become interwoven with and dependent upon the personal problems of individuals. We have, at all times, two kinds of processes going on in inextricable connection with each other: *interest politics,* the clash of material aims and needs among various groups and blocs; and *status politics,* the clash of various projective rationalizations arising from status aspirations and other personal motives. In times of depression and economic discontent—and by and large in times of acute national emergency—politics is more clearly a matter of interests, although of course status considerations are still present. In times of prosperity and general well-being on the material plane, status considerations among the masses can become much more influential in our politics. The two periods in our recent history in which status politics has been particularly prominent, the present era and the 1920's, have both been periods of prosperity.

During depressions, the dominant motif in dissent takes expression in proposals for reform or in panaceas. Dissent then tends to be highly programmatic—that is, it gets itself embodied in many kinds of concrete legislative proposals. It is also future-oriented and forward-looking, in the sense that it looks to a time when the adoption of this or that program will materially alleviate or eliminate certain discontents. In prosperity, however, when status politics becomes relatively more important, there is a tendency to embody discontent not so much in legislative proposals as in grousing. For the basic aspirations that underlie status discontent are only partially conscious; and, even so far as they are conscious, it is difficult to give them a programmatic expression. It is more difficult for the old lady who belongs to the D.A.R. and who sees her ancestral home swamped by new working-class dwellings to express her animus in concrete proposals of any degree of reality than it is, say, for the jobless worker during a slump to rally to a relief program. Therefore, it is the tendency of status politics to be expressed more in vindictiveness, in sour memories, in the search for scapegoats, than in realistic proposals for positive action.*

Paradoxically the intense status concerns of present-day politics are shared by two types of persons who arrive at them from opposite directions. The first are found among some types of old-family, Anglo-Saxon Protestants, and the second are found among many types of immigrant families, most notably among the Germans and Irish, who are very frequently Catholic. The Anglo-Saxons are most disposed toward pseudo-conservatism when they are losing caste, the immigrants when they are gaining.†

Consider first the old-family Americans. These people, whose stocks were once far more unequivocally dominant in America than they are

* Cf. Samuel Lubell's characterization of isolationism as a vengeful memory. *The Future of American Politics* (New York, 1952), Chapter VII. See also the comments of Leo Lowenthal and Norbert Guterman on the right-wing agitator: "The agitator seems to steer clear of the area of material needs on which liberal and democratic movements concentrate; his main concern is a sphere of frustration that is usually ignored in traditional politics. The programs that concentrate on material needs seem to overlook that area of moral uncertainties and emotional frustrations that are the immediate manifestations of malaise. It may therefore be conjectured that his followers find the agitator's statements attractive not because he occasionally promises to 'maintain the American standards of living' or to provide a job for everyone, but because he intimates that he will give them the emotional satisfactions that are denied them in the contemporary social and economic set-up. He offers attitudes, not bread." *Prophets of Deceit* (New York, 1949), pp. 91–92.

† Every ethnic group has its own peculiar status history, and I am well aware that my remarks in the text slur over many important differences. The status history of the older immigrant groups like the Germans and the Irish is quite different from that of ethnic elements like the Italians, Poles and Czechs, who have more recently arrived at the point at which they are bidding for wide acceptance in the professional and white-collar classes, or at least for the middle-class standards of housing and consumption enjoyed by these classes. The case of the Irish is of special interest, because the Irish, with their long-standing prominence in municipal politics, qualified as it has been by their relative non-acceptance in many other spheres, have an unusually ambiguous status. In many ways they have gained, while in others, particularly insofar as their municipal power has recently been challenged by other groups, especially the Italians, they have lost some status and power. The election of 1928, with its religious bigotry and social snobbery, inflicted upon them a status trauma from which they have never fully recovered, for it was a symbol of the Protestant majority's rejection of their ablest leadership on grounds quite irrelevant to merit. This feeling was kept alive by the breach between Al Smith and FDR, followed by the rejection of Jim Farley from the New Deal succession. A study of the Germans would perhaps emphasize the effects of uneasiness over national loyalties arising from the Hitler era and World War II, but extending back even to World War I.

today, feel that their ancestors made and settled and fought for this country. They have a certain inherited sense of proprietorship in it. Since America has always accorded a certain special deference to old families—so many of our families are *new*—these people have considerable claims to status by descent, which they celebrate by membership in such organizations as the D.A.R. and the S.A.R. But large numbers of them are actually losing their other claims to status. For there are among them a considerable number of the shabby genteel, of those who for one reason or another have lost their old objective positions in the life of business and politics and the professions, and who therefore cling with exceptional desperation to such remnants of their prestige as they can muster from their ancestors. These people, although very often quite well-to-do, feel that they have been pushed out of their rightful place in American life, even out of their neighborhoods. Most of them have been traditional Republicans by family inheritance, and they have felt themselves edged aside by the immigrants, the trade unions, and the urban machines in the past thirty years. When the immigrants were weak, these native elements used to indulge themselves in ethnic and religious snobberies at their expense.* Now the immigrant groups have developed ample means, political and economic, of self-defense, and the second and third generations have become considerably more capable of looking out for themselves. Some of the old-family Americans have turned to find new objects for their resentment among liberals, left-wingers, intellectuals and the like—for in true pseudo-conservative fashion they relish weak victims and shrink from asserting themselves against the strong.

New-family Americans have had their own peculiar status problem. From 1881 to 1900 over 8,800,000 immigrants came here, and during the next twenty years another 14,500,000. These immigrants, together with their descendants, constitute such a large portion of the population that Margaret Mead, in a stimulating analysis of our national character, has persuasively argued that the characteristic American outlook

* One of the noteworthy features of the current situation is that fundamentalist Protestants and fundamentalist Catholics have so commonly subordinated their old feuds (and for the first time in our history) to unite in opposition to what they usually describe as "godless" elements.

is now a third-generation point of view.* In their search for new lives and new nationality, these immigrants have suffered much, and they have been rebuffed and made to feel inferior by the "native stock," commonly being excluded from the better occupations and even from what has bitterly [been] called "first-class citizenship." Insecurity over social status has thus been mixed with insecurity over one's very identity and sense of belonging. Achieving a better type of job or a better social status and becoming "more American" have been practically synonymous, and the passions that ordinarily attach to social position have been vastly heightened by being associated with the need to belong.

The problems raised by the tasks of keeping the family together, disciplining children for the American race for success, trying to conform to unfamiliar standards, protecting economic and social status won at the cost of much sacrifice, holding the respect of children who grow American more rapidly than their parents, have thrown heavy burdens on the internal relationships of many new American families. Both new and old American families have been troubled by the changes of the past thirty years—the new because of their striving for middle-class respectability and American identity, the old because of their efforts to maintain an inherited social position and to realize under increasingly unfavorable social conditions imperatives of character and personal conduct deriving from nineteenth-century, Yankee-Protestant-rural backgrounds. The relations between generations, being cast in no stable mold, have been disordered, and the status anxieties of parents have been inflicted upon children.†

Often parents entertain status aspirations that they are unable to gratify, or that they can gratify only at exceptional psychic cost. Their children are expected to relieve their frustrations and redeem their

* Margaret Mead, *And Keep Your Powder Dry* (New York, 1942), Chapter III.

† See Else Frenkel-Brunswik's "Parents and Childhood As Seen Through the Interviews," *The Authoritarian Personality,* Chapter X. The author remarks (pp. 387–88) concerning subjects who were relatively *free* from ethnic prejudice that in their families "less obedience is expected of the children. Parents are less status-ridden and thus show less anxiety with respect to conformity and are less intolerant toward manifestations of socially unaccepted behavior. . . . Comparatively less pronounced status-concern often goes hand in hand with greater richness and liberation of emotional life. There is, on the whole, more affection, or more unconditional affection, in the families of unprejudiced subjects. There is less surrender to conventional rules. . . ."

lives. They become objects to be manipulated to that end. An extraordinarily high level of achievement is expected of them, and along with it a tremendous effort to conform and be respectable. From the standpoint of the children these expectations often appear in the form of an exorbitantly demanding authority that one dare not question or defy. Resistance and hostility, finding no moderate outlet in give-and-take, have to be suppressed, and reappear in the form of an internal destructive rage. An enormous hostility to authority, which cannot be admitted to consciousness, calls forth a massive overcompensation which is manifest in the form of extravagant submissiveness to strong power. Among those found by Adorno and his colleagues to have strong ethnic prejudices and pseudo-conservative tendencies, there is a high proportion of persons who have been unable to develop the capacity to criticize justly and in moderation the failings of parents and who are profoundly intolerant of the ambiguities of thought and feeling that one is so likely to find in real-life situations. For pseudo-conservatism is among other things a disorder in relation to authority, characterized by an inability to find other modes for human relationship than those of more or less complete domination or submission. The pseudo-conservative always imagines himself to be dominated and imposed upon because he feels that he is not dominant and knows of no other way of interpreting his position. He imagines that his own government and his own leaders are engaged in a more or less continuous conspiracy against him because he has come to think of authority only as something that aims to manipulate and deprive him. It is for this reason, among others, that he enjoys seeing outstanding generals, distinguished Secretaries of State, and prominent scholars browbeaten and humiliated.

Status problems take on a special importance in American life because a very large part of the population suffers from one of the most troublesome of all status questions: unable to enjoy the simple luxury of assuming their own nationality as a natural event, they are tormented by a nagging doubt as to whether they are really and truly and fully American. Since their forebears voluntarily left one country and embraced another, they cannot, as people do elsewhere, think of nationality as something that comes with birth; for them it is a matter of *choice,* and an object of striving. This is one reason why problems of "loyalty" arouse such an emotional response in many Americans and why it is so hard in the American climate of opinion to make any clear distinction between the problem of national security and the question of personal loyalty. Of course there is no real reason to doubt the loyalty to America of the immigrants and their descendants, or their willingness to serve the country as fully as if their ancestors had lived here for three centuries. Nonetheless, they have been thrown on the defensive by those who have in the past cast doubts upon the fullness of their Americanism. Possibly they are also, consciously or unconsciously, troubled by the thought that since their forebears have already abandoned one country, one allegiance, their own national allegiance might be considered fickle. For this I believe there is some evidence in our national practices. What other country finds it so necessary to create institutional rituals for the sole purpose of guaranteeing to its people the genuineness of their nationality? Does the Frenchman or the Englishman or the Italian find it necessary to speak of himself as "one hundred per cent" English, French or Italian? Do they find it necessary to have their equivalents of "I Am an American Day"? When they disagree with one another over national policies, do they find it necessary to call one another un-English, un-French or un-Italian? No doubt they too are troubled by subversive activities and espionage, but are their countermeasures taken under the name of committees on un-English, un-French or un-Italian activities?

The primary value that patriotic societies and anti-subversive ideologies have for their exponents can be found here. They provide additional and continued reassurance both to those who are of old American ancestry and have other status grievances and to those who are of recent American ancestry and therefore feel in need of reassurance about their nationality. Veterans' organizations offer the same satisfaction—what better evidence can there be of the genuineness of nationality and of *earned* citizenship than military service under the flag of one's country? Of course such organizations, once they exist, are liable to exploitation by vested interests that can use them as pressure groups on behalf of particular measures and interests. (Veterans' groups, since they lobby for the concrete interests of veterans, have a double role in this respect.) But the cement that holds them together is the status motivation and the desire for an identity.

Sociological studies have shown that there is a close relation between social mobility and ethnic prejudice. Persons moving downward in their social scale, and even upward under many circumstances, in the social scale tend to show greater prejudice against such ethnic minorities as the Jews and Negroes than commonly prevails in the social strata they have left or are entering.* While the existing studies in this field have been focused upon prejudice rather than the kind of hyper-patriotism and hyper-conformism that I am most concerned with, I believe that the typical prejudiced person and the typical pseudo-conservative dissenter are usually the same person, that the mechanisms at work in both complexes are quite the same,† and that it is merely the expediencies and the strategy of the situation today that cause groups that once stressed racial discrimination to find other scapegoats. Both the displaced old-American type and the new ethnic elements that are so desperately eager for reassurance of their fundamental Americanism can conveniently converge upon liberals, critics, and nonconformists of various sorts, as well as Communists and suspected Communists. To proclaim themselves vigilant in the pursuit of those who are even so much as accused of "disloyalty" to the United States is a way not only of reasserting but of advertising their own loyalty—and one of the chief characteristics of American super-patriotism is its constant inner urge toward self-advertisement. One notable quality in this new wave of conformism is that its advocates are much happier to have as their objects of hatred the Anglo-Saxon, Eastern, Ivy League intellectual gentlemen than they are to have such bedraggled souls as, say, Julius and Ethel Rosenberg. The reason, I believe, is that in the minds of the status-driven it is no special virtue to be more American than the Rosenbergs, but it is really something to be more American than Dean Acheson or John Foster Dulles—or Franklin Delano Roosevelt.‡ The status aspirations of some

* Cf. Joseph Greenblum and Leonard I. Pearlin, "Vertical Mobility and Prejudice" in Reinhard Bendix and Seymour M. Lipset, eds., *Class, Status and Power* (Glencoe, Illinois, 1953), pp. 480–91; Bruno Bettelheim and Morris Janowitz, "Ethnic Tolerance: A Function of Personal and Social Control," *American Journal of Sociology,* Vol. IV (1949), pp. 137–45.

† The similarity is also posited by Adorno, *op. cit.,* pp. 152 ff., and by others (see the studies cited by him, p. 152).

‡ I refer to such men to make the point that this animosity extends to those who are guilty of no wrongdoing. Of course a person like Alger Hiss, who has been guilty, suits much better. Hiss is the hostage the pseudo-conservatives hold from the New Deal generation. He is a heaven-sent gift. If he did not exist, the pseudo-conservatives would not have been able to invent him.

of the ethnic groups are actually higher than they were twenty years ago—which suggests one reason (there are others) why, in the ideology of the authoritarian right-wing, anti-Semitism and other blatant forms of prejudice have recently been soft-pedaled. Anti-Semitism, it has been said, is the poor man's snobbery. We Americans are always trying to raise the standard of living, and the same principle now seems to apply to standards of hating. So during the past fifteen years or so, the authoritarians have moved on from anti-Negroism and anti-Semitism to anti-Achesonianism, anti-intellectualism, anti-nonconformism, and other variants of the same idea, much in the same way as the average American, if he can manage it, will move on from a Ford to a Buick.

Such status-strivings may help us to understand some of the otherwise unintelligible figments of the pseudo-conservative ideology—the incredibly bitter feeling against the United Nations, for instance. Is it not understandable that such a feeling might be, paradoxically, shared at one and the same time by an old Yankee-Protestant American, who feels that his social position is not what it ought to be and that these foreigners are crowding in on his country and diluting its sovereignty just as "foreigners" have crowded into his neighborhood, and by a second- or third-generation immigrant who has been trying so hard to de-Europeanize himself, to get Europe out of his personal heritage, and who finds his own government mocking him by its complicity in these Old World schemes?

Similarly, is it not status aspiration that in good part spurs the pseudo-conservative on toward his demand for conformity in a wide variety of spheres of life? Conformity is a way of guaranteeing and manifesting respectability among those who are not sure that they are respectable enough. The nonconformity of others appears to such persons as a frivolous challenge to the whole order of things they are trying so hard to become part of. Naturally it is resented, and the demand for conformity in public becomes at once an expression of such resentment and a means of displaying one's own soundness. This habit has a tendency to spread from politics into intellectual and social spheres, where it can be made to challenge almost anyone whose pattern of life is different and who is imagined to enjoy a superior social position—notably, as one agitator put it, those in the "parlors of the sophisticated, the intellectuals, the so-called academic minds." Why has this tide of pseudo-conservative dissent risen to such heights in our time? To a considerable degree, we must remember, it is a response, however unrealistic, to realities. We do live in a disordered world, threatened by a great power and a powerful ideology, a world of enormous potential violence, which has already shown us the ugliest capacities of the human spirit. In our own country there has indeed been espionage, and laxity over security has in fact allowed some spies to reach high places. There is just enough reality at most points along the line to give a touch of credibility to the melodramatics of the pseudo-conservative imagination.

However, a number of developments in our recent history make this pseudo-conservative uprising more intelligible. For two hundred years and more, various conditions of American development—the process of settling the continent settlement, the continuous establishment in new areas of new status patterns in new areas, the arrival of continuous waves of new immigrants, each pushing the preceding waves upward in the ethnic hierarchy—made it possible to satisfy a remarkably large part of the extravagant status aspirations that were aroused. There was a sort of automatic built-in status elevator in the American social edifice. Today that elevator no longer operates automatically, or at least no longer operates in the same way.

Second, the growth of the mass media of communication and their use in politics have brought politics closer to the people than ever before and have made politics a form of entertainment in which the spectators feel themselves involved. Thus it has become, more than ever before, an arena into which private emotions and personal problems can be readily projected. Mass communications have made it possible to keep the mass man in an almost constant state of political mobilization.

Third, the long tenure in power of the liberal elements to which the pseudo-conservatives are most opposed and the wide variety of changes that have been introduced into our social, economic and administrative life have intensified the sense of powerlessness and victimization among the opponents of these changes and have widened the area of social issues over which they feel discontent. There has been, among other things, the emergence of a wholly new struggle: the conflict between businessmen of certain types and the New Deal bureaucracy, which has spilled over into a resentment of intellectuals and experts.

Finally, unlike our previous postwar periods, ours has been a period of continued crisis, from which the future promises no relief. In no foreign war of our history did we fight so long or make such sacrifices as in the Second World War. When it was over, instead of being able to resume our peace-time preoccupations, we were very promptly confronted with another war. It is hard for a certain type of American, who does not think much about the world outside and does not want to have to do so, to understand why we must become involved in such an unremitting struggle. It will be the fate of those in power for a long time to come to have to conduct the delicate diplomacy of the cold peace without the sympathy or understanding of a large part of their own people. From bitter experience, Eisenhower and Dulles are learning today what Truman and Acheson learned yesterday.

These considerations suggest that the pseudo-conservative political style, while it may already have passed the peak of its influence, is one of the long waves of twentieth-century American history and not a momentary mood. I do not share the widespread foreboding among liberals that this form of dissent will grow until it overwhelms our liberties altogether and plunges us into a totalitarian nightmare. Indeed, the idea that it is purely and simply fascist or totalitarian, as we have known these things in recent European history, is to my mind a false conception, based upon the failure to read American developments in terms of our peculiar American constellation of political realities. (It reminds me of the people who, because they found several close parallels between the N.R.A. and Mussolini's corporate state, were once deeply troubled at the thought that the N.R.A. was the beginning of American fascism.) However, in a populistic culture like ours, which seems to lack a responsible elite with political and moral autonomy, and in which it is possible to exploit the wildest currents of public sentiment for private purposes, it is at least conceivable that a highly organized, vocal, active and well-financed minority could create a political climate in which the rational pursuit of our well-being and safety would become impossible.

★ ★ ★

## "CERTAIN ETERNAL TRUTHS"
## Young Americans for Freedom, The Sharon Statement, Sharon, Connecticut—September 11, 1960

At a meeting of young conservatives at the Connecticut home of *National Review* founder William F. Buckley, Jr. (1925–2008), this statement was adopted as the guiding credo of the newly formed anti-Communist, pro-free market Young Americans for Freedom.

IN THIS TIME of moral and political crises, it is the responsibility of the youth of America to affirm certain eternal truths. We, as young conservatives, believe:

That foremost among the transcendent values is the individual's use of his God-given free will, whence derives his right to be free from the restrictions of arbitrary force;

That liberty is indivisible, and that political freedom cannot long exist without economic freedom;

That the purpose of government is to protect those freedoms through the preservation of internal order, the provision of national defense, and the administration of justice;

That when government ventures beyond these rightful functions, it accumulates power, which tends to diminish order and liberty;

That the Constitution of the United States is the best arrangement yet devised for empowering government to fulfill its proper role, while restraining it from the concentration and abuse of power;

That the genius of the Constitution—the division of powers—is summed up in the clause that reserves primacy to the several states, or to the people, in those spheres not specifically delegated to the Federal government;

That the market economy, allocating resources by the free play of supply and demand, is the single economic system compatible with the requirements of personal freedom and constitutional government, and that it is at the same time the most productive supplier of human needs;

That when government interferes with the work of the market economy, it tends to reduce the moral and physical strength of the nation;

That when it takes from one man to bestow on another, it diminishes the incentive of the first, the integrity of the second, and the moral autonomy of both;

That we will be free only so long as the national sovereignty of the United States is secure;

That history shows periods of freedom are rare, and can exist only when free citizens concertedly defend their rights against all enemies;

That the forces of international Communism are, at present, the greatest single threat to these liberties;

That the United States should stress victory over, rather than coexistence with, this menace; and

That American foreign policy must be judged by this criterion: does it serve the just interests of the United States?

★ ★ ★

## "COMPLICATED AND DISTURBING PARADOXES"
### Students for a Democratic Society, Port Huron Statement—June 15, 1962

Also known as the "Agenda for a Generation," the Port Huron Statement, authored for the Students for a Democratic Society by the activist Tom Hayden (1939–2016), was an articulation of progressive principles that would help fuel and shape the protest movements of the 1960s.

(1) We are people of this generation, bred in at least modest comfort, housed now in universities, looking uncomfortably to the world we inherit.

(2) When we were kids the United States was the wealthiest and strongest country in the world; the only one with the atom bomb, the least scarred by modern war, an initiator of the United Nations that we thought would distribute Western influence throughout the world. Freedom and equality for each individual, government of, by, and for the people—these American values we found good, principles by which we could live as men. Many of us began maturing in complacency.

THE

**PORT HURON STATEMENT**

*. . . we seek the establishment of a democracy of individual participation governed by two central aims: that the individual share in those social decisions determining the quality and direction of his life; that society be organized to encourage independence in men and provide the media for their common participation . . .*

**Students for a Democratic Society**

35¢

***Students for a Democratic Society!***

SDS is a movement of young people who study and participate in daily struggles for social change. Committed to change in many spheres of society, SDS members, in chapters, projects, and as individuals:

Organize the dispossessed in community movements for economic gains. During the summer of 1964, one hundred and fifty students provided the full-time staffs for 10 community projects in the urban North—40 of them continuing full-time in the fall. Movements of welfare mothers, the unemployed, tenants, and others have been organized around their particular grievances.

Participate in activity for peace through protest, research, education, and community organization. SDS organized protests and proposed peaceful solutions during the Cuba and Vietnam crises; sponsors peace research among students; and is undertaking pilot efforts to organize defense workers for economic conversion.

Work for civil rights through direct action, publication, and support of the Student Nonviolent Coordinating Committee. SDS projects in Chester, Pa., and Newark, N. J., serve as models for Negro movements in the North due to their mass support.

Inject controversy into a stagnant educational system. SDS participated in the mass demonstrations and organized national support for free speech at Berkeley; pioneered in the introduction of peace courses into college curricula; and initiated the union organization of student employees at the U. of Michigan.

Support political insurgents, such as Noel Day in Boston, in the fight for a government that would promote social justice. SDS produces studies of the political and electoral situation.

***Won't you join?***

(3) As we grew, however, our comfort was penetrated by events too troubling to dismiss. First, the permeating and victimizing fact of human degradation, symbolized by the Southern struggle against racial bigotry, compelled most of us from silence to activism. Second, the enclosing fact of the Cold War, symbolized by the presence of the Bomb, brought awareness that we ourselves, and our friends, and millions of abstract "others" we knew more directly because of our common peril, might die at any time. We might deliberately ignore, or avoid, or fail to feel all other human problems, but not these two, for these were too immediate and crushing in their impact, too challenging in the demand that we as individuals take the responsibility for encounter and resolution.

(4) While these and other problems either directly oppressed us or rankled our consciences and became our own subjective concerns, we began to see complicated and disturbing paradoxes in our surrounding America. The declaration "all men are created equal . . ." rang hollow before the facts of Negro life in the South and the big cities of the North. The proclaimed peaceful intentions of the United States contradicted its economic and military investments in the Cold War status quo.

(5) We witnessed, and continue to witness, other paradoxes. With nuclear energy whole cities can easily be powered, yet the dominant nation-states seem more likely to unleash destruction greater than that incurred in all wars of human history. Although our own technology is destroying old and creating new forms of social organization, men still tolerate meaningless work and idleness. While two-thirds of mankind suffers under nourishment, our own upper classes revel amidst superfluous abundance. Although world population is expected to double in forty years, the nations still tolerate anarchy as a major principle of international conduct and uncontrolled exploitation governs the sapping of the earth's physical resources. Although mankind desperately needs revolutionary leadership, America rests in national stalemate, its goals ambiguous and tradition-bound instead of informed and clear, its democratic system apathetic and manipulated rather than "of, by, and for the people."

(6) Not only did tarnish appear on our image of American virtue, not only did disillusion occur when the hypocrisy of American ideals was discovered, but we began to sense that what we had originally seen as the American Golden Age was actually the decline of an era. The worldwide outbreak of revolution against colonialism and imperialism, the entrenchment of totalitarian states, the menace of war, overpopulation, international disorder, supertechnology—these trends were testing the tenacity of our own commitment to democracy and freedom and our abilities to visualize their application to a world in upheaval.

(7) Our work is guided by the sense that we may be the last generation in the experiment with living. But we are a minority—the vast majority of our people regard the temporary equilibriums of our society and world as eternally functional parts. In this is perhaps the outstanding paradox; we ourselves are imbued with urgency, yet the message of our society is that there is no viable alternative to the present. Beneath the reassuring tones of the politicians, beneath the common opinion that America will "muddle through," beneath the stagnation of those who have closed their minds to the future, is the pervading feeling that there simply are no alternatives, that our times have witnessed the exhaustion not only of Utopias, but of any new departures as well. Feeling the press of complexity upon the emptiness of life, people are fearful of the thought that at any moment things might be thrust out of con-

trol. They fear change itself, since change might smash whatever invisible framework seems to hold back chaos for them now. For most Americans, all crusades are suspect, threatening. The fact that each individual sees apathy in his fellows perpetuates the common reluctance to organize for change. The dominant institutions are complex enough to blunt the minds of their potential critics, and entrenched enough to swiftly dissipate or entirely repel the energies of protest and reform, thus limiting human expectancies. Then, too, we are a materially improved society, and by our own improvements we seem to have weakened the case for further change.

(8) Some would have us believe that Americans feel contentment amidst prosperity—but might it not better be called a glaze above deeply felt anxieties about their role in the new world? And if these anxieties produce a developed indifference to human affairs, do they not as well produce a yearning to believe that there *is* an alternative to the present, that something *can* be done to change circumstances in the school, the workplaces, the bureaucracies, the government? It is to this latter yearning, at once the spark and engine of change, that we direct our present appeal. The search for truly democratic alternatives to the present, and a commitment to social experimentation with them, is a worthy and fulfilling human enterprise, one which moves us and, we hope, others today. On such a basis do we offer this document of our convictions and analysis: as an effort in understanding and changing the conditions of humanity in the late twentieth century, an effort rooted in the ancient, still unfulfilled conception of man attaining determining influence over his circumstances of life.

PART VIII

# RIGHTS AND REACTION

*1962–1968*

This Nation was founded by men of many nations and backgrounds. It was founded on the principle that all men are created equal, and that the rights of every man are diminished when the rights of one man are threatened.

—John F. Kennedy, 1963

PANY

PREVIOUS SPREAD: *Alabama state troopers attack John Lewis, the chairman of the Student Nonviolent Coordinating Committee, and other marchers in Selma, Alabama, on Sunday, March 7, 1965.*

SIX DAYS EARLIER EVERYTHING HAD SEEMED TO CHANGE. On Sunday, March 7, 1965, led by John Lewis, nonviolent demonstrators marching across the Edmund Pettus Bridge in Selma, Alabama, had been brutally attacked by Alabama authorities. Footage of the attack made a deep impression on the American public, and President Lyndon B. Johnson had asked the state's segregationist governor, George C. Wallace, to come to Washington. It was now Saturday, March 13, and the president, perched in a tall rocking chair, loomed over Wallace, who was seated on a cushioned sofa in the Oval Office.

"I kept my eyes directly on the Governor's face the entire time," LBJ recalled. "I saw a nervous, aggressive man; a rough, shrewd politician who had managed to touch the deepest chords of pride as well as prejudice among his people." The racist agenda was a loser, Johnson told Wallace—morally and historically. "George, why are you doing this?" Johnson asked Wallace. "You came into office a liberal—you spent your life trying to do things for the poor. Now, why are you working on this? Why are you off on this Negro thing? You ought to be down there calling for help for Aunt Susie in the nursing home." It was time, LBJ continued, for Wallace to get on board with the Great Society—with the future, not the past.

"Now, listen, George, don't think about 1968," Johnson said. "Think about 1988. You and me, we'll be dead and gone then, George. . . . What do you want left after you, when you die? Do you want a great big marble monument that reads, 'George Wallace—He Built.' Or do you want a little piece of scrawny pine board lying across that harsh caliche soil that reads, 'George Wallace—He Hated.' "

It worked, up to a point: Wallace agreed to allow the marchers to resume their journey from Selma to Montgomery. Johnson, meanwhile, would go before the Congress to call for historic voting-rights legislation; the bill would pass that summer. LBJ's capacity to cajole in the cause of reform was remarkable. James H. Rowe, who had advised FDR, once compared John Kennedy's and Johnson's negotiating styles. "A senator would come to Kennedy and say, 'I'd love to go along with you, Mr. President, but it would give me serious trouble back home,' "

Rowe said. "Kennedy would always say, 'I understand.' Now Johnson knew damn well the senator was going to tell him that, and he never let the senator get to the point of his troubles back home. He would tell him about the flag, and by God, the story of the country, and he'd get them by the lapels and they were out the door. That's why he got so much done so fast."

So much was moving so fast in the sixties. Assassinations; civil and voting rights; an expanded federal role in healthcare and in education; the prolonged and tragic war in Vietnam. Whole eras would seem to unfold in a single day. On Tuesday, June 11, 1963, for instance, Wallace would stand in the schoolhouse door to try to stop the desegregation of the University of Alabama; President Kennedy would address the nation on civil rights; and, in the early-morning hours of the next day, Medgar Evers of the NAACP would be shot to death in Jackson, Mississippi. Not long after, on Wednesday, August 28, 1963, the March on Washington for Jobs and Freedom would prove a pivotal point in the life of the country, with John Lewis and Martin Luther King, Jr., summoning America to a reckoning. And in testimony at the 1964 Democratic National Convention, Fannie Lou Hamer would courageously describe the realities facing Black Americans who wished to vote.

Reaction to the advances of the Great Society was swift and certain. Barry Goldwater won the 1964 Republican presidential nomination, a campaign notable not least for the national political debut of a former actor, television host, and General Electric corporate spokesman named Ronald Reagan. Lyndon Johnson's immense victory over Goldwater would be quickly followed by Republican victories in the 1966 midterm elections. Nineteen sixty-eight began with the North Vietnamese Tet Offensive and was followed by LBJ's withdrawal from that year's presidential campaign, the assassinations of Dr. King and of Robert F. Kennedy, the violent chaos of the Democratic convention in Chicago, and Richard Nixon's narrow margin over Democrat Hubert Humphrey and George Wallace, who sought the presidency, like Strom Thurmond twenty years before, on a segregationist third-party ticket.

In his last public appearance—on Tuesday, December 12, 1972, at his presidential library in Austin, Texas—Lyndon Johnson preached the old gospel once more. "The progress has been much too small," he said. "I'm kind of ashamed of myself that I had six years and couldn't do more than I did. . . . So let no one delude themselves that our work is done. . . . To be black in a white society is not to stand on level and equal ground." And, as ever, the former president was practical about making the ideal real. "Reason with the leadership and with the President!" Johnson said. "And you don't need to start off by saying he is terrible—because *he* doesn't think he's terrible. Start talking about how you believe that he wants to do what's right and how you believe *this* is right, and you'll be surprised how many who want to do what's right will try to help you." He would be dead within six weeks.

★ ★ ★

## "GOVERNMENTALLY COMPOSED PRAYERS"

**_Engel v. Vitale_, 370 U.S. 421 (1962) · Opinion of the Court by Justice Hugo L. Black; Dissent of Justice Potter Stewart—June 25, 1962**

The revolutionary work of the Supreme Court in the years Earl Warren (1891–1974) of California served as chief justice included the seminal 1962 decision that ruled mandatory school prayer was unconstitutional. FDR appointee Hugo Black (1886–1971) wrote the majority opinion; Eisenhower appointee Potter Stewart (1915–1985) dissented.

MR. JUSTICE BLACK delivered the opinion of the Court.

The respondent Board of Education of Union Free School District No. 9, New Hyde Park, New York, acting in its official capacity under state law, directed the School District's principal to cause the following prayer to be said aloud by each class in the presence of a teacher at the beginning of each school day: "Almighty God, we acknowledge our dependence upon Thee, and we beg Thy blessings upon us, our parents, our teachers and our Country."

This daily procedure was adopted on the recommendation of the State Board of Regents, a governmental agency created by the State Constitution to which the New York Legislature has granted broad supervisory, executive, and legislative powers over the State's public school system. These state officials composed the prayer which they recommended and published as a part of their "Statement on Moral and Spiritual Training in the Schools," saying: "We believe that this Statement will be subscribed to by all men and women of good will, and we call upon all of them to aid in giving life to our program."

Shortly after the practice of reciting the Regents' prayer was adopted by the School District, the parents of ten pupils brought this action in a New York State Court insisting that use of this official prayer in the public schools was contrary to the beliefs, religions, or religious practices of both themselves and their children. Among other things, these parents challenged the constitutionality of both the state law authorizing the School District to direct the use of prayer in public schools and the School District's regulation ordering the recitation of this particular prayer on the ground that these actions of official governmental agencies violate that part of the First Amendment of the Federal Constitution which commands that "Congress shall make no law respecting an establishment of religion"—a command which was "made applicable to the State of New York by the Fourteenth Amendment of the said Constitution." . . .

We think that, by using its public school system to encourage recitation of the Regents' prayer, the State of New York has adopted a practice wholly inconsistent with the Establishment Clause. There can, of course, be no doubt that New York's program of daily classroom invocation of God's blessings as prescribed in the Regents' prayer is a religious activity. It is a solemn avowal of divine faith and supplication for the blessings of the Almighty. The nature of such a prayer has always been religious, none of the respondents has denied this, and the trial court expressly so found. . . .

It is a matter of history that this very practice of establishing governmentally composed prayers for religious services was one of the reasons which caused many of our early colonists to leave England and seek religious freedom in America. The Book of Common Prayer, which was created under governmental direction and which was approved by Acts of Parliament in 1548 and 1549, set out in minute detail the accepted form and content of prayer and other religious ceremonies to be used in the established, tax supported Church of England. The controversies over the Book and what should be its content repeatedly threatened to disrupt the peace of that country as the accepted forms of prayer in the established church changed with the views of the particular ruler that happened to be in control at the time. Powerful groups representing some of the varying religious views of the people struggled among themselves to impress their particular views upon the Government and obtain amendments of the Book more suitable to their respective notions of how religious services should be conducted in order that the official religious establishment would advance their particular religious beliefs. Other groups, lacking the necessary political power to influence the Government on the matter, decided to leave England and its established church and seek freedom in America from England's governmentally ordained and supported religion.

It is an unfortunate fact of history that, when some of the very groups which had most strenuously opposed the established Church of England found themselves sufficiently in control of colonial governments in this country to write their own prayers into law, they passed laws making their own religion the official religion of their respective colonies. Indeed, as late as the time of the Revolutionary War, there were established churches in at least eight of the thirteen former colonies and established religions in at least four of the other five. But the successful Revolution against English political domination was shortly followed by intense opposition to the practice of establishing religion by law. This opposition crystallized rapidly into an effective political force in Virginia, where the minority religious groups such as Presbyterians, Lutherans, Quakers and Baptists had gained such strength that the adherents to the established Episcopal Church were actually a minority themselves. In 1785–1786, those opposed to the established Church, led by James Madison and Thomas Jefferson, who, though themselves not members of any of these dissenting religious groups, opposed all religious establishments by law on grounds of principle, obtained the enactment of the famous "Virginia Bill for Religious Liberty" by which all religious groups were placed on an equal footing so far as the State was concerned. Similar though less far-reaching legislation was being considered and passed in other states.

By the time of the adoption of the Constitution, our history shows that there was a widespread awareness among many Americans of the dangers of a union of Church and State. These people knew, some of them from bitter personal experience, that one of the greatest dangers to the freedom of the individual to worship in his own way lay in the Government's placing its official stamp of approval upon one particular kind of prayer or one particular form of religious services. They knew the anguish, hardship and bitter strife that could come when zealous religious groups struggled with one another to obtain the Government's stamp of approval from each King, Queen, or Protector that came to temporary power. The Constitution was intended to avert a part of this danger by leaving the government of this country in the hands of the people, rather than in the hands of any monarch. But this safeguard was not enough. Our Founders were no more willing to let the content of their prayers and their privilege of praying whenever they pleased be influenced by the ballot box than they were to let these vital matters of personal conscience depend upon the succession of monarchs. The First Amendment was added to the Constitution to stand as a guarantee that neither the power nor the prestige of the Federal Government would be used to control, support or influence the kinds of prayer the American people can say—that the people's religions must not be subjected to the pressures of government for change each time a new political administration is elected to office. Under that Amendment's prohibition against governmental establishment of religion, as reinforced by the provisions of the Fourteenth Amendment, government in this country, be it state or federal, is without power to prescribe by law any particular form of prayer which is to be used as an official prayer in carrying on any program of governmentally sponsored religious activity. . . .

MR. JUSTICE STEWART, dissenting.

A local school board in New York has provided that those pupils who wish to do so may join in a brief prayer at the beginning of each school day, acknowledging their dependence upon God and asking His blessing upon them and upon their parents, their teachers, and their country. The Court today decides that, in permitting this brief nondenominational prayer, the school board has violated the Constitution of the United States. I think this decision is wrong.

The Court does not hold, nor could it, that New York has interfered with the free exercise of anybody's religion. For the state courts have made clear that those who object to reciting the prayer must be entirely free of any compulsion to do so, including any "embarrassments and pressures." But the Court says that, in permitting school children to say this simple prayer, the New York authorities have established "an official religion."

With all respect, I think the Court has misapplied a great constitutional principle. I cannot see how an "official religion" is established by letting those who want to say a prayer say it. On the contrary, I think that to deny the wish of these school children to join in reciting this prayer is to deny them the opportunity of sharing in the spiritual heritage of our Nation.

The Court's historical review of the quarrels over the Book of Common Prayer in England throws no light for me on the issue before us in this case. England had then and has now an established church. Equally unenlightening, I think, is the history of the early establishment and later rejection of an official church in our own States. For we deal here not with the establishment of a state church, which would, of course, be constitutionally impermissible, but with whether school children who want to begin their day by joining in prayer must be prohibited from doing so. Moreover, I think that the Court's task, in this as in all areas of constitutional adjudication is not responsibly aided by the uncritical invocation of metaphors like the "wall of separation," a phrase nowhere to be found in the Constitution. What is relevant to the issue here is not the history of an established church in sixteenth century England or in eighteenth century America, but the history of the religious traditions of our people, reflected in countless practices of the institutions and officials of our government.

At the opening of each day's Session of this Court we stand, while one of our officials invokes the protection of God. Since the days of John Marshall, our Crier has said, "God save the United States and this Honorable Court." Both the Senate and the House of Representatives open their daily Sessions with prayer. Each of our Presidents, from George Washington to John F. Kennedy, has, upon assuming his Office, asked the protection and help of God.

The Court today says that the state and federal governments are without constitutional power to prescribe any particular form of words to be recited by any group of the American people on any subject touching religion. One of the stanzas of "The Star-Spangled Banner" made our National Anthem by Act of Congress in 1931, contains these verses:

"Blest with victory and peace, may the heav'n rescued land"
"Praise the Pow'r that hath made and preserved us a nation,"
"Then conquer we must, when our cause it is just."
"And this be our motto 'In God is our Trust.'"

In 1954, Congress added a phrase to the Pledge of Allegiance to the Flag so that it now contains the words "one Nation *under* God, indivisible, with liberty and justice for all." In 1952, Congress enacted legislation calling upon the President each year to proclaim a National Day of Prayer. Since 1865, the words "IN GOD WE TRUST" have been impressed on our coins.

Countless similar examples could be listed, but there is no need to belabor the obvious. It was all summed up by this Court just ten years ago in a single sentence: "We are a religious people whose institutions presuppose a Supreme Being."*

I do not believe that this Court, or the Congress, or the President has, by the actions and practices I have mentioned, established an "official religion" in violation of the Constitution. And I do not believe the State of New York has done so in this case. What each has done has been to recognize and to follow the deeply entrenched and highly cherished spiritual traditions of our Nation—traditions which come down to us from those who almost two hundred years ago avowed their "firm Reliance on the Protection of divine Providence" when they proclaimed the freedom and independence of this brave new world.

I dissent.

★ ★ ★

## "I DRAW THE LINE IN THE DUST"
## George C. Wallace, Inaugural Address, Montgomery, Alabama—January 14, 1963

Born in Barbour County, Alabama, George C. Wallace (1919–1998) lost a 1958 gubernatorial race, he believed, because his opponent, John Patterson, was a more outspoken segregationist. Running again in

* *Zorach v. Clauson*, 343 U. S. 306, 343 U. S. 313.

1962, Wallace prevailed, and he became the face of white Southern racism in the most dramatic years of the civil-rights movement.

*Nearly a decade after the U.S. Supreme Court's* Brown *decision, George Wallace, at the Alabama state capitol in Montgomery—once home to the Confederate government—pledges to fight integration.*

THIS IS THE day of my Inauguration as Governor of the State of Alabama. And on this day I feel a deep obligation to renew my pledges, my covenants with you . . . the people of this great state.

General Robert E. Lee said that "duty" is the sublimest word on the English language and I have come, increasingly, to realize what he meant. I SHALL do my duty to you, God helping . . . to every man, to every woman . . . yes, to every child in this state. I shall fulfill my duty toward honesty and economy in our State government so that no man shall have a part of his livelihood cheated and no child shall have a bit of his future stolen away. . . .

Today I have stood, where once Jefferson Davis stood, and took an oath to my people. It is very appropriate then that from this Cradle of the Confederacy, this very Heart of the Great Anglo-Saxon Southland, that today we sound the drum for freedom as have our generations of forebears before us done, time and time again through history. Let us rise to the call of freedom-loving blood that is in us and send our answer to the tyranny that clanks its chains upon the South. In the name of the greatest people that have ever trod this earth, I draw the line in the dust and toss the gauntlet before the feet of tyranny . . . and I say . . . segregation today . . . segregation tomorrow . . . segregation forever. . . .

Let us send this message back to Washington by our representatives who are with us today . . . that from this day we are standing up, and the heel of tyranny does not fit the neck of an upright man . . . that we intend to take the offensive and carry our fight for freedom across the nation, wielding the balance of power we know we possess in the Southland . . . that WE, not the insipid bloc of voters of some sections . . . will determine in the next election who shall sit in the White House of these United States. . . . That from this day, from this hour . . . from this minute . . . we give the word of a race of honor that we will tolerate their boot in our face no longer . . . and let those certain judges put that in their opium pipes of power and smoke it for what it is worth.

Hear me, Southerners! You sons and daughters who have moved north and west throughout this nation . . . we call on you from your native soil to join with us in national support and vote . . . and we know . . . wherever you are . . . away from the hearths of the Southland . . . that you will respond, for though you may live in the fartherest reaches of this vast country . . . your heart has never left Dixieland.

And you native sons and daughters of old New England's rock-ribbed patriotism . . . and you sturdy natives of the great Mid-West . . . and you descendants of the far West flaming spirit of pioneer freedom . . . we invite you to come and be with us . . . for you are of the Southern spirit . . . and the Southern philosophy . . . you are Southerners too and brothers with us in our fight. . . .

We have placed this sign, "In God We Trust," upon our State Capitol on this Inauguration Day as physical evidence of determination to renew the faith of our fathers and to practice the free heritage they bequeathed to us. We do this with the clear and solemn knowledge that such physical evidence is evidently a direct violation of the logic of that Supreme Court in Washington D.C., and if they or their spokesmen in this state wish to term this defiance . . . I say . . . then let them make the most of it.

This nation was never meant to be a unit of one . . . but a united of the many . . . that is the exact reason our freedom loving forefathers established the states, so as to divide the rights and powers among the states, insuring that no central power could gain master government control.

In united effort we were meant to live under this government . . . whether Baptist, Methodist, Presbyterian, Church of Christ, or whatever one's denomination or religious belief . . . each respecting the other's right to a separate denomination . . . each, by working to develop his own, enriching the total of all our lives through united effort. And so it was meant in our political lives . . . whether Republican, Democrat, Prohibition, or whatever political party . . . each striving from his separate political station . . . respecting the rights of others to be separate and work from within their political framework . . . and each separate political station making its contribution to our lives. . . .

And so it was meant in our racial lives . . . each race, within its own framework has the freedom to teach . . . to instruct . . . to develop . . . to ask for and receive deserved help from others of separate racial stations. This is the great freedom of our American founding fathers . . . but if we amalgamate into the one unit as advocated by the communist philosophers . . . then the enrichment of our lives . . . the freedom for our development . . . is gone forever. We become, therefore, a mongrel unit of one under a single all powerful government . . . and we stand for everything . . . and for nothing.

The true brotherhood of America, of respecting the separateness of others . . . and uniting in effort . . . has been so twisted and distorted from its original concept that there is a small wonder that communism is winning the world.

We invite the negro citizens of Alabama to work with us from his separate racial station . . . as we will work with him . . . to develop, to grow in individual freedom and enrichment. We want jobs and a good future for BOTH races . . . the tubercular and the infirm. This is the basic heritage of my religion, of which I make full practice . . . for we are all the handiwork of God.

But we warn those, of any group, who would follow the false doctrine of communistic amalgamation that we will not surrender our system of government . . . our freedom of race and religion . . . that freedom was won at a hard price and if it requires a hard price to retain it . . . we are able . . . and quite willing to pay it.

★ ★ ★

## "THIS IS ONE COUNTRY"
### John F. Kennedy, Address to the Nation on Civil Rights, Washington, D.C.—June 11, 1963

Confronted with Wallace's refusal to allow the court-ordered integration of the University of Alabama in Tuscaloosa, John F. Kennedy (1917–1963) authorized the commander of the Alabama National Guard, General Henry V. Graham, to, if necessary, move aside the governor, who was blocking the university building's door, to prevent two Black students from registering for classes. Wallace complied, and that evening President Kennedy addressed the country.

THIS AFTERNOON, FOLLOWING a series of threats and defiant statements, the presence of Alabama National Guardsmen was required on the University of Alabama to carry out the final and unequivocal order of the United States District Court of the Northern District of Alabama. That order called for the admission of two clearly qualified young Alabama residents who happened to have been born Negro.

That they were admitted peacefully on the campus is due in good measure to the conduct of the students of the University of Alabama, who met their responsibilities in a constructive way.

I hope that every American, regardless of where he lives, will stop and examine his conscience about this and other related incidents. This Nation was founded by men of many nations and backgrounds. It was founded on the principle that all men are created equal, and that the rights of every man are diminished when the rights of one man are threatened.

Today we are committed to a worldwide struggle to promote and protect the rights of all who wish to be free. And when Americans are sent to Viet-Nam or West Berlin, we do not ask for whites only. It ought to be possible, therefore, for American students of any color to attend any public institution they select without having to be backed up by troops.

It ought to be possible for American consumers of any color to receive equal service in places of public accommodation, such as hotels and restaurants and theaters and retail stores, without being forced to

*"We are confronted primarily with a moral issue," President Kennedy said of civil rights. "It is as old as the scriptures and is as clear as the American Constitution."*

resort to demonstrations in the street, and it ought to be possible for American citizens of any color to register and to vote in a free election without interference or fear of reprisal.

It ought to be possible, in short, for every American to enjoy the privileges of being American without regard to his race or his color. In short, every American ought to have the right to be treated as he would wish to be treated, as one would wish his children to be treated. But this is not the case.

The Negro baby born in America today, regardless of the section of the Nation in which he is born, has about one-half as much chance of completing high school as a white baby born in the same place on the same day, one-third as much chance of completing college, one-third as much chance of becoming a professional man, twice as much chance of becoming unemployed, about one-seventh as much chance of earning

$10,000 a year, a life expectancy which is 7 years shorter, and the prospects of earning only half as much.

This is not a sectional issue. Difficulties over segregation and discrimination exist in every city, in every State of the Union, producing in many cities a rising tide of discontent that threatens the public safety. Nor is this a partisan issue. In a time of domestic crisis men of good will and generosity should be able to unite regardless of party or politics. This is not even a legal or legislative issue alone. It is better to settle these matters in the courts than on the streets, and new laws are needed at every level, but law alone cannot make men see right.

We are confronted primarily with a moral issue. It is as old as the scriptures and is as clear as the American Constitution.

The heart of the question is whether all Americans are to be afforded equal rights and equal opportunities, whether we are going to treat our fellow Americans as we want to be treated. If an American, because his skin is dark, cannot eat lunch in a restaurant open to the public, if he cannot send his children to the best public school available, if he cannot vote for the public officials who represent him, if, in short, he cannot enjoy the full and free life which all of us want, then who among us would be content to have the color of his skin changed and stand in his place? Who among us would then be content with the counsels of patience and delay?

One hundred years of delay have passed since President Lincoln freed the slaves, yet their heirs, their grandsons, are not fully free. They are not yet freed from the bonds of injustice. They are not yet freed from social and economic oppression. And this Nation, for all its hopes and all its boasts, will not be fully free until all its citizens are free.

We preach freedom around the world, and we mean it, and we cherish our freedom here at home, but are we to say to the world, and much more importantly, to each other that this is a land of the free except for the Negroes; that we have no second-class citizens except Negroes; that we have no class or caste system, no ghettoes, no master race except with respect to Negroes?

Now the time has come for this Nation to fulfill its promise. The events in Birmingham and elsewhere have so increased the cries for equality that no city or State or legislative body can prudently choose to ignore them.

The fires of frustration and discord are burning in every city, North and South, where legal remedies are not at hand. Redress is sought in the streets, in demonstrations, parades, and protests which create tensions and threaten violence and threaten lives.

We face, therefore, a moral crisis as a country and as a people. It cannot be met by repressive police action. It cannot be left to increased demonstrations in the streets. It cannot be quieted by token moves or talk. It is a time to act in the Congress, in your State and local legislative body and, above all, in all of our daily lives.

It is not enough to pin the blame on others, to say this is a problem of one section of the country or another, or deplore the facts that we face. A great change is at hand, and our task, our obligation, is to make that revolution, that change, peaceful and constructive for all.

Those who do nothing are inviting shame as well as violence. Those who act boldly are recognizing right as well as reality.

Next week I shall ask the Congress of the United States to act, to make a commitment it has not fully made in this century to the proposition that race has no place in American life or law. The Federal judiciary has upheld that proposition in a series of forthright cases. The executive branch has adopted that proposition in the conduct of its affairs, including the employment of Federal personnel, the use of Federal facilities, and the sale of federally financed housing.

But there are other necessary measures which only the Congress can provide, and they must be provided at this session. The old code of equity law under which we live commands for every wrong a remedy, but in too many communities, in too many parts of the country, wrongs are inflicted on Negro citizens and there are no remedies at law. Unless the Congress acts, their only remedy is in the street.

I am, therefore, asking the Congress to enact legislation giving all Americans the right to be served in facilities which are open to the public—hotels, restaurants, theaters, retail stores, and similar establishments.

This seems to me to be an elementary right. Its denial is an arbitrary indignity that no American in 1963 should have to endure, but many do.

I have recently met with scores of business leaders urging them to take voluntary action to end this discrimination and I have been encouraged by their response, and in the last 2 weeks over 75 cities have seen progress made in desegregating these kinds of facilities. But many are unwilling to act alone, and for this reason, nationwide legislation is needed if we are to move this problem from the streets to the courts.

I am also asking Congress to authorize the Federal Government to participate more fully in lawsuits designed to end segregation in public education. We have succeeded in persuading many districts to desegregate voluntarily. Dozens have admitted Negroes without violence. Today a Negro is attending a State-supported institution in every one of our 50 States, but the pace is very slow.

Too many Negro children entering segregated grade schools at the time of the Supreme Court's decision 9 years ago will enter segregated high schools this fall, having suffered a loss which can never be restored. The lack of an adequate education denies the Negro a chance to get a decent job.

The orderly implementation of the Supreme Court decision, therefore, cannot be left solely to those who may not have the economic resources to carry the legal action or who may be subject to harassment.

Other features will be also requested, including greater protection for the right to vote. But legislation, I repeat, cannot solve this problem alone. It must be solved in the homes of every American in every community across our country.

In this respect, I want to pay tribute to those citizens North and South who have been working in their communities to make life better for all. They are acting not out of a sense of legal duty but out of a sense of human decency.

Like our soldiers and sailors in all parts of the world they are meeting freedom's challenge on the firing line, and I salute them for their honor and their courage.

My fellow Americans, this is a problem which faces us all—in every city of the North as well as the South. Today there are Negroes unemployed, two or three times as many compared to whites, inadequate in education, moving into the large cities, unable to find work, young people particularly out of work without hope, denied equal rights, denied the opportunity to eat at a restaurant or lunch counter or go to a movie theater, denied the right to a decent education, denied almost today the right to attend a State university even though qualified. It seems to me that these are matters which concern us all, not merely Presidents or

Congressmen or Governors, but every citizen of the United States.

This is one country. It has become one country because all of us and all the people who came here had an equal chance to develop their talents.

We cannot say to 10 percent of the population that you can't have that right; that your children can't have the chance to develop whatever talents they have; that the only way that they are going to get their rights is to go into the streets and demonstrate. I think we owe them and we owe ourselves a better country than that.

Therefore, I am asking for your help in making it easier for us to move ahead and to provide the kind of equality of treatment which we would want ourselves; to give a chance for every child to be educated to the limit of his talents.

As I have said before, not every child has an equal talent or an equal ability or an equal motivation, but they should have the equal right to develop their talent and their ability and their motivation, to make something of themselves.

We have a right to expect that the Negro community will be responsible, will uphold the law, but they have a right to expect that the law will be fair, that the Constitution will be color blind, as Justice Harlan said at the turn of the century.

This is what we are talking about and this is a matter which concerns this country and what it stands for, and in meeting it I ask the support of all our citizens.

★ ★ ★

## "WHITES ALARMED; VICTIM IS SHOT FROM AMBUSH"

**Claude Sitton on Medgar Evers's Assassination,**
***The New York Times*—June 13, 1963**

This longest of days—June 12, 1963—ended with the assassination, by a white supremacist, of Medgar Evers, the NAACP's field secretary in Mississippi.

JACKSON, MISS., JUNE 12—A sniper lying in ambush shot and fatally wounded a Negro civil rights leader early today.

The slaying touched off mass protests by Negroes in which 158 were arrested. It also roused widespread fear of further racial violence in this state capital.

The victim of the shooting was Medgar W. Evers, 37-year-old Mississippi field secretary of the National Association for the Advancement of Colored People. Struck in the back by a bullet from a high-powered rifle as he walked from his automobile to his home, he died less than an hour later—at 1:14 a.m. in University Hospital.

Agents of the Federal Bureau of Investigation joined Jackson, Hinds County, and state authorities in the search for the killer.

A 51-year-old white man was picked up, questioned for several hours and released. Investigators discovered a .30-06-caliber rifle with a newly attached telescopic sight in a vacant lot near the honeysuckle thicket from which they believed the fatal shot had been fired.

[In New York, the N.A.A.C.P. offered a $10,000 reward for information leading to the arrest and conviction of Mr. Evers's killer. The Rev. Dr. Martin Luther King Jr. mourned Mr. Evers as a "pure patriot."]

The first demonstration today occurred at 11:25 A.M., when 13 ministers left the Pearl Street African Methodist Episcopal Church and walked silently toward the City Hall.

The police, who refused to let them proceed by twos at widely spaced intervals, arrested all 13. The group included many of the Negro leaders who had been working with white officials in efforts to resolve this city's month-old racial crisis.

An hour and a half later, approximately 200 Negro teenagers marched out of the Masonic Building on Lynch Street, site of Mr. Evers's office. Some 100 city policemen, Hinds County deputy sheriffs, and state highway patrolmen, armed with riot guns and automatic rifles, halted them a block away.

A total of 145 demonstrators, including 74 aged 17 and under, were then arrested. One girl was struck in the face by a club, deputies wrestled a middle-aged woman spectator to the sidewalk and other Negroes were shoved back roughly.

Mrs. Evers spoke tonight to some 500 persons at a mass meeting in the Pearl Street church. Dressed in a pale green dress, she appeared

*The writer James Baldwin and Medgar Evers, who was assassinated in Jackson, Mississippi, a few hours after President Kennedy's address to the nation on civil rights.*

tired but composed. Many women in the audience wept openly.

Referring to her husband's death, she said, "It was his wish that this [Jackson] movement would be one of the most successful that this nation has ever known."

Mrs. Evers, who had requested that she be given the opportunity to speak, said that her husband had spoken of death last Sunday and said that he was ready to go.

"I am left with the strong determination to try to take up where he left off," she said. "I hope that by his death that all here and those [who] are not here will be able to draw some of his strength, some of his courage and some of his determination to finish this fight."

"Nothing can bring Medgar back, but the cause can live on."

Leaflets distributed at the meeting urged Negroes to return to the church tomorrow "prepared for action."

Other speakers also called on the audience to mourn Mr. Evers's death by wearing a black patch on their clothing for at least 30 days and by boycotting downtown white merchants.

A fund designed to provide money for the education of the Evers children was started here at the meeting. Speakers called for persons all over the nation to contribute to it.

The slaying, coupled with the arrests, led to sorrow mixed with anger among Negroes. Whites in this strongly segregationist community publicly expressed shock. But privately they showed more concern over the possibility of Negro retaliation.

The sentiment of Negroes seemed to be summed up by a slogan lettered on a white N.A.A.C.P. T-shirt worn by one of the demonstrators. "White Man. You May Kill the Body, but Not the Soul," it declared.

There were well-founded reports that a number of Negroes had armed themselves.

Gov. Ross R. Barnett and other officials issued statements deploring Mr. Evers's slaying and offering rewards for the arrest and conviction of the guilty.

Many of them, including Governor Barnett and Mayor Allen C. Thompson, are members of the Citizens Councils, a racist organization with national headquarters here.

The Mississippi Publishers Corporation, publisher of *The Clarion-Ledger* and *Jackson Daily News,* offered a $1,000 reward. These newspapers have spearheaded the campaign to maintain 100 per cent segregation throughout the state.

In a statement, Governor Barnett said of the killing:

"Apparently it was a dastardly act and as Governor of the State of Mississippi, I shall cooperate in every way to apprehend the guilty party.

"Too many such incidents are happening throughout the country, including the race riot last night in Cambridge, Md."

Governor Barnett and other officials here have frequently attacked the N.A.A.C.P. as an organization inspired by Communist aims and dedicated to the subversion of "the Southern way of life."

Mayor Thompson broke off a brief visit to a Florida resort to fly back to Jackson. He and City Commissioners D. L. Luckey and Tom Marshall announced the city was offering a $5,000 reward.

"Along with all of the citizens of Jackson, the commissioners and I are dreadfully shocked, humiliated and sick at heart that such a terrible tragedy should happen in our city," Mr. Thompson said in a statement.

"We will not stop working night or day until we find the person or persons who are responsible for such a cowardly act, and we urge the cooperation of everyone in this search," the Mayor said.

Mayor Thompson declined to comment on the mood of white residents of the state capital. He said he had been too busy with the investigation to talk to many of them.

However, one policeman said of the slayer:

"He destroyed in one minute everything we've been trying to do here."

He then asserted, "We're just scared to death. That's the truth."

Jimmy Ward, editor of *The Jackson Daily News,* expressed concern over the damage that the incident might cause to Jackson's reputation.

He did so in his daily front-page column, which frequently contains jokes aimed at the N.A.A.C.P., other civil rights organizations and their leaders and members.

"Despite numerous, most earnest appeals for law and order at all times and most especially during the current racial friction in Jackson," Mr. Ward wrote, "some conscienceless individual has stooped to violence and has greatly harmed the good relations that have existed in Jackson. All Mississippians and especially this shocked community are saddened by the dastardly act of inhuman behavior last night."

Mr. Evers, a native of Decatur, Miss., and an Army veteran of World War II, had been one of the key leaders in the Negroes' drive here to win a promise from the city to hire some Negro policemen and to appoint a biracial committee.

He left a mass meeting at a church last night, stopped at the residence of a Negro lawyer and then drove to his home on the city's northern edge. Before leaving the church, he remarked to a newsman that "tomorrow will be a big day."

He arrived at his neat, green-paneled and buff-brick ranch-style home on Guynes Street shortly after midnight. The accounts of the authorities, his wife and neighbors showed that the following series of events had taken place:

He parked his 1962 light blue sedan in the driveway, behind his wife's station wagon.

As he turned to walk into a side entrance opening into a carport, the sniper's bullet struck him just below the right shoulder blade.

The slug crashed through a front window of the home, penetrated an interior wall, ricocheted off a refrigerator and struck a coffee pot. The battered bullet was found beneath a watermelon on a kitchen cabinet.

Mr. Evers staggered to the doorway, his keys in his hand, and collapsed near the steps. His wife, Myrlie, and three children rushed to the door.

The screaming of the children, "Daddy! Daddy! Daddy!" awoke a neighbor, Thomas A. Young. Another neighbor, Houston Wells, said he had heard the shot and the screams of Mrs. Evers.

Mr. Wells, according to the police, said he had looked out a bedroom window, saw Mr. Evers's crumpled body in the carport and had rushed out into his yard. He said he had crouched behind a clump of shrubbery, fired a shot into the air and shouted for help.

The police, who arrived a short time later, helped neighbors place Mr. Evers in Mr. Wells's station wagon.

As the station wagon sped to University Hospital, those who accompanied the dying man said he had murmured weakly, "Sit me up," and later, "Turn me loose."

Dr. A. B. Britton, Mr. Evers's physician, a member of the Mississippi Advisory Committee to the Federal Civil Rights Commission, rushed to the hospital. He indicated that the victim had died from loss of blood and internal injuries.

Mr. Evers expressed a premonition several weeks ago that he might be shot, according to Dr. Britton. The physician said he and other friends believed that they should have taken steps then to protect him.

City detectives making the investigation found a newly cleared space in the honeysuckle thicket, some 200 feet southwest of Mr. Evers's home. They speculated the killer had hidden there while awaiting the arrival of his victim.

Lights in the carport, according to investigators, silhouetted Mr. Evers's body and enabled the sniper to see through the telescopic sight.

★ ★ ★

## "WE WANT TO BE FREE NOW!"
## John Lewis, Address to the March on Washington for Jobs and Freedom—August 28, 1963

---

Born in Pike County, Alabama, John Robert Lewis (1940–2020) grew up in a segregated America. As a teenager he heard radio sermons delivered by the young Martin Luther King, Jr., in nearby Montgomery and was moved to become part of the burgeoning civil-rights movement. While in Nashville attending the American Baptist Theological Seminary, Lewis was trained in the philosophy and the means of nonviolent protest. In the summer of 1963 he was the youngest speaker at the March on Washington.

WE MARCH TODAY for jobs and freedom, but we have nothing to be proud of. For hundreds and thousands of our brothers are not here. For they are receiving starvation wages, or no wages at all. While we stand here, there are sharecroppers in the Delta of Mississippi who are out in the fields working for less than three dollars a day, twelve hours a day. While we stand here there are students in jail on trumped-up charges. Our brother James Farmer, along with many others, is also in jail. We come here today with a great sense of misgiving.

It is true that we support the administration's civil rights bill. We support it with great reservations, however. Unless Title III is put in this bill, there is nothing to protect the young children and old women who must face police dogs and fire hoses in the South while they engage in peaceful demonstrations. In its present form, this bill will not protect the citizens of Danville, Virginia, who must live in constant fear of a police state. It will not protect the hundreds and thousands of people that have been arrested on trumped charges. What about the three young men, SNCC field secretaries in Americus, Georgia, who face the death penalty for engaging in peaceful protest?

As it stands now, the voting section of this bill will not help the thousands of black people who want to vote. It will not help the citizens of Mississippi, of Alabama and Georgia, who are qualified to vote, but lack a sixth-grade education. "One man, one vote" is the African cry. It is ours too. It must be ours!

We must have legislation that will protect the Mississippi sharecropper who is put off of his farm because he dares to register to vote. We need a bill that will provide for the homeless and starving people of this nation. We need a bill that will ensure the equality of a maid who earns five dollars a week in a home of a family whose total income is $100,000 a year. We must have a good FEPC [Fair Employment Practices Committee] bill.

My friends, let us not forget that we are involved in a serious social revolution. By and large, American politics is dominated by politicians who build their careers on immoral compromises and ally themselves with open forms of political, economic, and social exploitation. There are exceptions, of course. We salute those. But what political leader can stand up and say, "My party is the party of principles"? For the party of Kennedy is also the party of [James] Eastland [of Mississippi]. The party of [Jacob] Javits [of New York] is also the party of Goldwater. Where is our party? Where is the political party that will make it unnecessary to march on Washington?

Where is the political party that will make it unnecessary to march in the streets of Birmingham? Where is the political party that will protect the citizens of Albany, Georgia? Do you know that in Albany, Georgia, nine of our leaders have been indicted, not by the Dixiecrats, but by the federal government for peaceful protest? But what did the federal government do when Albany's deputy sheriff beat Attorney C. B. King and left him half-dead? What did the federal government do when local police officials kicked and assaulted the pregnant wife of Slater King, and she lost her baby?

To those who have said, "Be patient and wait," we have long said that we cannot be patient. We do not want our freedom gradually, but we want to be free now! We are tired. We are tired of being beaten by policemen. We are tired of seeing our people locked up in jail over and over again. And then you holler, "Be patient." How long can we be patient? We want our freedom and we want it now. We do not want to go to jail. But we will go to jail if this is the price we must pay for love, brotherhood, and true peace.

I appeal to all of you to get into this great revolution that is sweeping this nation. Get in and stay in the streets of every city, every village and hamlet of this nation until true freedom comes, until the revolution of 1776 is complete. We must get in this revolution and complete the revolution. For in the Delta in Mississippi, in southwest Georgia, in the Black Belt of Alabama, in Harlem, in Chicago, Detroit, Philadelphia, and all over this nation, the black masses are on the march for jobs and freedom.

They're talking about slow down and stop. We will not stop. All of the forces of Eastland, Barnett, Wallace, and Thurmond will not stop this revolution. If we do not get meaningful legislation out of this Congress, the time will come when we will not confine our marching to Washington. We will march through the South; through the streets of Jackson, through the streets of Danville, through the streets of Cambridge, through the streets of Birmingham. But we will march with the spirit of love and with the spirit of dignity that we have shown here today. By the force of our demands, our determination, and our numbers, we shall splinter the segregated South into a thousand pieces and put them together in the image of God and democracy. We must say: "Wake up America! Wake up!" For we cannot stop, and we will not and cannot be patient.

★ ★ ★

## "AMERICA GROWS, AMERICA CHANGES"

**Senator Everett M. Dirksen of Illinois, Speech on the Civil Rights Bill, United States Senate—June 10, 1964**

A distinguished lawmaker from Illinois, Everett McKinley Dirksen (1896–1969) was the Senate Republican Leader across the presidencies of Dwight Eisenhower, John F. Kennedy, Lyndon B. Johnson, and Richard Nixon. In 1964, with conservative senators blocking a final vote on civil-rights legislation that would strike a mortal blow against legalized Jim Crow, Dirksen delivered the following speech. "In this critical hour Senator Dirksen came through, as I had hoped he would," LBJ remarked. "He knew his country's future was at stake. He knew what he could do to help. He knew what he had to do as a leader."

IT IS A year ago this month that the late President Kennedy sent his civil rights bill and message to the Congress. For two years, we had been chiding him about failure to act in this field. At long last, and after many conferences, it became a reality.

After nine days of hearings before the Senate Judiciary Committee, it was referred to a subcommittee. There it languished and the administration leadership finally decided to await the House bill.

In the House, it traveled an equally tortuous road. But at long last, it reached the House floor for action. It was debated for 64 hours; 155 amendments were offered; 34 were approved. On February 10, 1964, it passed the House by a vote of 290 to 130. That was a 65-percent vote. . . .

It is now 4 months since it passed the House. It is 3½ months since it came to the Senate calendar. Three months have gone by since the motion to consider was made. We have acted on one intervening motion to send the bill back to the Judiciary Committee and a vote on the jury trial amendment. That has been the extent of our action.

Sharp opinions have developed. Incredible allegations have been made. Extreme views have been asserted. The mail volume has been heavy. The bill has provoked many long-distance telephone calls, many of them late at night or in the small hours of the morning. There has been unrestrained criticism about motives. Thousands of people have come to the Capitol to urge immediate action on an unchanged House bill.

For myself, I have had but one purpose and that was the enactment of a good, workable, equitable, practical bill having due regard for the progress made in the civil rights field at the state and local level.

I am no Johnnie-come-lately in this field. Thirty years ago, in the House of Representatives, I voted on anti-poll tax and anti-lynching measures. Since then, I have sponsored or co-sponsored scores of bills dealing with civil rights.

At the outset, I contended that the House bill was imperfect and deficient. That fact is now quite generally conceded. But the debate continued. The number of amendments submitted increased. They now number nearly four hundred. The stalemate continued. A backlog of work piled up. Committees could not function normally. It was an unhappy situation, and it was becoming a bit intolerable.

It became increasingly evident that to secure passage of a bill in the Senate would require cloture and a limitation on debate. Senate aversion to cloture is traditional. Only once in thirty-five years has cloture been voted. But the procedure for cloture is a standing rule of the Senate. It grew out of a filibuster against the Armed Ship bill in 1917 and has been part of the standing rules of the Senate for forty-seven years. To argue that cloture is unwarranted or unjustified is to assert that in

1917, the Senate adopted a rule which it did not intend to use when circumstances required or that it was placed in the rulebook only as to be repudiated. It was adopted as an instrument for action when all other efforts failed.

Today the Senate is stalemated in its efforts to enact a civil rights bill, one version of which has already been approved by the House by a vote of more than 2 to 1. That the Senate wishes to act on a civil rights bill can be divined from the fact that the motion to take up was adopted by a vote of 67 to 17.

There are many reasons why cloture should be invoked and a good civil rights measure enacted.

First. It is said that on the night he died, Victor Hugo wrote in his diary, substantially this sentiment: '*Stronger than all the armies is an idea whose time has come.*'

The time has come for equality of opportunity in sharing in government, in education, and in employment. It will not be stayed or denied. It is here.

The problem began when the Constitution makers permitted the importation of persons to continue for another twenty years. That problem was to generate the fury of civil strife seventy-five years later. Out of it was to come the Thirteenth Amendment ending servitude, the Fourteenth Amendment to provide equal protection of the laws and dual citizenship, the Fifteenth Amendment to prohibit government from abridging the right to vote.

Other factors had an impact. Two and three-quarter million young Negroes served in World Wars I, II, and Korea. Some won the Congressional Medal of Honor and the Distinguished Service Cross. Today they are fathers and grandfathers. They brought back impressions from countries where no discrimination existed. These impressions have been transmitted to children and grandchildren. Meanwhile, hundreds of thousands of colored [people] have become teachers and professors, doctors and dentists, engineers and architects, artists and actors, musicians and technicians. They have become status minded. They have sensed inequality. They are prepared to make the issue. They feel that the time has come for the idea of equal opportunity. To enact the pending measure by invoking cloture is imperative.

Second. Years ago, a professor who thought he had developed an incontrovertible scientific premise submitted it to his faculty associate. Quickly they picked it apart. In agony he cried out, "Is nothing eternal?" To this one of his associates replied, "Nothing is eternal except change."

Since the act of 1875 on public accommodations and the Supreme Court decision of 1883 which struck it down, America has changed. The population then was 45 million. Today it is 190 million. In the Pledge of Allegiance to the Flag we intone, "One nation, under God." And so it is. It is an integrated nation. Air, rail, and highway transportation make it so. A common language makes it so. A tax pattern which applies equally to white and nonwhites makes it so. Literacy makes it so. The mobility provided by eighty million autos makes it so. The accommodations laws in thirty-four states and the District of Columbia makes [sic] it so. The fair employment practice laws in thirty states make it so. Yes, our land has changed since the Supreme Court decision of 1883. . . .

To my friends from the South, I would refresh you on the words of a great Georgian named Henry W. Grady [editor of the Atlanta Constitution, 1879-1889]. On December 22, 1886, he was asked to respond to a toast to the new South at the New England society dinner. His words were dramatic and explosive. He began his toast by saying: *"There was a South of slavery and secession—that South is dead. There is a South of union and freedom—that South thank God is living, breathing, growing every hour."*

America grows, America changes. And on the civil rights issue we must rise with the occasion. That calls for cloture and for the enactment of a civil rights bill.

Third. There is another reason—our covenant with the people. For many years, each political party has given major consideration to a civil rights plank in its platform. Go back and reexamine our pledges to the country as we sought the suffrage of the people and for a grant of authority to manage and direct their affairs. Were these pledges so much campaign stuff or did we mean it? Were these promises on civil rights but idle words for vote-getting purposes or were they a covenant meant to be kept? If all this was mere pretense, let us confess the sin of hypocrisy now and vow not to delude the people again.

To you, my Republican colleagues, let me refresh you on the words of a great American. His name is Herbert Hoover. In his day he was reviled and maligned. He was castigated and calumniated. But today his views and his judgment stand vindicated at the bar of history. In 1952 he received a volcanic welcome as he appeared before our national convention in Chicago. On that occasion he commented on the Whig Party, predecessor of the Republican Party, and said: "*The Whig party temporized, compromised upon the issue of freedom for the Negro. That party disappeared. It deserved to disappear. Shall the Republican party receive or deserve any better fate if it compromises upon the issue of freedom for all men?*"

To those who have charged me with doing a disservice to my party because of my interest in the enactment of a good civil rights bill—and there have been a good many who have made that charge—I can only say that our party found its faith in the Declaration of Independence in which a great Democrat, Jefferson by name, wrote the flaming words: "*We hold these truths to be self-evident that all men are created equal.*"

That has been the living faith of our party. Do we forsake this article of faith, now that equality's time has come or do we stand up for it and ensure the survival of our party and its ultimate victory? There is no substitute for a basic and righteous idea. We have a duty—a firm duty—to use the instruments at hand—namely, the cloture rule—to bring about the enactment of a good civil rights bill.

Fourth. There is another reason why we dare not temporize with the issue which is before us. It is essentially moral in character. It must be resolved. It will not go away. Its time has come. Nor is it the first time in our history that an issue with moral connotations and implications has swept away the resistance, the fulminations, the legalistic speeches, the ardent but dubious arguments, the lamentations and the thought patterns of an earlier generation and pushed forward to fruition. . . .

Pending before us is another moral issue. Basically it deals with equality of opportunity in exercising the franchise, in securing an education, in making a livelihood, in enjoying the mantle of protection of the law. It has been a long, hard furrow and each generation must plow its share. Progress was made in 1957 and 1960. But the furrow does not end there. It requires the implementation provided by the substitute measure which is before us. And to secure that implementation requires cloture.

Let me add one thought to these observations. Today is an anniversary. It is in fact the one hundredth anniversary of the nomination of Abraham Lincoln for a second term for the presidency on the Republican ticket. Two documents became the blueprints for his life and his conduct. The first was the Declaration of Independence which proclaimed the doctrine that all men are created equal. The second was the Constitution, the preamble to which began with the words: *"We, the people . . . do ordain and establish this Constitution for the United States of America."*

These were the articles of his superb and unquenchable faith. Nowhere and at no time did he more nobly reaffirm that faith than at Gettysburg 101 years ago when he spoke of "a new nation, conceived in liberty and dedicated to the proposition that all men are created equal."

It is to take us further down that road that a bill is pending before us. We have a duty to get that job done. To do it will require cloture and a limitation on debate as provided by a standing rule of the Senate which has been in being for nearly fifty years. I trust we shall not fail in that duty.

That, from a great Republican, thinking in the frame of equality of opportunity—and that is all that is involved in this bill.

To those who have charged me with doing a disservice to my party—and there have been many—I can only say that our party found its faith in the Declaration of Independence, which was penned by a great Democrat, Thomas Jefferson by name. . . .

That has been the living faith of our party. Do we forsake this article of faith, now that the time for our decision has come?

There is no substitute for a basic ideal. We have a firm duty to use the instrument at hand; namely, the cloture rule, to bring about the enactment of a good civil rights bill.

I appeal to all senators. We are confronted with a moral issue. Today let us not be found wanting in whatever it takes by way of moral and spiritual substance to face up to the issue and to vote cloture.

★ ★ ★

## "THE GREAT SOCIETY"
### Lyndon B. Johnson, Remarks at the University of Michigan, Ann Arbor, Michigan—May 22, 1964

Lyndon B. Johnson (1908–1973) came to the presidency after President Kennedy's murder in Dallas, determined to make a lasting mark. In this commencement address, delivered as he was seeking election in his own right, Johnson laid out his sweeping vision of what government could do—an agenda to match, and perhaps surpass, his old hero Franklin Roosevelt.

THE PURPOSE OF protecting the life of our Nation and preserving the liberty of our citizens is to pursue the happiness of our people. Our success in that pursuit is the test of our success as a Nation.

For a century we labored to settle and to subdue a continent. For half a century we called upon unbounded invention and untiring industry to create an order of plenty for all of our people.

The challenge of the next half century is whether we have the wisdom to use that wealth to enrich and elevate our national life, and to advance the quality of our American civilization.

Your imagination, your initiative, and your indignation will determine whether we build a society where progress is the servant of our needs, or a society where old values and new visions are buried under unbridled growth. For in your time we have the opportunity to move not only toward the rich society and the powerful society, but upward to the Great Society.

The Great Society rests on abundance and liberty for all. It demands an end to poverty and racial injustice, to which we are totally committed in our time. But that is just the beginning.

The Great Society is a place where every child can find knowledge to enrich his mind and to enlarge his talents. It is a place where leisure is a welcome chance to build and reflect, not a feared cause of boredom and restlessness. It is a place where the city of man serves not only the needs of the body and the demands of commerce but the desire for beauty and the hunger for community.

It is a place where man can renew contact with nature. It is a place which honors creation for its own sake and for what it adds to the understanding of the race. It is a place where men are more concerned with the quality of their goals than the quantity of their goods.

But most of all, the Great Society is not a safe harbor, a resting place, a final objective, a finished work. It is a challenge constantly renewed, beckoning us toward a destiny where the meaning of our lives matches the marvelous products of our labor.

So I want to talk to you today about three places where we begin to build the Great Society—in our cities, in our countryside, and in our classrooms.

Many of you will live to see the day, perhaps 50 years from now, when there will be 400 million Americans, four-fifths of them in urban areas. In the remainder of this century urban population will double, city land will double, and we will have to build homes, highways, and facilities equal to all those built since this country was first settled. So in the next 40 years we must rebuild the entire urban United States.

Aristotle said: "Men come together in cities in order to live, but they remain together in order to live the good life." It is harder and harder to live the good life in American cities today.

The catalog of ills is long: there is the decay of the centers and the despoiling of the suburbs. There is not enough housing for our people or transportation for our traffic. Open land is vanishing and old landmarks are violated.

Worst of all, expansion is eroding the precious and time honored values of community with neighbors and communion with nature. The loss of these values breeds loneliness and boredom and indifference.

Our society will never be great until our cities are great. Today the frontier of imagination and innovation is inside those cities and not beyond their borders.

New experiments are already going on. It will be the task of your generation to make the American city a place where future generations will come, not only to live but to live the good life.

I understand that if I stayed here tonight I would see that Michigan students are really doing their best to live the good life.

This is the place where the Peace Corps was started. It is inspiring to see how all of you, while you are in this country, are trying so hard to live at the level of the people.

A second place where we begin to build the Great Society is in our countryside. We have always prided ourselves on being not only America the strong and America the free, but America the beautiful. Today that beauty is in danger. The water we drink, the food we eat, the very air that we breathe, are threatened with pollution. Our parks are overcrowded, our seashores overburdened. Green fields and dense forests are disappearing.

A few years ago we were greatly concerned about the "Ugly American." Today we must act to prevent an ugly America.

For once the battle is lost, once our natural splendor is destroyed, it can never be recaptured. And once man can no longer walk with beauty or wonder at nature his spirit will wither and his sustenance be wasted.

A third place to build the Great Society is in the classrooms of America. There your children's lives will be shaped. Our society will not be great until every young mind is set free to scan the farthest reaches of thought and imagination. We are still far from that goal.

Today, 8 million adult Americans, more than the entire population of Michigan, have not finished 5 years of school. Nearly 20 million have

*Lyndon Johnson's expansive ambitions helped him win an epic victory in 1964, but he and his party lost the 1966 midterms and then the White House in 1968.*

not finished 8 years of school. Nearly 54 million—more than one-quarter of all America—have not even finished high school.

Each year more than 100,000 high school graduates, with proved ability, do not enter college because they cannot afford it. And if we cannot educate today's youth, what will we do in 1970 when elementary school enrollment will be 5 million greater than 1960? And high school enrollment will rise by 5 million. College enrollment will increase by more than 3 million.

In many places, classrooms are overcrowded and curricula are outdated. Most of our qualified teachers are underpaid, and many of our paid teachers are unqualified. So we must give every child a place to sit and a teacher to learn from. Poverty must not be a bar to learning, and learning must offer an escape from poverty.

But more classrooms and more teachers are not enough. We must seek an educational system which grows in excellence as it grows in size. This means better training for our teachers. It means preparing youth to enjoy their hours of leisure as well as their hours of labor. It means exploring new techniques of teaching, to find new ways to stimulate the love of learning and the capacity for creation.

These are three of the central issues of the Great Society. While our Government has many programs directed at those issues, I do not pretend that we have the full answer to those problems.

But I do promise this: We are going to assemble the best thought and the broadest knowledge from all over the world to find those answers for America. I intend to establish working groups to prepare a series of White House conferences and meetings—on the cities, on natural beauty, on the quality of education, and on other emerging challenges. And from these meetings and from this inspiration and from these studies we will begin to set our course toward the Great Society.

The solution to these problems does not rest on a massive program in Washington, nor can it rely solely on the strained resources of local authority. They require us to create new concepts of cooperation, a creative federalism, between the National Capital and the leaders of local communities.

Woodrow Wilson once wrote: "Every man sent out from his university should be a man of his Nation as well as a man of his time."

Within your lifetime powerful forces, already loosed, will take us toward a way of life beyond the realm of our experience, almost beyond the bounds of our imagination.

For better or for worse, your generation has been appointed by history to deal with those problems and to lead America toward a new age. You have the chance never before afforded to any people in any age. You can help build a society where the demands of morality, and the needs of the spirit, can be realized in the life of the Nation.

So, will you join in the battle to give every citizen the full equality which God enjoins and the law requires, whatever his belief, or race, or the color of his skin?

Will you join in the battle to give every citizen an escape from the crushing weight of poverty?

Will you join in the battle to make it possible for all nations to live in enduring peace—as neighbors and not as mortal enemies?

Will you join in the battle to build the Great Society, to prove that our material progress is only the foundation on which we will build a richer life of mind and spirit?

There are those timid souls who say this battle cannot be won; that we are condemned to a soulless wealth. I do not agree. We have the power to shape the civilization that we want. But we need your will, your labor, your hearts, if we are to build that kind of society.

Those who came to this land sought to build more than just a new country. They sought a new world. So I have come here today to your campus to say that you can make their vision our reality. So let us from this moment begin our work so that in the future men will look back and say: It was then, after a long and weary way, that man turned the exploits of his genius to the full enrichment of his life.

⋆ ⋆ ⋆

## "THE EXTREMIST THREAT"

### Nelson A. Rockefeller, Speech to the 1964 Republican National Convention, San Francisco, California—July 14, 1964

Nelson A. Rockefeller (1908–1979), scion of an American fortune and governor of New York, was a pillar of the moderate-to-liberal wing of the Republican Party that in 1964 was losing ground to a conservative insurgency led by Senator Barry Goldwater of Arizona. In these remarks at the Republican National Convention, Rockefeller, facing boos and catcalls, spoke in favor of a platform plank that would denounce "extremism." The measure failed to pass.

IT IS ESSENTIAL that this Convention repudiate here and now any doctrinaire, militant minority, whether Communist, Ku Klux Klan or Bircher which would subvert this party to purposes alien to the very basic tenets which gave this party birth. . . .

During this year, I have criss-crossed this nation fighting . . . and warning of the extremist threat, its danger to the party and its danger to the nation.

The methods of these extremist elements I have experienced at first hand. Their tactics have ranged from cancellation by coercion of a speaking engagement before a college audience to outright threats of personal violence.

These things have no place in America. But I can personally testify to their existence. And so can countless others who have also experienced: anonymous midnight and early morning telephone calls, unsigned threatening letters, smear and hate literature, strongarm and goon tactics, bomb threats and bombings, infiltration and take-over of established political organizations by communist and Nazi methods.

These extremists feed on fear, hate and terror. They have no program for American—for the Republican party. They have no solutions for our problems of chronic unemployment, of education, of agriculture, of racial injustice or strife.

These extremists have no plan and no program to keep the peace and bring freedom to the world.

On the contrary, they spread distrust. They engender suspicion.

They encourage disunity. And they operated from the dark shadows of secrecy. . . .

They have called President Eisenhower "a dedicated, conscious agent of the Communist conspiracy."

They have labeled a great Republican Secretary of State, the late John Foster Dulles, "a Communist agent."

They have demanded that the United States get out of the United Nations and that the United Nations get out of the United States.

There is no place in this Republican party for such hawkers of hate, such purveyors of prejudice, such fabricators of fear, whether Communist, Ku Klux Klan or Bircher.

There is no place in this Republican party for those who would infiltrate its ranks, distort its aims, and convert it into a cloak of apparent respectability for a dangerous extremism.

And make no mistake about it—the hidden members of the John Birch Society and others like them are out to do just that!

These people have nothing in common with Republicanism.

These people have nothing in common with Americans.

The Republican Party must repudiate these people!

I move the adoption of this resolution.

⋆ ⋆ ⋆

## "EXTREMISM IN THE DEFENSE OF LIBERTY IS NO VICE"
**Barry Goldwater, Acceptance Speech to the Republican National Convention, San Francisco, California—July 16, 1964**

---

The nomination of Barry Goldwater (1909–1998) marked the ascendance of the right wing of the Republican Party after years of leadership by more moderate figures such as Thomas E. Dewey and Dwight D. Eisenhower.

IN THIS WORLD no person, no party can guarantee anything, but what we can do and what we shall do is to deserve victory, and victory will be ours. The good Lord raised this mighty Republic to be a home for the brave and to flourish as the land of the free—not to stagnate in the swampland of collectivism, not to cringe before the bully of communism.

Now, my fellow Americans, the tide has been running against freedom. Our people have followed false prophets. We must, and we shall, return to proven ways—not because they are old, but because they are true.

We must, and we shall, set the tide running again in the cause of freedom. And this party, with its every action, every word, every breath, and every heartbeat, has but a single resolve, and that is freedom.

Freedom made orderly for this nation by our constitutional government. Freedom under a government limited by laws of nature and of nature's God. Freedom balanced so that liberty lacking order will not become the slavery of the prison cell; balanced so that liberty lacking order will not become the license of the mob and of the jungle.

Now, we Americans understand freedom; we have earned it, we have lived for it, and we have died for it. This nation and its people are freedom's models in a searching world. We can be freedom's missionaries in a doubting world.

But, ladies and gentlemen, first we must renew freedom's mission in our own hearts and in our own homes.

During four futile years the administration which we shall replace has distorted and lost that faith. It has talked and talked and talked and talked the words of freedom, but it has failed and failed and failed in the works of freedom.

Now failure cements the wall of shame in Berlin; failures blot the sands of shame at the Bay of Pigs; failures marked the slow death of freedom in Laos; failures infest the jungles of Vietnam; and failures haunt the houses of our once great alliances and undermine the greatest bulwark ever erected by free nations, the NATO community.

Failures proclaim lost leadership, obscure purpose, weakening wills, and the risk of inciting our sworn enemies to new aggressions and to new excesses.

And because of this administration we are tonight a world divided. We are a nation becalmed. We have lost the brisk pace of diversity and the genius of individual creativity. We are plodding at a pace set by centralized planning, red tape, rules without responsibility, and regimentation without recourse.

Rather than useful jobs in our country, people have been offered bureaucratic make-work; rather than moral leadership, they have been given bread and circuses; they have been given spectacles, and, yes, they've even been given scandals.

Tonight there is violence in our streets, corruption in our highest offices, aimlessness among our youth, anxiety among our elderly; and there's a virtual despair among the many who look beyond material success toward the inner meaning of their lives. And where examples of morality should be set, the opposite is seen. Small men seeking great wealth or power have too often and too long turned even the highest levels of public service into mere personal opportunity. . . .

The growing menace in our country tonight, to personal safety, to life, to limb and property, in homes, in churches, on the playgrounds and places of business, particularly in our great cities, is the mounting concern—or should be—of every thoughtful citizen in the United States. Security from domestic violence, no less than from foreign aggression, is the most elementary and fundamental purpose of any government, and a government that cannot fulfill this purpose is one that cannot long command the loyalty of its citizens.

History shows us, demonstrates that nothing, nothing prepares the way for tyranny more than the failure of public officials to keep the streets from bullies and marauders.

Now, we Republicans see all this as more—much more—than the result of mere political differences or mere political mistakes. We see this as the result of a fundamentally and absolutely wrong view of man, his nature and his destiny.

Those who seek to live your lives for you, to take your liberty in return for relieving you of yours, those who elevate the state and downgrade the citizen, must see ultimately a world in which earthly power can be substituted for divine will. And this nation was founded upon the rejection of that notion and upon the acceptance of God as the author of freedom.

Now, those who seek absolute power, even though they seek it to do what they regard as good, are simply demanding the right to enforce their own version of heaven on earth, and let me remind you they are the very ones who always create the most hellish tyranny.

Absolute power does corrupt, and those who seek it must be suspect and must be opposed. Their mistaken course stems from false notions, ladies and gentlemen, of equality. Equality, rightly understood as our founding fathers understood it, leads to liberty and to the emancipation of creative differences; wrongly understood, as it has been so tragically in our time, it leads first to conformity and then to despotism.

Fellow Republicans, it is the cause of Republicanism to resist concentrations of power, private or public, which enforce such conformity and inflict such despotism.

It is the cause of Republicanism to ensure that power remains in the hands of the people—and, so help us God, that is exactly what a Republican president will do with the help of a Republican Congress.

It is further the cause of Republicanism to restore a clear understanding of the tyranny of man over man in the world at large. It is our cause to dispel the foggy thinking which avoids hard decisions in the delusion that a world of conflict will somehow resolve itself into a world of harmony, if we just don't rock the boat or irritate the forces of aggression—and this is hogwash.

It is further the cause of Republicanism to remind ourselves, and the world, that only the strong can remain free, that only the strong can keep the peace. . . .

And I needn't remind you—but I will—that it's been during Democratic years that our strength to deter war has been stilled and even gone into a planned decline. It has been during Democratic years that we have weakly stumbled into conflicts, timidly refusing to draw our own lines against aggression, deceitfully refusing to tell even our people of our full participation and tragically letting our finest men die on battlefields unmarked by purpose, unmarked by pride or the prospect of victory.

Yesterday it was Korea; tonight it is Vietnam. Make no bones of this. Don't try to sweep this under the rug. We are at war in Vietnam. And yet the president, who is the commander in chief of our forces, refuses to say—refuses to say, mind you—whether or not the objective over there is victory, and his secretary of defense continues to mislead and misinform the American people, and enough of it has gone by.

And I needn't remind you—but I will—it has been during Democratic years that a billion persons were cast into Communist captivity and their fate cynically sealed. . . .

Now, the Republican cause demands that we brand communism as the principal disturber of peace in the world today. Indeed, we should brand it as the only significant disturber of the peace. And we must make clear that until its goals of conquest are absolutely renounced and its relations with all nations tempered, communism and the governments it now controls are enemies of every man on earth who is or wants to be free. . . .

In our vision of a good and decent future, free and peaceful, there must be room, room for the liberation of the energy and the talent of the individual, otherwise our vision is blind at the outset.

We must assure a society here which while never abandoning the needy, or forsaking the helpless, nurtures incentives and opportunity for the creative and the productive.

We must know the whole good is the product of many single contributions.

And I cherish the day when our children once again will restore as heroes the sort of men and women who, unafraid and undaunted, pursue the truth, strive to cure disease, subdue and make fruitful our natural environment, and produce the inventive engines of production, science, and technology.

This nation, whose creative people have enhanced this entire span of history, should again thrive upon the greatness of all those things which we—we as individual citizens—can and should do. . . .

Anyone who joins us in all sincerity, we welcome. Those, those who do not care for our cause, we don't expect to enter our ranks, in any case. And let our Republicanism so focused and so dedicated not be made fuzzy and futile by unthinking and stupid labels.

I would remind you that extremism in the defense of liberty is no vice! And let me remind you also that moderation in the pursuit of justice is no virtue!

The beauty of the very system we Republicans are pledged to restore and revitalize, the beauty of this federal system of ours, is in its reconciliation of diversity with unity. We must not see malice in honest differences of opinion, and no matter how great, so long as they are not inconsistent with the pledges we have given to each other in and through our Constitution.

Our Republican cause is not to level out the world or make its people conform in computer-regimented sameness. Our Republican cause is to free our people and light the way for liberty throughout the world.

Ours is a very human cause for very humane goals. This party, its good people, and its unquestionable devotion to freedom will not fulfill the purposes of this campaign which we launch here now until our cause has won the day, inspired the world, and shown the way to a tomorrow worthy of all our yesteryears.

⋆ ⋆ ⋆

## "IS THIS AMERICA?"
## Fannie Lou Hamer, Testimony Before the Credentials Committee of the Democratic National Convention, Atlantic City, New Jersey—August 22, 1964

Fannie Lou Hamer (1917–1977) bravely testified on behalf of the Mississippi Freedom Democrats, an integrated delegation that had come to the national convention in Atlantic City in the wake of the passage of the Civil Rights Act of 1964 to argue that it, not the segregated all-white delegation of the state's regular Democrats, should be seated. Hamer's case did not carry the day, but a compromise brokered in part by Walter F. Mondale (1928–2021), the attorney general of Minnesota, decreed that there could be no segregated delegations in the future.

*Fannie Lou Hamer at the 1964 Democratic National Convention in Atlantic City, New Jersey.*

*[In June 1963, after a voter-registration workshop, Hamer and others were arrested in Winona, Mississippi. She was placed in a cell with two Black men who were also in custody; the authorities ordered the men to strike her with a blackjack while she lay face-down on a bunk.]*

I was beat by the first Negro until he was exhausted. . . . [Then] the State Highway Patrolman ordered the second Negro to take the blackjack. . . .

One white man . . . he walked over and pulled my dress—I pulled my dress down and he pulled my dress back up. . . .

All of this is on account of we want to register, to become first-class citizens. And if the Freedom Democratic Party is not seated now, I question America. Is this America, the land of the free and the home of the brave, where we have to sleep with our telephones off the hooks because our lives be threatened daily, because we want to live as decent human beings, in America?

ON OCTOBER 16, 2017, *Representative Sheila Jackson Lee, Democrat of Texas, delivered remarks honoring Hamer in the United States House of Representatives. Excerpts:*

Mr. Speaker, as a senior member of the Congressional Black Caucus and a Co-Chair of the Congressional Voting Rights Caucus, I rise in remembrance of Fannie Lou Hamer, a leading heroine of the Civil Rights Movement, a fearless fighter for voting rights and social justice who spoke truth to power and touched conscience of the nation.

On this day, exactly one hundred years ago, October 6, 1917, Fannie Lou Hamer was born in Montgomery County, Mississippi, to Lou Ella and James Lee Townsend, the youngest of twenty children.

Although she managed to complete several years of school, by adolescence Fannie Lou Hamer was picking hundreds of pounds of cotton a day.

She would later meet and marry Perry Hamer, known as Pap, and work alongside him as sharecroppers at W. D. Marlow's plantation near Ruleville, in Sunflower County, Mississippi.

From these humble beginnings Fannie Lou Hamer would go on to become one of the iconic figures of the Civil Rights Movement that succeeded in bringing down the Jericho walls of *de jure* segregation and winning passage of the Voting Rights Act of 1965, the greatest victory for civil rights and human dignity since the Emancipation Proclamation.

Mr. Speaker, one of our proudest boasts as Americans is that "one person can make a difference."

The life of Fannie Lou Hamer demonstrates that this is not an idle boast but a simple truth.

Fannie Lou Hamer dedicated her life to the fight for civil rights, working for the Student Nonviolent Coordinating Committee, an organization that engaged in acts of civil disobedience to fight racial segregation and injustice in the South.

During the 1950s, when Fannie Lou Hamer was in her thirties, she attended several annual conferences of the Regional Council of Negro Leadership (RCNL), a civil rights and self-help organization that ignited her passion for activism.

In 1962 Fannie Lou Hamer took up the call to try and register to vote in Mississippi, a state whose constitution and laws erected barriers such as poll taxes and literacy tests to disenfranchise African Americans.

It was on the bus trip to Indianola, Mississippi, to register to vote that, in what would become her signature trait as an activist, she began singing African American spirituals such as "Go Tell It on the Mountain" and "This Little Light of Mine."

Singing spirituals reflected her firm belief that the struggle for civil rights was a righteous cause and toiling in this vineyard was the Christian thing to do.

Fannie Lou Hamer's courage and leadership in Indianola came to the attention of SNCC organizer Bob Moses, who recruited her to travel around the South doing organizing work for the organization.

Being an African American activist at that time in that place was dangerous, but that did not deter the fierce Fannie Lou Hamer. . . .

During one of Fannie Lou Hamer's trips she and other civil rights activists were arrested and badly beaten on the orders of police officers.

After recovering from the assault she returned to activism and the task of organizing voter registration drives. . . .

In 1964, Fannie Lou Hamer helped organize "Freedom Summer," during which she was known by other activists as a motherly figure who strongly believed that the civil rights struggle should be broad-based and multi-racial.

Later that year, Fannie Lou Hamer helped to found and served as Vice-Chair of the Mississippi Freedom Democratic Party (MDFP), which challenged the seating of the all-white and anti-civil rights Mississippi delegation to the Democratic National Convention in Atlantic City, New Jersey.

*Amelia Boynton after being beaten and tear-gassed on Bloody Sunday.*

In Atlantic City, Fannie Lou Hamer addressed the Democratic National Convention's Credentials Committee, where she passionately recounted the problems she had encountered in voter registration, including the vicious beatings she received in jail. . . .

Fannie Lou Hamer's raw, authentic, and powerful testimony was so compelling that President Lyndon Johnson hastily called a White House press conference to divert media attention, which succeeded temporarily until the broadcast networks replayed her speech, unedited and uninterrupted, on the evening news.

Responding to Fannie Lou Hamer's speech, viewers flooded the Democratic National Credentials Committee with thousands of calls and letters demanding the seating of the Mississippi Freedom Democratic Party delegates.

Although the MDFP's delegates were not seated, as a compromise the Democratic Party changed its bylaws to require equality of representation of state delegations to the national convention, which led in turn to the selection of Fannie Lou Hamer as a delegate to the 1972 Democratic National Convention in Miami Beach, Florida.

Fannie Lou Hamer died on March 14, 1977, in Mound Bayou, Mississippi, at the age of 59, due to her poor health, a combination of a lifetime in poverty, her 1963 beating, and a 1976 cancer diagnosis.

Mr. Speaker, Fannie Lou Hamer was always about paying it forward. . . .

As the third African American woman elected to Congress from the State of Texas, the second to serve on the House Committee on the Judiciary, and the first to become the Ranking Democratic Member of the Judiciary Subcommittee on Crime, Terrorism, Homeland Security, and Investigations, I am ever mindful and grateful of the sacrifices made by giants like Fannie Lou Hamer so that persons like me have the opportunity to serve and contribute to the greatness of our country.

I ask the House to observe a moment of silence in memory of Fannie Lou Hamer on the one hundredth anniversary of her birth.

* * *

## "THE DESTINY OF DEMOCRACY"

### Lyndon B. Johnson, Special Message to the Congress: "The American Promise"—March 15, 1965

---

Eight days after Bloody Sunday in Selma, Alabama, Johnson went to Congress to urge the passage of voting-rights legislation.

I SPEAK TONIGHT FOR the dignity of man and the destiny of democracy.

I urge every member of both parties, Americans of all religions and of all colors, from every section of this country, to join me in that cause.

At times history and fate meet at a single time in a single place to shape a turning point in man's unending search for freedom. So it was at Lexington and Concord. So it was a century ago at Appomattox. So it was last week in Selma, Alabama.

There, long-suffering men and women peacefully protested the denial of their rights as Americans. Many were brutally assaulted. One good man, a man of God, was killed.

There is no cause for pride in what has happened in Selma. There is no cause for self-satisfaction in the long denial of equal rights of millions of Americans. But there is cause for hope and for faith in our democracy in what is happening here tonight.

For the cries of pain and the hymns and protests of oppressed people have summoned into convocation all the majesty of this great Government—the Government of the greatest Nation on earth.

Our mission is at once the oldest and the most basic of this country: to right wrong, to do justice, to serve man.

In our time we have come to live with moments of great crisis. Our lives have been marked with debate about great issues; issues of war and peace, issues of prosperity and depression. But rarely in any time does an issue lay bare the secret heart of America itself. Rarely are we met with a challenge, not to our growth or abundance, our welfare or our security, but rather to the values and the purposes and the meaning of our beloved Nation.

The issue of equal rights for American Negroes is such an issue. And should we defeat every enemy, should we double our wealth and conquer the stars, and still be unequal to this issue, then we will have failed as a people and as a nation.

For with a country as with a person, "What is a man profited, if he shall gain the whole world, and lose his own soul?"

There is no Negro problem. There is no Southern problem. There is no Northern problem. There is only an American problem. And we are met here tonight as Americans—not as Democrats or Republicans—we are met here as Americans to solve that problem.

This was the first nation in the history of the world to be founded with a purpose. The great phrases of that purpose still sound in every American heart, North and South: "All men are created equal"—"government by consent of the governed"—"give me liberty or give me death." Well, those are not just clever words, or those are not just empty theories. In their name Americans have fought and died for two centuries, and tonight around the world they stand there as guardians of our liberty, risking their lives.

Those words are a promise to every citizen that he shall share in the dignity of man. This dignity cannot be found in a man's possessions; it cannot be found in his power, or in his position. It really rests on his right to be treated as a man equal in opportunity to all others. It says that he shall share in freedom, he shall choose his leaders, educate his children, and provide for his family according to his ability and his merits as a human being.

To apply any other test—to deny a man his hopes because of his color or race, his religion or the place of his birth—is not only to do injustice, it is to deny America and to dishonor the dead who gave their lives for American freedom.

Our fathers believed that if this noble view of the rights of man was to flourish, it must be rooted in democracy. The most basic right of all was the right to choose your own leaders. The history of this country, in large measure, is the history of the expansion of that right to all of our people.

Many of the issues of civil rights are very complex and most difficult. But about this there can and should be no argument. Every American citizen must have an equal right to vote. There is no reason which can excuse the denial of that right. There is no duty which weighs more heavily on us than the duty we have to ensure that right.

Yet the harsh fact is that in many places in this country men and women are kept from voting simply because they are Negroes.

Every device of which human ingenuity is capable has been used to deny this right. The Negro citizen may go to register only to be told that the day is wrong, or the hour is late, or the official in charge is absent. And if he persists, and if he manages to present himself to the registrar, he may be disqualified because he did not spell out his middle name or because he abbreviated a word on the application.

And if he manages to fill out an application he is given a test. The registrar is the sole judge of whether he passes this test. He may be asked to recite the entire Constitution, or explain the most complex provisions of State law. And even a college degree cannot be used to prove that he can read and write.

For the fact is that the only way to pass these barriers is to show a white skin.

Experience has clearly shown that the existing process of law cannot overcome systematic and ingenious discrimination. No law that we now have on the books—and I have helped to put three of them there—can ensure the right to vote when local officials are determined to deny it.

In such a case our duty must be clear to all of us. The Constitution says that no person shall be kept from voting because of his race or his color. We have all sworn an oath before God to support and to defend that Constitution. We must now act in obedience to that oath.

Wednesday I will send to Congress a law designed to eliminate illegal barriers to the right to vote.

The broad principles of that bill will be in the hands of the Democratic and Republican leaders tomorrow. After they have reviewed it, it will come here formally as a bill. I am grateful for this opportunity to come here tonight at the invitation of the leadership to reason with my friends, to give them my views, and to visit with my former colleagues.

I have had prepared a more comprehensive analysis of the legislation which I had intended to transmit to the clerk tomorrow but which I will submit to the clerks tonight. But I want to really discuss with you now briefly the main proposals of this legislation.

This bill will strike down restrictions to voting in all elections—Federal, State, and local—which have been used to deny Negroes the right to vote.

This bill will establish a simple, uniform standard which cannot be used, however ingenious the effort, to flout our Constitution.

It will provide for citizens to be registered by officials of the United States Government if the State officials refuse to register them.

It will eliminate tedious, unnecessary lawsuits which delay the right to vote.

Finally, this legislation will ensure that properly registered individuals are not prohibited from voting.

I will welcome the suggestions from all of the Members of Congress—I have no doubt that I will get some—on ways and means to strengthen this law and to make it effective. But experience has plainly shown that this is the only path to carry out the command of the Constitution.

To those who seek to avoid action by their National Government in their own communities; who want to and who seek to maintain purely local control over elections, the answer is simple:

Open your polling places to all your people.

Allow men and women to register and vote whatever the color of their skin.

Extend the rights of citizenship to every citizen of this land.

There is no constitutional issue here. The command of the Constitution is plain.

There is no moral issue. It is wrong—deadly wrong—to deny any of your fellow Americans the right to vote in this country.

There is no issue of States' rights or national rights. There is only the struggle for human rights.

I have not the slightest doubt what will be your answer.

The last time a President sent a civil rights bill to the Congress it contained a provision to protect voting rights in Federal elections. That civil rights bill was passed after 8 long months of debate. And when that bill came to my desk from the Congress for my signature, the heart of the voting provision had been eliminated.

This time, on this issue, there must be no delay, no hesitation and no compromise with our purpose.

We cannot, we must not, refuse to protect the right of every American to vote in every election that he may desire to participate in. And we ought not and we cannot and we must not wait another 8 months before we get a bill. We have already waited a hundred years and more, and the time for waiting is gone.

So I ask you to join me in working long hours—nights and weekends, if necessary—to pass this bill. And I don't make that request lightly. For from the window where I sit with the problems of our country I recognize that outside this chamber is the outraged conscience of a nation, the grave concern of many nations, and the harsh judgment of history on our acts.

But even if we pass this bill, the battle will not be over. What happened in Selma is part of a far larger movement which reaches into every section and State of America. It is the effort of American Negroes to secure for themselves the full blessings of American life.

Their cause must be our cause too. Because it is not just Negroes, but really it is all of us, who must overcome the crippling legacy of bigotry and injustice. And we shall overcome.

As a man whose roots go deeply into Southern soil I know how agonizing racial feelings are. I know how difficult it is to reshape the attitudes and the structure of our society.

But a century has passed, more than a hundred years, since the Negro was freed. And he is not fully free tonight.

It was more than a hundred years ago that Abraham Lincoln, a great President of another party, signed the Emancipation Proclamation, but emancipation is a proclamation and not a fact.

A century has passed, more than a hundred years, since equality was promised. And yet the Negro is not equal.

A century has passed since the day of promise. And the promise is unkept.

The time of justice has now come. I tell you that I believe sincerely that no force can hold it back. It is right in the eyes of man and God that it should come. And when it does, I think that day will brighten the lives of every American.

For Negroes are not the only victims. How many white children have gone uneducated, how many white families have lived in stark poverty, how many white lives have been scarred by fear, because we have wasted our energy and our substance to maintain the barriers of hatred and terror?

So I say to all of you here, and to all in the Nation tonight, that those who appeal to you to hold on to the past do so at the cost of denying you your future.

This great, rich, restless country can offer opportunity and education and hope to all: black and white, North and South, sharecropper and city dweller. These are the enemies: poverty, ignorance, disease. They are the enemies and not our fellow man, not our neighbor. And these enemies too, poverty, disease and ignorance, we shall overcome.

Now let none of us in any sections look with prideful righteousness on the troubles in another section, or on the problems of our neighbors. There is really no part of America where the promise of equality has been fully kept. In Buffalo as well as in Birmingham, in Philadelphia as well as in Selma, Americans are struggling for the fruits of freedom.

This is one Nation. What happens in Selma or in Cincinnati is a matter of legitimate concern to every American. But let each of us look within our own hearts and our own communities, and let each of us put our shoulder to the wheel to root out injustice wherever it exists.

As we meet here in this peaceful, historic chamber tonight, men from the South, some of whom were at Iwo Jima, men from the North who have carried Old Glory to far corners of the world and brought it back without a stain on it, men from the East and from the West, are all fighting together without regard to religion, or color, or region, in Viet-Nam. Men from every region fought for us across the world 20 years ago.

And in these common dangers and these common sacrifices the South made its contribution of honor and gallantry no less than any other region of the great Republic—and in some instances, a great many of them, more.

And I have not the slightest doubt that good men from everywhere in this country, from the Great Lakes to the Gulf of Mexico, from the Golden Gate to the harbors along the Atlantic, will rally together now in this cause to vindicate the freedom of all Americans. For all of us owe this duty; and I believe that all of us will respond to it.

Your President makes that request of every American.

The real hero of this struggle is the American Negro. His actions and protests, his courage to risk safety and even to risk his life, have awakened the conscience of this Nation. His demonstrations have been designed to call attention to injustice, designed to provoke change, designed to stir reform.

He has called upon us to make good the promise of America. And who among us can say that we would have made the same progress were it not for his persistent bravery, and his faith in American democracy.

For at the real heart of battle for equality is a deep-seated belief in the democratic process. Equality depends not on the force of arms or tear gas but upon the force of moral right; not on recourse to violence but on respect for law and order.

There have been many pressures upon your President and there will be others as the days come and go. But I pledge you tonight that we intend to fight this battle where it should be fought: in the courts, and in the Congress, and in the hearts of men.

We must preserve the right of free speech and the right of free assembly. But the right of free speech does not carry with it, as has been said, the right to holler fire in a crowded theater. We must preserve the right to free assembly, but free assembly does not carry with it the right to block public thoroughfares to traffic.

We do have a right to protest, and a right to march under conditions that do not infringe the constitutional rights of our neighbors. And I intend to protect all those rights as long as I am permitted to serve in this office.

We will guard against violence, knowing it strikes from our hands the very weapons which we seek—progress, obedience to law, and belief in American values.

In Selma as elsewhere we seek and pray for peace. We seek order. We seek unity. But we will not accept the peace of stifled rights, or the order imposed by fear, or the unity that stifles protest. For peace cannot be purchased at the cost of liberty.

In Selma tonight, as in every—and we had a good day there—as in every city, we are working for just and peaceful settlement. We must all remember that after this speech I am making tonight, after the police and the FBI and the Marshals have all gone, and after you have promptly passed this bill, the people of Selma and the other cities of the Nation must still live and work together. And when the attention of the Nation has gone elsewhere they must try to heal the wounds and to build a new community.

This cannot be easily done on a battleground of violence, as the history of the South itself shows. It is in recognition of this that men of both races have shown such an outstandingly impressive responsibility in recent days—last Tuesday, again today.

The bill that I am presenting to you will be known as a civil rights bill. But, in a larger sense, most of the program I am recommending is a civil rights program. Its object is to open the city of hope to all people of all races.

Because all Americans just must have the right to vote. And we are going to give them that right.

All Americans must have the privileges of citizenship regardless of race. And they are going to have those privileges of citizenship regardless of race.

But I would like to caution you and remind you that to exercise these privileges takes much more than just legal right. It requires a trained mind and a healthy body. It requires a decent home, and the chance to find a job, and the opportunity to escape from the clutches of poverty.

Of course, people cannot contribute to the Nation if they are never taught to read or write, if their bodies are stunted from hunger, if their sickness goes untended, if their life is spent in hopeless poverty just drawing a welfare check.

So we want to open the gates to opportunity. But we are also going to give all our people, black and white, the help that they need to walk through those gates.

My first job after college was as a teacher in Cotulla, Texas, in a small Mexican-American school. Few of them could speak English, and I couldn't speak much Spanish. My students were poor and they often came to class without breakfast, hungry. They knew even in their youth the pain of prejudice. They never seemed to know why people disliked them. But they knew it was so, because I saw it in their eyes. I often walked home late in the afternoon, after the classes were finished, wishing there was more that I could do. But all I knew was to teach them the little that I knew, hoping that it might help them against the hardships that lay ahead.

Somehow you never forget what poverty and hatred can do when you see its scars on the hopeful face of a young child.

I never thought then, in 1928, that I would be standing here in 1965. It never even occurred to me in my fondest dreams that I might have the chance to help the sons and daughters of those students and to help people like them all over this country.

But now I do have that chance—and I'll let you in on a secret—I mean to use it. And I hope that you will use it with me.

This is the richest and most powerful country which ever occupied the globe. The might of past empires is little compared to ours. But I do not want to be the President who built empires, or sought grandeur, or extended dominion.

I want to be the President who educated young children to the wonders of their world. I want to be the President who helped to feed the hungry and to prepare them to be taxpayers instead of tax-eaters.

I want to be the President who helped the poor to find their own way and who protected the right of every citizen to vote in every election.

I want to be the President who helped to end hatred among his fellow men and who promoted love among the people of all races and all regions and all parties.

I want to be the President who helped to end war among the brothers of this earth.

And so at the request of your beloved Speaker and the Senator from

Montana; the majority leader, the Senator from Illinois; the minority leader, Mr. McCulloch, and other Members of both parties, I came here tonight—not as President Roosevelt came down one time in person to veto a bonus bill, not as President Truman came down one time to urge the passage of a railroad bill—but I came down here to ask you to share this task with me and to share it with the people that we both work for. I want this to be the Congress, Republicans and Democrats alike, which did all these things for all these people.

Beyond this great chamber, out yonder in 50 States, are the people that we serve. Who can tell what deep and unspoken hopes are in their hearts tonight as they sit there and listen. We all can guess, from our own lives, how difficult they often find their own pursuit of happiness, how many problems each little family has. They look most of all to themselves for their futures. But I think that they also look to each of us.

Above the pyramid on the great seal of the United States it says—in Latin—"God has favored our undertaking."

God will not favor everything that we do. It is rather our duty to divine His will. But I cannot help believing that He truly understands and that He really favors the undertaking that we begin here tonight.

* * *

## "PREACHERS ARE NOT CALLED TO BE POLITICIANS"

### Jerry Falwell, Sermon at the Thomas Road Baptist Church, Lynchburg, Virginia—March 21, 1965

---

The Reverend Jerry Falwell (1933–2007) was a founder of the contemporary religious right. As pastor of the Thomas Road Baptist Church, he opposed political activism by the clergy when the dominant issue facing the country was civil rights (as he preached in this excerpted 1965 sermon). After the Supreme Court's 1973 decision in *Roe v. Wade,* however, Falwell changed his mind and entered the arena.

UNDER THE CONSTITUTION of the United States, every American has the right to "peacefully" petition the government for a redress of grievances. This simply means that, in the present racial crises, all Americans, white, negro, or otherwise, have the legal right to "peacefully" demonstrate in order to obtain voting rights in Alabama—or elsewhere—if these rights are not allowed to the citizens. The purpose of this message is not to question such constitutional rights. Neither is it the intention of this message to discuss the subject of integration or segregation. It is my desire, in this sermon, to open the Bible and, from God's Word, answer the question—*"Does the 'CHURCH' have any command from God to involve itself in marches, demonstrations, or any other actions, such as many ministers and church leaders are so doing today in the name of civil rights reforms?"*

At the outset of this message, I do wish to speak frankly about one particular matter. There are, no doubt, many very sincere Christians who have felt a compulsion to join in civil rights efforts across the nation. At the same time, I must personally say that I do question the sincerity and non-violent intentions of some civil rights leaders such as Dr. Martin Luther King Jr., Mr. James Farmer, and others, who are known to have left-wing associations. It is very obvious that the Communists, as they do in all parts of the world, are taking advantage of a tense situation in our land, and are exploiting every incident to bring about violence and bloodshed. But I must repeat that I do believe many sincere persons are participating. I must also say that I believe these demonstrations and marches have done more to damage race relations and to engender hate than to help!

Since all orthodox Christians accept the Bible to be the verbally inspired Word of God, let us look into this Bible and see what the commands to the church are. In the first book of the New Testament, Matthew 28:18–20, Jesus commissioned the church to: "Go ye therefore and teach all nations, baptizing them in the name of the Father and of the Son and of the Holy Ghost: teaching them to observe all things whatsoever I have commanded you." You will notice here three specific commands: (1) Make disciples, or as we sometimes say, win souls; (2) baptize these new converts in the name of the Trinity; (3) teach them the Christ-life. In Mark 16, you will find the same command in slightly different words. In Luke 24 and in John 20, the same commands are given. As we move to the Book of the Acts of the Apostles, we find in the 1st chapter and the 8th verse the very same command. As we search through the letters of Paul, and all the other New Testament letters, we see that the church is given no command other than this Great Commission to take the message of Christ to a dying world. As far as the relationship of the church to the world, it can be expressed as simply as the three words which Paul gave to Timothy—"preach the Word." We have a message of redeeming grace through a crucified and risen Lord. This message is designed to go right to the heart of man and there meet his deep spiritual need. Nowhere are we commissioned to reform the externals. We are not told to wage wars against bootleggers, liquor stores, gamblers, murderers, prostitutes, racketeers, prejudiced persons or institutions, or any other existing evil as such. Our ministry is not reformation but transformation. The gospel does not clean up the outside but rather regenerates the inside. I have had no greater joy as a minister of the gospel than to witness the marvelous changes wrought in the lives of many people to whom I have preached the gospel. Right here in the Thomas Road Baptist Church, I look into the faces of many people each Sunday who once were involved in the worst kinds of sin. Today they are God-fearing servants of Christ Jesus. What changed them? Did we lead a march down to their bootlegging joint and demand that they stop selling liquor? Did we go to Richmond and try to get laws passed which would send these persons to jail? No! In Christian love, we went to them prayerfully with the message of a crucified Christ. They received this Christ as their own personal Lord and Savior. When Christ came in, sin went out. They no longer live their former lives. Not because we demanded they stop these things, but because now, they no longer want to do these things. As Paul says it in II Cor. 5:17: "Therefore if any man be in Christ, he is a new creature: old things are passed away; behold, all things are become new." . . .

The Christian has his citizenship in the Royal Nation in Heaven. While we are told to "render unto Caesar, the things that are Caesar's," in the true interpretation, we have very few ties on this earth. We pay our taxes, cast our votes as a responsibility of citizenship, obey the laws of the land, and other things demanded of us by the society in which we live. But, at the same time, we are cognizant that our only purpose on this earth is to know Christ and to make Him known. Believing the Bible as I do, I would find it impossible to stop preaching the pure saving gospel of Jesus Christ, and begin doing anything else—including fighting communism, or participating in civil rights reforms. As a God-called preacher, I find that there is no time left after I give the proper time and attention to winning people to Christ. Preachers are not called to be politicians but to be soul winners. . . . When the 2,000 members of Thomas Road Baptist Church attend our services, they do not hear sermons on communism, civil rights, or any other subject except the gospel of Christ. If the many thousands of churches and pastors of America would suddenly begin preaching the old fashioned gospel of Jesus Christ and the power that is in His atoning blood, a revival would grip our land such as we have never known before. If as much effort could be put into winning people to Jesus Christ across the land as is being exerted in the present civil rights movement, America would be turned upside down for God. Hate and prejudice would certainly be in a great measure overcome. Churches would be filled with sincere souls seeking God. Good relations between the races would soon be evidenced. God is Love, and when He is put first in the individual life and in the church, God's people become messengers of love. May we pray toward this goal. . . .

I feel that we need to get off the streets and back into the pulpits and into the prayer rooms. I believe we need to take our Bibles and go down into the highways and hedges and bring men to Christ. I believe we need to rededicate ourselves to the great task of turning this world back to God. The preaching of the gospel is the only means by which this can be done.

★ ★ ★

## "A MAN IS A MAN"

### James Baldwin, "The White Man's Guilt," *Ebony*—August 1965

James Baldwin (1924–1987) was an essayist and a novelist. Though born in New York, he spent much of his adult life in Paris.

I HAVE OFTEN WONDERED, and it is not a pleasant wonder, just what white Americans talk about with one another.

I wonder this because they do not, after all, seem to find very much to say to *me,* and I concluded long ago that they found the color of my skin inhibitory. This color seems to operate as a most disagreeable mirror, and a great deal of one's energy is expended in reassuring white Americans that they do not see what they see.

This is utterly futile, of course, since they *do* see what they see. And what they see is an appallingly oppressive and bloody history known all over the world. What they see is a disastrous, continuing, present condition which menaces them, and for which they bear an inescapable responsibility. But since, in the main, they seem to lack the energy to change this condition, they would rather not be reminded of it. Does this mean that, in their conversations with one another, they merely make reassuring sounds? It scarcely seems possible, and yet, on the other hand, it seems all too likely. In any case, whatever they bring to one another, it is certainly not freedom from guilt. The guilt remains, more deeply rooted, more securely lodged, than the oldest of old trees.

And to have to deal with such people can be unutterably exhausting, for they, with a really dazzling ingenuity, a tireless agility, are perpetually defending themselves against charges which one, disagreeable mirror though one may be, has not, really, for the moment, made. One does not *have* to make them. The record is there for all to read. It resounds all over the world. It might as well be written in the sky. One wishes that Americans, white Americans, would read, for their own sakes, this record, and stop defending themselves against it. Only then will they be enabled to change their lives.

The fact that they have not yet been able to do this—to face their history, to change their lives—hideously menaces this country. Indeed, it menaces the entire world.

White man, hear me! History, as nearly no one seems to know, is not merely something to be read. And it does not refer merely, or even principally, to the past. On the contrary, the great force of history comes from the fact that we carry it within us, are unconsciously controlled by it in many ways, and history is literally *present* in all that we do. It could scarcely be otherwise, since it is to history that we owe our frames of reference, our identities, and our aspirations. And it is with great pain and terror that one begins to realize this. In great pain and terror one begins to assess the history which has placed one where one is, and formed one's point of view. In great pain and terror because, thereafter, one enters into battle with that historical creation. Oneself, and attempts to re-create oneself according to a principle more humane and more liberating: one begins the attempt to achieve a level of personal maturity and freedom which robs history of its tyrannical power, and also changes history.

But, obviously, I am speaking as an historical creation which has had bitterly to contest its history, to wrestle with it, and finally accept it, in order to bring myself out of it. My point of view certainly is formed by my history, and it is probable that only a creature despised by history finds history a questionable matter. On the other hand, people who imagine that history flatters them (as it does, indeed, since they wrote it) are impaled on their history like a butterfly on a pin and become incapable of seeing or changing themselves, or the world.

This is the place in which, it seems to me, most white Americans find themselves. Impaled. They are dimly, or vividly, aware that the history they have fed themselves is mainly a lie, but they do not know how to release themselves from it, and they suffer enormously from the resulting personal incoherence. This incoherence is heard nowhere more plainly than in those stammering, terrified dialogues which white Americans sometime entertain with that black conscience, the black man in America. The nature of this stammering can be reduced to a plea: Do not blame *me,* I was not there. I did not do it. My history has nothing to do with Europe or the slave trade. Anyway, it was *your* chiefs who sold *you* to *me.* I was not present on the middle passage, I am not responsible for the textile mills of Manchester, or the cotton fields of Mississippi. Besides, consider how the English, too, suffered in those mills and in those awful cities! I *also* despise the governors of southern states and the sheriffs of southern counties, and I *also* want your child to have a decent education and rise as high as his capabilities will permit. I have nothing against you, nothing! What have *you* got against *me*? *What do you want?* But, on the same day, in another gathering, and in the most private chamber of his heart, always, the white American remains proud of that history for which he does not wish to pay, and from which, materially, he has profited so much.

On that same day, in another gathering, and in the most private chamber of his heart always, the black American finds *himself* facing the terrible roster of his lost: The dead, black junkie; the defeated, black father; the unutterably weary, black mother; the unutterably ruined, black girl. And one begins to suspect an awful thing: that people believe that they *deserve* their history, and that when they operate on this belief, they perish. But one knows that they can scarcely avoid believing that they deserve it: one's short time on this earth is very mysterious and very dark and very hard. I have known many black men and women and black boys and girls who really believed that it was better to be white than black, whose lives were ruined or ended by this belief; and I, myself, carried the seeds of this destruction within me for a long time.

Now if I, as a black man, profoundly believe that I deserve my history and deserve to be treated as I am, then I must also, fatally, believe that white people deserve their history and deserve the power and the glory which their testimony and the evidence of my own senses assure me that they have. And if black people fall into this trap, the trap of believing that they deserve their fate, white people fall into the yet more stunning and intricate trap of believing that they deserve *their* fate, and their comparative safety, and that black people, therefore, need only do as white people have done to rise to where white people now are. But this simply cannot be said, not only for reasons of politeness or charity, but also because white people carry in them a carefully muffled fear that black people long to do to others what has been done to them. Moreover, the history of white people has led them to a fearful, baffling place where they have begun to lose touch with reality—to lose touch, that is, with themselves—and where they certainly are not truly happy, for they know they are not truly safe. They do not know how this came about. On the one hand, they can scarcely dare to open a dialogue which must, if it is honest, become a personal confession—a cry for help and healing, which is, really, I think, the basis of all dialogues—and, on the other hand, the black man can scarcely dare to open a dialogue which must, if it is honest, become a personal confession which, fatally, contains an accusation. And yet, if neither of us cannot do this, each of us will perish in those traps in which we have been struggling for so long.

The American situation is very peculiar, and it may be without precedent in the world. No curtain under heaven is heavier than that curtain of guilt and lies behind which white Americans hide. That curtain may prove to be yet more deadly to the lives of human beings than that Iron Curtain of which we speak so much, and know so little. The

American curtain is color. Color. White men have used this word, this concept, to justify unspeakable crimes, not only in the past, but in the present. One can measure very neatly the white American's distance from his conscience—from himself—by observing the distance between White America and Black America. One has only to ask oneself who established this distance, who is this distance designed to protect, and from what is this distance designed to offer protection?

I have seen all this very vividly, for example, in the eyes of southern law enforcement officers barring, let us say, the door to a courthouse. There they stood, comrades all, invested with the authority of the community, with helmets, with sticks, with guns, with cattle prods. Facing them were unarmed black people—or, more precisely, they were faced by a group of unarmed people arbitrarily called black, whose color really ranged from the Russian steppes to the Golden Horn to Zanzibar. In a moment, because he could resolve the situation in no other way, this sheriff, this deputy, this honored American citizen, began to club these people down. Some of these people might have been related to him by blood. They are assuredly related to the black mammy of his memory and the black playmates of his childhood. And for a moment, therefore, he seemed nearly to be pleading with the people facing him not to force him to commit yet another crime and not to make yet deeper that ocean of blood in which his conscience was drenched, in which his manhood was perishing. The people did not go away, of course; once a people arise, they never go away (a fact which should be included in the Marine handbook). So the club rose, the blood came down, and his bitterness and his anguish and his guilt were compounded.

And I have seen it in the eyes of rookie cops in Harlem—rookie cops who were really the most terrified people in the world, and who had to pretend to themselves that the black junkie, the black mother, the black father, the black child were of different human species than themselves. The southern sheriff, the rookie cop, could, and I suspect still can only deal with their lives and their duties by hiding behind the color curtain—a curtain which, indeed, eventually becomes their principal justification for the lives they lead.

They thus will barricade themselves behind this curtain and continue in their crime, in the great unadmitted crime of what they have done to themselves.

White man, hear me! A man is a man, a woman is a woman, a child is a child. To deny these facts is to open the doors on a chaos deeper and deadlier, and, within the space of a man's lifetime, more timeless, more eternal, than the medieval vision of Hell. White man, you have already arrived at this unspeakable blasphemy in order to make money. You cannot endure the things you acquire—the only reason you continually acquire them, like junkies on hundred-dollar-a-day habits—and your money exists mainly on paper. God help you on that day when the population demands to know what is behind that paper. But, even beyond this, it is terrifying to consider the precise nature of the things you have bought with the flesh you have sold—of what you continue to buy with the flesh you continue to sell. To what, precisely, are you headed? To what human product, precisely, are you devoting so much ingenuity, so much energy?

In Henry James' novel *The Ambassadors,* published not long before James' death, the author recounts the story of a middle-aged New Englander, assigned by his middle-aged bride-to-be, a widow, the task of rescuing from the flesh-pots of Paris her only son. She wants him to come home to take over the direction of the family factory. In the event, it is the middle-aged New Englander, The Ambassador, who is seduced, not so much by Paris as by a new and less utilitarian view of life. He counsels the young man to "live, live all you can; it is a mistake not to." Which I translate as meaning "trust life, and it will teach you, in joy and sorrow, all you need to know." Jazz musicians know this. The old men and women of Montgomery—those who waved and sang and wept and could not join the marching, but had brought so many of us to the place where we could march—know this. But white Americans do not know this. Barricaded inside their history, they remain trapped in that factory to which, in Henry James' novel, the son returns. We never know what this factory produces, for James never tells us. He only conveys to us that the factory, at an unbelievable human expense, produces unnamable objects.

* * *

## "THE LIGHT OF AN INCREASED LIBERTY"
## Lyndon B. Johnson, Remarks on Signing the Immigration and Nationality Act, New York Harbor—October 3, 1965

The act LBJ signed on Liberty Island in the fall of 1965 ended the national quota system that had prevailed in the United States since the passage of restrictive legislation in 1924, an era of heightened anti-immigrant sentiment.

*President Johnson at the signing of the 1965 Immigration and Nationality Act.*

Our beautiful America was built by a nation of strangers. From a hundred different places or more they have poured forth into an empty land, joining and blending in one mighty and irresistible tide.

The land flourished because it was fed from so many sources—because it was nourished by so many cultures and traditions and peoples.

And from this experience, almost unique in the history of nations, has come America's attitude toward the rest of the world. We, because of what we are, feel safer and stronger in a world as varied as the people who make it up—a world where no country rules another and all countries can deal with the basic problems of human dignity and deal with those problems in their own way.

Now, under the monument which has welcomed so many to our shores, the American Nation returns to the finest of its traditions today.

The days of unlimited immigration are past.

But those who do come will come because of what they are, and not because of the land from which they sprung.

When the earliest settlers poured into a wild continent there was no one to ask them where they came from. The only question was: Were they sturdy enough to make the journey, were they strong enough to clear the land, were they enduring enough to make a home for freedom, and were they brave enough to die for liberty if it became necessary to do so?

And so it has been through all the great and testing moments of American history. Our history this year we see in Viet-Nam. Men there are dying—men named Fernandez and Zajac and Zelinko and Mariano and McCormick.

Neither the enemy who killed them nor the people whose independence they have fought to save ever asked them where they or their parents came from. They were all Americans. It was for free men and for America that they gave their all, they gave their lives and selves.

By eliminating that same question as a test for immigration the Congress proves ourselves worthy of those men and worthy of our own traditions as a Nation. . . .

Over my shoulders here you can see Ellis Island, whose vacant corridors echo today the joyous sound of long ago voices.

And today we can all believe that the lamp of this grand old lady is brighter today—and the golden door that she guards gleams more brilliantly in the light of an increased liberty for the people from all the countries of the globe.

★ ★ ★

## "TO END IN A STALEMATE"
### Walter Cronkite, Editorial on Vietnam and the Tet Offensive, *CBS Evening News*—February 27, 1968

CBS anchor Walter Cronkite (1916–2009) was an American fixture in the 1960s and 1970s, a trusted voice in a complex age. His commentary on the Vietnam War after the Tet Offensive in early 1968 reflected growing opinion that the war was unwinnable.

TONIGHT, BACK IN more familiar surroundings in New York, we'd like to sum up our findings in Vietnam, an analysis that must be speculative, personal, subjective.

*CBS's Walter Cronkite in the field in Vietnam.*

Who won and who lost in the great Tet Offensive against the cities? I'm not sure. The Viet Cong did not win by a knockout, but neither did we. The referees of history may make it a draw. Another standoff may be coming in the big battles expected south of the Demilitarized Zone. Khe Sanh could well fall, with a terrible loss in American lives, prestige and morale, and this is a tragedy of our stubbornness there; but the bastion no longer is a key to the rest of the northern regions, and it is doubtful that the American forces can be defeated across the breadth of the DMZ with any substantial loss of ground. Another standoff.

On the political front, past performance gives no confidence that the Vietnamese government can cope with its problems, now compounded by the attack on the cities. It may not fall, it may hold on, but it probably won't show the dynamic qualities demanded of this young nation. Another standoff.

We have been too often disappointed by the optimism of the American leaders, both in Vietnam and Washington, to have faith any longer in the silver linings they find in the darkest clouds. They may be right that Hanoi's winter-spring offensive has been forced by the Communist realization that they could not win the longer war of attrition, and that the Communists hope that any success in the offensive will improve their position for eventual negotiations. It would improve their position, and it would also require our realization, that we should have had all along, that any negotiations must be that—negotiations, not the dictation of peace terms.

For it seems now more certain than ever that the bloody experience of Vietnam is to end in a stalemate. This summer's almost certain standoff will either end in real give-and-take negotiations or terrible escalation; and for every means we have to escalate, the enemy can match us, and that applies to invasion of the North, the use of nuclear weapons, or the mere commitment of one hundred, or two hundred, or three hundred thousand more American troops to the battle. And with each escalation, the world comes closer to the brink of cosmic disaster.

To say that we are closer to victory today is to believe, in the face of the evidence, the optimists who have been wrong in the past. To suggest we are on the edge of defeat is to yield to unreasonable pessimism. To say that we are mired in stalemate seems the only realistic, yet unsatisfactory, conclusion.

On the off chance that military and political analysts are right, in the next few months we must test the enemy's intentions, in case this is indeed his last big gasp before negotiations. But it is increasingly clear to this reporter that the only rational way out then will be to negotiate, not as victors, but as an honorable people who lived up to their pledge to defend democracy and did the best they could.

This is Walter Cronkite.

Good night.

★ ★ ★

## "WE'VE GOT SOME DIFFICULT DAYS AHEAD"

**Martin Luther King, Jr., Mason Temple Church of God in Christ, Memphis, Tennessee—April 3, 1968**

---

Martin Luther King, Jr. (1929–1968), was in Memphis in the spring of 1968 at the invitation of the Reverend James M. Lawson, an architect of the nonviolent civil-rights movement. The occasion: a strike of the city's sanitation workers, a front in King's post–Jim Crow pursuit of economic justice. King was assassinated at the Lorraine Motel the day after delivering this speech.

THANK YOU VERY kindly, my friends. As I listened to Ralph Abernathy in his eloquent and generous introduction and then thought about myself, I wondered who he was talking about. It's always good to have your closest friend and associate say something good about you. And Ralph is the best friend that I have in the world.

I'm delighted to see each of you here tonight in spite of a storm warning. You reveal that you are determined to go on anyhow. Something is happening in Memphis, something is happening in our world.

As you know, if I were standing at the beginning of time, with the possibility of general and panoramic view of the whole human history up to now, and the Almighty said to me, "Martin Luther King, which age would you like to live in?"— I would take my mental flight by Egypt through, or rather across the Red Sea, through the wilderness on toward the promised land. And in spite of its magnificence, I wouldn't stop there. I would move on by Greece, and take my mind to Mount Olympus. And I would see Plato, Aristotle, Socrates, Euripides and Aristophanes assembled around the Parthenon as they discussed the great and eternal issues of reality.

But I wouldn't stop there. I would go on, even to the great heyday of the Roman Empire. And I would see developments around there, through various emperors and leaders. But I wouldn't stop there. I would even come up to the day of the Renaissance, and get a quick picture of all that the Renaissance did for the cultural and esthetic life of man. But I wouldn't stop there. I would even go by the way that the man for whom I'm named had his habitat. And I would watch Martin Luther as he tacked his ninety-five theses on the door at the church in Wittenberg.

But I wouldn't stop there. I would come on up even to 1863, and watch a vacillating president by the name of Abraham Lincoln finally come to the conclusion that he had to sign the Emancipation Proclamation. But I wouldn't stop there. I would even come up to the early thirties, and see a man grappling with the problems of the bankruptcy of his nation. And come with an eloquent cry that we have nothing to fear but fear itself.

But I wouldn't stop there. Strangely enough, I would turn to the Almighty, and say, "If you allow me to live just a few years in the second half of the twentieth century, I will be happy." Now that's a strange statement to make, because the world is all messed up. The nation is sick. Trouble is in the land. Confusion all around. That's a strange statement. But I know, somehow, that only when it is dark enough, can you see the stars. And I see God working in this period of the twentieth century in a way that men, in some strange way, are responding—something is happening in our world. The masses of people are rising up. And wherever they are assembled today, whether they are in Johannesburg, South Africa; Nairobi, Kenya: Accra, Ghana; New York City; Atlanta, Georgia; Jackson, Mississippi; or Memphis, Tennessee—the cry is always the same—"We want to be free."

And another reason that I'm happy to live in this period is that we have been forced to a point where we're going to have to grapple with the problems that men have been trying to grapple with through history, but the demands didn't force them to do it. Survival demands that we grapple with them. Men, for years now, have been talking about war and peace. But now, no longer can they just talk about it. It is no longer a choice between violence and nonviolence in this world; it's nonviolence or nonexistence.

That is where we are today. And also in the human rights revolution, if something isn't done, and in a hurry, to bring the colored peoples of the world out of their long years of poverty, their long years of hurt and neglect, the whole world is doomed. Now, I'm just happy that God has allowed me to live in this period, to see what is unfolding. And I'm happy that he's allowed me to be in Memphis.

I can remember, I can remember when Negroes were just going around as Ralph has said, so often, scratching where they didn't itch, and laughing when they were not tickled. But that day is all over. We mean business now, and we are determined to gain our rightful place in God's world.

And that's all this whole thing is about. We aren't engaged in any negative protest and in any negative arguments with anybody. We are saying that we are determined to be men. We are determined to be people. We are saying that we are God's children. And that we don't have to live like we are forced to live.

Now, what does all of this mean in this great period of history? It means that we've got to stay together. We've got to stay together and maintain unity. You know, whenever Pharaoh wanted to prolong the period of slavery in Egypt, he had a favorite, favorite formula for doing it. What was that? He kept the slaves fighting among themselves. But whenever the slaves get together, something happens in Pharaoh's court, and he cannot hold the slaves in slavery. When the slaves get together, that's the beginning of getting out of slavery. Now let us maintain unity.

Secondly, let us keep the issues where they are. The issue is injustice. The issue is the refusal of Memphis to be fair and honest in its dealings with its public servants, who happen to be sanitation workers. Now, we've got to keep attention on that. That's always the problem with a little violence. You know what happened the other day, and the press dealt only with the window-breaking. I read the articles. They very seldom got around to mentioning the fact that one thousand, three hundred sanitation workers were on strike, and that Memphis is not being fair to them, and that Mayor Loeb is in dire need of a doctor. They didn't get around to that.

Now we're going to march again, and we've got to march again, in order to put the issue where it is supposed to be. And force everybody to see that there are thirteen hundred of God's children here suffering, sometimes going hungry, going through dark and dreary nights wondering how this thing is going to come out. That's the issue. And we've got to say to the nation: we know it's coming out. For when people get caught up with that which is right and they are willing to sacrifice for it, there is no stopping point short of victory.

We aren't going to let any mace stop us. We are masters in our nonviolent movement in disarming police forces; they don't know what to do. I've seen them so often. I remember in Birmingham, Alabama, when we were in that majestic struggle there we would move out of the 16th Street Baptist Church day after day; by the hundreds we would move out. And Bull Connor would tell them to send the dogs forth and they did come; but we just went before the dogs singing, "Ain't gonna let nobody turn me round." Bull Connor next would say, "Turn the fire hoses on." And as I said to you the other night, Bull Connor didn't know history. He knew a kind of physics that somehow didn't relate to the transphysics that we knew about. And that was the fact that there was a certain kind of fire that no water could put out. And we went before the fire hoses; we had known water. If we were Baptist or some other denomination, we had been immersed. If we were Methodist, and some others, we had been sprinkled, but we knew water.

That couldn't stop us. And we just went on before the dogs and we would look at them; and we'd go on before the water hoses and we would look at it, and we'd just go on singing. "Over my head I see freedom in the air." And then we would be thrown in the paddy wagons, and sometimes we were stacked in there like sardines in a can. And they would throw us in, and old Bull would say, "Take them off," and they did; and we would just go in the paddy wagon singing, "We Shall Overcome." And every now and then we'd get in the jail, and we'd see the jailers looking through the windows being moved by our prayers, and being moved by our words and our songs. And there was a power there which Bull Connor couldn't adjust to; and so we ended up transforming Bull into a steer, and we won our struggle in Birmingham.

Now we've got to go on to Memphis just like that. I call upon you to be with us Monday. Now about injunctions: We have an injunction and we're going into court tomorrow morning to fight this illegal, unconstitutional injunction. All we say to America is, "Be true to what you said on paper." If I lived in China or even Russia, or any totalitarian country, maybe I could understand the denial of certain basic First Amendment privileges, because they hadn't committed themselves to that over there. But somewhere I read of the freedom of assembly. Somewhere I read of the freedom of speech. Somewhere I read of the freedom of the press. Somewhere I read that the greatness of America is the right to protest for right. And so just as I say, we aren't going to let any injunction turn us around. We are going on.

We need all of you. And you know what's beautiful to me, is to see all of these ministers of the Gospel. It's a marvelous picture. Who is it that is supposed to articulate the longings and aspirations of the people more than the preacher? Somehow the preacher must be an Amos, and say, "Let justice roll down like waters and righteousness like a mighty stream." Somehow, the preacher must say with Jesus, "The spirit of the Lord is upon me, because he hath anointed me to deal with the problems of the poor."

And I want to commend the preachers, under the leadership of these noble men: James Lawson, one who has been in this struggle for many years; he's been to jail for struggling; but he's still going on, fighting for the rights of his people. Rev. Ralph Jackson, Billy Kiles; I could just go right on down the list, but time will not permit. But I want to thank them all. And I want you to thank them, because so often, preachers aren't concerned about anything but themselves. And I'm always happy to see a relevant ministry.

It's alright to talk about "long white robes over yonder," in all of its symbolism. But ultimately people want some suits and dresses and shoes to wear down here. It's alright to talk about "streets flowing with milk and honey," but God has commanded us to be concerned about the slums down here, and his children who can't eat three square meals a day. It's alright to talk about the new Jerusalem, but one day, God's preacher must talk about the new New York, the new Atlanta, the new Philadelphia, the new Los Angeles, the new Memphis, Tennessee. This is what we have to do.

Now the other thing we'll have to do is this: Always anchor our external direct action with the power of economic withdrawal. Now, we are poor people, individually, we are poor when you compare us with white society in America. We are poor. Never stop and forget that collectively, that means all of us together, collectively we are richer than all the nations in the world, with the exception of nine. Did you ever think about that? After you leave the United States, Soviet Russia, Great Britain, West Germany, France, and I could name the others, the Negro collectively is richer than most nations of the world. We have an annual income of more than thirty billion dollars a year, which is more than all of the exports of the United States, and more than the national budget of Canada. Did you know that? That's power right there, if we know how to pool it.

We don't have to argue with anybody. We don't have to curse and go around acting bad with our words. We don't need any bricks and bottles, we don't need any Molotov cocktails, we just need to go around to these stores, and to these massive industries in our country, and say, "God sent us by here, to say to you that you're not treating his children right. And we've come by here to ask you to make the first item on your agenda fair treatment, where God's children are concerned. Now, if you are not prepared to do that, we do have an agenda that we must follow. And our agenda calls for withdrawing economic support from you."

And so, as a result of this, we are asking you tonight, to go out and tell your neighbors not to buy Coca-Cola in Memphis. Go by and tell them not to buy Sealtest milk. Tell them not to buy—what is the other bread?—Wonder Bread. And what is the other bread company, Jesse?

Tell them not to buy Hart's bread. As Jesse Jackson has said, up to now, only the garbage men have been feeling pain; now we must kind of redistribute the pain. We are choosing these companies because they haven't been fair in their hiring policies; and we are choosing them because they can begin the process of saying, they are going to support the needs and the rights of these men who are on strike. And then they can move on downtown and tell Mayor Loeb to do what is right.

But not only that, we've got to strengthen black institutions. I call upon you to take your money out of the banks downtown and deposit your money in Tri-State Bank—we want a "bank-in" movement in Memphis. So go by the savings and loan association. I'm not asking you something that we don't do ourselves at SCLC. Judge Hooks and others will tell you that we have an account here in the savings and loan association from the Southern Christian Leadership Conference. We're just telling you to follow what we're doing. Put your money there. You have six or seven black insurance companies in Memphis. Take out your insurance there. We want to have an "insurance-in."

Now there are some practical things we can do. We begin the process of building a greater economic base. And at the same time, we are putting pressure where it really hurts. I ask you to follow through here.

Now, let me say as I move to my conclusion that we've got to give ourselves to this struggle until the end. Nothing would be more tragic than to stop at this point, in Memphis. We've got to see it through. And when we have our march, you need to be there. Be concerned about your brother. You may not be on strike. But either we go up together, or we go down together.

Let us develop a kind of dangerous unselfishness. One day a man came to Jesus; and he wanted to raise some questions about some vital matters in life. At points, he wanted to trick Jesus, and show him that he knew a little more than Jesus knew, and through this, throw him off base. Now that question could have easily ended up in a philosophical and theological debate. But Jesus immediately pulled that question from mid-air, and placed it on a dangerous curve between Jerusalem and Jericho. And he talked about a certain man, who fell among thieves. You remember that a Levite and a priest passed by on the other side. They didn't stop to help him. And finally a man of another race came by. He got down from his beast, decided not to be compassionate by proxy. But with him, administered first aid, and helped the man in need. Jesus ended up saying, this was the good man, this was the great man, because he had the capacity to project the "I" into the "thou," and to be concerned about his brother.

Now you know, we use our imagination a great deal to try to determine why the priest and the Levite didn't stop. At times we say they were busy going to church meetings—an ecclesiastical gathering—and they had to get on down to Jerusalem so they wouldn't be late for their meeting. At other times we would speculate that there was a religious law that "One who was engaged in religious ceremonials was not to touch a human body twenty-four hours before the ceremony." And every now and then we begin to wonder whether maybe they were not going down to Jerusalem, or down to Jericho, rather to organize a "Jericho Road Improvement Association." That's a possibility. Maybe they felt that it was better to deal with the problem from the causal root, rather than to get bogged down with an individual effort.

But I'm going to tell you what my imagination tells me. It's possible that these men were afraid. You see, the Jericho road is a dangerous road. I remember when Mrs. King and I were first in Jerusalem. We rented a car and drove from Jerusalem down to Jericho. And as soon as we got on that road, I said to my wife, "I can see why Jesus used this as a setting for his parable." It's a winding, meandering road. It's really conducive for ambushing. You start out in Jerusalem, which is about 1200 miles, or rather 1200 feet above sea level. And by the time you get down to Jericho, fifteen or twenty minutes later, you're about 2200 feet below sea level. That's a dangerous road. In the day of Jesus it came to be known as the "Bloody Pass."

And you know, it's possible that the priest and the Levite looked over that man on the ground and wondered if the robbers were still around. Or it's possible that they felt that the man on the ground was merely faking. And he was acting like he had been robbed and hurt, in order to seize them over there, lure them there for quick and easy seizure. And so the first question that the Levite asked was, "If I stop to help this man, what will happen to me?" But then the Good Samaritan came by. And he reversed the question: "If I do not stop to help this man, what will happen to him?"

That's the question before you tonight. Not, "If I stop to help the sanitation workers, what will happen to all of the hours that I usually spend in my office every day and every week as a pastor?" The question is not, "If I stop to help this man in need, what will happen to me?" "If I do not stop to help the sanitation workers, what will happen to them?" That's the question.

Let us rise up tonight with a greater readiness. Let us stand with a greater determination. And let us move on in these powerful days, these days of challenge to make America what it ought to be. We have an opportunity to make America a better nation. And I want to thank God, once more, for allowing me to be here with you.

You know, several years ago, I was in New York City autographing the first book that I had written. And while sitting there autographing books, a demented black woman came up. The only question I heard from her was, "Are you Martin Luther King?"

And I was looking down writing, and I said yes. And the next minute I felt something beating on my chest. Before I knew it I had been stabbed by this demented woman. I was rushed to Harlem Hospital. It was a dark Saturday afternoon. And that blade had gone through, and the X-rays revealed that the tip of the blade was on the edge of my aorta, the main artery. And once that's punctured, you drown in your own blood—that's the end of you.

It came out in the *New York Times* the next morning, that if I had sneezed, I would have died. Well, about four days later, they allowed me, after the operation, after my chest had been opened, and the blade had been taken out, to move around in the wheel chair in the hospital. They allowed me to read some of the mail that came in, and from all over the states, and the world, kind letters came in. I read a few, but one of them I will never forget. I had received one from the President and the Vice-President. I've forgotten what those telegrams said. I'd received a visit and a letter from the Governor of New York, but I've forgotten what the letter said.

But there was another letter that came from a little girl, a young girl who was a student at the Whites Plains High School. And I looked at that letter, and I'll never forget it. It said simply, "Dear Dr. King: I am a ninth-grade student at the White Plains High School." She said, "While it should not matter, I would like to mention that I am a white girl. I read in the paper of your misfortune, and of your suffering. And I read that if you had sneezed, you would have died. And I'm simply writing you to say that I'm so happy that you didn't sneeze."

And I want to say tonight, I want to say that I am happy that I didn't sneeze. Because if I had sneezed, I wouldn't have been around here in 1960, when students all over the South started sitting-in at lunch counters. And I knew that as they were sitting in, they were really standing up for the best in the American dream. And taking the whole nation back to those great wells of democracy which were dug deep by the Founding Fathers in the Declaration of Independence and the Constitution. If I had sneezed, I wouldn't have been around in 1962, when Negroes in Albany, Georgia, decided to straighten their backs up. And whenever men and women straighten their backs up, they are going somewhere, because a man can't ride your back unless it is bent.

If I had sneezed, I wouldn't have been here in 1963, when the black people of Birmingham, Alabama, aroused the conscience of this nation, and brought into being the Civil Rights Bill. If I had sneezed, I wouldn't have had a chance later that year, in August, to try to tell America about a dream that I had had. If I had sneezed, I wouldn't have been down in Selma, Alabama, to see the great movement there. If I had sneezed, I wouldn't have been in Memphis to see a community rally around those brothers and sisters who are suffering. I'm so happy that I didn't sneeze.

And they were telling me, now it doesn't matter now. It really doesn't matter what happens now. I left Atlanta this morning, and as we got started on the plane, there were six of us, the pilot said over the public address system, "We are sorry for the delay, but we have Dr. Martin Luther King on the plane. And to be sure that all of the bags were checked, and to be sure that nothing would be wrong with the plane, we had to check out everything carefully. And we've had the plane protected and guarded all night."

And then I got to Memphis. And some began to say that threats, or talk about the threats that were out. What would happen to me from some of our sick white brothers?

Well, I don't know what will happen now. We've got some difficult days ahead. But it doesn't matter with me now. Because I've been to the mountaintop. And I don't mind. Like anybody, I would like to live a long life. Longevity has its place. But I'm not concerned about that now. I just want to do God's will. And He's allowed me to go up to the mountain. And I've looked over. And I've seen the promised land. I may not get there with you. But I want you to know tonight, that we, as a people, will get to the promised land. And I'm happy tonight. I'm not worried about anything. I'm not fearing any man. Mine eyes have seen the glory of the coming of the Lord.

★ ★ ★

## "SAY A PRAYER FOR OUR COUNTRY"

### Robert F. Kennedy, Remarks on the Assassination of Dr. King, Indianapolis, Indiana—April 4, 1968

Robert F. Kennedy (1925–1968) was campaigning for the Democratic presidential nomination when word of King's assassination reached him in Indianapolis. Kennedy himself would be killed two months later, in Los Angeles, just after winning the California primary.

I HAVE BAD NEWS for you, for all of our fellow citizens, and people who love peace all over the world, and that is that Martin Luther King was shot and killed tonight.

Martin Luther King dedicated his life to love and to justice for his fellow human beings, and he died because of that effort.

In this difficult day, in this difficult time for the United States, it is perhaps well to ask what kind of a nation we are and what direction we want to move in. For those of you who are black—considering the evidence there evidently is that there were white people who were responsible—you can be filled with bitterness, with hatred, and a desire for revenge. We can move in that direction as a country, in great polarization—black people amongst black, white people amongst white, filled with hatred toward one another.

Or we can make an effort, as Martin Luther King did, to understand and to comprehend, and to replace that violence, that stain of bloodshed that has spread across our land, with an effort to understand with compassion and love.

For those of you who are black and are tempted to be filled with hatred and distrust at the injustice of such an act, against all white people, I can only say that I feel in my own heart the same kind of feeling. I had a member of my family killed, but he was killed by a white man. But we have to make an effort in the United States, we have to make an effort to understand, to go beyond these rather difficult times.

My favorite poet was Aeschylus. He wrote: "In our sleep, pain which cannot forget falls drop by drop upon the heart until, in our own despair, against our will, comes wisdom through the awful grace of God."

What we need in the United States is not division; what we need in the United States is not hatred; what we need in the United States is not violence or lawlessness; but love and wisdom, and compassion toward one another, and a feeling of justice toward those who still suffer within our country, whether they be white or they be black.

So I shall ask you tonight to return home, to say a prayer for the family of Martin Luther King, that's true, but more importantly to say a prayer for our own country, which all of us love—a prayer for understanding and that compassion of which I spoke.

We can do well in this country. We will have difficult times; we've had difficult times in the past; we will have difficult times in the future. It is not the end of violence; it is not the end of lawlessness; it is not the end of disorder.

But the vast majority of white people and the vast majority of black people in this country want to live together, want to improve the quality of our life, and want justice for all human beings who abide in our land.

Let us dedicate ourselves to what the Greeks wrote so many years ago: to tame the savageness of man and make gentle the life of this world.

Let us dedicate ourselves to that, and say a prayer for our country and for our people.

PART IX

# FRAYING CONSENSUS

*1969–*

Our Constitution works; our great Republic is a government of laws and not of men. Here the people rule. But there is a higher Power, by whatever name we honor Him, who ordains not only righteousness but love, not only justice but mercy.

—Gerald R. Ford, 1974

Previous Spread: *On Friday, August 9, 1974, Richard Nixon, the thirty-seventh president of the United States, resigned the office and returned, with his wife, Pat, to California. Vice President Gerald R. Ford, here with his wife, Betty, succeeded Nixon in the hope, as Ford put it, that the nation would experience "a time to heal."*

Tom Wicker was a young correspondent in Washington for the *Winston-Salem Journal* when, one night in 1957, he encountered a solitary figure in the Capitol: the vice president of the United States, Richard Nixon. As Wicker recalled, Nixon was "walking along rather slowly, shoulders slumped, hands jammed in his trouser pockets, head down and his eyes apparently fixed—though perhaps on nothing—on the ornate Capitol floor. What I could see of his face seemed darker than could be accounted for by the trademark five o'clock shadow; it was preoccupied, brooding, gloomy, whether angry or merely disconsolate I was unable to tell. . . . I had expected Nixon to be taller, and of better posture, and would have thought he'd have a politician's ready greeting for a voter unexpectedly encountered. But as he went his way without the slightest recognition that someone else was in that shadowy hall, I realized that I was seeing a man bound up in his inner being . . . unaware of the impression he was making, unaware even that he was making an impression, too absorbed in himself to present the façade with which . . . most of us guard the truth of that inner self, that secret life, we rarely share with anyone."

As Wicker observed, Richard Milhous Nixon was a mysterious if ubiquitous figure in what Time-Life founder Henry Luce dubbed the American Century. Nixon ran on five national major-party tickets, a feat matched only by Franklin D. Roosevelt. Born in Yorba Linda, California, educated at Whittier College and at Duke Law School, Nixon served in World War II, was elected to the House in 1946, to the Senate in 1950, and became vice president under Dwight Eisenhower in 1953. He narrowly lost the presidency to John F. Kennedy in 1960 before staging a spectacular political comeback and winning the White House in 1968 and in 1972.

Then, of course, it all came crashing down, and Nixon was forced to resign from office in August 1974 after covering up political espionage within the White House and among his political operatives.

Who was Nixon, really? The great man who opened China? Who negotiated with the Soviet Union? Who created the Environmental Protection Agency and presided over a centrist domestic policy that valued government's role in the life of the nation? Or was he the crude pol who exploited race to win, who tried to use federal agencies to hound his opponents, who railed against anyone he thought a rival or a foe?

In truth he was all these things. An astute biographer, Evan Thomas, interviewed Brent Scowcroft, who served several presidents, and asked Scowcroft whether Nixon could ever see the true Nixon. "No," Scowcroft told Thomas, "but sometimes I think he took a peek." Thomas went on: "That sounds about right. At some deep, possibly subconscious level, Nixon seems to have understood that he was locked in a titanic battle between hope and fear, and he struggled, bravely if not always wisely, against the dark."

The fact that Nixon resigned—and the fact that the Congress seemed poised to impeach and convict him on a largely bipartisan basis—belongs to another political age. It was an age when, for all its ferocity, there was a sense of shame at the highest levels, a sense of duty to institutions.

And in some ways Nixon's essential policy centrism helped fuel a conservative reaction that would find its fullest expression in the presidential election of 2016. The presidents in between—Gerald R. Ford, Jimmy Carter, Ronald Reagan, George H. W. Bush, Bill Clinton, George W. Bush, and Barack Obama—all governed in an ethos that was based on commonly accepted realities.

The rise of Donald Trump can perhaps be best explained as a manifestation of the more virulent forces that have always been part of American life. There is, as this volume has shown, no happily ever after in a democracy, for there can be no happily ever after in human affairs, at least as reality is now constituted. The task is to nudge the world closer to the good while always understanding that the bad is the most formidable of foes.

★ ★ ★

## "THERE ARE NO FOUNDING MOTHERS"
### Shirley Chisholm of New York, "Equal Rights for Women," Address to the U.S. House of Representatives—May 21, 1969

The first African-American woman elected to Congress, Shirley Chisholm (1924–2005) sought the Democratic presidential nomination in 1972, played a central role in creating the food stamp program, and, in these remarks, made a landmark case for the passage of the Equal Rights Amendment.

MR. SPEAKER, HOUSE Joint Resolution 264, before us today, which provides for equality under the law for both men and women, represents one of the most clear-cut opportunities we are likely to have to declare our faith in the principles that shaped our Constitution. It provides a legal basis for attack on the most subtle, most pervasive, and most institutionalized form of prejudice that exists. Discrimination against women, solely on the basis of their sex, is so widespread that it seems to many persons normal, natural, and right.

Legal expression of prejudice on the grounds of religious or political belief has become a minor problem in our society. Prejudice on the basis of race is, at least, under systematic attack. There is reason for optimism that it will start to die with the present, older generation. It is time we act to assure full equality of opportunity to those citizens who, although in a majority, suffer the restrictions that are commonly imposed on minorities, to women.

The argument that this amendment will not solve the problem of sex discrimination is not relevant. If the argument were used against a civil rights bill, as it has been used in the past, the prejudice that lies behind it would be embarrassing. Of course laws will not eliminate prejudice from the hearts of human beings. But that is no reason to allow prejudice to continue to be enshrined in our laws—to perpetuate injustice through inaction.

The amendment is necessary to clarify countless ambiguities and inconsistencies in our legal system. For instance, the Constitution guarantees due process of law, in the 5th and 14th amendments. But the applicability of due process of sex distinctions is not clear. Women are excluded from some State colleges and universities. In some States, restrictions are placed on a married woman who engages in an independent business. Women may not be chosen for some juries. Women even receive heavier criminal penalties than men who commit the same crime. What would the legal effects of the equal rights amendment really be? The equal rights amendment would govern only the relationship between the State and its citizens—not relationships between private citizens. The amendment would be largely self-executing, that is, and Federal or State laws in conflict would be ineffective one year after date of ratification without further action by the Congress or State legislatures.

Opponents of the amendment claim its ratification would throw the law into a state of confusion and would result in much litigation to establish its meaning. This objection overlooks the influence of legislative history in determining intent and the recent activities of many groups preparing for legislative changes in this direction.

State labor laws applying only to women, such as those limiting hours of work and weights to be lifted would become inoperative unless the legislature amended them to apply to men. As of early 1970 most States would have some laws that would be affected. However, changes are being made so rapidly as a result of title VII of the Civil Rights Act of 1964, it is likely that by the time the equal rights amendment would become effective, no conflicting State laws would remain.

In any event, there has for years been great controversy as to the usefulness to women of these State labor laws. There has never been any doubt that they worked a hardship on women who need or want to work overtime and on women who need or want better paying jobs, and there has been no persuasive evidence as to how many women benefit from the archaic policy of the laws. After the Delaware hours law was repealed in 1966, there were no complaints from women to any of the State agencies that might have been approached.

Jury service laws not making women equally liable for jury service would have been revised. The selective service law would have to include women, but women would not be required to serve in the Armed Forces where they are not fitted any more than men are required to serve. Military service, while a great responsibility, is not without benefits, particularly for young men with limited education or training.

Since October 1966, 246,000 young men who did not meet the normal mental or physical requirements have been given opportunities for training and correcting physical problems. This opportunity is not open to their sisters. Only girls who have completed high school and meet high standards on the educational test can volunteer. Ratification of the amendment would not permit application of higher standards to women.

Survivorship benefits would be available to husbands of female workers on the same basis as to wives of male workers. The Social Security Act and the civil service and military service retirement acts are in conflict. Public schools and universities could not be limited to one sex and could not apply different admission standards to men and women. Laws requiring longer prison sentences for women than men would be invalid, and equal opportunities for rehabilitation and vocational training would have to be provided in public correctional institutions. Different ages of majority based on sex would have to be

*The battle over the Equal Rights Amendment reflected the competing forces of the age.*

harmonized. Federal, State, and other governmental bodies would be obligated to follow nondiscriminatory practices in all aspects of employment, including public school teachers and State university and college faculties.

What would be the economic effects of the equal rights amendment? Direct economic effects would be minor. If any labor laws applying only to women still remained, their amendment or repeal would provide opportunity for women in better-paying jobs in manufacturing. More opportunities in public vocational and graduate schools for women would also tend to open up opportunities in better jobs for women.

Indirect effects could be much greater. The focusing of public attention on the gross legal, economic, and social discrimination against women by hearings and debates in the Federal and State legislatures would result in changes in attitude of parents, educators, and employers that would bring about substantial economic changes in the long run.

Sex prejudice cuts both ways. Men are oppressed by the requirements of the Selective Service Act, by enforced legal guardianship of minors, and by alimony laws. Each sex, I believe, should be liable when necessary to serve and defend this country. Each has a responsibility for the support of children.

There are objections raised to wiping out laws protecting women workers. No one would condone exploitation. But what does sex have to do with it. Working conditions and hours that are harmful to women are harmful to men; wages that are unfair for women are unfair for men. Laws setting employment limitations on the basis of sex are irrational, and the proof of this is their inconsistency from State to State. The physical characteristics of men and women are not fixed, but cover two wide spans that have a great deal of overlap. It is obvious, I think, that a robust woman could be more fit for physical labor than a weak man. The choice of occupation would be determined by individual capabilities, and the rewards for equal works should be equal.

This is what it comes down to: artificial distinctions between persons must be wiped out of the law. Legal discrimination between the sexes is, in almost every instance, founded on outmoded views of society and the pre-scientific beliefs about psychology and physiology. It is time to sweep away these relics of the past and set further generations free of them.

Federal agencies and institutions responsible for the enforcement of equal opportunity laws need the authority of a Constitutional amendment. The 1964 Civil Rights Act and the 1963 Equal Pay Act are not enough; they are limited in their coverage—for instance, one excludes teachers, and the other leaves out administrative and professional women. The Equal Employment Opportunity Commission has not proven to be an adequate device, with its power limited to investigation, conciliation, and recommendation to the Justice Department. In its cases involving sexual discrimination, it has failed in more than one-half. The Justice Department has been even less effective. It has intervened in only one case involving discrimination on the basis of sex, and this was on a procedural point. In a second case, in which both sexual and racial discrimination were alleged, the racial bias charge was given far greater weight.

Evidence of discrimination on the basis of sex should hardly have to be cited here. It is in the Labor Department's employment and salary figures for anyone who is still in doubt. Its elimination will involve so many changes in our State and Federal laws that, without the authority and impetus of this proposed amendment, it will perhaps take another 194 years. We cannot be parties to continuing a delay. The time is clearly now to put this House on record for the fullest expression of that equality of opportunity which our founding fathers professed. They professed it, but they did not assure it to their daughters, as they tried to do for their sons.

The Constitution they wrote was designed to protect the rights of white, male citizens. As there were no black Founding Fathers, there were no founding mothers—a great pity, on both counts. It is not too late to complete the work they left undone. Today, here, we should start to do so.

★ ★ ★

## "THE GREAT SILENT MAJORITY"
### Richard Nixon, Address to the Nation on the War in Vietnam, Washington, D.C.—November 3, 1969

Richard Nixon (1913–1994) of California served in the House and in the Senate before becoming vice president under Dwight Eisenhower. He lost narrowly to John F. Kennedy in the 1960 presidential election, but came back to win the White House in 1968.

TONIGHT I WANT to talk to you on a subject of deep concern to all Americans and to many people in all parts of the world—the war in Vietnam. . . .

In San Francisco a few weeks ago, I saw demonstrators carrying signs reading: "Lose in Vietnam, bring the boys home."

Well, one of the strengths of our free society is that any American has a right to reach that conclusion and to advocate that point of view. But as President of the United States, I would be untrue to my oath of office if I allowed the policy of this Nation to be dictated by the minority who hold that point of view and who try to impose it on the Nation by mounting demonstrations in the street.

For almost 200 years, the policy of this Nation has been made under our Constitution by those leaders in the Congress and the White House elected by all of the people. If a vocal minority, however fervent its cause, prevails over reason and the will of the majority, this Nation has no future as a free society.

And now I would like to address a word, if I may, to the young people of this Nation who are particularly concerned, and I understand why they are concerned, about this war.

I respect your idealism.

I share your concern for peace.

I want peace as much as you do.

There are powerful personal reasons I want to end this war. This week I will have to sign 83 letters to mothers, fathers, wives, and loved ones of men who have given their lives for America in Vietnam. It is very little satisfaction to me that this is only one-third as many letters as I signed the first week in office. There is nothing I want more than to see the day come when I do not have to write any of those letters. . . .

I have chosen a plan for peace. I believe it will succeed.

If it does succeed, what the critics say now won't matter. If it does not succeed, anything I say then won't matter.

I know it may not be fashionable to speak of patriotism or national destiny these days. But I feel it is appropriate to do so on this occasion.

Two hundred years ago this Nation was weak and poor. But even then, America was the hope of millions in the world. Today we have become the strongest and richest nation in the world. And the wheel of destiny has turned so that any hope the world has for the survival of peace and freedom will be determined by whether the American people have the moral stamina and the courage to meet the challenge of free world leadership.

Let historians not record that when America was the most powerful nation in the world we passed on the other side of the road and allowed the last hopes for peace and freedom of millions of people to be suffocated by the forces of totalitarianism.

And so tonight—to you, the great silent majority of my fellow Americans—I ask for your support.

★ ★ ★

## "WE ARE A GOVERNMENT OF LAWS, NOT OF MEN"
## Gerald R. Ford, Remarks on Taking the Oath of Office, Washington, D.C.—August 9, 1974

Gerald R. Ford (1913–2006) was an unlikely president. A longtime member of the U.S. House from Grand Rapids, Michigan, Ford was elevated to the vice presidency in 1973 when his predecessor, Spiro T. Agnew, was forced to resign amid charges of corruption. The next year President Nixon resigned under threat of impeachment and conviction in the Watergate affair. Ford thus became the only American president never to have appeared on a national ballot.

THE OATH THAT I have taken is the same oath that was taken by George Washington and by every President under the Constitution. But I assume the Presidency under extraordinary circumstances never before experienced by Americans. This is an hour of history that troubles our minds and hurts our hearts.

Therefore, I feel it is my first duty to make an unprecedented compact with my countrymen. Not an inaugural address, not a fireside chat, not a campaign speech—just a little straight talk among friends. And I intend it to be the first of many.

I am acutely aware that you have not elected me as your President by your ballots, and so I ask you to confirm me as your President with your prayers. And I hope that such prayers will also be the first of many.

If you have not chosen me by secret ballot, neither have I gained office by any secret promises. I have not campaigned either for the Presidency or the Vice Presidency. I have not subscribed to any partisan platform. I am indebted to no man, and only to one woman—my dear wife—as I begin this very difficult job.

I have not sought this enormous responsibility, but I will not shirk it. Those who nominated and confirmed me as Vice President were my friends and are my friends. They were of both parties, elected by all the people and acting under the Constitution in their name. It is only fitting then that I should pledge to them and to you that I will be the President of all the people.

Thomas Jefferson said the people are the only sure reliance for the preservation of our liberty. And down the years, Abraham Lincoln renewed this American article of faith, asking, "Is there any better way or equal hope in the world?"

I intend, on Monday next, to request of the Speaker of the House of Representatives and the President pro tempore of the Senate the privilege of appearing before the Congress to share with my former colleagues and with you, the American people, my views on the priority business of the Nation and to solicit your views and their views. And may I say to the Speaker and the others, if I could meet with you right after these remarks, I would appreciate it.

Even though this is late in an election year, there is no way we can go forward except together and no way anybody can win except by serving the people's urgent needs. We cannot stand still or slip backwards. We must go forward now together.

To the peoples and the governments of all friendly nations, and I hope that could encompass the whole world, I pledge an uninterrupted and sincere search for peace. America will remain strong and united, but its strength will remain dedicated to the safety and sanity of the entire family of man, as well as to our own precious freedom.

I believe that truth is the glue that holds government together, not only our Government but civilization itself. That bond, though strained, is unbroken at home and abroad.

In all my public and private acts as your President, I expect to follow my instincts of openness and candor with full confidence that honesty is always the best policy in the end.

My fellow Americans, our long national nightmare is over.

Our Constitution works; our great Republic is a government of laws and not of men. Here the people rule. But there is a higher Power, by whatever name we honor Him, who ordains not only righteousness but love, not only justice but mercy.

As we bind up the internal wounds of Watergate, more painful and more poisonous than those of foreign wars, let us restore the golden rule to our political process, and let brotherly love purge our hearts of suspicion and of hate.

In the beginning, I asked you to pray for me. Before closing, I ask again your prayers, for Richard Nixon and for his family. May our former President, who brought peace to millions, find it for himself. May God bless and comfort his wonderful wife and daughters, whose love and loyalty will forever be a shining legacy to all who bear the lonely burdens of the White House.

I can only guess at those burdens, although I have witnessed at close hand the tragedies that befell three Presidents and the lesser trials of others.

With all the strength and all the good sense I have gained from life, with all the confidence my family, my friends, and my dedicated staff impart to me, and with the good will of countless Americans I have encountered in recent visits to 40 States, I now solemnly reaffirm my promise I made to you last December 6: to uphold the Constitution, to do what is right as God gives me to see the right, and to do the very best I can for America.

God helping me, I will not let you down.

★ ★ ★

## "I, BARBARA JORDAN, AM A KEYNOTE SPEAKER"

### Barbara Jordan, Keynote Address to the Democratic National Convention, Madison Square Garden, New York City—July 12, 1976

With her powerful voice, Barbara Jordan (1936–1996) captivated the 1976 Democratic National Convention with a keynote address that placed the congresswoman from Texas's own story in the context of the nation's.

It was one hundred and forty-four years ago that members of the Democratic Party first met in convention to select a Presidential candidate. Since that time, Democrats have continued to convene once every four years and draft a party platform and nominate a Presidential candidate. And our meeting this week is a continuation of that tradition.

But there is something different about tonight. There is something special about tonight. What is different? What is special? I, Barbara Jordan, am a keynote speaker.

A lot of years passed since 1832, and during that time it would have been most unusual for any national political party to ask that a Barbara Jordan deliver a keynote address, but tonight here I am. And I feel that notwithstanding the past that my presence here is one additional bit of evidence that the American Dream need not forever be deferred.

Now that I have this grand distinction what in the world am I supposed to say?

I could easily spend this time praising the accomplishments of this party and attacking the Republicans but I don't choose to do that.

I could list the many problems which Americans have. I could list the problems which cause people to feel cynical, angry, frustrated: problems which include lack of integrity in government; the feeling that the individual no longer counts; the reality of material and spiritual poverty; the feeling that the grand American experiment is failing or has failed. I could recite these problems and then I could sit down and offer no solutions. But I don't choose to do that either.

The citizens of America expect more. They deserve and they want more than a recital of problems.

We are a people in a quandary about the present. We are a people in search of our future. We are a people in search of a national community.

We are a people trying not only to solve the problems of the present—unemployment, inflation—but we are attempting on a larger scale to fulfill the promise of America. We are attempting to fulfill our national purpose; to create and sustain a society in which all of us are equal.

Throughout our history, when people have looked for new ways to solve their problems, and to uphold the principles of this nation, many times they have turned to political parties. They have often turned to the Democratic Party.

What is it, what is it about the Democratic Party that makes it the instrument that people use when they search for ways to shape their future? Well, I believe the answer to that question lies in our concept of governing. Our concept of governing is derived from our view of people. It is a concept deeply rooted in a set of beliefs firmly etched in the national conscience, of all of us.

Now what are these beliefs?

First, we believe in equality for all and privileges for none. This is a belief that each American regardless of background has equal standing in the public forum, all of us. Because we believe this idea so firmly, we are an inclusive rather than an exclusive party. Let everybody come.

I think it no accident that most of those immigrating to America in the nineteenth century identified with the Democratic Party. We are a heterogeneous party made up of Americans of diverse backgrounds.

We believe that the people are the source of all governmental power; that the authority of the people is to be extended, not restricted. This can be accomplished only by providing each citizen with every opportunity to participate in the management of the government. They must have that.

We believe that the government which represents the authority of all the people, not just one interest group, but all the people, has an obligation to actively—underscore actively—seek to remove those obstacles which would block individual achievement, obstacles emanating from race, sex, economic condition. The government must seek to remove them.

We are a party of innovation. We do not reject our traditions, but we are willing to adapt to changing circumstances, when change we must. We are willing to suffer the discomfort of change in order to achieve a better future.

We have a positive vision of the future founded on the belief that the gap between the promise and reality of America can one day be finally closed. We believe that.

This, my friends, is the bedrock of our concept of governing. This is a part of the reason why Americans have turned to the Democratic Party. These are the foundations upon which a national community can be built.

*Barbara Jordan of Texas at the rostrum of the Democratic National Convention that nominated Jimmy Carter for president and Walter Mondale for vice president in 1976.*

Let's all understand that these guiding principles cannot be discarded for short-term political gains. They represent what this country is all about. They are indigenous to the American idea. And these are principles which are not negotiable.

In other times, I could stand here and give this kind of exposition on the beliefs of the Democratic Party and that would be enough. But today that is not enough. People want more. That is not sufficient reason for the majority of the people of this country to decide to vote Democratic. We have made mistakes. We realize that. We admit our mistakes. In our haste to do all things for all people, we did not foresee the full consequences of our actions. And when the people raised their voices, we didn't hear. But our deafness was only a temporary condition, and not an irreversible condition.

Even as I stand here and admit that we have made mistakes I still believe that as the people of America sit in judgment on each party, they will recognize that our mistakes were mistakes of the heart. They'll recognize that.

And now we must look to the future. Let us heed the voice of the people and recognize their common sense. If we do not, we not only blaspheme our political heritage, we ignore the common ties that bind all Americans.

Many fear the future, many are distrustful of their leaders and believe that their voices are never heard. Many seek only to satisfy their private work wants to satisfy their private interests.

But this is the great danger America faces. That we will cease to be one nation and become instead a collection of interest groups: city against suburb, region against region, individual against individual. Each seeking to satisfy private wants.

If that happens, who then will speak for America?

Who then will speak for the common good?

This is the question which must be answered in 1976.

Are we to be one people bound together by common spirit sharing in a common endeavor or will we become a divided nation?

For all of its uncertainty, we cannot flee the future. We must not become the new Puritans and reject our society. We must address and master the future together. It can be done if we restore the belief that we share a sense of national community, that we share a common national endeavor. It can be done.

There is no executive order; there is no law that can require the American people to form a national community. This we must do as individuals and if we do it as individuals, there is no President of the United States who can veto that decision.

As a first step, we must restore our belief in ourselves. We are a generous people so why can't we be generous with each other? We need to take to heart the words spoken by Thomas Jefferson: "Let us restore to social intercourse that harmony and that affection without which liberty and even life are but dreary things."

A nation is formed by the willingness of each of us to share in the responsibility for upholding the common good.

A government is invigorated when each one of us is willing to participate in shaping the future of this nation.

In this election year we must define the common good and begin again to shape a common future. Let each person do his or her part. If one citizen is unwilling to participate, all of us are going to suffer. For the American idea, though it is shared by all of us, is realized in each one of us.

And now, what are those of us who are elected public officials supposed to do? We call ourselves public servants but I'll tell you this: we as public servants must set an example for the rest of the nation. It is hypocritical for the public official to admonish and exhort the people to uphold the common good if we are derelict in upholding the common good. More is required of public officials than slogans and handshakes and press releases. More is required. We must hold ourselves strictly accountable. We must provide the people with a vision of the future.

If we promise as public officials, we must deliver. If we as public officials propose, we must produce. If we say to the American people it is time for you to be sacrificial, sacrifice. If the public official says that, we must be the first to give. We must be. And again, if we make mistakes, we must be willing to admit them. We have to do that. What we have to do is strike a balance between the idea that government should do everything and the idea, the belief, that government ought to do nothing. Strike a balance.

Let there be no illusions about the difficulty of forming this kind of a national community. It's tough, difficult, not easy. But a spirit of harmony will survive in America only if each of us remembers that we share a common destiny. If each of us remembers—when self-interest and bitterness seem to prevail—that we share a common destiny.

I have confidence that we can form this kind of national community.

I have confidence that the Democratic Party can lead the way. I have that confidence. We cannot improve on the system of government handed down to us by the founders of the Republic, there is no way to improve upon that. But what we can do is to find new ways to implement that system and realize our destiny.

Now, I began this speech by commenting to you on the uniqueness of a Barbara Jordan making a keynote address. Well I am going to close my speech by quoting a Republican president and I ask you that as you listen to these words of Abraham Lincoln, relate them to the concept of national community in which every last one of us participates:

"As I would not be a *slave,* so I would not be a *master.* This expresses my idea of democracy. Whatever differs from this, to the extent of the difference, is no democracy."

★ ★ ★

## "A CRISIS OF CONFIDENCE"

### Jimmy Carter, Address to the Nation on Energy and National Goals, Washington, D.C.—July 15, 1979

Jimmy Carter (1924–2024) surprised the political class with his successful 1976 campaign for president, coming from national obscurity to the highest office in the wake of Vietnam and of Watergate. By 1979, however, the nation seemed adrift, and Carter spoke directly to the state of things in an Oval Office address.

THIS IS A special night for me. Exactly three years ago, on July 15, 1976, I accepted the nomination of my party to run for President of the United States. I promised you a President who is not isolated from the people, who feels your pain, and who shares your dreams and who draws his strength and his wisdom from you.

During the past three years I've spoken to you on many occasions about national concerns, the energy crisis, reorganizing the Government, our Nation's economy, and issues of war and especially peace. But over those years the subjects of the speeches, the talks, and the press conferences have become increasingly narrow, focused more and more on what the isolated world of Washington thinks is important. Gradually, you've heard more and more about what the Government thinks or what the Government should be doing and less and less about our Nation's hopes, our dreams, and our vision of the future.

Ten days ago I had planned to speak to you again about a very important subject—energy. For the fifth time I would have described the urgency of the problem and laid out a series of legislative recommendations to the Congress. But as I was preparing to speak, I began to ask myself the same question that I now know has been troubling many of you. Why have we not been able to get together as a nation to resolve our serious energy problem?

It's clear that the true problems of our Nation are much deeper—deeper than gasoline lines or energy shortages, deeper even than inflation or recession. And I realize more than ever that as President I need your help. So, I decided to reach out and listen to the voices of America.

I invited to Camp David people from almost every segment of our society—business and labor, teachers and preachers, Governors, mayors, and private citizens. And then I left Camp David to listen to other Americans, men and women like you. It has been an extraordinary ten days, and I want to share with you what I've heard.

First of all, I got a lot of personal advice. Let me quote a few of the typical comments that I wrote down.

This from a southern Governor: "Mr. President, you are not leading this Nation—you're just managing the Government."

"You don't see the people enough anymore."

"Some of your Cabinet members don't seem loyal. There is not enough discipline among your disciples."

"Don't talk to us about politics or the mechanics of government, but about an understanding of our common good."

"Mr. President, we're in trouble. Talk to us about blood and sweat and tears."

"If you lead, Mr. President, we will follow."

Many people talked about themselves and about the condition of our Nation. This from a young woman in Pennsylvania: "I feel so far from government. I feel like ordinary people are excluded from political power."

And this from a young Chicano: "Some of us have suffered from recession all our lives."

*President Carter and Ronald Reagan, the former governor of California, faced off in only one debate, in 1980; Reagan's polished performance helped him secure a landslide victory over the incumbent just a week later.*

"Some people have wasted energy, but others haven't had anything to waste."

And this from a religious leader: "No material shortage can touch the important things like God's love for us or our love for one another."

And I like this one particularly from a black woman who happens to be the mayor of a small Mississippi town: "The big-shots are not the only ones who are important. Remember, you can't sell anything on Wall Street unless someone digs it up somewhere else first."

This kind of summarized a lot of other statements: "Mr. President, we are confronted with a moral and a spiritual crisis."

Several of our discussions were on energy, and I have a notebook full of comments and advice. I'll read just a few.

"We can't go on consuming 40 percent more energy than we produce. When we import oil we are also importing inflation plus unemployment."

"We've got to use what we have. The Middle East has only 5 percent of the world's energy, but the United States has 24 percent."

And this is one of the most vivid statements: "Our neck is stretched over the fence and OPEC has a knife."

"There will be other cartels and other shortages. American wisdom and courage right now can set a path to follow in the future."

This was a good one: "Be bold, Mr. President. We may make mistakes, but we are ready to experiment."

And this one from a labor leader got to the heart of it: "The real issue is freedom. We must deal with the energy problem on a war footing."

And the last that I'll read: "When we enter the moral equivalent of war, Mr. President, don't issue us BB guns."

These ten days confirmed my belief in the decency and the strength and the wisdom of the American people, but it also bore out some of my long-standing concerns about our Nation's underlying problems.

I know, of course, being President, that government actions and legislation can be very important. That's why I've worked hard to put my campaign promises into law—and I have to admit, with just mixed success. But after listening to the American people I have been reminded again that all the legislation in the world can't fix what's wrong with America. So, I want to speak to you first tonight about a subject even more serious than energy or inflation. I want to talk to you right now about a fundamental threat to American democracy.

I do not mean our political and civil liberties. They will endure. And I do not refer to the outward strength of America, a nation that is at peace tonight everywhere in the world, with unmatched economic power and military might.

The threat is nearly invisible in ordinary ways. It is a crisis of confidence. It is a crisis that strikes at the very heart and soul and spirit of our national will. We can see this crisis in the growing doubt about the meaning of our own lives and in the loss of a unity of purpose for our Nation.

The erosion of our confidence in the future is threatening to destroy the social and the political fabric of America.

The confidence that we have always had as a people is not simply some romantic dream or a proverb in a dusty book that we read just on the Fourth of July. It is the idea which founded our Nation and has guided our development as a people. Confidence in the future has supported everything else—public institutions and private enterprise, our own families, and the very Constitution of the United States. Confidence has defined our course and has served as a link between generations. We've always believed in something called progress. We've always had a faith that the days of our children would be better than our own.

Our people are losing that faith, not only in government itself but in the ability as citizens to serve as the ultimate rulers and shapers of our democracy. As a people we know our past and we are proud of it. Our progress has been part of the living history of America, even the world. We always believed that we were part of a great movement of humanity itself called democracy, involved in the search for freedom, and that belief has always strengthened us in our purpose. But just as we are losing our confidence in the future, we are also beginning to close the door on our past.

In a nation that was proud of hard work, strong families, close-knit communities, and our faith in God, too many of us now tend to worship self-indulgence and consumption. Human identity is no longer defined by what one does, but by what one owns. But we've discovered that owning things and consuming things does not satisfy our longing for meaning. We've learned that piling up material goods cannot fill the emptiness of lives which have no confidence or purpose.

The symptoms of this crisis of the American spirit are all around us. For the first time in the history of our country a majority of our people believe that the next 5 years will be worse than the past 5 years. Two-thirds of our people do not even vote. The productivity of American workers is actually dropping, and the willingness of Americans to save for the future has fallen below that of all other people in the Western world.

As you know, there is a growing disrespect for government and for churches and for schools, the news media, and other institutions. This is not a message of happiness or reassurance, but it is the truth and it is a warning.

These changes did not happen overnight. They've come upon us gradually over the last generation, years that were filled with shocks and tragedy.

We were sure that ours was a nation of the ballot, not the bullet, until the murders of John Kennedy and Robert Kennedy and Martin Luther King, Jr. We were taught that our armies were always invincible and our causes were always just, only to suffer the agony of Vietnam. We respected the Presidency as a place of honor until the shock of Watergate.

We remember when the phrase "sound as a dollar" was an expression of absolute dependability, until 10 years of inflation began to shrink our dollar and our savings. We believed that our Nation's resources were limitless until 1973, when we had to face a growing dependence on foreign oil.

These wounds are still very deep. They have never been healed.

Looking for a way out of this crisis, our people have turned to the Federal Government and found it isolated from the mainstream of our Nation's life. Washington, D.C., has become an island. The gap between our citizens and our Government has never been so wide. The people are looking for honest answers, not easy answers; clear leadership, not false claims and evasiveness and politics as usual.

What you see too often in Washington and elsewhere around the country is a system of government that seems incapable of action. You see a Congress twisted and pulled in every direction by hundreds of well-financed and powerful special interests. You see every extreme position defended to the last vote, almost to the last breath by one unyielding group or another. You often see a balanced and a fair approach that demands sacrifice, a little sacrifice from everyone, abandoned like an orphan without support and without friends.

Often you see paralysis and stagnation and drift. You don't like it, and neither do I. What can we do?

First of all, we must face the truth, and then we can change our course. We simply must have faith in each other, faith in our ability to govern ourselves, and faith in the future of this Nation. Restoring that faith and that confidence to America is now the most important task we face. It is a true challenge of this generation of Americans.

One of the visitors to Camp David last week put it this way: "We've got to stop crying and start sweating, stop talking and start walking, stop cursing and start praying. The strength we need will not come from the White House, but from every house in America."

We know the strength of America. We are strong. We can regain our unity. We can regain our confidence. We are the heirs of generations who survived threats much more powerful and awesome than those that challenge us now. Our fathers and mothers were strong men and women who shaped a new society during the Great Depression, who fought world wars, and who carved out a new charter of peace for the world.

We ourselves are the same Americans who just 10 years ago put a man on the Moon. We are the generation that dedicated our society to the pursuit of human rights and equality. And we are the generation that will win the war on the energy problem and in that process rebuild the unity and confidence of America.

We are at a turning point in our history. There are two paths to choose. One is a path I've warned about tonight, the path that leads to fragmentation and self-interest. Down that road lies a mistaken idea of freedom, the right to grasp for ourselves some advantage over others. That path would be one of constant conflict between narrow interests ending in chaos and immobility. It is a certain route to failure.

All the traditions of our past, all the lessons of our heritage, all the promises of our future point to another path, the path of common purpose and the restoration of American values. That path leads to true freedom for our Nation and ourselves. We can take the first steps down that path as we begin to solve our energy problem.

Energy will be the immediate test of our ability to unite this Nation, and it can also be the standard around which we rally. On the battlefield of energy we can win for our Nation a new confidence, and we can seize control again of our common destiny.

In little more than two decades we've gone from a position of energy independence to one in which almost half the oil we use comes from foreign countries, at prices that are going through the roof. Our excessive dependence on OPEC has already taken a tremendous toll on our economy and our people. This is the direct cause of the long lines which have made millions of you spend aggravating hours waiting for gasoline. It's a cause of the increased inflation and unemployment that we now face. This intolerable dependence on foreign oil threatens our economic independence and the very security of our Nation.

The energy crisis is real. It is worldwide. It is a clear and present danger to our Nation. These are facts and we simply must face them.

What I have to say to you now about energy is simple and vitally important.

Point one: I am tonight setting a clear goal for the energy policy of the United States. Beginning this moment, this Nation will never use more foreign oil than we did in 1977—never. From now on, every new addition to our demand for energy will be met from our own production and our own conservation. The generation-long growth in our dependence on foreign oil will be stopped dead in its tracks right now and then reversed as we move through the 1980s, for I am tonight setting the further goal of cutting our dependence on foreign oil by one-half by the end of the next decade—a saving of over 4½ million barrels of imported oil per day.

Point two: To ensure that we meet these targets, I will use my Presidential authority to set import quotas. I'm announcing tonight that for 1979 and 1980, I will forbid the entry into this country of one drop of foreign oil more than these goals allow. These quotas will ensure a reduction in imports even below the ambitious levels we set at the recent Tokyo summit.

Point three: To give us energy security, I am asking for the most massive peacetime commitment of funds and resources in our Nation's history to develop America's own alternative sources of fuel—from coal, from oil shale, from plant products for gasohol, from unconventional gas, from the Sun.

I propose the creation of an energy security corporation to lead this effort to replace 2½ million barrels of imported oil per day by 1990. The corporation will issue up to $5 billion in energy bonds, and I especially want them to be in small denominations so that average Americans can invest directly in America's energy security.

Just as a similar synthetic rubber corporation helped us win World War II, so will we mobilize American determination and ability to win the energy war. Moreover, I will soon submit legislation to Congress calling for the creation of this Nation's first solar bank, which will help us achieve the crucial goal of 20 percent of our energy coming from solar power by the year 2000.

These efforts will cost money, a lot of money, and that is why Congress must enact the windfall profits tax without delay. It will be money well spent. Unlike the billions of dollars that we ship to foreign countries to pay for foreign oil, these funds will be paid by Americans to Americans. These funds will go to fight, not to increase, inflation and unemployment.

Point four: I'm asking Congress to mandate, to require as a matter of law, that our Nation's utility companies cut their massive use of oil by 50 percent within the next decade and switch to other fuels, especially coal, our most abundant energy source.

Point five: To make absolutely certain that nothing stands in the way of achieving these goals, I will urge Congress to create an energy mobilization board which, like the War Production Board in World War II, will have the responsibility and authority to cut through the red tape, the delays, and the endless roadblocks to completing key energy projects.

We will protect our environment. But when this Nation critically needs a refinery or a pipeline, we will build it.

Point six: I'm proposing a bold conservation program to involve every State, county, and city and every average American in our energy battle. This effort will permit you to build conservation into your homes and your lives at a cost you can afford.

I ask Congress to give me authority for mandatory conservation and for standby gasoline rationing. To further conserve energy, I'm proposing tonight an extra $10 billion over the next decade to strengthen our public transportation systems. And I'm asking you for your good and for your Nation's security to take no unnecessary trips, to use carpools or public transportation whenever you can, to park your car one extra day per week, to obey the speed limit, and to set your thermostats to save fuel. Every act of energy conservation like this is more than just common sense—I tell you it is an act of patriotism.

Our Nation must be fair to the poorest among us, so we will increase aid to needy Americans to cope with rising energy prices. We often think of conservation only in terms of sacrifice. In fact, it is the most painless and immediate way of rebuilding our Nation's strength. Every gallon of oil each one of us saves is a new form of production. It gives us more freedom, more confidence, that much more control over our own lives.

So, the solution of our energy crisis can also help us to conquer the crisis of the spirit in our country. It can rekindle our sense of unity, our confidence in the future, and give our Nation and all of us individually a new sense of purpose.

You know we can do it. We have the natural resources. We have more oil in our shale alone than several Saudi Arabias. We have more coal than any nation on Earth. We have the world's highest level of technology. We have the most skilled work force, with innovative genius, and I firmly believe that we have the national will to win this war.

I do not promise you that this struggle for freedom will be easy. I do not promise a quick way out of our Nation's problems, when the truth is that the only way out is an all-out effort. What I do promise you is that I will lead our fight, and I will enforce fairness in our struggle, and I will ensure honesty. And above all, I will act.

We can manage the short-term shortages more effectively and we will, but there are no short-term solutions to our long-range problems. There is simply no way to avoid sacrifice.

Twelve hours from now I will speak again in Kansas City, to expand and to explain further our energy program. Just as the search for solutions to our energy shortages has now led us to a new awareness of our Nation's deeper problems, so our willingness to work for those solutions in energy can strengthen us to attack those deeper problems.

I will continue to travel this country, to hear the people of America. You can help me to develop a national agenda for the 1980s. I will listen and I will act. We will act together. These were the promises I made three years ago, and I intend to keep them.

Little by little we can and we must rebuild our confidence. We can spend until we empty our treasuries, and we may summon all the wonders of science. But we can succeed only if we tap our greatest resources—America's people, America's values, and America's confidence.

I have seen the strength of America in the inexhaustible resources of our people. In the days to come, let us renew that strength in the struggle for an energy-secure nation.

In closing, let me say this: I will do my best, but I will not do it alone. Let your voice be heard. Whenever you have a chance, say something good about our country. With God's help and for the sake of our Nation, it is time for us to join hands in America. Let us commit ourselves together to a rebirth of the American spirit. Working together with our common faith we cannot fail.

★ ★ ★

## "THE INFRASTRUCTURE OF DEMOCRACY"
### Ronald Reagan, Address to the British Parliament, Westminster Hall, London—June 8, 1982

Ronald Reagan (1911–2004) was a sportscaster, Hollywood movie actor, network television host, and General Electric corporate spokesman who, by the early 1960s, had moved from New Deal–Fair Deal liberalism to anticommunist, antigovernment conservatism. Twice elected the Republican governor of California, he won the presidency in 1980 and again in 1984. (He was reelected by carrying forty-nine states.) In this 1982 address in London, Reagan articulated his understanding of the Cold War and his commitment to democratic values and institutions.

SPEAKING FOR ALL Americans, I want to say how very much at home we feel in your house. Every American would, because this is—as we have been so eloquently told—one of democracy's shrines. Here the rights of free people and the processes of representation have been debated and refined.

It has been said that an institution is the lengthening shadow of a man. This institution is the lengthening shadow of all the men and women who have sat here and all those who have voted to send representatives here.

This is my second visit to Great Britain as president of the United States. My first opportunity to stand on British soil occurred almost a year and a half ago when your prime minister graciously hosted a diplomatic dinner at the British Embassy in Washington. Mrs. Thatcher said then that she hoped that I was not distressed to find staring down at me from the grand staircase a portrait of His Royal Majesty King George III. She suggested it was best to let bygones be bygones and—in view of our two countries' remarkable friendship in succeeding years—she added that most Englishmen today would agree with Thomas Jefferson that "a little rebellion now and then is a very good thing."

Well, from here I will go on to Bonn and then Berlin, where there stands a grim symbol of power untamed. The Berlin Wall, that dreadful gray gash across the city, is in its third decade. It is the fitting signature of the regime that built it.

And a few hundred kilometers behind the Berlin Wall there is another symbol. In the center of Warsaw there is a sign that notes the distances to two capitals. In one direction it points toward Moscow. In the other it points toward Brussels, headquarters of Western Europe's tangible unity. The marker says that the distances from Warsaw to Moscow and Warsaw to Brussels are equal. The sign makes this point: Poland is not East or West. Poland is at the center of European civilization. It has contributed mightily to that civilization. It is doing so today by being magnificently unreconciled to oppression.

Poland's struggle to be Poland, and to secure the basic rights we often take for granted, demonstrates why we dare not take those rights for granted. Gladstone, defending the Reform Bill of 1866, declared: "You cannot fight against the future. Time is on our side." It was easier to believe in the march of democracy in Gladstone's day, in that high noon of Victorian optimism.

We are approaching the end of a bloody century plagued by a terrible political invention—totalitarianism. Optimism comes less easily today, not because democracy is less vigorous but because democracy's enemies have refined their instruments of repression. Yet optimism is in order because, day by day, democracy is proving itself to be a not-at-all fragile flower.

From Stettin on the Baltic to Varna on the Black Sea, the regimes planted by totalitarianism have had more than thirty years to establish their legitimacy. But none—not one regime—has yet been able to risk free elections. Regimes planted by bayonets do not take root.

The strength of the Solidarity movement in Poland demonstrates the truth told in an underground joke in the Soviet Union. It is that the Soviet Union would remain a one-party nation even if an opposition party were permitted, because everyone would join the opposition party.

America's time as a player on the stage of world history has been brief. I think understanding this fact has always made you patient with your younger cousins. Well, not always patient—I do recall that on one occasion Sir Winston Churchill said in exasperation about one of our most distinguished diplomats: "He is the only case I know of a bull who carries his china shop with him."

Witty as Sir Winston was, he also had that special attribute of great statesmen—the gift of vision, the willingness to see the future based on the experience of the past. It is this sense of history, this understanding of the past, that I want to talk with you about today, for it is in remembering what we share of the past that our two nations can make common cause for the future.

We have not inherited an easy world. If developments like the Industrial Revolution, which began here in England, and the gifts of science and technology have made life much easier for us, they have also made it more dangerous. There are threats now to our freedom, indeed, to our very existence, that other generations could never even have imagined.

There is, first, the threat of global war. No president, no congress, no prime minister, no parliament can spend a day entirely free of this threat. And I don't have to tell you that in today's world, the existence of nuclear weapons could mean, if not the extinction of mankind, then surely the end of civilization as we know it.

That's why negotiations on intermediate-range nuclear forces now underway in Europe and the START talks—Strategic Arms Reduction Talks—which will begin later this month, are not just critical to American or Western policy, they are critical to mankind. Our commitment to early success in these negotiations is firm and unshakable and our purpose is clear: reducing the risk of war by reducing the means of waging war on both sides.

At the same time, there is a threat posed to human freedom by the enormous power of the modern state. History teaches the dangers of government that overreaches: political control taking precedence over free economic growth, secret police, mindless bureaucracy—all combining to stifle individual excellence and personal freedom.

Now, I am aware that among us here and throughout Europe, there is legitimate disagreement over the extent to which the public sector should play a role in a nation's economy and life. But on one point all of us are united: our abhorrence of dictatorship in all its forms, but most particularly totalitarianism and the terrible inhumanities it has caused in our time: the great purge, Auschwitz and Dachau, the Gulag, and Cambodia.

Historians looking back at our time will note the consistent restraint and peaceful intentions of the West. They will note that it was the democracies who refused to use the threat of their nuclear monopoly in the 1940s and early 1950s for territorial or imperial gain. Had that nuclear monopoly been in the hands of the Communist world, the map of Europe—indeed, the world—would look very different today. And certainly they will note it was not the democracies that invaded Afghanistan or suppressed Polish solidarity or used chemical and toxin warfare in Afghanistan and Southeast Asia.

If history teaches anything, it teaches that self-delusion in the face of unpleasant facts is folly. We see around us today the marks of our terrible dilemma—predictions of doomsday, antinuclear demonstrations, an arms race in which the West must, for its own protection, be an unwilling participant. At the same time, we see totalitarian forces in the world who seek subversion and conflict around the globe to further their barbarous assault on the human spirit.

What, then, is our course? Must civilization perish in a hail of fiery atoms?

Must freedom wither in a quiet, deadening accommodation with totalitarian evil?

Sir Winston Churchill refused to accept the inevitability of war or even that it was imminent. He said:

> *"I do not believe that Soviet Russia desires war. What they desire is the fruits of war and the indefinite expansion of their power and doctrines. But what we have to consider here today, while time remains, is the permanent prevention of war and the establishment of conditions of freedom and democracy as rapidly as possible in all countries."*

This is precisely our mission today: to preserve freedom as well as peace. It may not be easy to see, but I believe we live now at a turning point.

In an ironic sense, Karl Marx was right. We are witnessing today a great revolutionary crisis—a crisis where the demands of the economic order are conflicting directly with those of the political order. But the crisis is happening not in the free, non-Marxist West but in the home of Marxism-Leninism, the Soviet Union. It is the Soviet Union that runs against the tide of history by denying human freedom and human dignity to its citizens. It also is in deep economic difficulty. The rate of growth in the national product has been steadily declining since the 1950s and is less than half of what it was then.

The dimensions of this failure are astounding. A country which employs one-fifth of its population in agriculture is unable to feed its own people. Were it not for the tiny private sector tolerated in Soviet agriculture, the country might be on the brink of famine. These private plots occupy a bare 3 percent of the arable land but account for nearly one-quarter of Soviet farm output and nearly one-third of meat products and vegetables.

Overcentralized, with little or no incentives, year after year the Soviet system pours its best resources into the making of instruments of destruction. The constant shrinkage of economic growth combined with the growth of military production is putting a heavy strain on the Soviet people. What we see here is a political structure that no longer corresponds to its economic base, a society where productive forces are hampered by political ones.

The decay of the Soviet experiment should come as no surprise to us. Wherever the comparisons have been made between free and closed societies—West Germany and East Germany, Austria and Czechoslovakia, Malaysia and Vietnam—it is the democratic countries that are prosperous and responsive to the needs of their people. And one of the simple but overwhelming facts of our time is this: of all the millions of refugees we've seen in the modern world, their flight is always away from, not toward, the Communist world. Today on the NATO line, our military forces face east to prevent a possible invasion. On the other side of the line, the Soviet forces also face East—to prevent their people from leaving.

The hard evidence of totalitarian rule has caused in mankind an uprising of the intellect and will. Whether it is the growth of the new schools of economics in America or England or the appearance of the so-called new philosophers in France, there is one unifying thread running through the intellectual work of these groups: rejection of the arbitrary power of the state, the refusal to subordinate the rights of the individual to the superstate, the realization that collectivism stifles all the best human impulses.

Since the exodus from Egypt, historians have written of those who sacrificed and struggled for freedom: the stand at Thermopylae, the revolt of Spartacus, the storming of the Bastille, the Warsaw uprising in World War II. More recently we have seen evidence of this same human impulse in one of the developing nations in Central America. For months and months the world news media covered the fighting in El Salvador. Day after day we were treated to stories and film slanted toward the brave freedom fighters battling oppressive government forces in behalf of the silent, suffering people of that tortured country.

Then one day those silent, suffering people were offered a chance to vote, to choose the kind of government they wanted. Suddenly the freedom fighters in the hills were exposed for what they really are: Cuban-backed guerrillas who want power for themselves and their backers, not democracy for the people. They threatened death to any who voted and destroyed hundreds of buses and trucks to keep people from getting to the polling places. But on election day the people of El Salvador, an unprecedented 1.4 million of them, braved ambush and gunfire and trudged miles to vote for freedom.

They stood for hours in the hot sun waiting for their turn to vote. Members of our Congress who went there as observers told me of a woman who was wounded by rifle fire who refused to leave the line to have her wound treated until after she had voted. A grandmother, who had been told by the guerrillas she would be killed when she returned from the polls, told the guerrillas: "You can kill me, kill my family, kill my neighbors, but you can't kill us all." The real freedom fighters of El Salvador turned out to be the people of that country—the young, the old, and the in-between.

Strange, but in my own country there has been little if any news coverage of that war since the election. Perhaps they'll say it's because there are newer struggles now—on distant islands in the South Atlantic young men are fighting for Britain.

And, yes, voices have been raised protesting their sacrifices for lumps of rock and earth so far away. But those young men aren't fighting for mere real estate. They fight for a cause, for the belief that armed aggression must not be allowed to succeed and that people must participate in the decisions of government under the rule of law. If there had been firmer support for that principle some forty-five years ago, perhaps our generation wouldn't have suffered the bloodletting of World War II.

In the Middle East now the guns sound once more, this time in Lebanon, a country that for too long has had to endure the tragedy of civil war, terrorism, and foreign intervention and occupation. The fighting in Lebanon on the part of all parties must stop, and Israel should bring its forces home. But this is not enough. We must all work to stamp out the scourge of terrorism that in the Middle East makes war an ever-present threat.

But beyond the trouble spots lies a deeper, more positive pattern. Around the world today the democratic revolution is gathering new strength. In India, a critical test has been passed with the peaceful change of governing political parties. In Africa, Nigeria is moving in remarkable and unmistakable ways to build and strengthen its democratic institutions. In the Caribbean and Central America, sixteen of twenty-four countries have freely elected governments. And in the United Nations, eight of the ten developing nations which have joined the body in the past five years are democracies.

In the Communist world as well, man's instinctive desire for freedom and self-determination surfaces again and again. To be sure, there are grim reminders of how brutally the police state attempts to snuff out this quest for self-rule: 1953 in East Germany, 1956 in Hungary, 1968 in Czechoslovakia, 1981 in Poland. But the struggle continues in Poland, and we know that there are even those who strive and suffer for freedom within the confines of the Soviet Union itself. How we conduct ourselves here in the Western democracies will determine whether this trend continues.

No, democracy is not a fragile flower; still, it needs cultivating. If the rest of this century is to witness the gradual growth of freedom and democratic ideals, we must take actions to assist the campaign for democracy.

Some argue that we should encourage democratic change in right-wing dictatorships but not in Communist regimes. To accept this preposterous notion—as some well-meaning people have—is to invite the argument that, once countries achieve a nuclear capability, they should be allowed an undisturbed reign of terror over their own citizens.

We reject this course.

As for the Soviet view, President Brezhnev repeatedly has stressed that the competition of ideas and systems must continue and that this is entirely consistent with relaxation of tensions and peace.

We ask only that these systems begin by living up to their own constitutions, abiding by their own laws, and complying with the international obligations they have undertaken. We ask only for a process, a direction, a basic code of decency—not for an instant transformation.

We cannot ignore the fact that even without our encouragement, there have been and will continue to be repeated explosions against repression in dictatorships. The Soviet Union itself is not immune to this reality. Any system is inherently unstable that has no peaceful means to legitimatize its leaders. In such crises, the very repressiveness of the state ultimately drives people to resist it—if necessary, by force.

While we must be cautious about forcing the pace of change, we must not hesitate to declare our ultimate objectives and to take concrete actions to move toward them. We must be staunch in our conviction that freedom is not the sole prerogative of a lucky few but the inalienable and universal right of all human beings. So states the U.N. Universal Declaration of Human Rights, which, among other things, guarantees free elections.

The objective I propose is quite simple to state: to foster the infrastructure of democracy—the system of a free press, unions, political parties, universities—which allows a people to choose their own way, to develop their own culture, to reconcile their own differences through peaceful means.

This is not cultural imperialism: it is providing the means for genuine self-determination and protection for diversity. Democracy already flourishes in countries with very different cultures and historical experiences. It would be cultural condescension, or worse, to say that any people prefer dictatorship to democracy. Who would voluntarily choose not to have the right to vote, decide to purchase government propaganda handouts instead of independent newspapers, prefer government to worker-controlled unions, opt for land to be owned by the state instead of those who till it, want government repression of religious liberty, a single political party instead of a free choice, a rigid cultural orthodoxy instead of democratic tolerance and diversity?

Since 1917 the Soviet Union has given covert political training and assistance to Marxist-Leninists in many countries. Of course, it also has promoted the use of violence and subversion by these same forces. Over the past several decades, West European and other social democrats . . . have offered open assistance to fraternal, political, and social institutions to bring about peaceful and democratic progress. Appropriately for a vigorous new democracy, the Federal Republic of Germany's political foundations have become a major force in this effort.

We in America now intend to take additional steps, as many of our allies have already done, toward realizing this same goal. The chairmen and other leaders of the national Republican and Democratic party organizations are initiating a study with the bipartisan American Political Foundation to determine how the United States can best contribute—as a nation—to the global campaign for democracy now gathering force. They will have the cooperation of congressional leaders of both parties along with representatives of business, labor, and other major institutions in our society.

I look forward to receiving their recommendations and to working with these institutions and the Congress in the common task of strengthening democracy throughout the world.

It is time that we committed ourselves as a nation—in both the public and private sectors—to assisting democratic development.

We plan to consult with leaders of other nations as well. There is a proposal before the Council of Europe to invite parliamentarians from democratic countries to a meeting next year in Strasbourg. That prestigious gathering would consider ways to help democratic political movements.

This November in Washington there will take place an international meeting on free elections. And next spring there will be a conference of world authorities on constitutionalism and self-government hosted by the chief justice of the United States. Authorities from a number of developing and developed countries—judges, philosophers, and politicians with practical experience—have agreed to explore how to turn principle into practice and further the rule of law.

At the same time, we invite the Soviet Union to consider with us how the competition of ideas and values—which it is committed to support—can be conducted on a peaceful and reciprocal basis. For example, I am prepared to offer President Brezhnev an opportunity to speak to the American people on our television if he will allow me the same opportunity with the Soviet people. We also suggest that panels of our newsmen periodically appear on each other's television to discuss major events.

I do not wish to sound overly optimistic, yet the Soviet Union is not immune from the reality of what is going on in the world. It has happened in the past: a small ruling elite either mistakenly attempts to ease domestic unrest through greater repression and foreign adventure or it chooses a wiser course. It begins to allow its people a voice in their own destiny.

Even if this latter process is not realized soon, I believe the renewed strength of the democratic movement, complemented by a global campaign for freedom, will strengthen the prospects for arms control and a world at peace.

I have discussed on other occasions . . . the elements of Western policies toward the Soviet Union to safeguard our interests and protect the peace. What I am describing now is a plan and a hope for the long term—the march of freedom and democracy which will leave Marxism-Leninism on the ash heap of history as it has left other tyrannies which stifle the freedom and muzzle the self-expression of the people.

And that is why we must continue our efforts to strengthen NATO even as we move forward with our Zero-Option initiative in the negotiations on intermediate-range forces and our proposal for a one-third reduction in strategic ballistic missile warheads.

Our military strength is a prerequisite to peace, but let it be clear we maintain this strength in the hope it will never be used. For the ultimate determinant in the struggle now going on for the world will not be bombs and rockets, but a test of wills and ideas, a trial of spiritual resolve: the values we hold, the beliefs we cherish, the ideals to which we are dedicated.

The British people know that, given strong leadership, time, and a little bit of hope, the forces of good ultimately rally and triumph over evil. Here among you is the cradle of self-government, the mother of parliaments. Here is the enduring greatness of the British contribution to mankind, the great civilized ideas: individual liberty, representative government, and the rule of law under God.

I have often wondered about the shyness of some of us in the West about standing for these ideals that have done so much to ease the plight of man and the hardships of our imperfect world. This reluctance to use those vast resources at our command reminds me of the elderly lady whose home was bombed in the Blitz. As the rescuers moved about they found a bottle of brandy she'd stored behind the staircase, which was all that was left standing. Since she was barely conscious, one of the workers pulled the cork to give her a taste of it. She came around immediately and said, "There now, put it back, that's for emergencies."

Well, the emergency is upon us. Let us be shy no longer—let us go to our strength. Let us offer hope. Let us tell the world that a new age is not only possible but probable.

During the dark days of the Second World War, when this island was incandescent with courage, Winston Churchill exclaimed about Britain's adversaries: "What kind of a people do they think we are?" Britain's adversaries found out what extraordinary people the British are. But all the democracies paid a terrible price for allowing the dictators to underestimate us. We dare not make that mistake again. So let us ask ourselves: What kind of people do we think we are? And let us answer: free people, worthy of freedom, and determined not only to remain so but to help others gain their freedom as well.

Sir Winston led his people to great victory in war and then lost an election just as the fruits of victory were about to be enjoyed. But he left office honorably—and, as it turned out, temporarily—knowing that the liberty of his people was more important than the fate of any single leader. History recalls his greatness in ways no dictator will ever know. And he left us a message of hope for the future, as timely now as when he first uttered it, as opposition leader in the Commons nearly twenty-seven years ago. He said, "When we look back on all the perils through which we have passed and at the mighty foes we have laid low and all the dark and deadly designs we have frustrated, why should we fear for our future? We have," he said, "come safely through the worst."

The task I have set forth will long outlive our own generation. But together, we, too, have come through the worst. Let us now begin a major effort to secure the best—a crusade for freedom that will engage the faith and fortitude of the next generation. For the sake of peace and justice, let us move toward a world in which all people are at last free to determine their own destiny.

★ ★ ★

## "THERE IS DESPAIR, MR. PRESIDENT"

### Mario Cuomo, Keynote Address to the Democratic National Convention, San Francisco, California—July 16, 1984

New York governor Mario Cuomo (1932–2015) offered an incisive critique of Ronald Reagan's America at the Democratic National Convention that nominated Walter Mondale and Geraldine Ferraro to challenge the popular fortieth president's reelection in 1984.

PLEASE ALLOW ME to skip the stories and the poetry and the temptation to deal in nice but vague rhetoric. Let me instead use this valuable opportunity to deal immediately with the questions that should determine this election and that we all know are vital to the American people.

Ten days ago, President Reagan admitted that although some people in this country seemed to be doing well nowadays, others were unhappy, even worried, about themselves, their families and their futures.

The President said that he didn't understand that fear. He said, "Why, this country is a shining city on a hill."

And the President is right. In many ways we are "a shining city on a hill."

But the hard truth is that not everyone is sharing in this city's splendor and glory.

A shining city is perhaps all the President sees from the portico of the White House and the veranda of his ranch, where everyone seems to be doing well.

But there's another city, there's another part to the shining city, the part where some people can't pay their mortgages and most young people can't afford one, where students can't afford the education they need and middle-class parents watch the dreams they hold for their children evaporate.

In this part of the city there are more poor than ever, more families in trouble. More and more people who need help but can't find it.

Even worse: There are elderly people who tremble in the basements of the houses there.

And there are people who sleep in the city's streets, in the gutter, where the glitter doesn't show.

There are ghettos where thousands of young people, without a job or an education, give their lives away to drug dealers every day.

There is despair, Mr. President, in the faces that you don't see, in the places that you don't visit in your shining city.

In fact, Mr. President, you ought to know that this nation is more a "Tale of Two Cities" than it is just a "Shining City on a Hill."

Maybe, Mr. President, if you visited some more places, maybe if you went to Appalachia where some people still live in sheds, maybe if you went to Lackawanna where thousands of unemployed steel workers wonder why we subsidize foreign steel; maybe, Mr. President, if you stopped in at a shelter in Chicago and talked with some of the homeless there; maybe, Mr. President, if you asked a woman who had been denied the help she needed to feed her children because you said you needed the money for a tax break for a millionaire or for a missile we couldn't afford to use—maybe then you'd understand.

Maybe, Mr. President. But I'm afraid not.

Because, the truth is, ladies and gentlemen, that this is how we were warned it would be.

President Reagan told us from the very beginning that he believed in a kind of social Darwinism. Survival of the fittest. "Government can't do everything," we were told. "So it should settle for taking care of the strong and hope that economic ambition and charity will do the rest. Make the rich richer and what falls from the table will be enough for the middle class and those who are trying desperately to work their way into the middle class."

You know, the Republicans called it trickle-down when Hoover tried it. Now they call it supply side. But it's the same shining city for those relative few who are lucky enough to live in its good neighborhoods.

But for the people who are excluded, for the people who are locked out, all they can do is to stare from a distance at that city's glimmering towers.

It's an old story. It's as old as our history.

The difference between Democrats and Republicans has always been measured in courage and confidence. The Republicans believe that the wagon train will not make it to the frontier unless some of the old, some of the young, some of the weak are left behind by the side of the trail.

The strong, the strong, they tell us, will inherit the land!

We Democrats believe in something else. We Democrats believe that we can make it all the way with the whole family intact.

And we have more than once.

Ever since Franklin Roosevelt lifted himself from his wheelchair to lift this nation from its knees. Wagon train after wagon train. To new frontiers of education, housing, peace. The whole family aboard. Constantly reaching out to extend and enlarge that family. Lifting them up into the wagon on the way. Blacks and Hispanics and people of every ethnic group and Native Americans—all those struggling to build their families and claim some small share of America.

For nearly 50 years we carried them all to new levels of comfort and security and dignity, even affluence.

And remember this, some of us in this room today are here only because this nation had that kind of confidence.

And it would be wrong to forget that.

So, here we are at this convention to remind ourselves where we come from and to claim the future for ourselves and for our children. Today, our great Democratic Party, which has saved this nation from depression, from fascism, from racism, from corruption, is called upon to do it again—this time to save the nation from confusion and division, from the threat of eventual fiscal disaster and most of all from the fear of a nuclear holocaust.

But that's not going to be easy. . . . And in order to succeed, we must answer our opponent's polished and appealing rhetoric with a more telling reasonableness and rationality.

We must win this case on the merits.

We must get the American public to look past the glitter, beyond the showmanship, to the reality, the hard substance of things.

And we'll do it not so much with speeches that sound good as with speeches that are good and sound.

Not so much with speeches that will bring people to their feet as with speeches that bring people to their senses.

We must make the American people hear our "tale of two cities."

We must convince them that we don't have to settle for two cities, that we can have one city, indivisible, shining for all of its people.

We will have no chance to do that if what comes out of this convention is a babel of arguing voices. If that's what's heard throughout the campaign, dissonant sounds from all sides, we will have no chance to tell our message.

To succeed we will have to surrender some small parts of our individual interests, to build a platform we can all stand on, at once, and comfortably, proudly singing out. We need a platform we can all agree to, so that we can sing out the truth for the nation to hear, in chorus, its logic so clear and commanding that no slick Madison Avenue commercial, no amount of geniality, no martial music will be able to muffle the sound of the truth.

We Democrats must unite. We Democrats must unite so that the entire nation can unite, because surely the Republicans won't bring this country together. Their policies divide the nation: into the lucky and the left-out, into the royalty and the rabble.

The Republicans are willing to treat that division as victory. They would cut this nation in half, into those temporarily better off and those worse off than before, and they would call that division recovery.

We should not be embarrassed or dismayed or chagrined if the process of unifying is difficult, even wrenching at times.

Remember that unlike any other party, we embrace men and women of every color, every creed, every orientation, every economic class. In our family are gathered everyone from the abject poor of Essex County in New York, to the enlightened affluent of the gold coasts at both ends of our nation. And in between is the heart of our constituency. The middle class, the people not rich enough to be worry-free but not poor enough to be on welfare, the middle class, those who work for a living because they have to, not because some psychiatrist told them it was a convenient way to fill the interval between birth and eternity. White collar and blue collar. Young professionals. Men and women in small business desperate for the capital and contracts that they need to prove their worth.

We speak for the minorities who have not yet entered the mainstream.

We speak for ethnics who want to add their culture to the magnificent mosaic that is America.

We speak for women who are indignant that this nation refuses to etch into our governmental commandments the simple rule "thou shalt not sin against equality," a rule so simple—I was going to say and I perhaps dare not, but I will—it's a commandment so simple it can be spelled in three letters: E.R.A.!

We speak for young people demanding an education and a future.

We speak for senior citizens. We speak for senior citizens who are terrorized by the idea that their only security, their Social Security, is being threatened.

We speak for millions of reasoning people fighting to preserve our environment from greed and from stupidity. And we speak for reasonable people who are fighting to preserve our very existence from a macho intransigence that refuses to make intelligent attempts to discuss the possibility of nuclear holocaust with our enemy. They refuse. They refuse because they believe we can pile missiles so high that they will pierce the clouds and the sight of them will frighten our enemies into submission.

We're proud of this diversity as Democrats. We're grateful for it. We don't have to manufacture it the way the Republicans will next month in Dallas, by propping up mannequin delegates on the convention floor.

But we, while we're proud of this diversity, we pay a price for it.

The different people that we represent have different points of view, and sometimes they compete and even debate and even argue. That's what our primaries were all about.

But now the primaries are over, and it is time when we pick our candidates and our platform here to lock arms and move into this campaign together.

If you need any more inspiration to put some small part of your own difference aside to create this consensus, all you need to do is to reflect on what the Republican policy of divide and cajole has done to this land since 1980.

The President has asked the American people to judge him on whether or not he's fulfilled the promises he made four years ago. I believe as Democrats we ought to accept that challenge, and just for a moment let us consider what he said and what he's done.

Inflation is down since 1980. But not because of the supply-side miracle promised to us by the President. Inflation was reduced the old-fashioned way, with a recession, the worst since 1932. Now how did we—we could have brought inflation down that way. How did he do it?—55,000 bankruptcies. Two years of massive unemployment. Two hundred thousand farmers and ranchers forced off the land. More homeless—more homeless than at any time since the Great Depression in 1932. More hungry, in this world of enormous affluence, the United States of America, more hungry, more poor—most of them women. And—and he paid one other thing—a nearly $200 billion deficit threatening our future. Now, we must make the American people understand this deficit because they don't.

The President's deficit is a direct and dramatic repudiation of his promise in 1980 to balance our budget by 1983.

How large is it? The deficit is the largest in the history of the universe; President Carter's last budget had a deficit less than one-third of this deficit.

It is a deficit that, according to the President's own fiscal adviser, may grow to as much as $300 billion a year, for "as far as the eye can see."

And ladies and gentlemen, it is a debt so large—that is almost one-half of the money we collect from the personal income tax each year goes just to pay the interest.

It is a mortgage on our children's future that can only be paid in pain and that could bring this nation to its knees.

Now don't take my word for it—I'm a Democrat.

Ask the Republican investment bankers on Wall Street what they think the chances of this recovery being permanent are. If they're not too embarrassed to tell you the truth, they'll say that they are appalled and frightened by the President's deficit. Ask them what they think of our economy, now that it has been driven by the distorted value of the dollar back to its colonial condition, now we're exporting agricultural products and importing manufactured ones.

Ask those Republican investment bankers what they expect the rate of interest to be a year from now. And ask them, if they dare tell you the truth, you'll learn from them what they predict for the inflation rate a year from now because of the deficit.

How important is this question of the deficit?

Think about it practically: What chance would the Republican candidate have had in 1980 if he had told the American people that he intended to pay for his so-called economic recovery with bankruptcies, unemployment, more homeless, more hungry, and the largest Government debt known to humankind? If he had told the voters in 1980 that truth, would American voters have signed the loan certificate for him on Election Day? Of course not! That was an election won under false pretenses. It was won with smoke and mirrors, and illusions. That's the kind of recovery we have now as well.

And what about foreign policy?

They said that they would make us and the whole world safer. They say they have.

By creating the largest defense budget in history, one that even they now admit is excessive. By escalating to a frenzy the nuclear arms race. By incendiary rhetoric. By refusing to discuss peace with our enemies. By the loss of 279 young Americans in Lebanon in pursuit of a plan and a policy that no one can find or describe.

We give money to Latin American governments that murder nuns, and then lie about it.

We have been less than zealous in our support of our only real friend, it seems to me, in the Middle East, the one democracy there, our flesh and blood ally, the state of Israel.

Our policy, our foreign policy, drifts with no real direction, other than an hysterical commitment to an arms race that leads nowhere, if we're lucky. And if we're not, it could lead us to bankruptcy or war.

Of course we must have a strong defense!

Of course Democrats are for a strong defense, of course Democrats believe that there are times that we must stand and fight. And we have. Thousands of us have paid for freedom with our lives. But always, when this country has been at our best, our purposes were clear.

Now they're not. Now our allies are as confused as our enemies.

Now we have no real commitment to our friends or to our ideals, not to human rights, not to the refuseniks, not to Sakharov, not to Bishop Tutu and the others struggling for freedom in South Africa.

We have in the last few years spent more than we can afford. We have pounded our chests and made bold speeches. But we lost 279 young Americans in Lebanon and we live behind sandbags in Washington.

How can anyone say that we are safer, stronger, or better?

That is the Republican record.

That its disastrous quality is not more fully understood by the American people I can only attribute to the President's amiability and the failure by some to separate the salesman from the product.

And now it's up to us, now it's up to you and to me, to make the case to America.

And to remind Americans that if they are not happy with all that the President has done so far, they should consider how much worse it will be if he is left to his radical proclivities for another four years unrestrained—unrestrained!

If July brings back Anne Gorsuch Burford, what can we expect of December? Where would another four years take us? Where would four years more take us? How much larger will the deficit be?

How much deeper the cuts in programs for the struggling middle class and the poor to limit that deficit? How high will the interest rates be? How much more acid rain killing our forests and fouling our lakes?

And, ladies and gentlemen, please think of this—the nation must think of this—what kind of Supreme Court will we have? We must ask ourselves what kind of court and country will be fashioned by the man who believes in having government mandate people's religion and morality.

The man who believes that trees pollute the environment, the man that believes that the laws against discrimination against people go too far. A man who threatens Social Security and Medicaid and help for the disabled.

How high will we pile the missiles?

How much deeper will the gulf be between us and our enemies?

And, ladies and gentlemen, will four years more make meaner the spirit of the American people?

This election will measure the record of the past four years. But more than that, it will answer the question of what kind of people we want to be.

We Democrats still have a dream. We still believe in this nation's future.

And this is our answer to the question, this is our credo:

We believe in only the government we need, but we insist on all the government we need.

We believe in a government that is characterized by fairness and reasonableness, a reasonableness that goes beyond labels, that doesn't distort or promise to do things that we know we can't do.

We believe in a government strong enough to use words like "love" and "compassion" and smart enough to convert our noblest aspirations into practical realities.

We believe in encouraging the talented, but we believe that while survival of the fittest may be a good working description of the process of evolution, a government of humans should elevate itself to a higher order. Our government should be able to rise to the level where it can fill the gaps that are left by chance or by a wisdom we don't understand.

We would rather have laws written by the patron of this great city, the man called the "world's most sincere Democrat," St. Francis of Assisi, than laws written by Darwin.

We believe, as Democrats, that a society as blessed as ours, the most affluent democracy in the world's history, one that can spend trillions on instruments of destruction, ought to be able to help the middle class in its struggle, ought to be able to find work for all who can do it, room at the table, shelter for the homeless, care for the elderly and infirm, and hope for the destitute.

And we proclaim as loudly as we can the utter insanity of nuclear proliferation and the need for a nuclear freeze, if only to affirm the simple truth that peace is better than war because life is better than death.

We believe in firm but fair law and order. We believe proudly in the union movement. We believe in privacy for people, openness by government, we believe in civil rights, and we believe in human rights.

We believe in a single fundamental idea that describes better than most textbooks and any speech that I could write what a

> proper government should be. The idea of family. Mutuality. The sharing of benefits and burdens for the good of all. Feeling one another's pain. Sharing one another's blessings. Reasonably, honestly, fairly, without respect to race, or sex, or geography or political affiliation. We believe we must be the family of America, recognizing that at the heart of the matter we are bound one to another, that the problems of a retired school teacher in Duluth are our problems. That the future of the child in Buffalo is our future. That the struggle of a disabled man in Boston to survive and live decently is our struggle. That the hunger of a woman in Little Rock is our hunger. That the failure anywhere to provide what reasonably we might, to avoid pain, is our failure.

For 50 years we Democrats created a better future for our children, using traditional democratic principles as a fixed beacon, giving us direction and purpose, but constantly innovating, adapting to new realities: Roosevelt's alphabet programs; Truman's NATO and the GI Bill of Rights; Kennedy's intelligent tax incentives and the Alliance for Progress; Johnson's civil rights; Carter's human rights and the nearly miraculous Camp David peace accords.

Democrats did it, and Democrats can do it again.

We can build a future that deals with our deficit.

Remember this, that 50 years of progress under our principles never cost us what the last four years of stagnation have. And we can deal with the deficit intelligently, by shared sacrifice, with all parts of the nation's family contributing, building partnerships with the private sector, providing a sound defense without depriving ourselves of what we need to feed our children and care for our people.

We can have a future that provides for all the young of the present by marrying common sense and compassion.

We know we can, because we did it for nearly 50 years before 1980.

And we can do it again. If we do not forget. If we do not forget that this entire nation has profited by these progressive principles. That they helped lift up generations to the middle class and higher: that they gave us a chance to work, to go to college, to raise a family, to own a house, to be secure in our old age and, before that, to reach heights that our own parents would not have dared dream of.

That struggle to live with dignity is the real story of the shining city. And it's a story, ladies and gentlemen, that I didn't read in a book, or learn in a classroom. I saw it, and lived it. Like many of you.

I watched a small man with thick calluses on both hands work 15 and 16 hours a day. I saw him once literally bleed from the bottoms of his feet, a man who came here uneducated, alone, unable to speak the language, who taught me all I needed to know about faith and hard work by the simple eloquence of his example. I learned about our kind of democracy from my father. I learned about our obligation to each other from him and from my mother. They asked only for a chance to work and to make the world better for their children and they asked to be protected in those moments when they would not be able to protect themselves. This nation and this nation's government did that for them.

And that they were able to build a family and live in dignity and see one of their children go from behind their little grocery store in South Jamaica on the other side of the tracks where he was born, to occupy the highest seat in the greatest state in the greatest nation in the only world we know, is an ineffably beautiful tribute to the democratic process.

And ladies and gentlemen, on January 20, 1985, it will happen again. Only on a much, much grander scale. We will have a new President of the United States, a Democrat born not to the blood of kings but to the blood of pioneers and immigrants.

We will have America's first woman Vice President, the child of immigrants, and she will open with one magnificent stroke a whole new frontier for the United States.

It will happen. It will happen if we make it happen, if you and I make it happen.

And I ask you now, ladies and gentlemen, brothers and sisters, for the good of all of us, for the love of this great nation, for the family of America, for the love of God. Please make this nation remember how futures are built.

★ ★ ★

## "THEY CAME FROM EVERY LAND"

### Ronald Reagan, Remarks at the Lighting of the Torch of the Statue of Liberty, New York Harbor—July 3, 1986

*Buoyant and eloquent, Reagan dominated the politics of the 1980s, remaining popular at home and pressing the Cold War to a victorious conclusion for the West.*

While we applaud those immigrants who stand out, whose contributions are easily discerned, we know that America's heroes are also those whose names are remembered by only a few. Many of them passed through this harbor, went by this lady, looked up at her torch, which we light tonight in their honor.

They were the men and women who labored all their lives so that their children would be well fed, clothed, and educated, the families that went through great hardship yet kept their honor, their dignity, and their faith in God. They passed on to their children those values, values that define civilization and are the prerequisites of human progress. They worked in our factories, on ships and railroads, in stores, and on road construction crews. They were teachers, lumberjacks, seamstresses, and journalists. They came from every land.

What was it that tied these profoundly different people together? What was it that made them not a gathering of individuals, but a nation? That bond that held them together, as it holds us together tonight, that bond that has stood every test and travail, is found deep in our national consciousness: an abiding love of liberty. For love of liberty, our forebears—colonists, few in number and with little to defend themselves—fought a war for independence with what was then the world's most powerful empire. For love of liberty, those who came before us tamed a vast wilderness and braved hardships which, at times, were beyond the limits of human endurance. For love of liberty, a bloody and heart-wrenching civil war was fought. And for love of liberty, Americans championed and still champion, even in times of peril, the cause of human freedom in far-off lands.

"The God who gave us life," Thomas Jefferson once proclaimed, "gave us liberty at the same time." But like all of God's precious gifts, liberty must never be taken for granted. Tonight we thank God for the many blessings He has bestowed on our land; we affirm our faithfulness to His rule and to our own ideals; and we pledge to keep alive the dream that brought our forefathers and mothers to this brave new land. . . .

We are the keepers of the flame of liberty. We hold it high tonight for the world to see, a beacon of hope, a light unto the nations.

★ ★ ★

## "THEY'RE SCARY . . . RIGHT-WINGED"

**Diary of George H. W. Bush, Presidential Campaign—February 28, 1988**

---

In the 1988 campaign season, George H. W. Bush (1924–2018), then the vice president of the United States, worried that the extremes were growing ever louder. Bush was a party man—to a point. He believed—though he probably wouldn't have put it this way—that the parties played an important intermediary role in American politics by bringing more unifying nominees to the country for the ultimate choice in November. Harry Truman had seen this, observing that it was good for the country to have both liberals and conservatives in both parties: That way, the eventual candidates who were presented to the country had already been vetted by voters of different philosophical dispositions. For Bush in 1988, the hard right was largely embodied by hardcore evangelicals who believed they had found their messenger in the Reverend Pat Robertson. Once, on the campaign trail in Kingsport, Tennessee, a Robertson true believer refused to shake Bush's hand. To his diary, Bush dictated his response to the moment.

STILL THIS STARING, glaring ugly—there's something terrible about those who carry it to extremes. They're scary. They're there for spooky, extraordinary right-winged reasons. They don't care about party. They don't care about anything. They're the excesses. They could be Nazis, they could be Communists, they could be whatever. In this case, they're religious fanatics and they're spooky. They will destroy this party if they're permitted. There is not enough of them, in my opinion, but this woman reminded me of my John Birch days in Houston. The lights go out and they pass out the ugly literature. Guilt by association. Nastiness. Ugliness. Believing the Trilateral Commission, the conspiratorial theories. And I couldn't tell—it may not be fair to that one woman, but that's the problem that Robertson brings to bear on the agenda.

★ ★ ★

## "TAKE BACK OUR CULTURE"

### Patrick J. Buchanan, Address to the Republican National Convention, Houston, Texas—August 17, 1992

A speechwriter for Richard Nixon, communications director for Ronald Reagan, columnist, and cable-news commentator, Patrick J. Buchanan (1938–) ran a nativist and protectionist campaign against the renomination of George H. W. Bush in 1992. Bush defeated Buchanan, but the themes Buchanan articulated appealed to many increasingly disaffected voters.

WELL, WE TOOK the long way home, but we finally got here.

And I want to congratulate President Bush, and remove any doubt about where we stand: The primaries are over, the heart is strong again, and the Buchanan brigades are enlisted—all the way to a great comeback victory in November.

Like many of you last month, I watched that giant masquerade ball at Madison Square Garden—where 20,000 radicals and liberals came dressed up as moderates and centrists—in the greatest single exhibition of cross-dressing in American political history.

One by one, the prophets of doom appeared at the podium. The Reagan decade, they moaned, was a terrible time in America; and the only way to prevent even worse times, they said, is to entrust our nation's fate and future to the party that gave us McGovern, Mondale, Carter and Michael Dukakis.

No way, my friends. The American people are not going to buy back into the failed liberalism of the 1960s and '70s—no matter how slick the package in 1992.

The malcontents of Madison Square Garden notwithstanding, the 1980s were not terrible years. They were great years. You know it. I know it. And the only people who don't know it are the carping critics who sat on the sidelines of history, jeering at one of the great statesmen of modern time.

Out of Jimmy Carter's days of malaise, Ronald Reagan crafted the longest peacetime recovery in U.S. history—3 million new businesses created, and 20 million new jobs.

Under the Reagan Doctrine, one by one, the communist dominos began to fall. First, Grenada was liberated, by U.S. troops. Then, the Red Army was run out of Afghanistan, by U.S. weapons. In Nicaragua, the Marxist regime was forced to hold free elections—by Ronald Reagan's contra army—and the communists were thrown out of power.

Have they forgotten? It was under our party that the Berlin Wall came down, and Europe was reunited. It was under our party that the Soviet Empire collapsed, and the captive nations broke free.

It is said that each president will be recalled by posterity with but a single sentence. George Washington was the father of our country. Abraham Lincoln preserved the Union. And Ronald Reagan won the

*Media-savvy and ideologically pugnacious, Pat Buchanan roiled Republican presidential politics in both 1992 and 1996 with a nationalist message.*

Cold War. And it is time my old colleagues, the columnists and commentators, looking down on us tonight from their anchor booths and sky boxes, gave Ronald Reagan the credit he deserves—for leading America to victory in the Cold War.

Most of all, Ronald Reagan made us proud to be Americans again. We never felt better about our country; and we never stood taller in the eyes of the world.

But we are here, not only to celebrate, but to nominate. And an American president has many, many roles.

He is our first diplomat, the architect of American foreign policy. And which of these two men is more qualified for that role? George Bush has been UN ambassador, CIA director, envoy to China. As vice president, he coauthored the policies that won the Cold War. As president, George Bush presided over the liberation of Eastern Europe and the termination of the Warsaw Pact. And Mr. Clinton? Well, Bill Clinton couldn't find 150 words to discuss foreign policy in an acceptance speech that lasted an hour. As was said of an earlier Democratic candidate, Bill Clinton's foreign policy experience is pretty much confined to having had breakfast once at the International House of Pancakes.

The presidency is also America's bully pulpit.... George Bush is a defender of right-to-life, and lifelong champion of the Judeo-Christian values and beliefs upon which this nation was built.

Mr. Clinton, however, has a different agenda.

At its top is unrestricted abortion on demand. When the Irish-Catholic governor of Pennsylvania, Robert Casey, asked to say a few words on behalf of the 25 million unborn children destroyed since *Roe v. Wade,* he was told there was no place for him at the podium of Bill Clinton's convention, no room at the inn.

Yet a militant leader of the homosexual rights movement could rise at that convention and exult: "Bill Clinton and Al Gore represent the most pro-lesbian and pro-gay ticket in history." And so they do.

Bill Clinton supports school choice—but only for state-run schools. Parents who send their children to Christian schools, or Catholic schools, need not apply.

Elect me, and you get two for the price of one, Mr. Clinton says of his lawyer-spouse. And what does Hillary believe? Well, Hillary believes that 12-year-olds should have a right to sue their parents, and she has compared marriage as an institution to slavery—and life on an Indian reservation.

Well, speak for yourself, Hillary.

Friends, this is radical feminism. The agenda Clinton and Clinton would impose on America—abortion on demand, a litmus test for the Supreme Court, homosexual rights, discrimination against religious schools, women in combat—that's change, all right. But it is not the kind of change America wants. It is not the kind of change America needs. And it is not the kind of change we can tolerate in a nation that we still call God's country.

A president is also commander in chief, the man we empower to send sons and brothers, fathers and friends, to war.

George Bush was 17 when they bombed Pearl Harbor. He left his high school class, walked down to the recruiting office, and signed up to become the youngest fighter pilot in the Pacific war. And Mr. Clinton? When Bill Clinton's turn came in Vietnam, he sat up in a dormitory in Oxford, England, and figured out how to dodge the draft.

Which of these two men has won the moral authority to call on Americans to put their lives at risk? I suggest, respectfully, it is the patriot and war hero, Navy Lieutenant j.g. George Herbert Walker Bush.

My friends, this campaign is about philosophy, and it is about character; and George Bush wins on both counts—going away; and it is time all of us came home and stood beside him.

As running mate, Mr. Clinton chose Albert Gore. And just how moderate is Prince Albert? Well, according to the Taxpayers Union, Al Gore beat out Teddy Kennedy, two straight years, for the title of biggest spender in the Senate.

And Teddy Kennedy isn't moderate about anything.

In New York, Mr. Gore made a startling declaration. Henceforth, he said, the "central organizing principle" of all governments must be: the environment.

Wrong, Albert!

The central organizing principle of this republic is freedom. And from the ancient forests of Oregon, to the Inland Empire of California, America's great middle class has got to start standing up to the environmental extremists who put insects, rats and birds ahead of families, workers and jobs.

One year ago, my friends, I could not have dreamt I would be here. I was then still just one of many panelists on what President Bush calls "those crazy Sunday talk shows."

But I disagreed with the president; and so we challenged the president in the Republican primaries and fought as best we could. From February to June, he won 33 primaries. I can't recall exactly how many we won.

But tonight I want to talk to the 3 million Americans who voted for me. I will never forget you, nor the great honor you have done me. But I do believe, deep in my heart, that the right place for us to be now—in this presidential campaign—is right beside George Bush. The party is our home; this party is where we belong. And don't let anyone tell you any different.

Yes, we disagreed with President Bush, but we stand with him for freedom to choose religious schools, and we stand with him against the amoral idea that gay and lesbian couples should have the same standing in law as married men and women.

We stand with President Bush for right-to-life, and for voluntary prayer in the public schools, and against putting American women in combat. And we stand with President Bush in favor of the right of small towns and communities to control the raw sewage of pornography that pollutes our popular culture.

We stand with President Bush in favor of federal judges who interpret the law as written, and against Supreme Court justices who think they have a mandate to rewrite our Constitution.

My friends, this election is about much more than who gets what. It is about who we are. It is about what we believe. It is about what we stand for as Americans. There is a religious war going on in our country for the soul of America. It is a cultural war, as critical to the kind of nation we will one day be as was the Cold War itself. And in that struggle for the soul of America, Clinton and Clinton are on the other side, and George Bush is on our side. And so, we have to come home, and stand beside him.

My friends, in those 6 months, from Concord to California, I came to know our country better than ever before in my life, and I collected memories that will be with me always.

There was that daylong ride through the great state of Georgia in a bus Vice President Bush himself had used in 1988—a bus they called Asphalt One. The ride ended with a 9:00 P.M. speech in front of a magnificent southern mansion, in a town called Fitzgerald.

There were the workers at the James River Paper Mill, in the frozen North Country of New Hampshire—hard, tough men, one of whom was silent, until I shook his hand. Then he looked up in my eyes and said, "Save our jobs!" There was the legal secretary at the Manchester airport on Christmas Day who told me she was going to vote for me, then broke down crying, saying, "I've lost my job, I don't have any money; they're going to take away my daughter. What am I going to do?"

My friends, even in tough times, these people are with us. They don't read Adam Smith or Edmund Burke, but they came from the same schoolyards and playgrounds and towns as we did. They share our beliefs and convictions, our hopes and our dreams. They are the conservatives of the heart.

They are our people. And we need to reconnect with them. We need to let them know we know they're hurting. They don't expect miracles, but they need to know we care.

There were the people of Hayfork, the tiny town high up in California's Trinity Alps, a town that is now under a sentence of death because a federal judge has set aside 9 million acres for the habitat of the spotted owl—forgetting about the habitat of the men and women who live and work in Hayfork. And there were the brave people of Koreatown who took the worst of the L.A. riots, but still live the family values we treasure, and who still believe deeply in the American dream.

Friends, in those wonderful 25 weeks, the saddest days were the days of the bloody riot in L.A., the worst in our history. But even out of that awful tragedy can come a message of hope.

Hours after the violence ended I visited the Army compound in south L.A., where an officer of the 18th Cavalry, that had come to rescue the city, introduced me to two of his troopers. They could not have been 20 years old. He told them to recount their story.

They had come into L.A. late on the 2nd day, and they walked up a dark street, where the mob had looted and burned every building but one, a convalescent home for the aged. The mob was heading in, to ransack and loot the apartments of the terrified old men and women. When the troopers arrived, M16s at the ready, the mob threatened and cursed, but the mob retreated. It had met the one thing that could stop it: force, rooted in justice, backed by courage.

Greater love than this hath no man than that he lay down his life for his friend. Here were 19-year-old boys ready to lay down their lives to stop a mob from molesting old people they did not even know. And as they took back the streets of L.A., block by block, so we must take back our cities, and take back our culture, and take back our country.

★ ★ ★

## "JUSTICE WILL PREVAIL"

### Bill Clinton, Remarks at Oklahoma City Memorial Prayer Service—April 23, 1995

Bill Clinton (1946–) defeated President Bush and independent candidate Ross Perot in 1992. In the 1994 midterms, however, Republicans made historic gains, including winning control of the U.S. House for the first time in forty years. At a time of rising antigovernment sentiment, the white-supremacist Timothy McVeigh and others attacked the Alfred P. Murrah Federal Building in Oklahoma City, killing 168 people, including 19 children. Clinton flew to the city four days later to speak at a memorial service for the victims.

TODAY OUR NATION joins with you in grief. We mourn with you. We share your hope against hope that some may still survive. We thank all those who have worked so heroically to save lives and to solve this crime—those here in Oklahoma and those who are all across this great land, and many who left their own lives to come here to work hand in hand with you.

We pledge to do all we can to help you heal the injured, to rebuild this city, and to bring to justice those who did this evil.

This terrible sin took the lives of our American family, innocent children in that building, only because their parents were trying to be good parents as well as good workers; citizens in the building going about their daily business; and many there who served the rest of us—who worked to help the elderly and the disabled, who worked to support our farmers and our veterans, who worked to enforce our laws and to protect us. Let us say clearly, they served us well, and we are grateful.

But for so many of you they were also neighbors and friends. You saw them at church or the PTA meetings, at the civic clubs, at the ballpark. You know them in ways that all the rest of America could not.

And to all the members of the families here present who have suffered loss, though we share your grief, your pain is unimaginable, and we know that. We cannot undo it. That is God's work.

Our words seem small beside the loss you have endured. But I found a few I wanted to share today. I've received a lot of letters in these last terrible days. One stood out because it came from a young widow and a mother of three whose own husband was murdered with over 200 other Americans when Pan Am 103 was [brought] down. Here is what that woman said I should say to you today: "The anger you feel is valid, but you must not allow yourselves to be consumed by it. The hurt you feel must not be allowed to turn into hate, but instead into the search for justice. The loss you feel must not paralyze your own lives. Instead, you must try to pay tribute to your loved ones by continuing to do all the things they left undone, thus ensuring they did not die in vain."

Wise words from one who also knows.

You have lost too much, but you have not lost everything. And you have certainly not lost America, for we will stand with you for as many tomorrows as it takes. . . .

If anybody thinks that Americans are mostly mean and selfish, they ought to come to Oklahoma. If anybody thinks Americans have lost the capacity for love and caring and courage, they ought to come to Oklahoma.

To all my fellow Americans beyond this hall, I say, one thing we owe those who have sacrificed is the duty to purge ourselves of the dark forces which gave rise to this evil. They are forces that threaten our common peace, our freedom, our way of life.

Let us teach our children that the God of comfort is also the God of righteousness. Those who trouble their own house will inherit the wind. Justice will prevail.

Let us let our own children know that we will stand against the forces of fear. When there is talk of hatred, let us stand up and talk against it. When there is talk of violence, let us stand up and talk against it. In the face of death, let us honor life. As St. Paul admonished us, let us not be overcome by evil, but overcome evil with good.

Yesterday Hillary and I had the privilege of speaking with some children of other federal employees—children like those who were lost here. And one little girl said something we will never forget. She said, we should all plant a tree in memory of the children. So this morning before we got on the plane to come here, at the White House, we planted that tree in honor of the children of Oklahoma.

It was a dogwood with its wonderful spring flower and its deep, enduring roots. It embodies the lesson of the Psalms—that the life of a good person is like a tree whose leaf does not wither.

My fellow Americans, a tree takes a long time to grow, and wounds take a long time to heal. But we must begin. Those who are lost now belong to God. Some day we will be with them. But until that happens, their legacy must be our lives.

★ ★ ★

## "A VICIOUS SLANDER ON GOOD PEOPLE"
### George H. W. Bush, Letter Resigning from the National Rifle Association—May 3, 1995

In retirement, George H. W. Bush resigned from the National Rifle Association after seeing a fundraising appeal from the group attacking federal agents. It had been a difficult season: federal law-enforcement officials had been involved in tragic episodes in Ruby Ridge, Idaho, and in Waco, Texas. Particularly after the Oklahoma City bombing, the slur on federal officials struck Bush as unacceptable, and he said so.

I WAS OUTRAGED WHEN, even in the wake of the Oklahoma City tragedy, Mr. Wayne LaPierre, executive vice president of N.R.A., defended his attack on federal agents as "jack-booted thugs." To attack Secret Service agents or A.T.F. people or any government law enforcement people as "wearing Nazi bucket helmets and black storm trooper uniforms" wanting to "attack law abiding citizens" is a vicious slander on good people.

Alan G. Whicher, who served on my [United States Secret Service] detail when I was Vice President and President, was killed in Oklahoma City. He was no Nazi. He was a kind man, a loving parent, a man dedicated to serving his country—and serve it well he did.

In 1993, I attended the wake for A.T.F. agent Steve Willis, another dedicated officer who did his duty. I can assure you that this honorable man, killed by weird cultists, was no Nazi.

John Magaw, who used to head the U.S.S.S. and now heads A.T.F., is one of the most principled, decent men I have ever known. He would be the last to condone the kind of illegal behavior your ugly letter charges. The same is true for the F.B.I.'s able Director Louis Freeh. I appointed Mr. Freeh to the Federal Bench. His integrity and honor are beyond question.

Both John Magaw and Judge Freeh were in office when I was President. They both now serve in the current administration. They both have badges. Neither of them would ever give the government's "go ahead to harass, intimidate, even murder law abiding citizens." (Your words)

I am a gun owner and an avid hunter. Over the years I have agreed with most of N.R.A.'s objectives, particularly your educational and training efforts, and your fundamental stance in favor of owning guns.

However, your broadside against Federal agents deeply offends my own sense of decency and honor; and it offends my concept of service to country. It indirectly slanders a wide array of government law enforcement officials, who are out there, day and night, laying their lives on the line for all of us.

You have not repudiated Mr. LaPierre's unwarranted attack. Therefore, I resign as a Life Member of N.R.A., said resignation to be effective upon your receipt of this letter. Please remove my name from your membership list.

Sincerely,
George Bush

★ ★ ★

## "LET THEM LISTEN TO THE VOICES OF WOMEN"

### Hillary Rodham Clinton, Address to the United Nations Conference on Women, Beijing, China—September 5, 1995

As First Lady, Hillary Rodham Clinton (1947–) spoke at the Fourth World Conference on Women in Beijing on the issues of women and human rights around the world.

This is truly a celebration—a celebration of the contributions women make in every aspect of life: in the home, on the job, in the community, as mothers, wives, sisters, daughters, learners, workers, citizens, and leaders.

It is also a coming together, much the way women come together every day in every country.

We come together in fields and factories. In village markets and supermarkets. In living rooms and boardrooms. Whether it is while playing with our children in the park or washing clothes in a river or taking a break at the office watercooler, we come together and talk about our

*Hillary Rodham Clinton would be elected to the U.S. Senate from New York in 2000, and later serve as Barack Obama's secretary of state before winning the 2016 Democratic presidential nomination.*

aspirations and concerns. And time and again, our talk turns to our children and our families.

However different we may appear, there is far more that unites us than divides us. We share a common future. And we are here to find common ground so that we may help bring new dignity and respect to women and girls all over the world—and in so doing, bring new strength and stability to families as well.

By gathering in Beijing, we are focusing world attention on issues that matter most in our lives, the lives of women and their families: access to education, health care, jobs, and credit, the chance to enjoy basic legal and human rights and participate fully in the political life of our countries.

There are some who question the reason for this conference. Let them listen to the voices of women in their homes, neighborhoods, and workplaces.

There are some who wonder whether the lives of women and girls matter to economic and political progress around the globe. Let them look at the women gathered here and at Huairou, the homemakers and nurses, the teachers and lawyers, the policymakers and women who run their own businesses.

It is conferences like this that compel governments and peoples everywhere to listen, look, and face the world's most pressing problems.

Wasn't it, after all, after the women's conference in Nairobi 10 years ago that the world focused for the first time on the crisis of domestic violence?

Earlier today, I participated in a World Health Organization forum. In that forum, we talked about ways that government officials, NGOs, and individual citizens are working to address the health problems of women and girls.

Tomorrow, I will attend a gathering of the United Nations Development Fund for Women. There, the discussion will focus on local and highly successful programs that give hardworking women access to credit so they can improve their own lives and the lives of their families.

What we are learning around the world is that if women are healthy and educated, their families will flourish. If women are free from violence, their families will flourish. If women have a chance to work and earn as full and equal partners in society, their families will flourish. And when families flourish, communities and nations do as well. That is why every woman, every man, every child, every family, and every nation on our planet does have a stake in the discussion that takes place here.

Over the past 25 years, I have worked persistently on issues relating to women, children, and families. Over the past two-and-a-half years, I have had the opportunity to learn more about the challenges facing women in my own country and around the world.

I have met new mothers in Indonesia who come together regularly in their village to discuss nutrition, family planning, and baby care.

I have met working parents in Denmark who talk about the comfort they feel in knowing that their children can be cared for in safe and nurturing after-school centers.

I have met women in South Africa who helped lead the struggle to end apartheid and are now helping to build a new democracy.

I have met with the leading women of my own hemisphere who are working every day to promote literacy and better health care for children in their countries.

I have met women in India and Bangladesh who are taking out small loans to buy milk cows, or rickshaws, or thread in order to create a livelihood for themselves and their families.

I have met the doctors and nurses in Belarus and Ukraine who are trying to keep children alive in the aftermath of Chernobyl.

The great challenge of this conference is to give voice to women everywhere whose experiences go unnoticed, whose words go unheard.

Women comprise more than half the world's population, 70 percent of the world's poor, and two-thirds of those who are not taught to read and write. We are the primary caretakers for most of the world's children and elderly. Yet much of the work we do is not valued—not by economists, not by historians, not by popular culture, not by government leaders.

At this very moment, as we sit here, women around the world are giving birth, raising children, cooking meals, washing clothes, cleaning houses, planting crops, working on assembly lines, running companies, and running countries.

Women also are dying from diseases that should have been prevented or treated; they are watching their children succumb to malnutrition caused by poverty and economic deprivation; they are being denied the right to go to school by their own fathers and brothers; they are being forced into prostitution; and they are being barred from the bank-lending offices and banned from the ballot box.

Those of us who have the opportunity to be here have the responsibility to speak for those who could not. As an American, I want to speak for women in my own country—women who are raising children on the minimum wage, women who can't afford health care or child care, women whose lives are threatened by violence, including violence in their own homes.

I want to speak up for mothers who are fighting for good schools, safe neighborhoods, clean air, and clean airwaves; for older women, some of them widows, who find that after raising their families, their skills and life experiences are not valued in the marketplace; for women who are working all night as nurses, hotel clerks, or fast-food chefs so that they can be at home during the day with their children; and for women everywhere who simply don't have time to do everything they are called upon to do each and every day.

Speaking to you today, I speak for them, just as each of us speaks for women around the world who are denied the chance to go to school, or see a doctor, or own property, or have a say about the direction of their lives, simply because they are women. The truth is that most women around the world work both inside and outside the home, usually by necessity.

We need to understand there is no one formula for how women should lead our lives. That is why we must respect the choices that each woman makes for herself and her family. Every woman deserves the chance to realize her own God-given potential.

We also must recognize that women will never gain full dignity until their human rights are respected and protected.

Our goals for this conference—to strengthen families and societies by empowering women to take greater control over their own destinies—cannot be fully achieved unless all governments, here and around the world, accept their responsibility to protect and promote internationally recognized human rights.

The international community has long acknowledged—and recently reaffirmed at Vienna—that both women and men are entitled to a range of protections and personal freedoms, from the right of personal security to the right to determine freely the number and spacing of the children they bear.

No one should be forced to remain silent for fear of religious or political persecution, arrest, abuse, or torture. Tragically, women are most often the ones whose human rights are violated. Even now, in the late 20th century, the rape of women continues to be used as an instrument of armed conflict. Women and children make up a large majority of the world's refugees. And when women are excluded from the political process, they become even more vulnerable to abuse.

I believe that, now on the eve of a new millennium, it is time to break the silence. It is time for us to say here in Beijing, and for the world to hear, that it is no longer acceptable to discuss women's rights as separate from human rights.

These abuses have continued because, for too long, the history of women has been a history of silence. Even today, there are those who are trying to silence our words.

But the voices of this conference and of the women at Huairou must be heard loudly and clearly:

> It *is* a violation of human rights when babies are denied food, or drowned, or suffocated, or [have] their spines broken, simply because they are born girls.
>
> It *is* a violation of human rights when women and girls are sold into the slavery of prostitution for human greed, and the kinds of reasons that are used to justify this practice should no longer be tolerated.
>
> It is a violation of human rights when women are doused with gasoline, set on fire, and burned to death because their marriage dowries are deemed too small.
>
> It is a violation of human rights when individual women are raped in their own communities and when thousands of women are subjected to rape as a tactic or prize of war.
>
> It is a violation of human rights when a leading cause of death worldwide among women ages 14 to 44 is the violence they are subjected to in their own homes, by their own relatives.
>
> It is a violation of human rights when young girls are brutalized by the painful and degrading practice of genital mutilation.
>
> It is a violation of human rights when women are denied the right to plan their own families, and that includes being forced to have abortions or being sterilized against their will.

If there is one message that echoes forth from this conference, let it be that human rights are women's rights and women's rights are human rights, once and for all.

And among those rights are the right to speak freely and the right to be heard. Women must enjoy the right to participate fully in the social and political lives of their countries if we want freedom and democracy to thrive and endure. It is indefensible that many women in nongovernmental organizations who wished to participate in this conference have not been able to attend or have been prohibited from fully taking part.

Let me be clear: Freedom means the right of people to assemble, organize, and debate openly. It means respecting the views of those who may disagree with the views of their governments. It means not taking citizens away from their loved ones and jailing them, mistreating them, or denying them their freedom or dignity because of the peaceful expression of their ideas and opinions.

In my country, we recently celebrated the 75th anniversary of women's suffrage. It took 150 years after the signing of our Declaration of Independence for women to win the right to vote. It took 72 years of organized struggle before that happened on the part of many courageous women and men. It was one of America's most divisive philosophical wars. But it was a bloodless war. Suffrage was achieved without a shot being fired.

But we have also been reminded, in V-J Day observances last weekend, of the good that comes when men and women join together to combat the forces of tyranny and to build a better world. We have seen peace prevail in most places for a half century. We have avoided another world war. But we have not solved older, deeply rooted problems that continue to diminish the potential of half the world's population.

Now it is time to act on behalf of women everywhere.

If we take bold steps to better the lives of women, we will be taking bold steps to better the lives of children and families too. Families rely on mothers and wives for emotional support and care; families rely on women for labor in the home; and increasingly everywhere, families rely on women for income needed to raise healthy children and care for other relatives.

As long as discrimination and inequities remain so commonplace everywhere in the world, as long as girls and women are valued less, fed less, fed last, overworked, underpaid, not schooled, subjected to violence in and out of their homes, the potential of the human family to create a peaceful, prosperous world will not be realized.

Let this conference be our—and the world's—call to action.

Let us heed that call so that we can create a world in which every woman is treated with respect and dignity, every boy and girl is loved and cared for equally, and every family has the hope of a strong and stable future.

That is the work before you; that is the work before all of us who have a vision of the world we want to see for our children and our grandchildren. The time is now. We must move beyond rhetoric; we must move beyond recognition of problems to working together to have the common efforts to build that common ground we hope to see.

God's blessings on you, your work, and all who will benefit from it.

★ ★ ★

## "COUNTRY BEFORE PARTY"
### Al Gore, Presidential Concession Speech, Washington, D.C.—December 13, 2000

It was the closest of elections, and everything came down to Florida. With grace, Al Gore (1948–) conceded the 2000 presidential race to George W. Bush after the U.S. Supreme Court, in a party-line decision, stopped further recounts, awarding the state's electors to Bush. The popular-vote margin was 537 votes out of nearly six million ballots cast.

JUST MOMENTS AGO, I spoke with George W. Bush and congratulated him on becoming the 43rd president of the United States. And I promised him that I wouldn't call him back this time. I offered to meet with him as soon as possible so that we can start to heal the divisions of the campaign and the contest through which we've just passed.

Almost a century and a half ago, Senator Stephen Douglas told Abraham Lincoln, who had just defeated him for the presidency, "Partisan feeling must yield to patriotism. I'm with you, Mr. President, and God bless you." Well, in that same spirit, I say to President-elect Bush that what remains of partisan rancor must now be put aside, and may God bless his stewardship of this country. Neither he nor I anticipated this long and difficult road. Certainly neither of us wanted it to happen. Yet it came, and now it has ended, resolved, as it must be resolved, through the honored institutions of our democracy.

*Al Gore's concession after the disputed 2000 election, delivered in the Old Executive Office Building, being broadcast in New York City's Times Square.*

Over the library of one of our great law schools is inscribed the motto, "Not under man but under God and law." That's the ruling principle of American freedom, the source of our democratic liberties. I've tried to make it my guide throughout this contest, as it has guided America's deliberations of all the complex issues of the past five weeks.

Now the U.S. Supreme Court has spoken. Let there be no doubt, while I *strongly* disagree with the court's decision, I accept it. I accept the finality of this outcome which will be ratified next Monday in the Electoral College. And tonight, for the sake of our unity as a people and the strength of our democracy, I offer my concession. I also accept my responsibility, which I will discharge unconditionally, to honor the new President-elect and do everything possible to help him bring Americans together in fulfillment of the great vision that our Declaration of Independence defines and that our Constitution affirms and defends.

Let me say how grateful I am to all those who supported me and supported the cause for which we have fought. Tipper and I feel a deep gratitude to Joe and Hadassah Lieberman, who brought passion and high purpose to our partnership and opened new doors, not just for our campaign but for our country.

This has been an extraordinary election. But in one of God's unforeseen paths, this belatedly broken impasse can point us all to a new common ground, for its very closeness can serve to remind us that we are one people with a shared history and a shared destiny. Indeed, that history gives us many examples of contests as hotly debated, as fiercely fought, with their own challenges to the popular will. Other disputes have dragged on for weeks before reaching resolution. And each time, both the victor and the vanquished have accepted the result peacefully and in a spirit of reconciliation.

So let it be with us.

I know that many of my supporters are disappointed. I am too. But our disappointment must be overcome by our love of country.

And I say to our fellow members of the world community, let no one see this contest as a sign of American weakness. The strength of American democracy is shown most clearly through the difficulties it can overcome. Some have expressed concern that the unusual nature of this election might hamper the next president in the conduct of his office. I do not believe it need be so.

President-elect Bush inherits a nation whose citizens will be ready to assist him in the conduct of his large responsibilities. I, personally, will be at his disposal, and I call on all Americans—I particularly urge all who stood with us—to unite behind our next president. This is America. Just as we fight hard when the stakes are high, we close ranks and come together when the contest is done. And while there will be time enough to debate our continuing differences, now is the time to recognize that that which unites us is greater than that which divides us. While we yet hold and do not yield our opposing beliefs, there is a higher duty than the one we owe to political party. This is America and we put country before party; we will stand together behind our new president.

As for what I'll do next, I don't know the answer to that one yet. Like many of you, I'm looking forward to spending the holidays with family and old friends. I know I'll spend time in Tennessee and mend some fences, literally and figuratively.

Some have asked whether I have any regrets, and I do have one regret: that I didn't get the chance to stay and fight for the American people over the next four years, especially for those who need burdens lifted and barriers removed, especially for those who feel their voices have not been heard. I heard you. And I will not forget.

I've seen America in this campaign, and I like what I see. It's worth fighting for and that's a fight I'll never stop. As for the battle that ends tonight, I do believe, as my father once said, that "No matter how hard the loss, defeat might serve as well as victory to shape the soul and let the glory out."

So for me this campaign ends as it began: with the love of Tipper and our family; with faith in God and in the country I have been so proud to serve, from Vietnam to the vice presidency; and with gratitude to our truly tireless campaign staff and volunteers, including all those who worked so hard in Florida for the last 36 days.

Now the political struggle is over and we turn again to the unending struggle for the common good of all Americans and for those multitudes around the world who look to us for leadership in the cause of freedom.

In the words of our great hymn "America, America": "Let us crown thy good with brotherhood, from sea to shining sea."

And now, my friends, in a phrase I once addressed to others: It's time for me to go.

★ ★ ★

## "THAT'S NOT THE AMERICA I KNOW"

### George W. Bush, Remarks at the Islamic Center of Washington, D.C.— September 17, 2001

Six days after the devastating terror attacks on the United States by Al Qaeda on Tuesday, September 11, 2001, George W. Bush (1946–) spoke briefly at the Islamic Center in Washington, urging Americans to view Muslims and Islam with a sense of proportion and of generosity.

THANK YOU ALL very much for your hospitality. We've just had a wide-ranging discussion on the matter at hand. Like the good folks standing with me, the American people were appalled and outraged at last Tuesday's attacks. And so were Muslims all across the world. Both Americans, our Muslim friends and citizens, taxpaying citizens . . . were just appalled and could not believe what we saw on our TV screens.

These acts of violence against innocents violate the fundamental tenets of the Islamic faith. And it's important for my fellow Americans to understand that.

The English translation is not as eloquent as the original Arabic, but let me quote from the Koran itself: "In the long run, evil in the extreme will be the end of those who do evil. For that they rejected the signs of Allah and held them up to ridicule."

The face of terror is not the true faith of Islam. That's not what Islam is all about. Islam is peace. These terrorists don't represent peace. They represent evil and war.

When we think of Islam, we think of a faith that brings comfort to a billion people around the world—billions of people find comfort and solace and peace—and that's made brothers and sisters out of every race—out of every race.

America counts millions of Muslims amongst our citizens, and Muslims make an incredibly valuable contribution to our country. Muslims are doctors, lawyers, law professors, members of the military, entrepreneurs, shopkeepers, moms and dads. And they need to be treated with respect. In our anger and emotion, our fellow Americans must treat each other with respect.

Women who cover their heads in this country must feel comfortable going outside their homes. Moms who wear cover must not be intimidated in America. That's not the America I know. That's not the America I value.

I've been told that some fear to leave; some don't want to go shopping for their families; some don't want to go about their ordinary daily routines because, by wearing cover, they're afraid they'll be intimidated. That should not and that will not stand in America.

Those who feel like they can intimidate our fellow citizens to take out their anger don't represent the best of America. They represent the worst of humankind, and they should be ashamed of that kind of behavior.

This is a great country. It's a great country because we share the same values of respect and dignity and human worth. And it is my honor to be meeting with leaders who feel just the same way I do. They're outraged; they're sad. They love America just as much as I do.

★ ★ ★

## "LOVE IS LOVE"

### Barack Obama, Remarks on the Supreme Court Decision on Marriage Equality, the White House—June 26, 2015

In the Rose Garden of the White House, Barack Obama (1961–) welcomed the U.S. Supreme Court's ruling, in *Obergefell v. Hodges,* that states could no longer prohibit same-sex marriage.

*A sweet moment between George W. Bush and Michelle Obama at the opening of the National Museum of African American History and Culture in Washington, D.C., in 2016.*

OUR NATION WAS founded on a bedrock principle that we are all created equal. The project of each generation is to bridge the meaning of those founding words with the realities of changing times—a never-ending quest to ensure those words ring true for every single American.

Progress on this journey often comes in small increments, sometimes two steps forward, one step back, propelled by the persistent effort of dedicated citizens. And then sometimes, there are days like this when that slow, steady effort is rewarded with justice that arrives like a thunderbolt.

This morning, the Supreme Court recognized that the Constitution guarantees marriage equality. In doing so, they've reaffirmed that all Americans are entitled to the equal protection of the law. That all people should be treated equally, regardless of who they are or who they love.

This decision will end the patchwork system we currently have. It will end the uncertainty hundreds of thousands of same-sex couples face from not knowing whether their marriage, legitimate in the eyes of one state, will remain if they decide to move [to] or even visit another. This ruling will strengthen all of our communities by offering to all loving same-sex couples the dignity of marriage across this great land.

In my second inaugural address, I said that if we are truly created equal, then surely the love we commit to one another must be equal as well. It is gratifying to see that principle enshrined into law by this decision.

This ruling is a victory for Jim Obergefell and the other plaintiffs in the case. It's a victory for gay and lesbian couples who have fought so long for their basic civil rights. It's a victory for their children, whose families will now be recognized as equal to any other. It's a victory for the allies and friends and supporters who spent years, even decades, working and praying for change to come.

And this ruling is a victory for America. This decision affirms what millions of Americans already believe in their hearts: When all Americans are treated as equal we are all more free.

My administration has been guided by that idea. It's why we stopped defending the so-called Defense of Marriage Act, and why we were pleased when the Court finally struck down a central provision of that discriminatory law. It's why we ended "Don't Ask, Don't Tell." From extending full marital benefits to federal employees and their spouses, to expanding hospital visitation rights for LGBT patients and their loved ones, we've made real progress in advancing equality for LGBT Americans in ways that were unimaginable not too long ago.

I know change for many of our LGBT brothers and sisters must have seemed so slow for so long. But compared to so many other issues, America's shift has been so quick. I know that Americans of goodwill continue to hold a wide range of views on this issue. Opposition in some cases has been based on sincere and deeply held beliefs. All of us who welcome today's news should be mindful of that fact; recognize different viewpoints; revere our deep commitment to religious freedom.

But today should also give us hope that on the many issues with which we grapple, often painfully, real change is possible. Shifts in hearts and minds is possible. And those who have come so far on their journey to equality have a responsibility to reach back and help others join them. Because for all our differences, we are one people, stronger together than we could ever be alone. That's always been our story.

We are big and vast and diverse; a nation of people with different backgrounds and beliefs, different experiences and stories, but bound by our shared ideal that no matter who you are or what you look like, how you started off, or how and who you love, America is a place where you can write your own destiny.

We are a people who believe that every single child is entitled to life and liberty and the pursuit of happiness.

There's so much more work to be done to extend the full promise of America to every American. But today, we can say in no uncertain terms that we've made our union a little more perfect.

That's the consequence of a decision from the Supreme Court, but, more importantly, it is a consequence of the countless small acts of courage of millions of people across decades who stood up, who came out, who talked to parents—parents who loved their children no matter what. Folks who were willing to endure bullying and taunts, and stayed strong, and came to believe in themselves and who they were, and slowly made an entire country realize that love is love.

What an extraordinary achievement. What a vindication of the belief that ordinary people can do extraordinary things. What a reminder of what Bobby Kennedy once said about how small actions can be like pebbles being thrown into a still lake, and ripples of hope cascade outwards and change the world.

Those countless, often anonymous heroes—they deserve our thanks. They should be very proud. America should be very proud.

★ ★ ★

## "AMERICAN CARNAGE"

### Donald J. Trump, First Inaugural Address—January 20, 2017

His was perhaps the unlikeliest rise in American presidential history. A media-savvy New York real-estate developer and reality-television star (NBC's prime-time *The Apprentice*), Donald Trump (1946–) announced his candidacy for the Republican nomination in the early summer of 2015. Capitalizing on anti-immigrant sentiment and reviving the isolationism of the "America First" movement of the pre–World War II period, Trump captured the GOP and prevailed over Hillary Clinton with an Electoral College victory in the 2016 general election. In 2020, Joseph R. Biden, Jr., the longtime U.S. senator from Delaware and vice president under Barack Obama, defeated President Trump, who, against all evidence, denied the legitimacy of Biden's win, leading to an attempted insurrection by Trump supporters at the United States Capitol on Wednesday, January 6, 2021. Four years later, in 2024, Trump would regain the White House in an abbreviated contest against Vice President Kamala Harris (1964–), who became the Democratic nominee after President Biden, who had been seeking reelection at age eighty-one, left the race in the wake of a disastrous debate performance that raised fundamental questions about his capacity to govern for another term. This is Trump's first inaugural address.

Chief Justice Roberts, President Carter, President Clinton, President Bush, President Obama, fellow Americans, and people of the world: Thank you.

We, the citizens of America, are now joined in a great national effort to rebuild our country and to restore its promise for all of our people.

Together, we will determine the course of America and the world for years to come.

We will face challenges. We will confront hardships. But we will get the job done.

Every four years, we gather on these steps to carry out the orderly and peaceful transfer of power, and we are grateful to President Obama and First Lady Michelle Obama for their gracious aid throughout this transition. They have been magnificent.

Today's ceremony, however, has very special meaning. Because today we are not merely transferring power from one Administration to another, or from one party to another—but we are transferring power from Washington, D.C., and giving it back to you, the American People.

For too long, a small group in our nation's Capital has reaped the rewards of government while the people have borne the cost.

Washington flourished—but the people did not share in its wealth.

Politicians prospered—but the jobs left, and the factories closed.

The establishment protected itself, but not the citizens of our country.

Their victories have not been your victories; their triumphs have not been your triumphs; and while they celebrated in our nation's Capital, there was little to celebrate for struggling families all across our land.

That all changes—starting right here, and right now, because this moment is your moment: it belongs to you.

It belongs to everyone gathered here today and everyone watching all across America.

This is your day. This is your celebration.

And this, the United States of America, is your country.

What truly matters is not which party controls our government, but whether our government is controlled by the people.

January 20th, 2017, will be remembered as the day the people became the rulers of this nation again.

The forgotten men and women of our country will be forgotten no longer.

Everyone is listening to you now.

You came by the tens of millions to become part of a historic movement the likes of which the world has never seen before.

At the center of this movement is a crucial conviction: that a nation exists to serve its citizens.

Americans want great schools for their children, safe neighborhoods for their families, and good jobs for themselves.

These are the just and reasonable demands of a righteous public.

But for too many of our citizens, a different reality exists: Mothers and children trapped in poverty in our inner cities; rusted-out factories scattered like tombstones across the landscape of our nation; an education system, flush with cash, but which leaves our young and beautiful students deprived of knowledge; and the crime and gangs and drugs that have stolen too many lives and robbed our country of so much unrealized potential.

This American carnage stops right here and stops right now.

We are one nation—and their pain is our pain. Their dreams are our dreams; and their success will be our success. We share one heart, one home, and one glorious destiny.

The oath of office I take today is an oath of allegiance to all Americans.

For many decades, we've enriched foreign industry at the expense of American industry;

Subsidized the armies of other countries while allowing for the very sad depletion of our military;

We've defended other nations' borders while refusing to defend our own;

And spent trillions of dollars overseas while America's infrastructure has fallen into disrepair and decay.

We've made other countries rich while the wealth, strength, and confidence of our country has disappeared over the horizon.

One by one, the factories shuttered and left our shores, with not even a thought about the millions upon millions of American workers left behind.

The wealth of our middle class has been ripped from their homes and then redistributed across the entire world.

But that is the past. And now we are looking only to the future.

We assembled here today are issuing a new decree to be heard in every city, in every foreign capital, and in every hall of power.

From this day forward, a new vision will govern our land.

From this moment on, it's going to be America First.

Every decision on trade, on taxes, on immigration, on foreign affairs, will be made to benefit American workers and American families.

We must protect our borders from the ravages of other countries making our products, stealing our companies, and destroying our jobs. Protection will lead to great prosperity and strength.

I will fight for you with every breath in my body—and I will never, ever let you down.

America will start winning again, winning like never before.

We will bring back our jobs. We will bring back our borders. We will bring back our wealth. And we will bring back our dreams.

We will build new roads, and highways, and bridges, and airports, and tunnels, and railways all across our wonderful nation.

We will get our people off of welfare and back to work—rebuilding our country with American hands and American labor.

We will follow two simple rules: Buy American and Hire American.

We will seek friendship and goodwill with the nations of the world—but we do so with the understanding that it is the right of all nations to put their own interests first.

We do not seek to impose our way of life on anyone, but rather to let it shine as an example for everyone to follow.

We will reinforce old alliances and form new ones—and unite the civilized world against Radical Islamic Terrorism, which we will eradicate completely from the face of the Earth.

At the bedrock of our politics will be a total allegiance to the United States of America, and through our loyalty to our country, we will rediscover our loyalty to each other.

When you open your heart to patriotism, there is no room for prejudice.

The Bible tells us, "how good and pleasant it is when God's people live together in unity."

We must speak our minds openly, debate our disagreements honestly, but always pursue solidarity.

When America is united, America is totally unstoppable.

There should be no fear—we are protected, and we will always be protected.

We will be protected by the great men and women of our military and law enforcement and, most importantly, we are protected by God.

Finally, we must think big and dream even bigger.

In America, we understand that a nation is only living as long as it is striving.

We will no longer accept politicians who are all talk and no action—constantly complaining but never doing anything about it.

The time for empty talk is over.

Now arrives the hour of action.

Do not let anyone tell you it cannot be done. No challenge can match the heart and fight and spirit of America.

We will not fail. Our country will thrive and prosper again.

We stand at the birth of a new millennium, ready to unlock the mysteries of space, to free the Earth from the miseries of disease, and to harness the energies, industries, and technologies of tomorrow.

A new national pride will stir our souls, lift our sights, and heal our divisions.

It is time to remember that old wisdom our soldiers will never forget: that whether we are black or brown or white, we all bleed the same red blood of patriots, we all enjoy the same glorious freedoms, and we all salute the same great American Flag.

And whether a child is born in the urban sprawl of Detroit or the windswept plains of Nebraska, they look up at the same night sky, they fill their heart with the same dreams, and they are infused with the breath of life by the same almighty Creator.

So to all Americans, in every city near and far, small and large, from mountain to mountain, and from ocean to ocean, hear these words:

You will never be ignored again.

Your voice, your hopes, and your dreams, will define our American destiny. And your courage and goodness and love will forever guide us along the way.

Together, We Will Make America Strong Again.

We Will Make America Wealthy Again.

We Will Make America Proud Again.

We Will Make America Safe Again.

And, Yes, Together, We Will Make America Great Again. Thank you, God Bless You, And God Bless America.

★ ★ ★

## "THE SOURCE OF AMERICA'S GREATNESS"
### J. D. Vance, Address Accepting the Vice-Presidential Nomination at the Republican National Convention, Milwaukee, Wisconsin—July 17, 2024

Born in Appalachia's Middletown, Ohio, J. D. Vance (1984–) was raised largely by his grandmother as his mother struggled with addiction, a story he told in his bestselling book *Hillbilly Elegy: A Memoir of a Family and Culture in Crisis,* published in 2016. A military journalist in the Marine Corps, he served in Iraq and was educated at Ohio State University and Yale Law School. Vance was elected to the United States Senate in 2022 and as vice president in 2024.

My friends, tonight is a night of hope. A celebration of what America once was, and with God's grace, what it will soon be again. And it is a reminder of the sacred duty we have to preserve the American experiment, to choose a new path for our children and grandchildren.

But as we meet tonight, we cannot forget that this evening could have been so much different. Instead of a day of celebration, this could have been a day of heartache and mourning. For the last eight years, President Trump has given everything he has to fight for the people of our country. He didn't need politics, but the country needed him.

Now, prior to running for president, he was one of the most successful businessmen in the world. He had everything anyone could ever want in a life. And yet, instead of choosing the easy path, he chose to endure abuse, slander and persecution. And he did it because he loves this country. I want all Americans to watch the video of a would-be assassin coming a quarter of an inch from taking his life. Consider the lies they told you about Donald Trump. And then look at that photo of him defiant—fist in the air. When Donald Trump rose to his feet in that Pennsylvania field—all of America stood with him. And what did he call for us to do for his country? To fight. To fight for America.

Even in his most perilous moment we were on his mind. His instinct was for us, for our country. To call us to something higher. To something greater. To once again be citizens who ask what our country needs of us. Now consider what they said. They said he was a tyrant. They said he must be stopped at all costs. But how did he respond? He called for national unity, for national calm literally right after an assassin nearly took his life. He remembered the victims of the terrible attack, especially the brave Corey Comperatore, who gave his life to protect his family. God bless him.

And then President Trump flew to Milwaukee and got back to work.

Now that's the man I've gotten to know personally over the last few years. He is tough, and he is, but he cares about people. He can stand defiant against an assassin one moment and call for national healing the next. He is a beloved father and grandfather, and, of course, a once-in-a-generation business leader. He's the man who's feared by America's adversaries, but two nights ago, and I'll share a moment, said good night to his two boys, told them he loved them, and made sure to give each of them a kiss on the cheek. And I will say, Don and Eric squirmed the same way my four-year-old does when his daddy tries to give him a kiss on the cheek. Sorry, guys.

He is all those things, but tonight, we celebrate. He is our once and future president of the United States of America.

Now, I want to respond to his call for unity myself. We have a big tent on this party, on everything from national security to economic policy.

But my message to you, my fellow Republicans, is—we love this country and we are united to win.

Now I think our disagreements actually make us stronger. That's what I've learned in my time in the United States Senate, where sometimes I persuade my colleagues and sometimes they persuade me. And my message to my fellow Americans, those watching from across the country, is shouldn't we be governed by a party that is unafraid to debate ideas and come to the best solution?

That's the Republican Party of the next four years: united in our love for this country, and committed to free speech and the open exchange of ideas.

And so tonight, Mr. Chairman, I stand here humbled, and I'm overwhelmed with gratitude to say I officially accept your nomination to be vice president of the United States of America.

Now, never in my wildest imagination could I have believed that I could be standing here tonight.

I grew up in Middletown, Ohio, a small town where people spoke their minds, built with their hands, and loved their God, their family, their community and their country with their whole hearts.

But it was also a place that had been cast aside and forgotten by America's ruling class in Washington.

When I was in the fourth grade, a career politician by the name of Joe Biden supported NAFTA, a bad trade deal that sent countless good jobs to Mexico.

When I was a sophomore in high school, that same career politician named Joe Biden gave China a sweetheart trade deal that destroyed even more good American middle-class manufacturing jobs.

When I was a senior in high school, that same Joe Biden supported the disastrous invasion of Iraq.

And at each step of the way, in small towns like mine in Ohio, or next door in Pennsylvania or Michigan, in other states across our country, jobs were sent overseas and our children were sent to war.

And somehow, a real estate developer from New York City by the name of Donald J. Trump was right on all of these issues while Biden was wrong. President Trump knew, even then, that we needed leaders who would put America first.

Now, thanks to these policies that Biden and other out-of-touch politicians in Washington gave us, our country was flooded with cheap Chinese goods, with cheap foreign labor—and in the decades to come, deadly Chinese fentanyl.

Joe Biden screwed up, and my community paid the price. Now, I was lucky. Despite the closing factories and the growing addiction in towns like mine, in my life, I had a guardian angel by my side. She was an old woman who could barely walk but she was tough as nails.

I called her "Mamaw," the name we hillbillies gave to our grandmothers.

Mamaw raised me as her own. . . .

Mamaw raised me as my mother struggled with addiction. Mamaw was in so many ways a woman of contradictions. She loved the Lord, ladies and gentlemen. She was a woman of very deep Christian faith.

But she also loved the f-word. I'm not kidding. She could make a sailor blush.

Now, she once told me, when she found out that I was spending too much time with a local kid who was known for dealing drugs, that if I ever hung out with that kid again, she would run him over with her car.

That's true. And she said, "J.D., no one will ever find out about it."

Now, now thanks to that Mamaw, things worked out for me.

After 9/11, I did what thousands of other young men my age did in that time of soaring patriotism and love of country: I enlisted in the United States Marines. *Semper Fi* to my fellow Marines.

Now I left the Marines after four years and went to The Ohio State University. I'm sorry, Michigan, I had to get that in there.

Now after Ohio State I went to Yale Law School, where I met my beautiful wife, and I then started businesses to create jobs in the kinds of places I grew up in.

Now, my work taught me that there is still so much talent and grit in the American heartland. There really is. But for these places to thrive, we need a leader who fights for the people who built this country.

We need a leader who's not in the pocket of big business, but answers to the working man, union and nonunion alike. A leader who won't sell out to multinational corporations, but will stand up for American companies and American industry. A leader who rejects Joe Biden and Kamala Harris's Green New Scam and fights to bring back our great American factories.

We need President Donald J. Trump.

Some people tell me I've lived the American dream, and of course they're right. And I'm so grateful for it.

But the American dream that always counted most was not starting a business or becoming a senator or even being here with you fine people, though it's pretty awesome. My most important American dream was becoming a good husband and a good dad.

I wanted to give my kids the things that I didn't have when I was growing up.

And that's the accomplishment that I'm proudest of. That tonight I'm joined by my beautiful wife, Usha, an incredible lawyer and a better mom. And our three beautiful kids, Ewan, who's seven, Vivek, who's four, Mirabel, who's two.

Now they're back at the hotel, and kids, if you're watching, Daddy loves you very much but get your butts in bed. It's ten o'clock.

But, my friends, things did not work out well for a lot of kids I grew up with. Every now and then I will get a call from a relative back home who asks, "Did you know so-and-so?"

And I'll remember a face from years ago, and then I'll hear, "They died of an overdose."

As always, America's ruling class wrote the checks. Communities like mine paid the price.

For decades, that divide between the few, with their power and comfort in Washington, and the rest of us only widened.

From Iraq to Afghanistan, from the financial crisis to the Great Recession, from open borders to stagnating wages, the people who govern this country have failed and failed again.

That is, of course, until a guy named President Donald J. Trump came along.

President Trump represents America's last best hope to restore what—if lost—may never be found again. A country where a working-class boy born far from the halls of power can stand on this stage as the next vice president of the United States of America.

But, my fellow Americans, here in this stage and watching at home, this moment is not about me; it's about all of us, and it's about who we're fighting for.

It's about the auto worker in Michigan, wondering why out-of-touch politicians are destroying their jobs.

It's about the factory worker in Wisconsin who makes things with their hands and is proud of American craftsmanship.

It's about the energy worker in Pennsylvania and Ohio who doesn't understand why Joe Biden is willing to buy energy from tinpot dictators across the world, when he could buy it from his own citizens right here in our own country.

And our movement is about single moms like mine, who struggled with money and addiction but never gave up.

And I'm proud to say that tonight my mom is here, ten years clean and sober.

I love you, Mom.

And, you know, Mom, I was thinking. It'll be ten years officially in January of 2025, and if President Trump's OK with it, let's have the celebration in the White House.

And our movement, ladies and gentlemen, it's about grandparents all across this country, who are living on Social Security and raising grandchildren they didn't expect to raise.

And while we're on the topic of grandparents, let me tell you another Mamaw story. Now, my Mamaw died shortly before I left for Iraq, in 2005. And when we went through her things, we found nineteen loaded handguns.

Now, the thing is, they were stashed all over her house. Under her bed, in her closet. In the silverware drawer. And we wondered what was going on, and it occurred to us that towards the end of her life, Mamaw couldn't get around very well. And so this frail old woman made sure that no matter where she was, she was within arm's length of whatever she needed to protect her family. That's who we fight for. That's American spirit.

Now, Joe Biden has been a politician in Washington for longer than I've been alive. Thirty-nine years old. Kamala Harris is not much further behind.

For half a century, he's been the champion of every major policy initiative to make America weaker and poorer.

And in four short years, Donald Trump reversed decades of betrayals inflicted by Joe Biden and the rest of the corrupt Washington insiders.

He created the greatest economy in history for workers. It really was amazing. There's this chart that shows worker wages. And they stagnated for pretty much my entire life, until President Donald J. Trump came along. Workers' wages went through the roof. And just imagine what he can do with four more years in the White House.

Months ago, I heard some young family member observe that their parents' generation—the baby boomers—could afford to buy a home when they first entered the workforce. "But I don't know," this person observed, "if I'll ever be able to afford a home."

The absurd cost of housing is the result of so many failures. And it reveals so much about what's broken in Washington. I can tell you exactly how it happened.

Wall Street barons crashed the economy and American builders went out of business.

As tradesmen scrambled for jobs, houses stopped being built.

The lack of good jobs, of course, led to stagnant wages.

And then the Democrats flooded this country with millions of illegal aliens.

So citizens had to compete—with people who shouldn't even be here—for precious housing.

Joe Biden's inflation crisis, my friends, is really an affordability crisis.

And many of the people that I grew up with can't afford to pay more for groceries, more for gas, more for rent, and that's exactly what Joe Biden's economy has given them. So prices soared, dreams were shattered.

And China and the cartels sent fentanyl across the border, adding addiction to the heartache.

But ladies and gentlemen, that is not the end of our story.

We've heard about the villains and their victims; I've talked a lot about that. I've talked a lot about that. But let me tell you about the future.

President Trump's vision is so simple and yet so powerful. We're done, ladies and gentlemen, catering to Wall Street. We'll commit to the working man.

We're done importing foreign labor. We're going to fight for American citizens and their good jobs and their good wages.

We're done buying energy from countries that hate us; we're going to get it right here, from American workers in Pennsylvania and Ohio and across the country.

We're done sacrificing supply chains to unlimited global trade, and we're going to stamp more and more products with that beautiful label "Made in the U.S.A."

We're going to build factories again, put people to work making real products for American families, made with the hands of American workers.

Together, we will protect the wages of American workers—and stop the Chinese Communist Party from building their middle class on the backs of American citizens.

Together, we will make sure our allies share in the burden of securing world peace. No more free rides for nations that betray the generosity of the American taxpayer.

Together, we will send our kids to war only when we must. But as

President Trump showed with the elimination of ISIS and so much more, when we punch, we're going to punch hard.

Together, we will put the citizens of America first, whatever the color of their skin.

We will, in short, make America great again.

You know, one of the things that you hear people say sometimes is that America is an idea. And to be clear, America was indeed founded on brilliant ideas, like the rule of law and religious liberty. Things written into the fabric of our Constitution and our nation. But America is not just an idea. It is a group of people with a shared history and a common future. It is, in short, a nation.

Now, it is part of that tradition, of course, that we welcome newcomers. But when we allow newcomers into our American family, we allow them on our terms. That's the way we preserve the continuity of this project from two hundred and fifty years past to hopefully two hundred and fifty years in the future. And let me illustrate this with a story, if I may.

I am, of course, married to the daughter of South Asian immigrants to this country. Incredible people. People who genuinely have enriched this country in so many ways.

And, of course, I'm biased, because I love my wife and her family, but it's true.

Now when I proposed to my wife, we were in law school, and I said, "Honey, I come with $120,000 worth of law school debt, and a cemetery plot on a mountainside in Eastern Kentucky."

And I guess standing here tonight it's just gotten weirder and weirder, honey. But that's what she was getting. Now that cemetery plot in Eastern Kentucky is near my family's ancestral home. And like a lot of people, we came from the mountains of Appalachia into the factories of Ohio, Pennsylvania, Michigan and Wisconsin.

Now that's Kentucky coal country, one of the ten poorest counties in the entire United States of America.

They're very hardworking people, and they're very good people. They're the kind of people who would give you the shirt off their back even if they can't afford enough to eat.

And our media calls them privileged and looks down on them.

But they love this country, not only because it's a good idea, but because in their bones they know that this is their home, and it will be their children's home, and they would die fighting to protect it.

That is the source of America's greatness.

As a United States senator, I get to represent millions of people in the great state of Ohio with similar stories, and it is the great honor of my life.

Now in that cemetery, there are people who were born around the time of the Civil War. And if, as I hope, my wife and I are eventually laid to rest there, and our kids follow us, there will be seven generations just in that small mountain cemetery plot in eastern Kentucky. Seven generations of people who have fought for this country. Who have built this country. Who have made things in this country. And who would fight and die to protect this country if they were asked to.

Now that's not just an idea, my friends. That's not just a set of principles. Even though the ideas and the principles are great, that is a homeland. That is our homeland. People will not fight for abstractions, but they will fight for their home. And if this movement of ours is going to succeed, and if this country is going to thrive, our leaders have to remember that America is a nation, and its citizens deserve leaders who put its interests first.

Now we won't agree on every issue, of course, not even in this room. We may disagree from time to time about how best to reinvigorate American industry and renew American family. That's fine. In fact it's more than fine, it's good.

But never forget that the reason why this united Republican Party exists, why we do this, why we care about those great ideas and that great history, is that we want this nation to thrive for centuries to come.

Now eventually, in that mountain cemetery, my children will lay me to rest.

And when they do, I would like them to know that thanks to the work of this Republican Party, the United States of America is strong, and as proud and as great as ever.

That is who we serve, my friends. That is who we fight for. And the only thing that we need to do right now, the most important thing that we can do for those people, for that American nation that we all love, is to reelect Donald J. Trump president of the United States.

Mr. President, I will never take for granted the trust you have put in me.

And what an honor it is to help achieve the extraordinary vision that you have for this country.

Now I pledge to every American, no matter your party, I will give you everything I have. To serve you and to make this country a place where every dream you have for yourself, your family and your country will be possible once again.

And I promise you one more thing. To the people of Middletown, Ohio, and all the forgotten communities in Michigan, Wisconsin, Pennsylvania and Ohio, and every corner of our nation:

I promise you this—I will be a vice president who never forgets where he came from.

And every single day for the next four years, when I walk into that White House to help President Trump, I will be doing it for you. For your family, for your future and for this great country.

Thank you, God bless all of you, and God bless our great country.

★ ★ ★

## "THE PATH TO AMERICAN AUTHORITARIANISM: WHAT COMES AFTER DEMOCRATIC BREAKDOWN"

**Steven Levitsky and Lucan A. Way, *Foreign Affairs*—March/April 2025**

---

The Trump presidencies featured notable breaks from American political and constitutional norms. For many of his supporters, such novel grasps for—and assertions of—power were welcome. For many others, however, the autocratic tendencies and targeted retributions against Trump's rivals and critics marked the beginning of a dark chapter in which the rule of law was being supplanted by the will of a single man and of a particular political movement. In this essay, the scholars Steven Levitsky (1968–) and Lucan A. Way (1968–) explored the implications of a second Trump presidency as it began in 2025.

Donald Trump's first election to the presidency in 2016 triggered an energetic defense of democracy from the American establishment. But his return to office has been met with striking indifference. Many of the politicians, pundits, media figures, and business leaders who viewed Trump as a threat to democracy eight years ago now treat those concerns as overblown—after all, democracy survived his first stint in office. In 2025, worrying about the fate of American democracy has become almost passé.

The timing of this mood shift could not be worse, for democracy is in greater peril today than at any time in modern U.S. history. America has been backsliding for a decade: between 2014 and 2021, Freedom House's annual global freedom index, which scores all countries on a scale of zero to 100, downgraded the United States from 92 (tied with France) to 83 (below Argentina and tied with Panama and Romania), where it remains.

The country's vaunted constitutional checks are failing. Trump violated the cardinal rule of democracy when he attempted to overturn the results of an election and block a peaceful transfer of power. Yet neither Congress nor the judiciary held him accountable, and the Republican Party—coup attempt notwithstanding—renominated him for president. Trump ran an openly authoritarian campaign in 2024, pledging to prosecute his rivals, punish critical media, and deploy the army to repress protest. He won, and thanks to an extraordinary Supreme Court decision, he will enjoy broad presidential immunity during his second term.

Democracy survived Trump's first term because he had no experience, plan, or team. He did not control the Republican Party when he took office in 2017, and most Republican leaders were still committed to democratic rules of the game. Trump governed with establishment Republicans and technocrats, and they largely constrained him. None of those things are true anymore. This time, Trump has made it clear that he intends to govern with loyalists. He now dominates the Republican Party, which, purged of its anti-Trump forces, now acquiesces to his authoritarian behavior.

U.S. democracy will likely break down during the second Trump administration, in the sense that it will cease to meet standard criteria for liberal democracy: full adult suffrage, free and fair elections, and broad protection of civil liberties.

The breakdown of democracy in the United States will not give rise to a classic dictatorship in which elections are a sham and the opposition is locked up, exiled, or killed. Even in a worst-case scenario, Trump will not be able to rewrite the Constitution or overturn the constitutional order.

He will be constrained by independent judges, federalism, the country's professionalized military, and high barriers to constitutional reform. There will be elections in 2028, and Republicans could lose them.

But authoritarianism does not require the destruction of the constitutional order. What lies ahead is not fascist or single-party dictatorship but competitive authoritarianism—a system in which parties compete in elections but the incumbent's abuse of power tilts the playing field against the opposition. Most autocracies that have emerged since the end of the Cold War fall into this category, including Alberto Fujimori's Peru, Hugo Chávez's Venezuela, and contemporary El Salvador, Hungary, India, Tunisia, and Turkey. Under competitive authoritarianism, the formal architecture of democracy, including multiparty elections, remains intact. Opposition forces are legal and above ground, and they contest seriously for power. Elections are often fiercely contested battles in which incumbents have to sweat it out. And once in a while, incumbents lose, as they did in Malaysia in 2018 and in Poland in 2023. But the system is not democratic, because incumbents rig the game by deploying the machinery of government to attack opponents and co-opt critics. Competition is real but unfair.

Competitive authoritarianism will transform political life in the United States. As Trump's early flurry of dubiously constitutional executive orders made clear, the cost of public opposition will rise considerably: Democratic Party donors may be targeted by the IRS; businesses that fund civil rights groups may face heightened tax and legal scrutiny or find their ventures stymied by regulators. Critical media outlets will likely confront costly defamation suits or other legal actions as well as retaliatory policies against their parent companies. Americans will still be able to oppose the government, but opposition will be harder and riskier, leading many elites and citizens to decide that the fight is not worth it. A failure to resist, however, could pave the way for authoritarian entrenchment—with grave and enduring consequences for global democracy.

## The Weaponized State

The second Trump administration may violate basic civil liberties in ways that unambiguously subvert democracy. The president, for example, could order the army to shoot protesters, as he reportedly wanted to do during his first term. He could also fulfill his campaign promise to launch the "largest deportation operation in American history," targeting millions of people in an abuse-ridden process that would inevitably lead to the mistaken detention of thousands of U.S. citizens.

But much of the coming authoritarianism will take a less visible form: the politicization and weaponization of government bureaucracy. Modern states are powerful entities. The U.S. federal government employs over two million people and has an annual budget of nearly $7 trillion. Government officials serve as important arbiters of political, economic, and social life. They help determine who gets prosecuted for crimes, whose taxes are audited, when and how rules and regulations are enforced, which organizations receive tax-exempt status, which private agencies get contracts to accredit universities, and which companies obtain critical licenses, concessions, contracts, subsidies, tariff waivers, and bailouts. Even in countries such as the United States that have relatively small, laissez-faire governments, this authority creates a plethora of opportunities for leaders to reward allies and punish opponents. No democracy is entirely free of such politicization. But when governments weaponize the state by using its power to systematically disadvantage and weaken the opposition, they undermine liberal democracy. Politics becomes like a soccer match in which the referees, the groundskeepers, and the scorekeepers work for one team to sabotage its rival.

This is why all established democracies have elaborate sets of laws, rules, and norms to prevent the state's weaponization. These include independent judiciaries, central banks, and election authorities and civil services with employment protections. In the United States, the 1883 Pendleton Act created a professionalized civil service in which hiring is based on merit. Federal workers are barred from participating in political campaigns and cannot be fired or demoted for political reasons. The vast majority of the over two million federal employees have long enjoyed civil service protection. At the start of Trump's second term, only about 4,000 of these were political appointees.

The United States has also developed an extensive set of rules and norms to prevent the politicization of key state institutions. These include the Senate's confirmation of presidential appointees, lifetime tenure for Supreme Court justices, tenure security for the chair of the

Federal Reserve, ten-year terms for FBI directors, and five-year terms for IRS directors. The armed forces are protected from politicization by what the legal scholar Zachary Price describes as "an unusually thick overlay of statutes" governing the appointment, promotion, and removal of military officers. Although the Justice Department, the FBI, and the IRS remained somewhat politicized through the 1970s, a series of post-Watergate reforms effectively ended partisan weaponization of these institutions.

Professional civil servants often play a critical role in resisting government efforts to weaponize state agencies. They have served as democracy's frontline of defense in recent years in Brazil, India, Israel, Mexico, and Poland, as well as in the United States during the first Trump administration. For this reason, one of the first moves undertaken by elected autocrats such as Nayib Bukele in El Salvador, Chávez in Venezuela, Viktor Orban in Hungary, Narendra Modi in India, and Recep Tayyip Erdogan in Turkey has been to purge professional civil servants from public agencies responsible for things such as investigating and prosecuting wrongdoing, regulating the media and the economy, and overseeing elections—and replace them with loyalists. After Orban became prime minister in 2010, his government stripped public employees of key civil service protections, fired thousands, and replaced them with loyal members of the ruling Fidesz party. Likewise, Poland's Law and Justice party weakened civil service laws by doing away with the competitive hiring process and filling the bureaucracy, the judiciary, and the military with partisan allies.

Trump and his allies have similar plans. For one, Trump has revived his first-term effort to weaken the civil service by reinstating Schedule F, an executive order that allows the president to exempt tens of thousands of government employees from civil service protections in jobs deemed to be "of a confidential, policy-determining, policy-making, or policy-advocating character." If implemented, the decree will transform tens of thousands of civil servants into "at will" employees who can easily be replaced with political allies. The number of partisan appointees, already higher in the U.S. government than in most established democracies, could increase more than tenfold. The Heritage Foundation and other right-wing groups have spent millions of dollars recruiting and vetting an army of up to 54,000 loyalists to fill government positions. These changes could have a broader chilling effect across the government, discouraging public officials from questioning the president. Finally, Trump's declaration that he would fire the director of the FBI, Christopher Wray, and the director of the IRS, Danny Werfel, before the end of their terms led both to resign, paving the way for their replacement by loyalists with little experience in their respective agencies.

Once key agencies such as the Justice Department, the FBI, and the IRS have been packed with loyalists, governments can harness them for three antidemocratic ends: investigating and prosecuting rivals, co-opting civil society, and shielding allies from prosecution.

## Shock and Law

The most visible means of weaponizing the state is through targeted prosecution. Virtually all elected autocratic governments deploy justice ministries, public prosecutors' offices, and tax and intelligence agencies to investigate and prosecute rival politicians, media companies, editors, journalists, business leaders, universities, and other critics. In traditional dictatorships, critics are often charged with crimes such as sedition, treason, or plotting insurrection, but contemporary autocrats tend to prosecute critics for more mundane offenses, such as corruption, tax evasion, defamation, and even minor violations of arcane rules. If investigators look hard enough, they can usually find petty infractions such as unreported income on tax returns or noncompliance with rarely enforced regulations.

Trump has repeatedly declared his intention to prosecute his rivals, including former Republican Representative Liz Cheney and other lawmakers who served on the House committee that investigated the January 6, 2021, attack on the U.S. Capitol. In December 2024, House Republicans called for an FBI investigation into Cheney. The first Trump administration's efforts to weaponize the Justice Department were largely thwarted from within, so this time, Trump sought appointees who shared his goal of pursuing perceived enemies. His nominee for attorney general, Pam Bondi, has declared that Trump's "prosecutors will be prosecuted," and his choice for FBI director, Kash Patel, has repeatedly called for the prosecution of Trump's rivals. In 2023, Patel even published a book featuring an "enemies list" of public officials to be targeted.

Because the Trump administration will not control the courts, most targets of selective prosecution will not end up in prison. But the government need not jail its critics to inflict harm on them. Targets of investigation will be forced to devote considerable time, energy, and resources to defending themselves; they will spend their savings on lawyers, their lives will be disrupted, their professional careers will be sidetracked, and their reputations will be damaged. At a minimum, they and their families will suffer months or years of anxiety and sleepless nights.

Trump's efforts to use government agencies to harass his perceived adversaries will not be limited to the Justice Department and the FBI. A variety of other departments and agencies can be deployed against critics. Autocratic governments, for example, routinely use tax authorities to target opponents for politically motivated investigations. In Turkey, the Erdogan government gutted the Dogan Yayin media group, whose newspapers and TV networks were reporting on government corruption, by charging it with tax evasion and imposing a crippling $2.5 billion fine that forced the Dogan family to sell its media empire to government cronies. Erdogan also used tax audits to pressure the Koc Group, Turkey's largest industrial conglomerate, to abandon its support for opposition parties.

The Trump administration could similarly deploy the tax authorities against critics. The Kennedy, Johnson, and Nixon administrations all politicized the IRS before the 1970s Watergate scandal led to reforms. An influx of political appointees would weaken those safeguards, potentially leaving Democratic donors in the cross hairs. Because all individual campaign donations are publicly disclosed, it would be easy for the Trump administration to identify and target those donors; indeed, fear of such targeting could deter individuals from contributing to opposition politicians in the first place.

Tax-exempt status may also be politicized. As president, Richard Nixon worked to deny or delay tax-exempt status for organizations and think tanks he viewed as politically hostile. Under Trump, such efforts could be facilitated by antiterrorism legislation passed in November

2024 by the House of Representatives that empowers the Treasury Department to withdraw tax-exempt status from any organization it suspects of supporting terrorism without having to disclose evidence to justify such an act. Because "support for terrorism" can be defined very broadly, Trump could, in the words of Democratic Representative Lloyd Doggett, "use it as a sword against those he views as his political enemies."

The Trump administration will almost certainly deploy the Department of Education against universities, which as centers of opposition activism are frequent targets of competitive authoritarian governments' ire. The Department of Education hands out billions of dollars in federal funding for universities, oversees the agencies responsible for college accreditation, and enforces compliance with Title VI and Title IX, laws that prohibit educational institutions from discriminating based on race, color, national origin, or sex. These capacities have rarely been politicized in the past, but Republican leaders have called for their deployment against elite schools.

Elected autocrats also routinely use defamation suits and other forms of legal action to silence their critics in the media. In Ecuador in 2011, for example, President Rafael Correa won a $40 million lawsuit against a columnist and three executives at a leading newspaper for publishing an editorial calling him a "dictator." Although public figures rarely win such suits in the United States, Trump has made ample use of a variety of legal actions to wear down media outlets, targeting ABC News, CBS News, *The Des Moines Register,* and Simon & Schuster. His strategy has already borne fruit. In December 2024, ABC made the shocking decision to settle a defamation suit brought by Trump, paying him $15 million to avoid a trial in which it probably would have prevailed. The owners of CBS are also reportedly considering settling a lawsuit by Trump, showing how spurious legal actions can prove politically effective.

The administration need not directly target all its critics to silence most dissent. Launching a few high-profile attacks may serve as an effective deterrent. A legal action against Cheney would be closely watched by other politicians; a suit against *The New York Times* or Harvard would have a chilling effect on dozens of other media outlets or universities.

## Honey Trap

A weaponized state is not merely a tool to punish opponents. It can also be used to build support. Governments in competitive authoritarian regimes routinely use economic policy and regulatory decisions to reward politically friendly individuals, firms, and organizations. Business leaders, media companies, universities, and other organizations have as much to gain as they have to lose from government antitrust decisions, the issuing of permits and licenses, the awarding of government contracts and concessions, the waiving of regulations or tariffs, and the conferral of tax-exempt status. If they believe that these decisions are made on political rather than technical grounds, they have a strong incentive to align themselves with incumbents.

The potential for co-optation is clearest in the business sector. Major American companies have much at stake in the U.S. government's antitrust, tariff, and regulatory decisions and in the awarding of government contracts. (In 2023, the federal government spent more than $750 billion, or nearly three percent of the United States' GDP, on awarding contracts.) For aspiring autocrats, policy and regulatory decisions can serve as powerful carrots and sticks to attract business support. This kind of patrimonial logic helped autocrats in Hungary, Russia, and Turkey secure private-sector cooperation. If Trump sends credible signals that he will behave in a similar manner, the political consequences will be far-reaching. If business leaders become convinced that it is more profitable to avoid financing opposition candidates or investing in independent media, they will change their behavior.

Indeed, their behavior has already begun to change. In what the *New York Times* columnist Michelle Goldberg termed "the Great Capitulation," powerful CEOs who had once criticized Trump's authoritarian behavior are now rushing to meet with him, praise him, and give him money. Amazon, Google, Meta, Microsoft, and Toyota each gave $1 million to fund Trump's inauguration, more than double their previous inaugural donations. In early January, Meta announced it was abandoning its fact-checking operations—a move that Trump bragged "probably" resulted from his threats to take legal action against Meta's owner, Mark Zuckerberg. Trump himself has recognized that in his first term, "everyone was fighting me," but now "everybody wants to be my friend."

A similar pattern is emerging in the media sector. Nearly all major U.S. media outlets—ABC, CBS, CNN, NBC, *The Washington Post*—are owned and operated by larger parent corporations. Although Trump cannot carry out his threat to withhold licenses from national television networks because they are not licensed nationally, he can pressure media outlets by pressuring their corporate owners. *The Washington Post,* for instance, is controlled by Jeff Bezos, whose largest company, Amazon, competes for major federal contracts. Likewise, the owner of the *Los Angeles Times,* Patrick Soon-Shiong, sells medical products subject to review by the Food and Drug Administration. Ahead of the 2024 presidential election, both men overruled their papers' planned endorsements of Kamala Harris.

## Protection Racket

Finally, a weaponized state can serve as a legal shield to protect government officials or allies who engage in antidemocratic behavior. A loyalist Justice Department, for example, could turn a blind eye to acts of pro-Trump political violence, such as attacks on or threats against journalists, election officials, protesters, or opposition politicians and activists. It could also decline to investigate Trump supporters for efforts to intimidate voters or even manipulate the results of elections.

This has happened before in the United States. During and after Reconstruction, the Ku Klux Klan and other armed white supremacist groups with ties to the Democratic Party waged violent terror campaigns across the South, assassinating Black and Republican politicians, burning Black homes, businesses, and churches, committing election fraud, and threatening, beating, and killing Black citizens who attempted to vote. This wave of terror, which helped establish nearly a century of single-party rule across the South, was made possible by the collusion of state and local law enforcement authorities, who routinely turned a blind eye to the violence and systematically failed to hold its perpetrators accountable.

The United States experienced a marked rise in far-right violence during the first Trump administration. Threats against members of Congress increased more than tenfold. These threats had consequences: according to Republican Senator Mitt Romney, fear of Trump supporters' violence dissuaded some Republican senators from voting for Trump's impeachment after the January 6, 2021, attack.

By most measures, political violence subsided after January 2021, in part because hundreds of participants in the January 6 attack were convicted and imprisoned. But Trump's pardon of nearly all the January 6 insurrectionists on returning to office has sent a message that violent or antidemocratic actors will be protected under his administration. Such signals encourage violent extremism, which means that during Trump's second term, critics of the government and independent journalists will almost certainly face more frequent threats and even outright attacks.

Governments need not jail their critics to silence dissent.

None of this would be entirely new for the United States. Presidents have weaponized government agencies before. The FBI director J. Edgar Hoover deployed the agency as a political weapon for the six presidents he served. The Nixon administration wielded the Justice Department and other agencies against perceived enemies. But the contemporary period differs in important ways. For one, global democratic standards have risen considerably. By any contemporary measure, the United States was considerably less democratic in the 1950s than it is today. A return to mid-twentieth-century practices would, by itself, constitute significant democratic backsliding.

More important, the coming weaponization of government will likely go well beyond mid-twentieth-century practices. Fifty years ago, both major U.S. parties were internally heterogeneous, relatively moderate, and broadly committed to democratic rules of the game. Today, these parties are far more polarized, and a radicalized Republican Party has abandoned its long-standing commitment to basic democratic rules, including accepting electoral defeat and unambiguously rejecting violence.

Moreover, much of the Republican Party now embraces the idea that America's institutions—from the federal bureaucracy and public schools to the media and private universities—have been corrupted by left-wing ideologies. Authoritarian movements commonly embrace the notion that their country's institutions have been subverted by enemies; autocratic leaders including Erdogan, Orban, and Venezuela's Nicolás Maduro routinely push such claims. Such a worldview tends to justify—even motivate—the kind of purging and packing that Trump promises. Whereas Nixon worked surreptitiously to weaponize the state and faced Republican opposition when that behavior came to light, today's GOP now openly encourages such abuses. Weaponization of the state has become Republican strategy. The party that once embraced President Ronald Reagan's campaign dictum that the government was the problem now enthusiastically embraces the government as a political weapon.

Using executive power in this way is what Republicans learned from Orban. Orban taught a generation of conservatives that the state should not be dismantled but rather wielded in pursuit of right-wing causes and against opponents. This is why tiny Hungary has become a model for so many Trump supporters. Weaponizing the state is not some new feature of conservative philosophy—it is an age-old feature of authoritarianism.

## Natural Immunity?

The Trump administration may derail democracy, but it is unlikely to consolidate authoritarian rule. The United States possesses several potential sources of resilience. For one, American institutions are stronger than those in Hungary, Turkey, and other countries with competitive authoritarian regimes. An independent judiciary, federalism, bicameralism, and midterm elections—all absent in Hungary, for instance—will likely limit the scope of Trump's authoritarianism.

Trump is also weaker politically than many successful elected autocrats. Authoritarian leaders do the most damage when they enjoy broad public support: Bukele, Chávez, Fujimori, and Russia's Vladimir Putin all boasted approval ratings above 80 percent when they launched authoritarian power grabs. Such overwhelming public support helps leaders secure the legislative supermajorities or landslide plebiscite victories needed to impose reforms that entrench autocratic rule. It also helps deter challenges from intraparty rivals, judges, and even much of the opposition.

Less popular leaders, by contrast, face greater resistance from legislatures, courts, civil society, and even their own allies. Their power grabs are thus more likely to fail. Peruvian President Pedro Castillo and South Korean President Yoon Suk-yeol each had approval ratings below 30 percent when they attempted to seize extraconstitutional power, and both failed. Brazilian President Jair Bolsonaro's approval rating was well below 50 percent when he tried to orchestrate a coup to overturn his country's 2022 presidential election. He, too, was defeated and forced out of office.

Trump's approval rating never surpassed 50 percent during his first term, and a combination of incompetence, overreach, unpopular policies, and partisan polarization will likely limit his support during his second. An elected autocrat with a 45 percent approval rating is dangerous, but less dangerous than one with 80 percent support.

Civil society is another potential source of democratic resilience. One major reason that rich democracies are more stable is that capitalist development disperses human, financial, and organizational resources away from the state, generating countervailing power in society. Wealth cannot wholly inoculate the private sector from the pressures imposed by a weaponized state. But the larger and richer a private sector is, the harder it is to fully capture or bully into submission. In addition, wealthier citizens have more time, skills, and resources to join or create civic or opposition organizations, and because they depend less on the state for their livelihoods than poor citizens do, they are in a better position to protest or vote against the government. Compared with those in other competitive authoritarian regimes, opposition forces in the United States are well-organized, well-financed, and electorally viable, which makes them harder to co-opt, repress, and defeat at the polls. American opposition will therefore be harder to sideline than it was in countries such as El Salvador, Hungary, and Turkey.

## Chinks in the Armor

But even a modest tilting of the playing field could cripple American democracy. Democracies require robust opposition, and robust oppositions must be able to draw on a large and replenishable pool of politicians, activists, lawyers, experts, donors, and journalists.

A weaponized state imperils such opposition. Although Trump's critics won't be jailed, exiled, or banned from politics, the heightened cost of public opposition will lead many of them to retreat to the political sidelines. In the face of FBI investigations, tax audits, congressional hearings, lawsuits, online harassment, or the prospect of losing business opportunities, many people who would normally oppose the government may conclude that it simply is not worth the risk or effort.

This process of self-sidelining may not attract much public attention, but it can be highly consequential. Facing looming investigations, promising politicians—Republicans and Democrats alike—leave public life. CEOs seeking government contracts, tariff waivers, or favorable antitrust rulings stop contributing to Democratic candidates, funding civil rights or democracy initiatives, and investing in independent media. News outlets whose owners worry about lawsuits or government harassment rein in their investigative teams and their most aggressive reporters. Editors engage in self-censorship, softening headlines and opting not to run stories critical of the government. And university leaders fearing government investigations, funding cuts, or punitive endowment taxes crack down on campus protest, remove or demote outspoken professors, and remain silent in the face of growing authoritarianism.

Weaponized states create a difficult collective action problem for establishment elites who, in theory, would prefer democracy to competitive authoritarianism. The politicians, CEOs, media owners, and university presidents who modify their behavior in the face of authoritarian threats are acting rationally, doing what they deem best for their organizations by protecting shareholders or avoiding debilitating lawsuits, tariffs, or taxes. But such acts of self-preservation have a collective cost. As individual actors retreat to the sidelines or censor themselves, societal opposition weakens. The media environment grows less critical. And pressure on the authoritarian government diminishes.

The depletion of societal opposition may be worse than it appears. We can observe when key players sideline themselves—when politicians retire, university presidents resign, or media outlets change their programming and personnel. But it is harder to see the opposition that might have materialized in a less threatening environment but never did—the young lawyers who decide not to run for office; the aspiring young writers who decide not to become journalists; the potential whistleblowers who decide not to speak out; the countless citizens who decide not to join a protest or volunteer for a campaign.

## Hold the Line

America is on the cusp of competitive authoritarianism. The Trump administration has already begun to weaponize state institutions and deploy them against opponents. The Constitution alone cannot save U.S. democracy. Even the best-designed constitutions have ambiguities and gaps that can be exploited for antidemocratic ends. After all, the same constitutional order that undergirds America's contemporary liberal democracy permitted nearly a century of authoritarianism in the Jim Crow South, the mass internment of Japanese Americans, and McCarthyism. In 2025, the United States is governed nationally by a party with greater will and power to exploit constitutional and legal ambiguities for authoritarian ends than at any time in the past two centuries.

Trump will be vulnerable. The administration's limited public support and inevitable mistakes will create opportunities for democratic forces—in Congress, in courtrooms, and at the ballot box.

But the opposition can win only if it stays in the game. Opposition under competitive authoritarianism can be grueling. Worn down by harassment and threats, many of Trump's critics will be tempted to retreat to the sidelines. Such a retreat would be perilous. When fear, exhaustion, or resignation crowds out citizens' commitment to democracy, emergent authoritarianism begins to take root.

# *Acknowledgments*

This anthology grew out of the work undertaken for *The Soul of America: The Battle for Our Better Angels,* which I published in 2018. The *Soul* volume was the result of the wise suggestions of two formidable friends and colleagues. Nancy Gibbs, then the editor of *Time* magazine, first asked me to write about the history of fear in American politics amid the white-supremacist violence in Charlottesville, Virginia, in the summer of 2017. Shortly thereafter, on a drive from our house in Nashville to Andrew Jackson's Hermitage, Gina Centrello, at the time the publisher of Random House, told me that I should expand on the themes of the *Time* essay in a book. I am forever grateful to Nancy and to Gina.

At Random House, Kate Medina brought grace and insight to this and to so many other projects through the years. I am also grateful to Andy Ward, Monica Rae Brown, Julia Harrison, Alison Rich, Michelle Jasmine, Milena Brown, Rebecca Berlant, Dennis Ambrose, Richard Elman, Simon Sullivan, Carol Poticny, and Lucas Heinrich. Random House has been my publishing home across four decades, and I am fortunate to be in such good hands. Amanda Urban remains a steadfast friend and advocate.

As always, my thanks to Margaret Shannon for her counsel and friendship. With her eye for detail, encyclopedic grasp of the American past, and good cheer, Margaret was a vital partner on this project. And I cannot imagine life without Mike Hill, my friend and colleague of many years' standing.

At Vanderbilt University, I owe much to my longtime colleague John Geer. Thanks as well to Daniel Diermeier, Nicholas Zeppos, Alan Wiseman, John Sides, Nicole Hemmer, and Joshua Clinton.

For kindnesses large and small, my thanks to Rachel Adler, Graham Allison, Michael Beschloss, David Blight, Sidney Blumenthal, Christopher Buckley, Ken Burns, Eddie Glaude, Jr., Doris Kearns Goodwin, Annette Gordon-Reed, Billy Hallock, Bill Haslam, Matthew Hiltzik, Harold Holzer, Walter Isaacson, Jamie Kabler, Jonathan Karp, Harrison Kidd, Alex Korson, Beth Laski, Betsy and Jonathan Martin, Priscilla Painton, Bill Prezant, Andrew Roberts, Gray Sasser, Joe Scarborough,

John Seigenthaler, Oscie and Evan Thomas, Marianne Wanamaker, Sean Wilentz, and Fareed Zakaria.

My family—Keith, Mary, Maggie, and Sam—makes all things possible.

This book is dedicated to the memory of Charles Peters, the founder of *The Washington Monthly.* For more than thirty years, Charlie's care, concern, and—inevitably—candor were sustaining and illuminating. I owe him more than I can say.

# *Text Permissions*

Grateful acknowledgment is made to the following for permission to reprint previously published material:

Arizona State University Library: RNC Acceptance speech by Barry Goldwater, July 16,1964, from the Personal and Political Papers of Senator Barry M. Goldwater, Greater Arizona Collection, Arizona State University Library. Reprinted by permission.

Patrick Buchanan: 1992 RNC Convention address by Pat Buchanan. Reprinted by permission of Patrick Buchanan.

CBS News: Excerpts from "We Must Not Confuse Dissent with Disloyalty" by Edward R. Murrow (March 9, 1954) and excerpts from "To End in a Stalemate" by Walter Cronkite (February 27, 1968). Reprinted by permission of CBS News.

Jonathan Falwell: "Ministers and Marches" by Jerry Falwell. Reprinted by permission of Jonathan Falwell.

*Foreign Affairs:* "The Path to American Authoritarianism: What Comes After Democratic Breakdown" by Steven R. Levitsky and Lucan A. May (*Foreign Affairs,* vol. 104, no. 2, March/April 2025, 468–482), copyright © 2025 by the Council on Foreign Relations, Inc. Reprinted by permission.

The Russell Kirk Legacy, LLC: Excerpts from *The Conservative Mind,* 3rd Edition by Russell Kirk, copyright © The Russell Kirk Legacy, LLC. Reprinted by permission.

Alfred A. Knopf, an imprint of the Knopf Doubleday Publishing Group, a division of Penguin Random House LLC: "The Pseudo-Conservative Revolt—1954" from *The Paranoid Style in America Politics and Other Essays* by Richard Hofstadter, copyright © 1952, 1964, 1965 by Richard Hofstadter. Reprinted by permission of Alfred A. Knopf, an imprint of the Knopf Doubleday Publishing Group, a division of Penguin Random House LLC.

The Estate of John Lewis: "March on Washington, 1963" by John Lewis. Reprinted by permission.

*The New York Times:* "Butler Bares 'Fascist Plot' " (*The New York Times,* November 21, 1934) copyright © 1934 The New York Times; "Whites Alarmed; Victim Is Shot" by Claude Sitton (*The New York Times,* June 13, 1963), copyright © 1963 The New York Times. Used by permission and protected by the Copyright Laws of the United States. The printing, copying, redistribution, or retransmission of this content without express written permission is prohibited.

The Permissions Company LLC on behalf of the James Baldwin Estate: "The White Man's Guilt" by James Baldwin (*Ebony,* 1965), copyright © 1965 by James

Baldwin. Reprinted by permission of The Permissions Company LLC on behalf of the James Baldwin Estate.

White Literary LLC: Excerpt from *The Meaning of Democracy* by E. B. White, copyright © 1943 by White Literary LLC. Reprinted by permission of White Literary LLC.

Writers House: "I've Been to the Mountaintop" by Martin Luther King, Jr., copyright © 1968 by Dr. Martin Luther King, Jr., and copyright renewed 1996 by Coretta Scott King. Reprinted by arrangement with the Heirs to the Estate of Martin Luther King, Jr. c/o Writers House, New York, New York, as agent for the proprietor.

# *Illustration List and Credits*

# *Index*

Page numbers of photographs appear in *italics*.

Key to abbreviations: DNC = Democratic National Convention; FDR = Franklin Delano Roosevelt; JFK = John F. Kennedy; LBJ = Lyndon B. Johnson; RFK = Robert F. Kennedy; RNC = Republican National Convention; TR = Theodore Roosevelt

# *About the Author*

JON MEACHAM is a Pulitzer Prize–winning biographer. The Rogers Chair in the American Presidency at Vanderbilt University, he is the author of the *New York Times* bestsellers *And There Was Light: Abraham Lincoln and the American Struggle; His Truth Is Marching On: John Lewis and the Power of Hope; The Soul of America: The Battle for Our Better Angels; The Hope of Glory: Reflections on the Last Words of Jesus from the Cross; Destiny and Power: The American Odyssey of George Herbert Walker Bush; Thomas Jefferson: The Art of Power; American Lion: Andrew Jackson in the White House; American Gospel: God, the Founding Fathers, and the Making of a Nation;* and *Franklin and Winston: An Intimate Portrait of an Epic Friendship.*

# *About the Type*

This book was set in Requiem, a typeface designed by the Hoefler Type Foundry. It is a modern typeface inspired by inscriptional capitals in Ludovico Vicentino degli Arrighi's 1523 writing manual, *Il modo de temperare le penne*. An original lowercase, a set of figures, and an italic in the chancery style that Arrighi (fl. 1522) helped popularize were created to make this adaptation of a classical design into a complete font family.

HENDERSON
TRACTORS
IMPLEMENT